The Meaning
of Protestant
Theology

The Meaning
of Protestant
Theology

Luther, Augustine,
and the Gospel That Gives Us
CHRIST

PHILLIP CARY

Baker Academic

a division of Baker Publishing Group
Grand Rapids, Michigan

© 2019 by Phillip Cary

Published by Baker Academic
a division of Baker Publishing Group
PO Box 6287, Grand Rapids, MI 49516-6287
www.bakeracademic.com

Printed in the United States of America

Library of Congress Cataloging-in-Publication Data

Names: Cary, Phillip, 1958– author.
Title: The meaning of Protestant theology : Luther, Augustine, and the Gospel that gives us Christ / Phillip Cary.
Description: Grand Rapids : Baker Publishing Group, 2019. | Includes bibliographical references and index.
Identifiers: LCCN 2018037006 | ISBN 9780801039454 (pbk. : alk. paper)
Subjects: LCSH: Luther, Martin, 1483–1546. | Theology, Doctrinal–History–16th century. | Protestantism. | Protestant churches—Doctrines—History.
Classification: LCC BR333.3 .C37 2019 | DDC 230/.044—dc23
LC record available at https://lccn.loc.gov/2018037006

ISBN 978-1-5409-6161-7 (casebound)

19 20 21 22 23 24 25   7 6 5 4 3 2 1

In gratitude for the students and faculty
of the Templeton Honors College
at Eastern University,
where I have had so much to learn

Contents

Abbreviations

CR   *Corpus Reformatorum*. Edited by K. G. Bretschneider et al. Halle, 1834–.

KJV   King James Version of the Bible, originally 1611.

LW   *Luther's Works*, standard American edition. Jaroslav Pelikan, general editor. St. Louis: Concordia (vols. 1–30); Philadelphia: Fortress (vols. 31–55), 1955–76.

PG   *Patrologia Graeca*. Edited by J.-P. Migne. 162 vols. Paris, 1857–66.

PL   *Patrologia Latina*. Edited by J.-P. Migne. 217 vols. Paris, 1844–55.

ST   Thomas Aquinas. *Summa Theologica*. Translated by Fathers of the English Dominican Province. 5 vols. Westminster, MD: Christian Classics, 1981.

WA   *Weimarer Ausgabe* = Luther, Martin. *D. Martin Luthers Werke*. Weimar: H. Böhlau, 1883–1993.

A Note on Citations

I have done my best to make it possible for readers to locate the passages I cite from ancient, medieval, and Reformation texts, even when they use a different edition than I do. This makes for some abstruse citations at times, which I must explain.

I cite ancient writers either by standard pagination (noted in the margins of most editions of Plato and Aristotle, for example) or by book, chapter, and paragraph (as in "Augustine, *Confessions* 7:10.16," which is book 7, chapter 10, paragraph 16). Whenever possible, I cite medieval and even modern writers the same way (for example, "Locke, *Essay*, 4:16.13"), and sometimes to avoid ambiguity I spell it out (for example, "Anselm, *Proslogion*, chap. 1"). Citations with only two numbers refer to book and chapter, except for Augustine, where they usually refer to chapter and paragraph in texts that consist of only one book (for example, "Augustine, *Teacher* 11.38," refers to chapter and paragraph, respectively). The exception to the exception is Augustine's *City of God*, which has only book and chapter numbers. It is useful also to note that some English translations of Augustine indicate only chapter or paragraph numbers, not both.

Letters, sermons, and orations, when they belong to a standard numbered collection, are cited in a similar manner. For example, "Augustine, Letter 147:2.7" refers to the 147th letter in the standard collection of Augustine's letters, second chapter, seventh paragraph. "Augustine, Sermon 52:2" refers to the fifty-second sermon in the standard collection of his sermons (a different set of sermons from his sermon series on John or the Psalms), the second paragraph. (Augustine's sermons, unlike his letters, don't have chapters.) Luther's sermons, on the other hand, are often cited by date or by their place in a collected edition, such as *WA* or Lenker (see below).

Like most scholars working on Plato, Aristotle, Augustine, or Luther, I use standard editions and anthologies that contain a multitude of writings between one set of covers. As a reader, however, I always want to know which particular work is being cited, not just which volume of a multivolume set it can be found in. Hence in the footnotes I have always given the name of the work to which I am referring or from which I am quoting. For works of Luther, whose development as a thinker I am tracing, I will often give the date when the work was originally published. For some works, such as the Galatians commentaries, the date has to be given every time, because the 1535 Galatians Commentary is an entirely different work from the 1519 Galatians Commentary.

Readers should be warned that the titles of Augustine's treatises are rendered differently by different translators, which can easily cause confusion. I have used the titles indicated in the bibliography, but I have often translated the text directly from the Latin available at http://www.augustinus.it/latino, which gives the *Patrologia Latina* edition of Augustine's complete works (*Opera Omnia*).

For Luther, I use the standard American edition, *Luther's Works* (abbreviated *LW*), as well as the collection of Luther's church postil sermons edited by Lenker (which are by no means all of Luther's sermons). Often I have translated directly from Luther's Latin or German when a closer or more literal translation makes a point clearer, or when *LW* simply needs to be corrected. When I make my own translations of Luther, I refer first to the standard critical edition of Luther's works in the original languages, the Weimar Edition or *Weimarer Ausgabe* (abbreviated *WA*), and then indicate in parentheses the corresponding passage in *LW* or Lenker's edition of the sermons, if there is one, like so: "(= *LW* 34:170)" or "(= Luther, *Sermons* 1:190)." Not all of Luther's works have been translated into English, however, so some references in *WA* have no corresponding reference in an English edition. Also, I sometimes use the *LW* translation but insert key phrases in the original language in brackets, like so: "in hope [*in spe*]." In that case I cite *LW* first and then indicate the corresponding place in *WA*, like so: "(= *WA* 56:269)." Similarly, when I give the French or Latin for Calvin, I refer to the editions of his works given in the *Corpus Reformatorum* series (abbreviated *CR*), like so: "(= *CR* 33:438)."

All italics in quotations are mine, added occasionally for emphasis but more often just to highlight the key phrases on which my interpretation turns.

Introduction

Why Protestantism?

s there a reason to be Protestant? For many people I know, this has become an urgent and life-changing question, as they consider that the answer might be "No." It is a question that often arises for Protestants having their first robust encounter with the Great Tradition of the church, its admirable Christians, its profound writers, its beautiful liturgies. They discover that their own particular, sometimes narrow Protestant upbringing is missing the riches they find in more ancient ways of being a disciple of Jesus Christ.

Today's ecumenical setting, in which members of the various churches and traditions have come to understand each other in a far more friendly way than before, makes the question all the more urgent. Apart from strenuous efforts to remain ignorant, no Protestant body today can plausibly claim to be the one true church or the only community that possesses the way to salvation. A Protestant learning the Great Tradition today soon realizes that not only other types of Protestants but Roman Catholics and Eastern Orthodox can truly be Christians—that they in fact include some of the most wonderful Christians in history, people from whom it would be foolish not to learn something about the way of Christ. Meanwhile, an older kind of urgency has begun to fade out of people's lives. For many reasons—even some good ones—Christians today are much less anxious about their own individual salvation or damnation than people in the sixteenth century, when Protestantism first arose. So if you don't have to be Protestant to be saved or to be a true Christian, why be Protestant?

Another level of urgency stems from dismay at Protestant theology and practice having fallen on hard times, with the drift toward a post-Christian future in some sectors of mainline Protestantism and the anxious narcissism of much contemporary evangelicalism.[1] I have in mind the evangelicals who are taught in church to answer the question, What is your faith about? by making it fundamentally about themselves: it's about "the experience of a transformed heart" or "having a relationship with God" or "God working in my life." God is part of the story, but it's my story and my job is to make God to fit in it. This kind of teaching is enough to drive many Protestants to Catholicism or Orthodoxy, or to a high-church sacramental Protestantism. What they're looking for is worship that is not about me, my life, my experience, my heart, my relationship with God, and so on. The great sacramental liturgies give us Christ, not advice about how to live the Christian life. In Luther's terms, they preach Gospel, not law. They focus not on telling us what to do but on telling us what Christ does, thus directing our attention away from our own works to Christ himself. The story they tell does include me, but that is because I get to be part of Christ's story, not the other way round. Sacramental faith does not mean trying to fit Christ into my life but rather finding that I belong in his life.[2]

In my experience, this is the most palpable source of the question: Why be Protestant? The Gospel, as Protestant theology has understood it ever since Luther, is found much more reliably and gloriously in the ancient liturgies than in any modern preaching you could name, including the kind you regularly find in various Protestant churches. Even Christians who have never heard of Luther's law/Gospel distinction can feel the difference between a church service that is all about me and one that is about Christ, and they can recognize where the good news is: in words that direct our attention to our Beloved, who is God in the flesh. These are the words of the Gospel, which makes us new from the inside, not by telling us how to transform our lives but by giving us Christ in person.

The Protestant exodus to liturgical churches shows us something crucial, I think, about the meaning of Protestant theology: the central concept of Protestantism is not sheer innovation, as if it emerged full-blown in the sixteenth century having nothing to do with the Great Tradition of Christian thought, life, and worship that came before it. Rather, it is an insight about what the Gospel word has always done when received in faith. The Gospel, Protestant

---

1. Cary, *Good News for Anxious Christians*, addresses the anxieties of American evangelicals, but chap. 9 also contains a brief analysis of the post-Christian drift in mainline Protestantism.

2. In this way Luther's concept of the Gospel exemplifies the premodern "direction of interpretation" identified by Hans Frei, *Eclipse of Biblical Narrative*, 3–6.

theology has taught ever since Luther, is God's way of giving us nothing less than his own beloved Son. That is why believing the Gospel is how you accept Christ. This concept of the Gospel as giving us Christ is the most important contribution Protestant theology makes to the thinking of the Great Tradition. If we set this concept at the center of our understanding of the meaning of Protestant theology, we can see the best of Protestant preaching, teaching, and practice as a gift as well as a challenge—a contribution to the life of the whole church that need not divide the church.

Putting the Gospel at the center of Protestant theology means putting Christ at the center. This is hardly a new idea, but it is not done often enough. It means emphasizing what is most Christian about Protestantism rather than what is most distinctive about it. There are of course things that make Protestantism different from other Christian traditions, especially its distinctive doctrine of justification by faith alone. But these ought to be presented in light of its center in the Gospel of Jesus Christ. And the aim of the presentation should be to offer a gift of self-understanding to all Christians, asking, in effect: Isn't this how things actually go? Isn't it always the Gospel word that gives you Christ, and thus builds you up in faith, hope, and love? Hasn't it always been this way, since the day the apostles began to preach and teach?

Making the Gospel central decenters the doctrine of justification by faith alone, precisely by locating its center in Christ, not in our faith or our justification. After all, what the doctrine teaches is that we are justified simply by faith in the Gospel, not by faith in faith nor by faith in the doctrine of justification by faith alone. So you don't have to believe in justification by faith alone in order to be justified by faith alone. Justification is what happens simply because, as Christians have always done, you believe in the Gospel that gives you Christ. What believing the Protestant doctrine of justification adds to this is a measure of self-understanding and assurance: I really can count on Christ alone to be my savior, because it is not what I do but what he does that saves and justifies me, and he has indeed promised to save and justify me. Therefore I am free to confess myself a sinner and repent of my sins—even my sins of unbelief—without fear that my sin and unbelief merely prove that I am not a Christian, that I am lost and damned. It is a great consolation not to have to put faith in my good works or even in my own faith.

This consolation, it turns out, is particularly important for Protestants. It is Protestants who have done the most to keep alive the fear of damnation—what Luther describes as terror of conscience—that had grown to monstrous proportions by the time Luther was a young man in the early sixteenth century. The doctrine of justification by faith alone says, in effect: believe the Gospel rather than your fears. The word of God, not your conscience, is telling you the truth about yourself: that you are one of those for whose sake Christ shed his blood, for whom he intercedes with the Father, and to whom he presents his own life-giving flesh.

If you don't have a terrified sixteenth-century conscience, you don't have quite so much need for the doctrine of justification by faith alone. But of course that does not mean you have no need or desire for the Gospel of Jesus Christ. What Protestant theology has to offer the whole church, in this and all times, is a piety of the word of God that clings to the Gospel alone as the way God gives us his own Son, along with a set of doctrines and practices designed to make that piety central to our lives. The most important reason to remain Protestant in our day is so that there may be communities that continue to present that piety to the whole church.

The aim of this book is to show why Protestantism is best understood as a form of piety based on faith in the Gospel as the word of God that gives us Christ. Its central claim is that Luther initiated the Protestant tradition when he came to understand the Gospel in this way. The book tells a story, some parts of which will be familiar, some not—and different parts will be familiar to different readers. So in this introduction I am providing a preview, allowing you to jump into the parts of the story you find most rewarding, whether that be the familiar or the unfamiliar. Many readers, I suppose, will want to go straight to the middle of the story in part 2, beginning in chapter 7, where the Gospel takes center stage. I would much rather have you do that than be bogged down in part 1 with my exposition of ancient Platonism and its presence in Christian thought, in case you don't find that of interest. But by the time you get to the end of part 3, I hope you will see why you need to understand the presence of Platonism in Christianity in order to appreciate what Luther's concept of the Gospel adds to the Western Christian heritage stemming from Augustine, that great Christian Platonist.

I should also warn you, there will be some difficult bits. Understanding always means seeing connections, and that is hard work—especially if what you're seeing is unfamiliar. This is why I want to make it possible for readers to start with the bits that interest them, where they will find the hard work most rewarding and thus have an incentive to go on to the work needed for understanding things elsewhere. The hard work has two main dimensions. First, I often get into the weeds, aiming to furnish a convincing reading of particular texts by Augustine, Luther, and others, tying them to their pastoral work as teachers of the faith. Second, I'm interested in the exact lay of the land: I spend time setting out the logic that gets an author from point A to point B and point C and beyond, so as to clarify not just what he thinks but why he thinks it's true—and why you might agree that it's true (or not).

Throughout all this hard work I aim to keep three central threads in view: (1) the divine carnality of Christ in the flesh, which is the central thread of Christian faith itself, (2) the desire for the intellectual vision of God as Truth, which is the central thread of Augustine's Platonist spirituality, and (3) the hearing of the Gospel by which we take hold of Christ in faith, which is the central thread of Luther's theology. The thesis that weaves them all together is that the third thread does justice to the first thread in a way that the second thread can't. This is why the Augustinian tradition needs a Luther.

And now for the preview: first, part by part, then chapter by chapter. At the heart of the book is the concept of the Gospel as the word of God that gives us Christ, which is the topic of part 2, where I argue that it was by arriving at this concept of the Gospel that Luther gave us Protestant theology. It is important, however, to set Luther's concept of the Gospel in the context of the Western Christian tradition before him, as well as to trace some of its most important consequences in the later history of Protestantism. Hence the story I tell proceeds in three stages, focusing on context, concept, and consequences. Part 1 presents the *context*, the Christian tradition within which Luther's theology arose, focusing on the spirituality of Augustine, the great Western church father who was Luther's favorite theologian. This part begins with ancient Platonism, because Augustine's spirituality was built on a critical appropriation of Platonist philosophy, which I think was not critical enough. Part 2 presents the key *concept*, the Gospel that gives us Christ, examining how it arises out of the Augustinian context and leads Luther in a new direction that has deeper affinities with medieval sacramental theology and its faith in external means of grace than with Augustine's Platonist spirituality and its inward turn to intellectual vision. Part 3 turns to the *consequences* of Luther's teaching that receiving Christ by faith in the Gospel is how we know God. Luther steers Protestant theology away from the Augustinian spirituality of intellectual vision by teaching that the deepest knowledge of God comes from hearing the word of God, not from seeing for ourselves; for this is how we receive God in person, in the flesh of Christ hidden at the right hand of God. But because our knowledge depends on an external word, it does not give us the kind of certainty that Protestants themselves have often wanted.

In chapter 1, I begin with a very basic explanation of Platonism, which may be familiar to some readers but very unfamiliar to others. Platonist spirituality plays a much larger role in the familiar beliefs of the Christian tradition than most Christians realize. Modern theologians have often obscured this by drawing a far too easy and ill-defined distinction between Christian theology and Platonist philosophy. In its thinking about the spiritual being of God, his immateriality and eternity, the Christian tradition has genuinely benefited from Platonist metaphysics. But the Platonist contribution to Western spirituality, along with its role in Christian ethics and epistemology, is a different matter. In a nutshell, I argue that Platonism is often right about God, but wrong about how we know God and are united with him. Above all, I suggest we should be critical of the Platonist notion that there is a kind of mind's eye or intellectual vision that gives us a deep understanding of the eternal Truth that is God. There is a great deal that is attractive about this Platonist notion, but it directs our attention differently from the Gospel that gives us Christ.

Chapter 2 turns to the fundamental point at which Christianity differs most clearly from Platonism or any other philosophy: the faith it puts in one particular human being, Jesus Christ, as God in the flesh. In place of human spirituality bringing us to God in a kind of ascent of heart and mind, the Gospel tells the story of a divine carnality, a descent of God to us. This is something too enormous and anomalous to be contained in any philosophy, and it ends up fracturing every conceptual framework you try to put it in. It demands its own distinctive form of thought, which is the task of Christian theology to develop as it works out the doctrines of Trinity and incarnation. The result is good news based not on the immortality of the soul but on the resurrection of the body, and a spirituality that is based not on intellectual vision but on the Holy Spirit, who is the Spirit of Christ, with whom heaven descends to us in the end.

But human spirituality is stubborn, especially in the conceptually and emotionally powerful form of Platonism. Chapter 3 presents the most powerful form of it in Western Christianity, the Platonist spirituality of Augustine, the most influential theologian in the Western Church. In Augustine's spirituality faith seeks understanding, which means faith in Christ and his words sets us on a journey by the road of love to the destination of seeing God in Platonist intellectual vision. The meaning of Christ's incarnation is thus defined by a Platonist goal, and the journey has no place for what Luther calls Gospel, an external word that gives us salvation and the ultimate knowledge of God in Christ incarnate. We can see this in depth by looking closely at an important programmatic statement of Augustine's theology in his great treatise *City of God*.

Chapter 4 explains how Augustine's spirituality develops into his doctrine of grace, which becomes the context of the sixteenth-century anxieties that Luther's theology addressed. Above all, Augustine gives us an extraordinarily powerful picture of the dynamic of Christian love as a force of attraction and of union, which is fundamental to his account of the spiritual life of the church, but which also leads to a view of grace that makes the problem of predestination inescapable. Augustine's robust doctrine of predestination has often been blamed anachronistically on John Calvin, but it is shared by Luther and Thomas Aquinas as well. The deep disagreement between Luther and Augustine arises not from the doctrine of predestination but from Luther's thinking about how external things such as word and sacrament can be means of grace. If you were to extend Luther's concept of the Gospel so that it over-shadowed and redefined Augustine's concept of predestination, you would get something very much like Karl Barth's doctrine of election, according to which predestination means that God has chosen from the beginning that the Gospel of Christ is the true story of the world.

Part 2 tells the story of how Luther's concept of the Gospel arose, starting with two chapters on Luther's early theology, where the concept is lacking. Chapter 5 looks at what Augustine's spiritual journey had turned into by the sixteenth century, and how it generated anxieties and terrors of conscience that Augustinian theology was not equipped to handle. The journey had become a fundamentally penitential process, shaped by practices of con-fession that did not exist in Augustine's time, which constantly confronted believers with their damnable moral imperfection. Young Luther developed an Aristotelian account of the Augustinian journey of justification that in-sisted we must be "always in motion," never resting in the imperfection that is inevitably present in any process so long as it is still going on. At the same time, Luther repudiated the commonsense Aristotelian notion that virtue and righteousness could become a reliable habit of the soul, which meant there was nothing in ourselves we could build on in the effort to become righteous in God's sight.

In chapter 6 we shall see how fiercely young Luther wanted us to internalize the sense of sin and penitence, to the point of hating ourselves and wishing to be damned. This was the core of his early doctrine of justification. At this point he already taught that we are justified by faith alone, but without a concept of Gospel as a word of grace, "faith alone" means putting faith in a divine word of accusation and agreeing that God is right to condemn and damn us. In a paradoxical joining of opposites (*coincidentia oppositorum*), we are justified in God's sight to the extent that we sincerely agree with God's judgment against us. The result is a kind of spiritual masochism that could only accentuate the anxieties of the terrified conscience.

Chapters 7 and 8 tell how Luther came to think of the Gospel as the gra-cious word of God that gives us Christ. These are the central chapters of the book and the basis for the corrections I seek to make in how the meaning and history of Protestant theology are understood. Chapter 7 focuses on Luther's concept of the Gospel as the promise of God authorizing a sacramental word that says "you" and means me. The concept emerges in Luther's thinking about the sacraments beginning in 1518, starting with the word of absolution in the sacrament of penance. In a kind of double structure of God's word, this sacramental word is based on Christ's promise in Scripture, with the result that when I hear the absolution, I should be as certain my sins are absolved as if God himself had absolved my sins in person. My inward penitence or contrition is not what matters but only the fact that God is true to his word. The basis for everything is *Deus verax*, which means that God is true, though every man be a liar, as Paul says in Romans 3:4. Likewise in baptism, my faith should not be based on any reflective confidence in my own belief, but simply on the truth of the sacramental word, based on the promise of Christ in Scripture, so that it is Christ himself who makes me a Christian by telling me, "I baptize you in the name of the Father, and of the Son, and of the Holy Spirit." Finally, in the Eucharist what I am to believe is that I am united with Christ and receive every good thing that is his, including justification, salvation, and eternal life, in a wondrous exchange, in which all my evils, sin, and death become his and all his goods, blessings, and benefits become mine.

Chapter 8 traces how the concept of Gospel, expanding from the promise of Christ to the whole story of Christ, becomes the basis of Luther's mature doctrine of justification. Luther adds a kind of codicil to the heritage of the Augustinian theology of grace, teaching that the Gospel is the external means by which God gives the inward grace of Christ, so that Augustine's law/grace contrast becomes Luther's law/Gospel contrast. Unlike later Lutheranism, however, Luther still thinks of justification as a process. It is a process that makes progress by always returning to square one, returning to one's baptism and taking hold of Christ once again in the Gospel. Because the process is ongoing and therefore always incomplete in this life, believers are not only righteous by faith but also sinners by their remaining unbelief, and thus every Christian is "righteous and sinner at the same time" (*simul justus et peccator*). Therefore it is important that God, for Christ's sake, does not count our sins against us or impute them to us. However, this "forensic" justification, as it is called, is not the foundation or the core of Luther's doctrine but rather is a third element coming after union with Christ and then the wondrous exchange in which we receive every good thing that is his. This includes the righteousness of Christ, which is not simply his human merits imputed to us but the very righteousness of God (*justitia Dei*), which becomes our possession because Christ himself is our possession, like a bridegroom belonging to a bride with all that is his.

Part 3 considers some of the consequences of Luther's theology of the Gospel as they unfold in the history of Protestantism. It begins, in chapter 9, by focusing on a serious bad consequence: the Protestant obsession with the wrong kind of certainty. Faith in the Gospel is grounded on the certainty that God will be true to his word, not the certainty of our theology and its interpretation of Scripture. These two kinds of certainty can and should be separated, for two reasons. One is illustrated by Luther's vicious polemics against theological opponents, whom he accused of lying against their own conscience when they claimed certainty for *their* theological interpretations. This led to the sheer wickedness of Luther's polemics against the Jews, which cannot be excused as a reflection of his times but are grounded in Luther's distinctive demand for conscientious certainty in Scriptural interpretation. The other reason is that Protestant certainties, which looked plausible in the sixteenth century, generated all sorts of unintended *un*certainties due to the ongoing squabbles of theologians in the seventeenth and eighteenth centuries, and then ran altogether aground with the rise of modern biblical criticism in the eighteenth and nineteenth centuries. The future of Protestant theology depends on remembering its place within the Christian tradition rather than being captive to the assumptions of the modern research university, which harbors a tradition of biblical scholarship that has no particular commitment to the Gospel of Jesus Christ. Protestant theology can benefit from the postmodern insight that even modern rationality is traditional, which should lead to an understanding of the rationality of traditions that I call "right-wing postmodernism."

Chapter 10 focuses on a distinctively Protestant anxiety. Whereas Catholics get anxious about whether they are in a state of mortal sin, Protestants worry about whether they really have faith. Different worries stem from the logic of different theologies, which I illustrate for Protestantism by way of two sets of syllogisms, one Calvinist and one Lutheran. The Calvinist syllogisms represent the logic of pastoral care in pursuit of what Calvinists call the assurance of salvation, while the Lutheran syllogisms represent the logic of sacramental faith clinging to the word of God in the midst of what Luther calls *Anfechtungen*, or the trials and temptations of faith. The reason I prefer Luther as representative of Protestant theology is that his faith is logically unreflective, which is to say it does not require us to put faith in faith. Luther is more successful than any other theologian in showing us how to put our faith in the word of God alone, which is a fundamental intention of Protestant theology. This is illustrated by the fact that the Lutheran syllogisms do not mention faith but are premised solely on the truth of God's word. This in turn is closely related to the fact that for Luther the Christian life is based not on a conversion experience but on the word of God given to each of us personally in baptism.

In contrast to Augustinian inwardness, Luther's faith is based on an outward turn to the Gospel as an external word. Chapter 11 connects Luther's outward turn with his epistemology of hearing, his teaching that we must find God where we hear God's word tell us to find him—above all in Christ's flesh, which we must believe is present externally in the bread of the Eucharist, even though of course we do not see it. The difference between Luther's sacramental theology and the teaching of other Protestant theologians who do not want us believing that God's flesh is present in bread is therefore no trivial matter. To clarify the difference, it helps to understand the assumptions of Augustine's sacramental semiotics, his account of sacraments as signs, which all parties to this sixteenth-century debate had in common. The crucial difference, which usually goes unnoticed, is that for Luther, following the view of medieval Catholicism, the body and blood of Christ is not just the thing signified by the sacrament (its *res*) but is also the external sign in the sacrament (its *signum*), which means it is present wherever there is a valid sacrament, even when unbelief separates the sacrament from the grace it signifies. The underlying assumption for Luther, as for medieval Catholicism, is that an external sign can by the will of God be the site of spiritual power, giving what it signifies. In this regard Luther is closer to Thomas Aquinas than to Augustine, whereas Calvin is closer to Augustine than Luther is.

Chapter 12 turns to the doctrine of the Trinity as the most important ground on which to contrast the epistemology of hearing, as a way of describing how God's word gives us God in person, with the epistemology of intellectual vision championed by Augustine. As before, Augustine's Platonism gives us an apt metaphysics (despite unconvincing attacks by twentieth-century theologians who thought his metaphysics of the Trinity was too "Western") but not an apt epistemology. The point of the doctrine of the Trinity is not found in an Augustinian spiritual ascent to an understanding of the Trinity, but in the good news that the Son of God has chosen to descend to us by being none other than the baby born of Mary and the man crucified under Pontius Pilate. Faith seeks understanding not by ascending to beatific vision of the being of God but by awaiting the kingdom where we shall see in full how Christ keeps his word.

I came to the thoughts in this book over the course of many years, and it is worth saying a few words about the path that brought me here. It began with a philosophical thought: that we come to know other persons by hearing their word and believing it. Persons have a right to a say in how we know them, so we are dependent on their willingness to give themselves to be known in what they say, and especially on their ability to be true to their word and keep their promises.[3] So I have never been happy with the "expressionist" picture of our knowledge of another person, in which our task is to penetrate through the outer shell of words to get at the inner self that words signify and express. In reality the movement of knowledge goes in the opposite direction: we come to know people by letting their words into our hearts, so that what they say can reshape us. Such knowledge requires an outward turn, putting faith in the external authority of those we desire to know. We should respect and cherish this authority precisely in its externality, because externality is the mark of the otherness of other persons.

That philosophical thought was for me always in partnership with Protestant theologies of the hearing of the word, which fit biblical thinking about how we know God. I was much attracted to Karl Barth's robust theology of the word of God, as well as his corrective to liberal Protestant versions of the inward turn, the turn to experience or "experiential-expressivism."[4] But I found myself dissatisfied with Barth's "actualism," his way of turning the word of God into an event that changes us but eludes our grasp. Luther's sacramental conception of the word, by contrast, directs our attention to something we can cling to. Sacraments and preaching are indeed events, taking place at particular times and locations, yet they do not elude our grasp but give us something to cling to: promises we can count on and always return to, so that through them we may take hold of Christ himself (*apprehendere Christum*), as Luther loves to say.

So my studies led me back from Barth to Luther. And then unexpectedly to Augustine. I knew I would find in Augustine the semiotics or theory of signs that underlay Luther's treatment of both words and sacraments. I also expected that Augustine would provide the foundation for the medieval notion of sacramental efficacy that was indispensable for Luther's arriving at the concept of the saving power of the Gospel. So I was surprised to find that Augustine actually had no place for the sacramental concept of external signs giving the inward grace they signify, and that he had his own version of the inward turn, and that more than anyone else, he deserved the title of inventor of the Western conception of the inner self.[5] The motive for these developments in Augustine's thought came from ancient Platonism rather than liberal Protestantism, but they did give liberal theology some of its key ideas

3. Cary, "Believing the Word."
4. For this term used to describe liberal theology, see Lindbeck, *Nature of Doctrine*, chaps. 1 and 2.
5. Cary, *Outward Signs*; Cary, *Augustine's Invention*.

many centuries later. More importantly, his devotion to the Platonist project of intellectual vision became the basis of the Roman Catholic spirituality of beatific vision. I became a critic of Augustine as well as an advocate of Luther because I think we know God by hearing, not seeing: by believing the word of the Gospel in which we hear of Christ coming to us, not by ascending to the vision of the supreme Good as in Plato's allegory of the cave.

Yet I am not urging everyone to become Lutheran (I am not Lutheran myself but Anglican) nor even to become Protestant. I think the church, the one Body of Christ, needs Catholics and Orthodox as well as Protestants of various kinds, and that when the day comes that we properly understand the oneness of the church, we will be able to honor our differences without creating division between ourselves. Luther himself was not good at this, of course; he often failed to discern the presence of the Gospel among Christians who didn't join his cause. But surely he was right about the centrality of the Gospel and its power to give us Christ. The more we bring Protestant theology into focus around that center, the less divisive Protestantism will be. Luther is my guide to the meaning of Protestant theology because I find him being clearer than any other theologian about this central point, which makes him more successful than any other theologian at carrying out the fundamental Protestant intention of putting faith in the word of God alone. This is why I take Luther's thinking to be necessary to any properly Protestant self-understanding, and thus to the gift and challenge Protestant piety offers to the whole church.

One sign for me of the oneness of the church, from which I have benefited in ways past telling, is the myriad conversations I have had with all sorts of Protestants, Catholics, and Orthodox who helped give shape to the thoughts in this book. In addition to my teachers Hans Frei, George Lindbeck, Robert Johnson, and Nicholas Wolterstorff, I want to thank especially my fellow student David Yeago for conversations that got much of my learning about Luther started many years ago. More recently, I have learned a great deal from my own students, including long arguments with Jeremiah Barker about Luther and Cajetan, which sharpened my thinking about important matters in chapter 7, and one particularly thought-provoking discussion of the doctrine of the Trinity with Kate Bresee that fed into chapter 12. Much of the initial shaping of this book took place while I was a fellow at the Center of Theological Inquiry in Princeton, and the book got into its final shape with help from students in my senior seminar: Daniel Ennis, Madeleine Harris, Zachary Nelson, Anne Nussbaum, Jack Shephard, and Mason Waldhauser. I owe many years of intellectual challenge and stimulation to my colleagues R. J. Snell, Randall Colton, Ben Richards, and Amy Gilbert Richards, philosophers to whom theology is dear. My colleague and dean, Jonathan Yonan, was remarkably protective of our time, as well as being a supportive listener and a long-suffering Reformed theologian. The dedication of this book honors him in honoring the school to whose life he devoted so much of his remarkable creative energy.

Spirituality
and the Being
of God

1

Philosophical Spirituality

The drama of Protestant theology begins on a stage set in large part by Augustinian spirituality, which is why we shall spend a good deal of time with the great church father Augustine in part 1 before we get to Luther, the founding figure of Protestantism, in part 2. The stage is furnished with many taken-for-granted beliefs in the background, which include not only the teachings of Scripture but elements of ancient philosophy, especially Platonism. Augustine has set this stage by combining Bible and philosophy in ways that have become so familiar over the centuries that people in the drama have not always noticed the difference. Part 1 of this book is an exercise in noticing the difference, beginning in this chapter by introducing some of the Platonist elements, and then proceeding to examine Christian appropriations of Platonism, especially in Augustine.

Critical Appropriation

The aim is not to eliminate the Platonism that has found its way into Christian thinking. On the contrary, as the church fathers recognized, Plato and his followers got some things right, and some of their stock of concepts can be useful for Christian thought if critically appropriated.[1] This means, of course,

---

1. For good introductions to Platonism in early Christian thought, see Allen and Springstead, *Philosophy for Understanding Theology*, chaps. 1–3; Stead, *Philosophy in Christian Antiquity*; Louth, *Origins of the Christian Mystical Tradition*, especially chaps. 1–5; McGinn, *Foundations of Mysticism*, chap. 2. It should be noted that when Louth and McGinn write about "mysticism," their focus is not on altered states of consciousness but on what the Christian tradition

both appropriation and criticism—making something our own precisely by asking the critical question, Is it really true? The reason for recognizing the difference between Platonism and Christianity is not that the two have nothing to do with each other, but rather in order to pursue this critical question well, with eyes open, knowing that there can be both truth in Platonism and falsehood in the Christian tradition. In that way we may discern not only how the Christian faith and Platonist philosophy have been allies over the centuries but also why their alliance has been more valuable in some respects than in others.

This chapter shall not present anything like a full or adequate account of Platonism, but only some key concepts that were important to the church fathers, the orthodox theologians of the early centuries of the Christian church. The church fathers are the first Christian theologians whose writings are found outside the Bible: Gentile writers, for the most part, figuring out how to teach the Gospel on the basis of Jewish scriptures—including the New Testament, which was written almost entirely by Jews. Those of the fathers who lived within the Roman Empire came to this task equipped with a classical Greek or Latin education, which was focused especially on rhetoric but included at least a passing familiarity with the philosophical tradition stemming from ancient Athens, including Plato and Aristotle and the Stoics. The church fathers have sometimes been criticized for "Hellenizing" Christianity, making it too Greek—as if thinking in Greek were foreign to the New Testament. This "Hellenization" thesis is rightly repudiated by most theologians today, but it is important to recognize that when ancient Gentile thinkers taught Jewish scriptures, there were inevitably some losses. Much of the life and lore of ancient Israel up to and including the time of Jesus was unknown to the church fathers and needs to be retrieved by modern scholars in order to arrive at a robust understanding of the New Testament in its original historical context. Church fathers like Augustine could bring immense conceptual sophistication to their task—and frankly, they are often much smarter than the scholars who write about them—but they seldom sympathized with or even understood how Israel thought of its own relation to God, as we shall see at the end of part 1.

In general, I shall be arguing that the metaphysics of Platonism has proved most valuable for Christian thinking, its ethics less so, and its epistemology less still. That is to say, the Platonists got many things right when it comes to abstract questions about the being of God, but not so many when it comes to our relation to God, and especially not when it comes to how we know God. Their key epistemological concept, which I shall label "intellectual vision,"

---

calls "mystical theology," which concerns the nature and destiny of the soul in its relation to God. This puts it in the ballpark of what I am calling "spirituality."

concerns a power of the soul that I think we do not actually have, and it shaped Augustine's spirituality in a way that displaces faith in the Gospel of Jesus Christ as the fundamental form of the knowledge of God. Since epistemology and ethics—how we know and how we live—profoundly shape each other, especially in the area of spirituality, this concept is at the center of what I shall be critical about in the critical appropriation of Augustinian Platonism.

But I shall begin at the other end, with the things that the Platonist tradition gets right about the being of God. I use the word "being" as equivalent to the Greek philosophical term *ousia*, which can also be translated "essence." The term was incorporated into the Nicene Creed, in which the church confesses that Jesus Christ, the eternal Son of God, is "of one being [*homoousios*] with the Father." This little phrase illustrates what I mean by critical appropriation: using a Platonist vocabulary, it says something subtly but profoundly different from anything an ordinary Platonist could accept. The orthodox doctrine of the Trinity, to which this phrase makes a central contribution, is in fact the most fundamental reckoning the Christian tradition has had with Platonism. The church fathers who formulated this creed appropriated Platonist concepts of the eternity and immateriality of God, then used them to say something about Jesus Christ that would have astounded Plato: that this particular man has the same being as the God who created heaven and earth.

What the Platonists got wrong stems from all the things Plato could not possibly have known about Christ, who was born four hundred years after his death. This includes not just the humanity of Jesus but the fact that he is the Son of God, eternally begotten from the Father and of one being with him. Not knowing this or else not believing it, the later pagan Platonists ended up getting some things right, conceptually, about the being of God, but they were ignorant of who God is. What they get wrong about ethics and especially epistemology follows from this ignorance. They did not really ask *who* God is, for they thought of God as a principle, power, and goal, but not as someone who chose to act for a particular people such as Israel, and certainly not as someone who could be crucified under Pontius Pilate. Hence they were in no position to recognize that knowing God requires believing in Jesus Christ whom he has sent (John 17:3). In the Platonist tradition knowing God came to mean knowing the being or essence of God, which is a rather less important thing to know than who Jesus is. However, as the church fathers recognized, knowing Christ does have implications for what we know about the being of God, and there the Platonists were right about some things. To distinguish what they got right from what they got wrong is precisely the task of critical appropriation that was carried out in the doctrines of the Trinity and incarnation formulated by the church fathers.

To highlight the difficulties of this task of critical appropriation, I will talk about "spirituality," which is an important term in part because of its treacherous ambiguity. We can speak of the "spirituality" of God, meaning that God is nonphysical, transcending the world of space and time. (Because the content of the discipline of physics has changed so much since ancient times, we get closer to these ancient thinkers if we avoid the term "nonphysical" and say instead "incorporeal," meaning not a bodily thing, or "immaterial," meaning not made up of any kind of material.) But I shall focus on "spirituality" in another sense of the term, which we encounter when it is used to describe human devotional practices, the forms of piety or spiritual journeys that are meant to bring people closer to God. Much of what we today call "spirituality" stems ultimately from the Platonist philosophical tradition. The area where Christians should be most critical in their appropriation of Platonism has to do with this sense of spirituality, where the focus of the word is not on God so much as on our relationship with God.

Of course these two senses of the term "spirituality" are connected, and that is why the term is ambiguous and sometimes treacherous: it is so easy to try deriving human spirituality from the spirituality of God. This is where I shall urge us to be especially critical, since I believe our relationship to God must be formed not by human spirituality but by divine carnality—not by our spirit but by Christ's flesh (*carnem* in Latin). I want to heed Martin Luther's warning against "making spiritual what God has made bodily and outward."[2] At the end of chapter 2, we shall arrive at a specifically Christian sense of "spirituality" based on the Holy Spirit, who is the Spirit of Christ incarnate. And I shall often use the phrase "divine carnality," in order to emphasize the way God has made himself bodily and outward, according to the Christian doctrine of incarnation (which means literally "enfleshment"). The term "incarnation" is easily confused with terms for quite different concepts, such as reincarnation (the non-Christian idea that souls are reborn in many bodies) and embodiment, which applies to all living creatures that have bodies, whereas the Christian doctrine of incarnation applies solely to Jesus Christ, the only person in all creation who is God incarnate.

Platonists against Materialism

If you want to work out a coherent account of the incorporeal being of God, then the Platonist tradition is the place to go. Other traditions of philosophy

2. Luther, *Against the Heavenly Prophets*, LW 40:192.

are not so helpful on this point. When ancient philosophers, for instance, spoke of "spirit" (*spiritus* in Latin, *pneuma* in Greek, both of which could literally mean "breath"), most of them thought of material things such as breath or fire or some extrafine "spiritual" material such as light or the aetherial stuff of heaven. (Light, after all, is perfectly physical, something observed and investigated in both ancient and modern physics.) Cicero spoke for a great many ancient writers when he described *spiritus* as a "fiery breath" and identified it as the material the soul was made of.[3] He was following the Stoic philosophers, who identified *pneuma* or *spiritus* with the heavenly fire that made up the being of the stars and gave light to the earth. In other words, because most philosophers in those days were materialists, they thought of "spirit" in material terms. They had a lot to say about soul as well as spirit, but they thought of both as made out of a distinctive, "spiritual" kind of material, perhaps light or the aether of heaven. After all, they thought, how could anything have being if it was not made out of *something*? Or, in Augustine's version of the problem, how could a thing have being if it did not take up space somehow?[4]

As Augustine came to see, the Platonists were the philosophers to learn from if you wanted to find a nonmaterialist (or as we would now say, "nonphysical") answer to these questions. They were the ones who were intent on seeing how there could be a being that was not made up of some material or other and that was not located somewhere in physical space the way bodily things are. To understand Platonist spirituality, which is all about seeing what is spiritual, we need to get some familiarity with this radical concept of immaterial or incorporeal being and what it has to do with the life of the soul.

We can start with the notion of "form," which is the key term to contrast with "material." It is a deceptively simple term, which does not mean quite what we now think of when we use the word. The Platonist contrast between *form* and *material* is different from the modern contrast between *form* and *content*, where the form is like the external shell or container and the content is the real stuff inside. Platonist philosophy, on the contrary, thinks of form as real being, the enduring structure or pattern of things, whereas matter or material (for Platonists, the two words mean the same thing) is less real, something changeable and unstable, the source of a thing's decaying and dying.

To see why, think about it for a moment the same way as Aristotle, Plato's student, who modified Platonism in important ways but remained a Platonist in many respects. Think about the being of a bowl. What is it that makes a

3. Cicero, *Tusculan Disputations* 1:42.
4. Augustine, *Confessions* 7:1.1.

bowl to *be* a bowl? It would obviously be a mistake to answer that it's simply the material the bowl is made of. A bowl can be made of any number of materials—wood, stone, or plastic, just to name a few—but none of these are what makes it a bowl, for of course these same materials could be used to make many other things besides bowls. Something is a bowl when the material it is made of has the shape of a bowl. In other words, it is a bowl because of its form, not its material. So according to Aristotelian philosophy the essence or being of a bowl is its form. Having the right form is what it is for the bowl to *be* a bowl. The form, not the matter, is its true being or *ousia*.

Now take a more complicated example. What is it that makes a house *be* a house? Once again, it's not the materials it's made of (stone or brick or wood), because these could take some form other than a house. Unlike the form of a bowl, however, the form of a house is something more than its shape. There is a kind of general structure that all houses have in common, which stems from the purpose a house serves—what Aristotle calls its end or *telos*. The purpose of a house is to provide long-term shelter for human beings, so its structure includes an inside, an outside, a roof, and walls. The form of a house is the kind of structure that serves that purpose well.

Here we come upon a fundamental connection. The form of a thing is what makes it *good* for something, the way a bowl is good at holding liquid or a house is good for shelter. This means there is a deep connection between being and goodness. The same form that makes something *be* a bowl makes it a *good* bowl. Just think about what happens when a bowl begins to lose its form. When it's cracked, it is not such a good bowl, because it's not so good at doing what a bowl does—holding water or other things. Then if it splits into several pieces or is shattered, it loses the form of a bowl altogether. It ceases to be a bowl because it is simply no good at doing what bowls do. The same thing can be said for a house when it falls into disrepair and eventually collapses in ruin: as it loses the form of a house, it stops being a good house and eventually stops being a house at all.

So form is not only what makes something be what it is; it's what makes it able to do what it does, and do it well. It is the source of all powers and abilities, all capacity to do good things. To shift to a new set of examples that get us closer to our own being: think about a skill and how it gives shape or form to what we do. If you're a musician—a pianist for example—your fingers move in a well-formed way over the instrument, not at random like someone unskilled or unmusical. The skill shapes your movements but also forms your knowledge: because of your musical skill, you hear the piano's sounds with more accuracy and depth than when you were just a beginner. You can discern patterns that the unskilled don't notice. In that way, skills shape not only our perceptions but our minds or souls—or, in biblical language, our hearts. This shape or form in our hearts is a kind of power, an ability to do what the unskilled can't do. Thus form does not merely constrain us or restrict our freedom; it empowers us. Someone who knows how to move her fingers over the keys in a well-formed way rather than at random has the power to make music. She is formed in a way that makes her good at it. That is why we can describe learning to get good at something as a kind of formation—why we can speak of discipleship, for example, as Christian formation.

Think now about how you might get to be good, not at this or that skill, but at being human. This is what ancient culture called a virtue. The classical philosophers, especially in the Aristotelian tradition, described it as the form of a good soul. We could also say: it is the shape of a good life. Think of how an honest person's life is shaped, for example: the boundaries she won't cross, the corners she won't cut, the places she won't go with her words. All these are ways of talking about the virtue of honesty. Other virtues, like courage or kindness or justice, also give a definite shape to a person's life. Here, too, form is the basis of power, the ability to accomplish things that are good and worthwhile. Because you can trust an honest man, for example, he can accomplish good things that a corrupt politician cannot. The fundamental insight here is that goodness affords us both power and being that evil lacks. Virtuous people are like good musicians in a way, bringing harmony to a community. They keep a society healthy, so that it does not fall into ruin like a house divided, torn apart by civil strife and unable to accomplish anything good together.

At this point Plato takes one further step, which takes us beyond Aristotle and gets us to the goal of Platonist spirituality. He insists that the form or structure of things has being apart from any material. Think of how in geometry you can study concave shapes—the shape of a bowl without the material of a bowl. Or think of the blueprint of a house, and how that information may be transferred to various media or materials: from paper to a computer disk to the mind of an architect, for example, or embodied in the wood and stone of an actual house. The information, the form that can be found on the disk or on paper, in a mind or in wood and stone, is fundamentally independent of the material. And then consider the form or structure common to all houses, the pure form that makes any house to be a house. Plato's writings propose that there is such a thing, and that it has always existed just like mathematical truths. Platonist metaphysics is a development of this key notion of form existing independent from matter and the physical world.

And then consider what it would mean for there to be a form of honesty, courage, or justice, independent of the particular people who had those virtues. You could think of it as an unchanging truth about what these virtues really are, a truth that is as unchanging and certain as geometry. If you're willing to think that way, then you're beginning to think like a Platonist, and beginning to see why many people, including Christians, thought this might tell us something about what is truly divine. If there is an unchanging truth of justice, for example, and we can know something about what it is, then we can know something about the mind of God—not the thinking of silly, vicious little pagan gods, but the divine principle that is the source of every good thing, all being and goodness.

Spirituality against Corruptibility

Think again about what happens when a bowl gets worn out, cracked, or broken. Its form is marred or (to use a key Platonist term) corrupted. But in a deeper sense, the Platonists thought, the form itself is fine: the pure form of a bowl, its shape as studied in geometry, is what it always has been, unchanged. What has changed is the material, the wood or stone or plastic that once held the shape of the bowl but now fails to do so. Something similar happens when a house falls into ruin: the materials, the wood and stone, have begun to collapse into a disordered heap, losing the form of a house. Thus for Platonism, materiality is the source of change and corruption.[5] Every material thing, everything that has a body, is transient, perishable, corruptible, precisely because it is material, made out of some kind of matter or stuff, which cannot hold its form forever.

The Greek word for corruption, *phthora*, refers to ruin and destruction. In philosophical usage, it includes natural processes of aging and decay, as well as anything that goes bad or goes wrong: a cracked bowl, a ruined house, a rotten apple, a vicious soul, a divided community. Applied to the human body, it refers to sickness and frailty as well as what happens to your corpse as it rots and decomposes and gradually loses all human form. Thus in Platonist usage, the term "corruption" links materiality and mortality, drawing a line that connects decay and death, highlighting all the changes we are afraid of and seeing them as grounded in the instability of all material things. Anxiety about the corruptibility of everything in the material world, reflected and enhanced by Platonist thinking, pervaded the culture of late antiquity—the culture into which the Gospel entered when

---

5. Hence Plotinus, a very influential pagan Platonist, identifies pure matter (apart from how it is formed into bodily things) as evil itself, the source of corruption and all that goes wrong, in his essay "On the Nature and Source of Evil," *Enneads* 1:8.

the Christian mission first came to the Gentiles—and led it to look with misgiving at change itself. Whereas nowadays "change" and "transformation" are optimistic-sounding words used to convey hope for better things, growth, and progress, in the ancient world it made people think first of loss, corruption, and destruction: death rather than birth, decay rather than growth, changing for the worse rather than the better. This is an anxiety Paul addresses when he writes that, according to the Gospel of Christ, "this corruptible must put on incorruption, and this mortal must put on immortality" (1 Cor. 15:53 KJV).[6] He is talking about our bodies, raised in Christ and clothed with eternal life, so that they are no longer subject to any kind of corruption or change for the worse.

This is good news meant for ancient Greek ears, but it is not what Plato could have expected. He lacked any concept of everlasting life for the human body, which is a material thing that is bound eventually to decay and die and rot. So his hopes for escape from corruption were more spiritual. (Here we begin to deal with concepts about which we shall need to think quite critically later on.) In the *Phaedo*, which is one of the most famous things he wrote, Plato produced a kind of drama about the day his teacher Socrates was executed. He portrays him spending his last hours engaged in a cheerful philosophical discussion of life after death. For Plato, such a life was based on the immortality of the soul, not the resurrection of the body.[7] Writing long before the birth of Christ, he had no inkling of the event Christians celebrate on Easter, in which a man who had been dead and buried was raised to life— not merely a ghost or soul going to heaven but a living human being, body and all, no longer to be found in the tomb because he was no longer dead, no longer even capable of death—an event in which death itself was defeated and overcome in his own body.

Plato's notion was different. It did not occur to him that a human body could escape death or overcome the corruption of the grave. So his hope was not that death could be defeated but that it could be welcomed, because there is a part of us that is not material—not a body—and therefore does not actually die. He meant the soul, of course, the most "spiritual" part of us (as we could now put it), which is also what we most truly are—as Socrates insists in a touching moment near the end of the *Phaedo*, when he tells his disciples that

6. The term Paul uses here stems from the same Greek term, *phthora*, that is commonplace in Platonist philosophy and that is usually translated into Latin as *corruptio*. More recent translations obscure this connection by using the word "perishable" instead of "corruptible."

7. The importance of this contrast, as well as its narrative setting in the deaths of Socrates and Jesus, was highlighted in a now classic essay, originally in 1955, by biblical scholar Oscar Cullmann, *Immortality of the Soul or Resurrection of the Dead?*

once he is executed they can bury his body, but they cannot bury *him*.[8] They will be able to find his corpse but they won't find Socrates, for his real self, his soul, will be gone, escaping this whole realm of materiality and mortality. In this Platonic view of things, death is the liberation that true philosophers are practicing for their whole lives. It is something that we can be philosophical about, in the original sense of the phrase, because it frees our souls from bondage to corruptible bodies.[9] According to this spiritual understanding of death, the corruptible does not put on incorruption but rather is shed like worn-out clothing that the immortal soul is finally rid of. The mortal does not put on immortality, but rather the immortal puts off mortality. For the human body, Socrates argues in Plato's text, is like a prison—or perhaps like a soldier's post where we have been stationed for a time by someone in authority over us. The body is an evil the soul must put up with until finally separated from it at death.[10]

Death, then, defined by Plato as the separation of the soul from the body, is a kind of liberation from what is mortal and material.[11] That is one of the great claims of spirituality, a claim that has been immensely influential in the West, not least in the history of Christian thought. But at the start it required a deep revision of our usual notion of ourselves, including the notion that Plato had inherited from Homer, which pictures souls being breathed out with our dying breath and then dissolved and scattered on the wind, never to return.[12] The soul has a better destiny than that, according to Plato's argument, because it has a better nature than that. It is not like a breath, something composed of material that can be dissolved, scattered, or blown away, but rather is akin to pure, immortal form.[13] This earth is not its home, for its true origin—and the place to which the pure soul ultimately returns—is a place beyond all places, the realm of pure form. By reconceiving the soul in this way Plato invents a

8. Plato, *Phaedo* 115c–d.

9. "To be philosophical" about death was also a major aim of the Stoic philosophers, which is why we still speak in the same vein of "being stoical" about it. Though the Stoics were not Platonists, they admired Socrates' philosophical attitude toward suffering and death as Plato portrayed it; see for example Epictetus, *Discourses* 1:4.24; 3:23.21; 4:1.159–66. This Stoic admiration for Socrates, often shared by Christians, is an example of how Platonist spirituality has had an effect well beyond the bounds of Platonism.

10. The key passages from Plato's *Phaedo*: philosophy as practicing to die (64a), the body as worn-out clothing (87b–d), as prison (82d–e), as post (62b–c), as an evil (66b).

11. Death is defined as the separation of soul and body in *Phaedo* 64c; it is thus the culmination of the philosopher's efforts to liberate the soul from the body in 64e. Augustine is describing his mother's death in Platonist terms when he says "that devout and holy soul was released from the body" (*Confessions* 9:11.28). But Augustine is far from the only Christian writer who thinks of death in these basically Platonist terms.

12. Plato, *Phaedo* 70a and 77d.

13. Plato, *Phaedo* 78b–80d.

rigorous version of what has come to be called soul-body dualism, where the soul is not just a breath in the body but a different kind of being from any bodily thing, with a different origin, nature, and destiny. We could call it the fully spiritual notion of the soul.

Spirituality as Intelligibility

Spirituality, in the deep sense that derives from Plato, is about the soul's relation to what is spiritual, where "spiritual" is a word that contrasts with "material." However, to describe Platonism in these terms is to use specifically Christian vocabulary, for Plato didn't use the Greek word for "spirit" in this way, in part because (as we have seen) the word for "spirit" in Greek philosophy typically meant something material like breath or fire. To begin talking about spirituality in Plato's own terms, we need to return to the notion of form and consider what it means to say that form is pure or free from all material.

Consider once again the form of a bowl. You might think that when a bowl is broken into little pieces its form is gone. Aristotle thought that way, arguing that the form of things was inseparable from the material in which it was, we might say, "embodied." This has consequences for his notion of the human body and soul, including the fact that he did not support Plato's version of immortality. The soul for Aristotle was the form of the body, the formative power that gave the body not just its outward shape but its anatomical structure and its living physiological processes, as well as its powers of motion and perception. In this case form is much more than mere shape, but it is still inseparable from matter; without flesh and blood, there is no human form, and therefore no soul.[14]

Plato thought, on the contrary, that form was inherently separate from matter. In Platonism the form of a bowl is not stuck, as it were, in the bowl, but is best understood in its pure form, as a geometrical shape that needs no material embodiment. The true form is not what you see by looking at wooden bowls, for example, but by learning to understand curves and concavities in geometry.[15] For form is, by its nature, intelligible not sensible: it is what you

14. This is the conclusion reached by one line of interpretation of Aristotle, who is cryptic on the subject of the immortality of the soul. Other interpretations are possible, but the status of the soul separated from the body—and how it can have any life or activity in this separated state—remains a serious problem for Aristotelian philosophers, as can be seen in Aquinas's discussion of the "separated soul" in *ST* I, 89 and Supp. 70. See also the discussion of Dante in Cary, "Weight of Love."

15. See the geometrical illustration used by Augustine in his spiritual quest at the end of *Soliloquies* 2:18.32.

understand with your intellect, not what you perceive with one of your five senses. Thus the original Platonist word for spirituality was "intelligibility," designating the kind of being that is understood by the intellect (i.e., the word "intelligible" refers to objects perceived by the intellect, just as the word "visible" refers to objects perceived by the power of vision and the word "sensible" refers to objects perceived by one of the five senses).

Intelligible Form and Intellectual Vision

If the connection between spirit and intellect seems a little odd, that may be in part because you are thinking in English. In French or German, where the word for mind is also the word for spirit (*esprit* or *Geist*), the connection does not seem so strange. Still, it takes some getting used to. Therefore, lest you think we are talking about something abstract or "merely intellectual" (to use a phrase deeply alien to Platonist thinking), try remembering the kind of experience you had while learning something difficult but rewarding, an experience of intellectual insight. Perhaps it was a math class where you were studying geometrical curves. Suppose at first that you had a hard time "getting" it. Maybe you drew curves on a piece of paper, or imagined the curve of a bowl, or remembered curves that your teacher drew on a blackboard—but that didn't really help, because of course these curves were not really what you were trying to understand; at best they were reminders, which you and your teacher were using to get you to see something that you could never see on a blackboard or a piece of paper. So you kept working at it until, suddenly, in a moment of insight, you *got* it. At that point, you might have said something like, "Aha! Now I see it!" It is a moment of sheer intellectual joy, like finding something you love.

What is it you're seeing in that "Aha!" moment? According to the Platonist view of things, it is pure intelligible form. Unlike a bowl you hold in your hand or a curve you draw on paper, it is something that never came into being and will never cease to be, because the truth of it never *began* to be true and will never stop being true. It is an eternal being and truth that cannot be seen with the physical eyes in your head but only—to introduce a key Platonist metaphor—with the mind's eye, the eye of your soul. It is important to be clear that the mind's eye, in the Platonist view, is not simply imagination. It is not like imagining a curve your teacher drew on a blackboard, which is something you saw with your bodily eyes.[16] Imagination, the ancient philosophers

16. Distinguishing pure intellectual understanding from mere imagination requires a moral purity of soul, Augustine argues in *Soliloquies* 2:20.34—a point to which we shall return in chap. 3.

thought, always makes use of mental images derived from the senses, the way an imagined unicorn has, for example, the look of a white horse with a golden horn, or an imagined curve has the color of chalk on a blackboard. Pure intelligible form is quite different: it has no colors, nothing that could ever be visible to the eyes of your body. It is the object of a distinctively *intellectual* vision.

Thus for Platonism, a pure form is not merely an abstraction; it is a real, eternal being.[17] It is an ultimate reality that you "see" with your intellect, not a mental image abstracted or "pulled off" (a literal translation of the Latin word *abstractus*) from material things such as bowls and curves drawn on blackboards. It has true being because it has always been and always will be—unlike bowls and curves drawn on blackboards and images in your mind. The pagan Platonists called it divine, because it is immortal, and in Greek "an immortal" was a term for a god. Of course it is not a person with desires and fears and jealousies, like the gods of traditional pagan mythology, which the Platonists never took literally.[18] But it is divine because of its eternal being, its superiority to things that are mortal and corruptible, and because it gives form and being to these lower things, such as bowls and horses and even our imaginary unicorns, all of which would be impossible without the spatial world that gets its form from the truths of geometry.

Love and the Supreme Good

But of course the intelligible realm includes much more than geometry. When Plato speaks of forms, he tends to think first of virtues, such as justice, piety, and wisdom as well as even higher principles like Beauty and the Good. Later Platonists in the Christian tradition, such as Augustine, will speak also of

17. A note about a particularly confusing piece of terminology is necessary here. Plato's forms have often been called "ideas" or even "ideals." This can be misleading if it leads you to think of them as less than fully real, for Plato thinks of them as more real than anything in the physical world. Plato did use the Greek word *idea*, which originally meant the "look" of physical things, to describe the "look" of forms as objects of intellectual vision. In that sense, Plato's ideas are simply Platonic forms. But that means the phrase "Plato's ideas" does not refer to Plato's thoughts or concepts. "Ideas," in the sense of the term used by Plato, are not ideals we strive for, nor are they thoughts in our heads. Rather, they are the unchanging essence and deep truth of things. For medieval philosophers, their proper location is not in any human mind but in the mind of God (as Augustine argued in *Eighty-Three Different Questions*, question 46). It was therefore a radical change in the meaning of the word when modern philosophers like Descartes started talking about "ideas" as if we human beings had them in our minds. That's not how the term was used in ancient or medieval thought.

18. See Socrates' skepticism about stories of gods misbehaving and fighting with each other in Plato, *Euthyphro* 6a.

eternal Truth and supreme Being. And all of these of course are terms for God. These divine things give form not only to bodies in space but also to souls with their desires and thoughts. Any power that can form human life for the good is something that Platonist philosophy seeks to grasp by rising above merely sensible things and using the intellect to understand what is to be seen in the intelligible realm of pure form. Hence true education for the intellectual soul is inseparable from formation in virtue, justice, and wisdom.

Platonist spirituality thus has a very large place for love of truth and the pursuit of wisdom, as well as a love of neighbor centered on the kind of friendship that promotes justice, virtue, and the common good. The fear of God, however, does not have a natural place in Platonism, because the Platonist kind of spirituality does not conceive of the divine as a person, like a king who comes to render judgment and set things right, vindicating the oppressed and punishing the wicked. Rather, the divine appears to the soul as fundamentally an object of desire, something we seek to know and be united with, like when a bright, earnest young person falls in love with mathematics or music, the virtuous life or the beauty of wisdom. Augustine, for example, describes how he fell in love with divine Wisdom as a young man after reading a pagan philosophy text.[19] Hence Platonism has had much more influence on how Christians love God than on how they fear him. It tends to produce a set of anxieties centered on the transience of this life and corruptibility of this world, rather than on the judgment of God. The two sets of anxieties can certainly be combined, as the moral corruption of our souls is a good reason to fear the judgment of God, but the roots of the anxieties are different. And the difference shows, as we shall see when we come to look at Augustine more closely in chapter 3.

Plato does have some things to say about punishment after death for souls not formed in virtue, but his conception of this is much more like medieval purgatory than like hell. The purpose of punishment, in his view, is fundamentally remedial. It is a kind of harsh medicine for the soul, to purge it of its vices, its foul desires and earthly attachments.[20] The ultimate aim of all punishment, in this life and the next, is not retribution but restoration of the soul to virtue. Such punishment is certainly an experience worth avoiding, but it is more like a long, painful process of healing and cleansing than like facing an angry judge. It is not at root an encounter with a person, and it is in that way less personal, as well as less fearsome, than biblical notions of divine judgment.

19. Augustine, *Confessions* 3:4.7–8. The text was Cicero's *Hortensius*, which owed a great deal to the Platonist tradition.

20. The remedial and purgative purpose of punishment for souls after death is particularly clear in the myth in Plato, *Phaedo* 113d–114b.

In any case, Plato's philosophy is not motivated by fear of punishment but by love of wisdom. What he has to say about punishment for the soul after this life never became as important in Platonist spirituality as the things he has to say about the soul's education in wisdom, virtue, and the love of true beauty. We have some idea of what he thinks this education looks like in practice, because it is illustrated in the philosophical dialogues he writes, many of which are carefully crafted dramas of education. Punishment, on the other hand, is depicted at length only in Plato's myths, the stories he makes up about the destiny of the soul that take us beyond anything we can observe with our eyes and ears.

The Allegory of the Cave

Plato in fact deliberately composes a number of myths, which are located in his dialogues at places where he wants our minds to catch sight of things that lie beyond ordinary human language and experience. Since ultimately we must see things for ourselves (like students who ought not to be content with memorizing formulas given by their teacher), Plato the teacher tells allegorical stories about what the soul experiences when it sees more than he can say. These Platonic myths are immensely suggestive and have been enormously influential. Like Plato's soul-body dualism and his concept of the immortality of the soul, they have had an impact far beyond the bounds of the Platonist tradition itself. If, for example, you are someone who hopes your soul will go to heaven when you die, then your thinking is under the influence of Plato's mythology. So the quickest way to come to an appreciation of how influential Platonist spirituality has been in Christianity is to get acquainted with these myths. (What follows is merely an introduction, highlighting some aspects of Plato's mythology that have been influential in Christian thought. It is not a complete interpretation of the myths nor even an adequate summary.)

The most famous of Plato's myths has been called the allegory of the cave.[21] Plato tells us at the outset that it is about the effects of education on our souls, but it turns out that its greatest influence has been on the history of spirituality and mysticism (which, on a Christian Platonist view, are not so different from educating the soul). Education, in the allegory, is like climbing

---

21. Plato, *Republic* 514a–521b. There is a somewhat similar myth of ascent from the lower earth to the True Earth in Plato, *Phaedo* 109d–111c. The latter is probably what C. S. Lewis had in mind in the finale to the Narnia books, where life after death is pictured as a movement "further up and further in" to a true Narnia that is more real than the Shadowlands of mortal, visible Narnia. When the children are surprised at this, the Professor remarks, "It's all in Plato, all in Plato; bless me, what *do* they teach them at these schools!" (*Last Battle*, 195 [chap. 15]).

out of a shadowy cave into the light of day, as you gradually learn to see for yourself the true forms of things. The cave contains everything we see with the eyes of our bodies or perceive with any of our senses. The shadows it contains are symbolic of material things, which we mistakenly suppose are ultimately real things, because in our uneducated and unspiritual state we don't know any better. As the soul climbs out of the cave, it ascends by degrees to what Plato calls the "intelligible place" (and later Platonists called "the intelligible world"), which is the realm of pure forms, the things we see with the intellect alone.

Plato's imagery is brilliantly suggestive. It tells us that the physical world (what ancient Platonists called "the sensible world") is real in its own inferior way, but has less reality than the intelligible world. The shadows in the cave, representing corporeal things or what we would now call "physical objects," have being only insofar as they imitate the shape of the fully real things in the world above. They have a share in the goodness of form, but no true reality of their own. To use another key Platonist term: they have form and being only insofar as they *participate* in intelligible forms above them. This participation means that bodily things have a share in higher things, not materially, the way you have a share in a piece of pie (which leaves less of the pie for others) but formally, the way a shadow or reflection shares the form of the real thing it resembles. Form can thus be shared or participated in by any number of material things, with no diminution or loss to the form itself. One form thus has limitless power to give form to lower things. The goodness of intelligible form is therefore infinite (later Platonists like Plotinus will say) not because it is endlessly extended in space or of infinite bulk, but because there is no limit to how it may share its goodness with lesser things.

Because intelligible form gives being to things, it is always a good; and the form of all forms, which is like the sun in the intelligible realm above the cave, is called by Plato "the Good itself." If you call it "the supreme Good," then you can readily see the connection with Christian thought, and how it becomes a term for God. The Good is what gives intelligibility to all other forms, as the literal, visible sun gives visibility to things on earth, making them visible by its light. And it gives being to things also, just as the literal sun provides the energy that causes plants to grow and makes all life and existence on earth possible. The Good is thus the source or principle (*arche*) of both being and understanding (or we could say, equivalently, of both reality and intelligibility).

The Good is the origin of all things, but it is also the end of all things, in the sense that it is the ultimate goal, the final object of desire and love and understanding. In the allegory, it is the last thing we are able to see in our ascent, because it is so full of light that at first we can't stand to look at it. It dazzles every eye that tries to look at it—especially those that have just come from the darkness of the cave, accustomed to gazing at shadows. The source of being and knowledge is thus beyond all being and knowledge, transcending even the intelligibility of form, not because it is unintelligible but because it is, as it were, superintelligible—again like the sun, which is hard to see not because it is dark or invisible but because it is so much brighter than everything else. It takes a while for the dazzled eye of the mind to get used to so much light, as Augustine explains for example in his *Soliloquies*, using the same metaphor of dazzlement as Plato,[22] and as Dante illustrates in his *Paradiso*, where the soul ascends to the heights of heavenly vision precisely as it is repeatedly strengthened to see more and more of the divine light.[23]

Between the shadows and the sun, and moving between them, is the soul, which in Platonist thinking occupies a peculiar place in the middle of things, neither a bodily thing nor a pure form. Unlike the eternal forms in the world above the cave, it is changeable, able to turn from bad to worse but also from worse to better: from ignorance to wisdom or from vice to virtue. In the allegory of the cave, this turn to the better is the movement from darkness to light, the ascent from the cave toward the supreme Good. The picture develops, over the centuries, into a full-blown notion of the soul going to heaven.

The Myth of the Fall

Plato, however, does not want us to think that we start in the cave as if we naturally belonged there. So something more needs to be said about the soul's movements: in addition to its ultimate ascent there is its primal descent, which Plato describes in another myth, the story of the Fall in the *Phaedrus*[24] (not to be confused with the *Phaedo*, which is a different dialogue). The myth of the Fall offers an explanation of how our souls came to be imprisoned in bodies, beginning with a picture of the life of pure souls in their original, heavenly home. Plato's notion of heaven draws on the new astronomy of his day (worked out in more detail in Ptolemaic astronomy, a few centuries

22. Augustine, *Soliloquies* 1:13.23, as well as 1:6.12–13, which established the metaphor of vision; both passages deploy imagery that seems clearly derived, whether directly or indirectly, from Plato's allegory of the cave.

23. See the pattern of dazzling light followed by strengthened eye as Dante ascends in *Paradiso* 1:46–63; 5:1–6; 14:76–84; 23:22–48; 26:70–79; 28:16–18; 30:46–60; 33:76–78. The pattern began in his encounters with angels at each new level of ascent in *Purgatorio* 8:34–36; 9:79–81; 15:10–12; 17:52–54; 24:142–44; 27:59–60.

24. Plato, *Phaedrus* 243a–256e.

later), which recognized that the earth is not flat but spherical, and explained the movements of the planets and the stars by positing a series of concentric spheres that revolved around the earth. Christian readers might be most familiar with it as the astronomy of Dante's *Paradiso*. In the myth of the Fall, as in the *Paradiso*, the souls of the blessed are pictured inhabiting the realm above the revolving spheres of heaven,[25] and thus in a sense outside time as well as space, because times and seasons on earth are all derived from the revolution of the heavenly spheres (days from the revolving of the sphere containing the sun, months from the revolving of the sphere containing the moon, and so on).

What souls are doing in their heavenly home, together with the gods (for in this myth, Plato is willing to talk about celestial gods), is contemplating the forms. "Contemplation" is a word for vision—in Greek, *theoria*, which gives us the word "theater" as well as "theory." In the Platonist tradition contemplation is an experience of enjoyment, which means that *theoria* and its opposite, which is the practical life or *praxis*, are related in a way quite different from the contrast of theory and practice in modern thought. They are two modes of the soul's activity (medieval Christians called them the contemplative life and the active life), which are related to one another as the enjoyment of a good thing is related to the hard work needed to produce it: as living in a house contrasts with building it, or enjoying music contrasts with learning how to play it, or celebrating a civic festival contrasts with working at civic government. The souls in heaven, in other words, have it good: they do not work and strive and seek, but join the gods in enjoying the sights. They contemplate pure beauty, beholding the intelligible loveliness of the forms that are the source of everything good and beautiful on earth.

Unlike the gods, however, they have trouble maintaining their concentration—and that is where the souls' evil begins. Plato compares human souls to charioteers whose chariots are pulled by two horses, one of which is unruly and hard to control. These horses symbolize the lower aspects of the soul, which are like beasts in that they are not rational. One of them, however, can listen to reason, like a good-tempered and well-trained animal obeying its master. It gladly submits to the guidance of the charioteer, who represents reason, the part of the soul that properly rules over the whole. The unruly horse, on the other hand, causes the charioteer no end of trouble, because it

25. It is a "place beyond heaven . . . visible only to intelligence" (Plato, *Phaedrus* 247c). Likewise in Dante, although souls manifest themselves at various levels in the heavens, their true home is in the empyrean, the heaven of fire (*Paradiso* 4:28–39), which is "not in space" (22:76) because it is beyond the outermost of the revolving spheres, so that it "has no other *where* than the Divine Mind" (27:109–10).

is unable to listen or obey. To make a long story short, human souls eventually lose control of their chariots altogether and fall from their high place in heaven. They are assigned to bodies on earth and thus (to combine Plato's myths) they come to be imprisoned in the cave, the material world.

The pagan Platonist tradition had an interestingly ambivalent attitude toward the descent of the soul into bodies. On the one hand, it is the soul's own fault, due to its moral weakness, loss of self-control, and failure to cling to the best, most rational kind of life. On the other hand, it is a very good thing for the material world to have souls in it, for without souls bodies have no life. Plotinus argued, in fact, that the descent of the soul into embodiment is due both to the necessity of animating the material world and to the soul's moral failing.[26] This is a telling example of the characteristically two-sided attitude of Platonism to this material world. On the one hand it is a world of shadows, less real than the world above. On the other hand, the shadows themselves imitate the shape of higher things, participating in their form and thus their reality and goodness. Hence the *Timaeus*, the Platonic dialogue that, more than any other, won the appreciation of orthodox Christians, contains a creation myth in which the material world is unmistakably good through and through, for it is a kind of visible image of divine beauty. This two-sidedness is important for understanding the diverse and complex roles Platonism has played in the history of Christian thought, as we are about to see.

26. Plotinus works out this two-sided view in his essay "On the Descent of the Soul," *Enneads* 4:8; cf. also *Enneads* 1:1.12; 4:3.9–18. On the evil of the Fall, see *Enneads* 1:8.14 (where matter is ultimately to blame) and 5:1.1 (where the fault seems to lie in the soul itself).

2

Divine Carnality

Platonist spirituality has given Christian thought some of its most widespread and taken-for-granted concepts. Plato, not the Bible, is at the root of our concept of the immortality of the soul, the notion that death is the separation of soul and body, and the hope of our soul going to heaven when we die. All these concepts belong to a spirituality of ascent to the divine, which shall be the focus of my criticism beginning in this chapter. The problem with such spirituality, I shall argue, is that it moves in a different direction from the incarnation of God in Jesus Christ, which is a descent into flesh rather than an ascent of the spirit. In the light of Christian faith, we should recognize that the fundamental relation between God and us is established not by human spirituality but by a kind of divine carnality. We should be looking to Christ's life-giving flesh rather than the power of the human spirit.

There are, to be sure, problems with flesh, which is at the basis of human weakness and corruptibility, including our vulnerability to disease, suffering, sin, and death. But in the flesh of Christ, God took up these problems and made them his own. So Christian faith is properly about his carnal descent rather than our spiritual ascent. In our spirituality we are all too prone to be like Zacchaeus, wanting to climb high to see the Son of God. But the first thing Jesus says to him is "Zacchaeus, hurry and come down!" (Luke 19:5). I imagine him saying this with a friendly laugh, as if to say: "What are you doing up there, Zacchaeus? I'm down here, and I mean to come have supper with you. But how can I eat with you if you're way up there?"

Christian Versions of the Fall

Descent into flesh is not what Platonism wants. Its name for this descent is the Fall of the soul, as we have seen. This is a good place to start seeing the complexities in the church fathers' critical appropriation of Platonist spirituality in the first few centuries of the Christian tradition.

The Platonic myth of the Fall has been influential enough in Christianity to give its name to the story of the first sin and disobedience in the garden of Eden. It's not actually an appropriate name, however, because the story of Adam and Eve never describes a fall or any kind of downward movement—no literal or symbolic descent from a higher place to a lower—unlike, say, the story of Lucifer falling from heaven in Isaiah 14:12–15 or Satan cast down from heaven in Revelation 12:7–11. The difference is that Lucifer or Satan is originally an angel, the kind of immortal being who belongs in heaven, whereas on a biblical view human beings belong on earth, just like fish in the sea, birds in the air, and cattle on the ground—as the first chapter of Genesis makes quite clear. In ancient thinking, both Greek and Israelite, heaven is for immortals, which is to say it is home for gods or angels or (Platonism suggests) disembodied souls, not for things that die. Again, it is helpful to think of Dante's astronomy, where the heavenly bodies are not made of earth but of pure crystal filled with light. There is literally no dirt up there, no perishable material—nothing at all like what we now think of when we talk about life on other planets. For Dante's astronomy, like Plato's and the Bible's, is still shaped by the contrast between heaven and earth, with no notion of what modern people call "outer space." Mortal things have no natural home up there on high.

We call the narrative about Adam and Eve and the forbidden fruit by the name "the Fall" because, ironically, it invited Platonist speculations about the Fall of the soul that were entertained but eventually rejected by orthodox Christianity. Origen, the great biblical exegete and Christian Platonist of the third century, whose spirituality was extremely influential but also went too far by orthodox reckoning, had suggested ways of combining Christian notions of sin with the Platonist notion that our souls inhabit mortal bodies because of their fall from a heavenly, disembodied state. Our souls originated long before our bodies, Origen suggested, and may well be reincarnated in a series of bodies (as Plato had suggested in another myth) before they are perfected and freed to return to their original heavenly life.[1] In the end, Origen's speculative

---

1. Plato appears willing to adopt a version of the ancient mythic notion of reincarnation or (as it is also called) transmigration of souls in *Meno* 81a–d; *Phaedo* 81b–82b; *Phaedrus* 248d–249b; *Republic* 614b–621d. This becomes an important element in later Platonist accounts of how souls are purified as they pass through a series of different kinds of bodies. Origen's speculations

suggestions were rejected by the church because they stood too much in tension with the message of Genesis about the original goodness of the material world as God created it. Augustine, the great Christian Platonist of the West, seems to have been the last major church father who entertained—at least for a while in his early years—the possibility that our souls existed before our bodies and came into them through a Fall.[2]

Both Origen and Augustine were trying to strike a distinctive balance required by Christian Platonism. For in Platonist spirituality the relation between spiritual and material can go in two opposite directions, as indicated by the ambiguity of the shadows in Plato's allegory. If you think of the emptiness of the shadows, their lack of true being, and the fact that our souls are nonetheless imprisoned with them and captivated by them, then the material world can look very evil indeed. But if you think of material things as formed by participation in higher things, like shadows or reflections shaped by their likeness to the form of things more real than themselves, then you can affirm that the whole material world is good, so far as it goes. Plato himself does this in the *Timaeus*, which, as mentioned at the end of chapter 1, was a treatise that orthodox Christians liked because it described a divine creative activity that fit the affirmation in Genesis that the whole visible world is good. In the *Timaeus*, the harmoniously revolving spheres of the visible heavens are "the most beautiful of all things that have come to be" because they are "a moving image of eternity." In their movement we see "time that imitates eternity."[3]

Hence, on the one hand, orthodox Christian Platonists go very far in the direction of affirming the goodness of all creation. Augustine, for instance, can say quite flatly that "everything that is, is good,"[4] because evil has no being of its own and the only evil in the world is the corruption of good things, so that every evil thing in the world is actually a good thing partially corrupted—and there can be no such thing as pure evil because pure corruption, like pure

---

along these lines, including both Fall and transmigration of souls, are developed in his treatise *On First Principles* 1:5–8. Since there are inconsistencies in this text (in part because we have much of it only in an unreliable Latin translation), it helps to have an overview from someone who has surveyed the whole of Origen's surviving writings, such as Crouzel, *Origen*, chap. 11. For Origen's relationship to his Platonist milieu in these matters, see Dillon, "Origen and Plotinus."

2. For a controversial but, to my mind, convincing argument that Augustine accepted a fallen-soul theory of human embodiment in his early works, see O'Connell, *St. Augustine's Early Theory of Man* and *St. Augustine's Confessions*, as well as the summary of O'Connell's arguments in Rombs, *Saint Augustine and the Fall of the Soul*. For the story of how Augustine changed his mind as he learned of the church's rejection of Origen's views, see O'Connell, *Origin of the Soul in St. Augustine's Later Works*.

3. Plato, *Timaeus* 29a, 37d, 38a. For the influence of this dialogue on Christian thought, see Pelikan, *Christianity and Classical Culture*, 95–98.

4. Augustine, *Confessions* 7:12.18.

darkness, is nothing at all.[5] Even the devil is only a corrupted angel, fallen from heaven. On the other hand, however, are the gnostics, the most important unorthodox Christians of the first few centuries, who came to think of the material world as irredeemably evil. To gain an appreciation of the strengths of orthodox Christian Platonism, it is useful to look briefly at the radical spirituality of the gnostics, whom even the pagan Platonist Plotinus found shockingly irreverent in their contempt for the visible world.[6]

Gnosticism

The label "gnosticism" has been used to describe a wide variety of ancient spiritualities, most of which owe something to Platonism.[7] (Readers unfamiliar with the term "gnostic" should be aware that the term has the opposite meaning from "agnostic," a modern term referring to those who claim not to know whether God exists. The ancient gnostics claimed a special, higher knowledge—*gnosis* in Greek—that gave them entry to spiritual realms inaccessible to others.) One central strand of gnosticism condemns the visible heavens themselves as a habitation of evil powers called *archons*, celestial rulers who block the soul's journey up beyond the heavens to escape the material world altogether. The gnostics aimed to take that journey, for they thought of themselves as pure spirits who needed to return to the *pleroma* (literally "the fullness") consisting of spiritual beings called *aeons*, which are something like personified Platonic forms, existing above the visible heavens and thus outside the material universe. Gnosticism seems to have arisen as the new astronomy that originated in the generation before Plato became part of popular consciousness, making the earth seem like a prison at the bottom of the cosmos, hemmed in by hostile heavenly spheres above and around it, which blocked access to the pure spiritual realm beyond.[8]

5. For a fuller exposition of the nature of evil by Augustine, see also *Enchiridion*, chaps. 12–14; *On the Nature of the Good*, chaps. 1–17. On the corruption of the devil, which took place by his evil use of God's good gift of free will, see *City of God* 11:11–17; 12:1–9.

6. Plotinus, *Enneads* 2:9.16–18. This essay has been given two titles, which are mutually illuminating: "Against the Gnostics" and "Against those who say the maker of the universe is evil and the universe is evil."

7. Though many scholars see something alien to the classical Greek spirit in gnosticism, the fact that gnostics often used Platonist language and forms of thought is not in dispute. In addition to the studies collected by Wallis and Bregman in *Neoplatonism and Gnosticism*, see Turner, *Sethian Gnosticism and the Platonic Tradition*, chap. 1, for a useful survey of scholarly approaches to the issue of the relation of gnosticism and Platonism. Dillon, *Middle Platonists*, 384–89, briefly but very helpfully locates Valentinian gnosticism in its Platonist milieu.

8. In evoking and explaining the sense of cosmic alienation characteristic of gnosticism, Jonas's *Gnostic Religion* is still unsurpassed; see especially his summary at the end of the second chapter, 42–47.

Gnostics, you could say, were people who wanted to go to heaven with a vengeance—to escape forever from the filth of earth and of the prison of their own bodies. They did not think highly of the God of the Jews, the creator of the material world. In their view he is the most arrogant of the archons, ignorant and not spiritually minded, who makes the ugly mistake of bringing into being the lowest and least honorable part of the cosmos, the ball of dirt called earth, where we humans are now imprisoned. He is so proud of this repulsive feat that he boasts of being the only God, not knowing that above him there is a whole realm of divine beings more spiritual than he is, the *pleroma* of the aeons.[9]

Gnostics can be thought of as one-sided Christian Platonists who see the world of the cave as all bad, something simply to escape from. They have been called "pessimistic," but that doesn't quite catch the poignancy of their belief, which is in one sense very optimistic, that they are pure spirits belonging to the eternal realm beyond the dirt and suffering of earth and above even the visible splendor of the stars. To appreciate the attraction of the gnostics' radical spirituality, consider what the church fathers tell us about Simon Magus, whom they identify as the first of the gnostics.[10] He went about like any old religious charlatan, performing fake miracles and magic tricks and claiming to be the most high God in person, the supreme Mind with secret spiritual knowledge (*gnosis*) to impart. He was accompanied by a woman named Helena, whom he picked up from a brothel where she had been a slave. He claimed she was the Thought of his divine Mind, trapped in flesh, and he told a story about how she had been reborn time after time into women's bodies, always subjected to abuse and degradation. Hearing of this story so many centuries later, it is not hard to understand why a woman in Helena's circumstances would want to escape the material world altogether, freed from the body that

9. See Dahl, "Arrogant Archon." The portrayal of the creator god in Sethian gnosticism as the arrogant archon Ialdabaoth (a perversion of the sacred name of the God of Israel) can be found in ancient gnostic documents in Robinson, *Nag Hammadi Library* (for example, *The Apocryphon of John* 10.20–13.14 and *On the Origin of the World* 101.1–103.29) and also in Irenaeus's report in *Against Heresies* 1:30.5–14. Dillon, "*Pleroma* and Noetic Cosmos," shows why the gnostic *pleroma* of aeons is a version of the Platonist intelligible world. It is worth noting that when the Nicene Creed, borrowing from biblical language about Christ in Col. 1:16, says that God the Father is Creator of all things visible *and invisible*, this was meant as an affirmation that the God of Israel creates not just the visible world of material things but the invisible world of angels and whatever rulers, archons, aeons, or spiritual beings there are above or below, in whatever *pleroma* or intelligible world there may be—which means that all of them are subjected to the Son of God, Jesus Christ (Eph. 1:21).

10. The story is most fully told in Irenaeus, *Against Heresies* 1:23 (cf. Jonas, *Gnostic Religion*, chap. 4). Irenaeus's identification of this Samaritan charlatan with Simon the magician (traditionally named Simon Magus) in Acts 8:9–24 may not be historically accurate, but the sense of longing that lies behind this kind of spirituality is no less poignantly on display.

made her vulnerable to repeated abuse. For her, gnostic spirituality must have come as good news.

Jesus Is LORD

The Gospel of Jesus Christ is a different kind of good news, which may at first sight seem impossibly optimistic. It announces the defeat of death itself, the glorification of our human bodies, and the renewal of the whole material world rather than escape from it. For the God of the Jews, who is the Father of our Lord Jesus Christ, did indeed create the material world, and since it belongs rightly to him he has no intention of letting it remain in bondage to death and decay. Hence our bodies themselves will, like Christ's resurrected body, put on incorruption and immortality, as Paul tells us (1 Cor. 15:53), so that they are no longer vulnerable to harm, to suffering and abuse. One might wonder how ancient Christians thought they could get away with believing this. Yet their worship—from the beginning, so far as we can tell—centered on proclaiming the truth of it: that Jesus Christ was raised bodily from the dead and exalted to eternal life at the right hand of God the Father almighty, so that in him death is defeated, resurrection of the body is promised to us, and the material world itself is to be "set free from its bondage to corruption" (Rom. 8:21). Christianity as a religion, a form of social life not just a conviction of the heart, began with the worship of this one man, whose flesh belongs on the throne of God.[11]

Such worship points to something extraordinary that is not easily contained in any conceptual framework. In biblical terms it means that the LORD, the God of Israel, Creator of all things, who gives his glory to no other, has given his glory and even his name to this man, Jesus. We see this in the earliest forms of Christian worship, as for instance in the writings of Paul, the first Christian whose writings we have (he wrote before the four gospels were written), who quotes a hymn that was already familiar to his Christian readers—perhaps the very earliest piece of Christian literature known to us—which praises Christ in his humiliation and exaltation, and concludes by offering him worship in terms fit only for the God of Israel:

11. For what follows, see Hurtado, *Lord Jesus Christ*, and Bauckham, *Jesus and the God of Israel*, both of which present historical evidence for a high Christology, including worship of the exalted Jesus, in the very earliest stages of Christianity. Bauckham brings a particular conceptual clarity to the subject, arguing that the highest possible Christology was characteristic of Christianity from its Jewish beginnings, precisely because Jewish monotheism had no conceptual room for worship of Jesus to be equivalent to worship of lesser divine beings or anything less than worship of the God of Israel, the Creator of heaven and earth.

> that at the name of Jesus every knee should bow
>> in heaven and on earth and under the earth,
> and every tongue confess
>> that Jesus Christ is Lord, to the glory of God the Father.
>> (Phil. 2:10–11)

The phrase "in heaven and on earth and under the earth" echoes the Ten Commandments, where it is meant to include everything in the created world, including the angels and all celestial beings, none of which Israel may worship, because only the LORD, who brought them out of Egypt, is their God (Exod. 20:2–4).

The term "LORD" (when spelled with small capital letters in translations of Old Testament Hebrew) is not merely a title, as if all it meant were "master." It represents the name of the God of Israel, by referring to the name without actually saying it. Since before Christianity arose and to this day, pious Jews have not uttered the name of God; so when reading Scripture aloud and coming upon the name of the God of Israel (transliterated into English as YHWH, without the vowels added, so as to prevent people from saying it aloud), they say instead the Hebrew word "Adonai," which means "Lord" (translated into Greek as *Kyrios*, the same word as in *Kyrie eleison*, "Lord have mercy"). This is the name given to Jesus in the hymn Paul quotes, as part of an act of worship giving glory to God the Father. The hymn is clearly meant to remind us of the proclamation of the name of God in Isaiah:

> I am the LORD; that is my name;
>> my glory I give to no other.
>> (Isa. 42:8)

Likewise the passage a little further on:

> I am God, and there is no other.
>> By myself I have sworn . . .
>>> a word that shall not return:
> "To me every knee shall bow,
>> every tongue shall swear allegiance."
>> (Isa. 45:22–23)

Worshiping God with the hymn in Paul's letter to the Philippians clearly means believing that Jesus Christ has the name and glory of the LORD, the God of Israel, who gives his name and glory to no other. The logical implication, of which the early Christians must have been fully aware, is that this man is rightly given the worship, faith, and obedience that belong to the LORD alone.

To confess that Jesus is Lord (in Greek, *Kyrios*) in the context of such a hymn is a way of saying that he is none other than the God of the Jews, the Creator of heaven and earth.[12] From the beginning of Christianity this has been the meaning of his exaltation, his being raised bodily not only from death but up to the throne in heaven, where he sits at the right hand of God or, as the book of Revelation pictures it, as the Lamb "in the midst of the throne" (Rev. 7:17). The throne is the symbol of God's rule over all things, which is why it is pictured as located *above* the heavens, superior to both heaven and earth. Thus the picture of Jesus on the throne envisions the same truth that is spoken in the early Christian confession that "Jesus is Lord." It means that to Jesus belong the glory and power, the kingdom and rule that belong to God alone. Either this is sheer idolatry or it requires Christians to say what the Gospel of John says: that the man on the cross is none other than the Word who is God, who was with God in the beginning, and who was not one of the things God created because it was through him that all things were made (John 1:1–3). This same Word is the Word made flesh (John 1:14) in the womb of Mary, and it is this same flesh that hung on a cross, was buried in a tomb, and was raised from death—the same human flesh of the same living man who is now on the throne in heaven, whence he pours out upon his people on earth the Spirit he has received from the Father, as Peter teaches at Pentecost (Acts 2:33).

When we set this Gospel beside Platonism, what we get is not so much human spirituality as divine materiality—or more specifically, divine carnality, God in flesh. Instead of the human soul or spirit turning its attention away from bodily things to ascend to higher things, the divine Word of God descends into flesh in the incarnation. As a result, not only is the human flesh of Jesus on the throne of God, exalted above all creation, but it is that same flesh which was once lifted up on the cross when Christ our Lord was, as the Gospel of John puts it, "glorified" there (John 12:23–24; 13:31–32). If the throne of God is a strange place for human flesh, then the cross is certainly a strange place for the glory of the LORD God. If we insert this good

---

12. This way of confessing the divinity of Christ is also implicit in the many New Testament passages that refer to something the Old Testament says about the LORD and apply it to the Lord Jesus, as for instance when Paul in Rom. 10:13 quotes Joel 2:32, "Everyone who calls on the name of the LORD shall be saved," and takes it to be about confessing Jesus as Lord (Rom. 10:9–13). This kind of thing happens so often in the New Testament that its import is easily missed, as is its logical consequence: that the primal Christian confession, "Jesus is Lord," is in effect a Jewish way of saying that Jesus is the one true God. For a catalog of relevant texts, see Bauckham, *Jesus and the God of Israel*, 186–90, 219–21.

news about Christ into the framework of the allegory of the cave, we have to imagine that a human body, not just the soul, can rise up out of the cave. But not only that. We must also say that the Good has come among us, as if the sun itself had entered into the cave with its light, so that we can behold its glory in the face of a crucified Jew (cf. 2 Cor. 4:6). With Christ in it, the conceptual framework of Platonism cracks open like a cave trying to contain the sun. There's something here that is too big for it to hold.

The Eternally Begotten Son

Platonist spirituality cannot accommodate the confession of Jesus as LORD without at least partially cracking, which is why Christian thinkers had to take so much time and energy developing the doctrines of the Trinity and incarnation, once they started thinking rigorously in terms of Greek philosophy. By the time of the fourth century, all the church fathers accepted a broadly Platonist framework for understanding the spiritual being of God. According to this framework, whatever is truly divine is not only immortal but unchangeable, beyond every possibility of defect, failure, or corruption. Most importantly, the divine is impassible, which is to say unaffected by outside forces, beyond any vulnerability to suffering or harm. To be impassible means literally to be without passion, in the root sense of passivity: it is to be never passive or acted upon but always active in affecting others, "unchangeable, but changing all things," as Augustine puts it.[13] It means always being the mover, never the moved; always forming other things, never being formed by them; always the doer, never the done-to. And that means never *suffering*—a word that used to be equivalent to "passion" in the sense of passivity, as we see in the old English phrase "doing and suffering," which was a way of referring to the originally Latin conceptions of action and passion, or activity and passivity, or what would now be conveyed by the words "doing and being done to."

It is because suffering is equivalent to passion, in this original sense of the word, that we speak of Good Friday as the day of Christ's *passion*, when a great deal was done to him and he did little but suffer it. The notion of divine impassibility does seem, on the face of it, to prevent us from speaking of the passion or suffering of God on a cross. But a similar thing is true of the less controversial notion of divine immortality, which seems to prevent us from saying that God died on a cross. Yet the doctrines of Trinity and incarnation, as developed in the series of ecumenical (i.e., "worldwide") church councils

---

13. Augustine, *Confessions* 1:4.4. I translate the elegant Latin as closely as I can: *immutabilis, mutans omnia.*

beginning at Nicaea in 325, led the orthodox church fathers to say both these things, even while they retained the Platonist framework of the spirituality of God. But the framework cracked, because Jesus Christ remained in the middle of it.

There are unfathomable depths here, but the basic conceptual developments, as reflected and anticipated in the Nicene Creed,[14] can be summarized in one paragraph. To begin with, Jesus Christ is the only begotten Son of God, which means he originates from the Father as "God from God," precisely because he is begotten from the Father, not created. Yet this eternally begotten God, fully divine and having exactly the same divine being (*ousia*) as the Father, is the same one who takes flesh of the virgin Mary and thus becomes a created being. He is both Creator and created, both fully divine and fully human, because he has two births, one eternal and one temporal: he is begotten of the Father in eternity and born of the virgin Mary in time. This is the narrative logic of the creed: the same one (i.e., the same person, the same grammatical subject) who is "eternally begotten from the Father, God from God," is also "born of the virgin Mary and made man." Hence the doctrine of incarnation implied in the Nicene Creed is that Jesus Christ is both God and man, divine and human, Creator and creature in one. In the words of Gregory of Nazianzus, the church father who presided over the opening of the Council of Nicaea: "What he was, he remained; what he was not, he assumed."[15] That is to say: while remaining fully God, eternal and uncreated, beyond time and change, and impassible, he assumed human creatureliness, body and soul, with its fleshly vulnerability to suffering, passion, and death—that is, he took it up and made it his own. Thus he became one of us, sharing our humanity, corruptibility, and mortality, so that we might become like him, sharing the incorruptibility of his divine and eternal life. Put in fully trinitarian form, this is the gist of the patristic formulation of the Gospel of Jesus Christ: that the Son of God became one with us so that we might become one with him, incorporated into his Body by the working of his Spirit and thus brought to share in the eternal life and glory of God his Father.

14. I refer here to the creed by its traditional name. It is in fact the creed attributed to the First Council of Constantinople in 381, an expanded and modified version of the original creed of Nicaea in 325. Scholars have called it the "Constantinopolitan" or "Nicaeno-Constantinopolitan" creed. It can be found in Leith, *Creeds of the Churches*, 33; Schaff, *Creeds of Christendom* 1:57–60 (including Greek and Latin versions); and is compared with the original creed of Nicaea in Hanson, *Search for the Christian Doctrine of God*, 812–20. It is also found in the prayer books and service books of many churches, which use it regularly in worship.

15. Gregory of Nazianzus, Oration 29:19 (the third "Theological Oration"). The formula is echoed frequently by Augustine, as we shall see in the next chapter.

The key question for the Nicene doctrine of the Trinity was how the eternal begetting of the Son is related to his suffering in the flesh.[16] The answer that was rejected at Nicaea was an extreme version of an answer that had been popular among Christian intellectuals for some time, as it was the most natural answer for a Christian Platonist to give—the one that does the least to crack the Platonist conceptual framework. Since the Good shines above all intelligible forms, Platonists of that era had come to think of the intelligible world as consisting of many ideas in the divine Mind or Intellect (*Nous*), which is lower on the scale of being than the perfect, indivisible unity of the Good, which was also called the One because of its perfect unity. Therefore, many Christians were inclined to identify the divine Word or *Logos* (which is Greek for Reason as well as Word) with the divine Intellect, which was a step lower than God the Father, who is the fully divine One. This second-level divinity, the Mind of God, contained the eternal forms or ideas or reasons that emanate from the Father as most high God. Precisely because the *Logos*, the divine Reason, originates from the Father, they thought, he must be less than the Father. For their thinking was that anything that is originated in any way, such as the Son who is begotten from the Father, must at some point have come into being—and if the *Logos* came into being, then he cannot be absolutely eternal. And if he is not absolutely eternal, then he is changeable and therefore not completely impassible. That's why he can take on passible human flesh and suffer, and the Father can't. The Father is too powerful and perfect to suffer. For the same reason, quite apart from the incarnation—that is to say, without any need for the divine to take on flesh—the Word or *Logos* can act as mediator between God and creation, because he occupies an intermediary level of being between the supreme One and the visible world, giving form, being, and knowledge to what is below him in the light of what he receives from above, from his Father.

A great many Christian writers before Nicaea had assumed some such subordination of the *Logos* to God the Father, but Arius, the man whose heresy was specifically rejected at Nicaea, took this subordinationism one step further. Like previous subordinationists, he explained the subordination of the *Logos* as being due to his having an origin. But then he added: since the

16. The history of the debate over the Nicene understanding of the eternal begetting of the Son is told briefly in Kelly, *Early Christian Doctrines*, 223–51; Pelikan, *Emergence of the Catholic Tradition*, 191–210; and much more comprehensively in Hanson, *Search for the Christian Doctrine of God*. The key documents are found in Hanson and also in Stevenson, *Creeds, Councils and Controversies*. Ayres, *Nicaea and Its Legacy*, makes major improvements to the historiography of the controversy, but does not change the fundamentals of the conceptual map. John Behr, *Nicene Faith*, provides a theological overview of the key figures in the development of Nicene trinitarianism.

Logos has an origin, he must be a created being, not the Creator. And that means that there must have been "once when he was not."[17]

This became the most famous thing Arius ever said. It got the attention of the orthodox, who explicitly condemned the phrase at the Council of Nicaea. The key aim of the council was to affirm that Jesus Christ, as the eternal *Logos* of God, is God in the fullest possible sense, which means he is the Creator, not a creature. They saw that Arius's view has the implication that Jesus is not deserving of exactly the same worship as the Father, and they realized that this implication violates the fundamental logic of Christian worship (that Christ is on the throne *of God*) and therefore the fundamental logic of Christian faith. So they insisted that Jesus Christ, as the eternal *Logos*, has exactly the same being (*ousia*) as God the Father. The famous term in the creed is that he is *homoousios*, "of one being," with the Father. The point of this term is that every divine attribute of the Father belongs equally, not in any inferior way, to Christ the Son. So for example, since God the Father is the supreme Good, so is the Son. Since God the Father is impassible, so is the Son. And since God the Father is eternal, so is the Son.

How can he be eternal if he has an origin? That was the key conceptual problem, encapsulated in a striking phrase in the creed: "eternally begotten." The church fathers at Nicaea were committed to saying the Son is begotten from the Father, but without saying "there was once when he was not." They insisted that he is not a creature, created out of nothing like you and me and the whole world, but originates in an entirely different way, not created but begotten (using the same term that is used for ordinary fathers begetting their children, the Greek word translated with the famous "begats" of the King James Bible in the first chapter of Matthew). But, they added, this eternal begetting or eternal generation (as it is sometimes translated) is utterly unique and incomprehensible, because it is not a process in time; it makes no change in God or division in his being. Rather, the whole being (*ousia*) of the Father, all his divine essence, including everything that makes him divine, is given to the Son, so that it eternally belongs to him. Thus the Son is both originated and eternal, for the Father begets him precisely by giving him the fullness of the Father's own eternal being. The only differences between them stem from the fact that the Father begets the Son, not vice versa. This has the strikingly beautiful implication that the Father becomes who he distinctively is—not just God, but God *the Father*—precisely by giving his whole being to the Son. To give all of his being to another in love is precisely to be eternally himself.

17. See the anathemas attached to the original creed of Nicaea in 325, in Schaff, *Creeds of Christendom* 1:28–29.

The eternal begetting of the Son is thus in a way the eternal becoming of both Father and Son, a becoming that has always been, never began to be, and will never end.

You can find the concept beautiful but you can also find it startlingly incomprehensible. The fathers regularly insisted on the incomprehensibility of the eternal begetting,[18] which for them was the central mystery of the doctrine of the Trinity. (As the full divinity of the Holy Spirit also came into view, they would later go on to say that God was in some sense both three and one, but that was more like a conceptual puzzle than a deep mystery of the faith—it was not what they meant by "the mystery of the Trinity.") Most importantly, it is the fully worked-out concept of eternal begetting or generation that showed what was wrong with Arius's theology. But it turned out to be overkill, for in addition to ruling out Arius's teaching, it ended up excluding every kind of subordination in what is divine. This kicked up a fierce controversy that raged for decades after the Council of Nicaea. The concept of eternal generation was in fact not a new one; the greatest pagan Platonist of the previous century, Plotinus, had already used it to describe the origination of the divine Intellect from the supreme Good.[19] But when the Nicene fathers said the Begotten had the same being (*ousia*) as the Begetter, they went further than Plotinus. They meant that in the being of God, you cannot locate what is originated at a level lower than what originates it. Having an origin or source does not give the *Logos* a subordinate status. Hence the *Logos* cannot be seen as somehow less impassible and incorruptible than the Father and thus more suitable for subjection to suffering and death. This generated new conceptual problems, focused specifically on the doctrine of incarnation.

The Suffering of God

Whereas the doctrine of the Trinity focuses on the divine being of the Son, the doctrine of the incarnation focuses on his humanity. The impassibility of the *Logos*, which follows from the Nicene doctrine of the Trinity, makes this all the harder to conceive. The key formula from Gregory of Nazianzus follows the narrative logic of the Nicene Creed, as we have seen. "What he was, he remained": that is to say, he never ceased to be the eternal, unchangeable,

18. See Cary, "Incomprehensibility of God."

19. Plotinus, *Enneads* 5:1.6. Porphyry, who edited Plotinus's work, gave this essay the title "On the Three Primary Hypostases." The three primary hypostases or divine beings, in descending order, are the Good, the divine Intellect or Mind, and the universal Soul. Replace "Soul" with "Spirit" and you get something very close to the subordinationist Trinity that Nicaea implicitly rejected. See Dillon, "Origen and Plotinus."

impassible God, beyond all change and suffering and death. "What he was not, he assumed": that is to say, he took up our passibility and mortality, suffering and death, and made it his own. To put the issue in these terms is to identify what is most paradoxical about the Christian claim that God became man. This is not a mythological story of a god like Zeus taking on human form. It is the eternal God who died, the impassible One who suffered, the supreme Good who entered the cave. It is the source of all being that is subjected to human corruptibility so that, as Paul teaches, human corruptibility may put on divine incorruption. So great must be the humiliation of the only begotten Son of God, if he is to raise up adopted sons and daughters of God in whom mortality puts on immortality.

This is the key intellectual achievement of Christian theology: to reckon seriously with the way Christ's incarnation—divine carnality rather than human spirituality—unites humanity to God. Instead of a Platonist intermediary that is midway between the supreme Good and the material creation (not quite either, but a little like both) providing a ladder for the human spirit's ascent out of the cave, orthodox Christianity finds its mediator in the man Jesus Christ, God who has descended to take on flesh, who is both *fully* divine and *fully* human (not just a little like both), a mortal inhabitant of the cave just as truly as we are—so that we may be truly incorruptible as he is, sharing in his eternal life by being incorporated into his Body. In contrast to subordinationist theology, he is not our mediator in his divine being, for in his divine being he is equal to the Father, not a lower, intermediary level of being—he does not exist at some level *between* God and man. He is mediator because he exists fully at both levels, truly God and truly man. Logically speaking, he is not a *tertium quid* (i.e., a third category) between Creator and creature, but a both/and—both Creator and creature in one.

Precisely by insisting on the (Platonist) impassibility of the *Logos*, the church fathers ended up affirming most powerfully the carnality of Christian faith rather than the spirituality of Platonism. Only the true God in the flesh can mediate between Creator and creature. The church fathers after Nicaea never backed down on the point that the Word is impassible, and remains so even as he takes up passible human flesh: he continues to be what he was even as he takes up what he was not and makes it his own. Since the same one who is impassible takes up our passibility, Cyril of Alexandria (a Greek-speaking church father who wrote about the same time as Augustine was writing his works in Latin) can say that the impassible one suffered— even "suffered impassibly."[20] It is like saying the immortal one died, which is

---

20. See Weinandy, *Does God Suffer?*, chap. 8; Gavrilyuk, *Suffering of the Impassible God*, chap. 6; and the texts of Cyril anthologized in McGuckin, *Saint Cyril of Alexandria*, 264 (the

in fact another implication of the Nicene doctrine. Thus the church fathers, often against their own original inclinations, ended up affirming what can be called Deipassionism, the doctrine that God suffers. The key formulation was "one of the Trinity suffered in the flesh."[21] For if the man suffering on the cross is truly God, one of the Trinity, then it is truly God who is suffering.

We could compare this with a parallel point brought up by Cyril: if the baby that Mary bears in her womb is truly God in the flesh, then she is truly the God-bearer (*theotokos*). She is the mother of God, not in the sense that she originated his divine nature, but in the sense that the human baby she bears is fully and truly God. As in the womb, so on the cross: if this man is truly God, then God truly died, just as he was truly born. The creed says as much: for the same one who is "God from God" is also the same one who "was born of the virgin Mary" and "suffered under Pontius Pilate."

It is not that God ever ceases to be the living God—for as Gregory's formula reminds us, he always remains what he is—but rather that this dead man is none other than the ever-living God, the second person of the Trinity. Just as Mary does not originate his divine nature, so the cross does not destroy it. The way the church fathers often put it is that God dies as man, not as God—in his human nature, not in his divine nature. The easiest way to picture this is in terms of Plato's definition of death as the separation of soul and body.[22] For three days Jesus was a dead man, which means his soul was separated from his body—the body lying in the tomb and the soul descending to the underworld. The eternal Son of God, being united to this one man, soul and body, remains united both to his soul and to his body even in their separation. More generally—whatever your definition of death—what it means for God to be dead is for the second person of the Trinity to be the same as this man Jesus, even in the three days when he was a dead man.

Because God suffers and dies only in his human nature, it is only the incarnate God who suffers and dies. Hence another point on which the church fathers never backed down was that the Father does not suffer or die. To put it in a neat Latin formula, they affirmed Deipassionism (God's suffering) but not Patripassionism (the Father's suffering). God suffers, for the man on the cross is the Son of God, who is truly God. But the Father does not suffer, for he is not the Son. The Father and the Son are of one being (*ousia*), having the same divine attributes, but in the narrative logic of the creed, they are not the

---

second letter to Nestorius), 270 (the third letter to Nestorius), and 301, 308, 327–35 ("Scholia on the Incarnation"). The phrase "suffered impassibly" appears on page 332.

21. This formula is implicitly accepted at the Second Council of Constantinople in 553. See Meyendorff, *Christ in Eastern Christian Thought*, chap. 4.

22. Plato, *Phaedo* 64e.

same grammatical subject. The Father is not the same one who is eternally begotten of the Father, not the same one who is incarnate of the virgin Mary, not the same one who dies on the cross and is raised and exalted to sit at the right hand of the Father. So the Father is not the one who suffers. The modern impulse to say that the Father must have suffered sympathetically with his suffering Son is not shared by the church fathers, because they see no honor to God or benefit to us in making God subject to suffering and thus inherently corruptible. Unlike modern thinkers such as Hegel, they did not believe the eternal had to find itself in the sufferings of history in order to become real and concrete. They had no desire to see God suffer, and they saw no way this could help us in our suffering.

To use an analogy I have found helpful: the church fathers are like the kind of lifeguards who warn you that it does no good to jump in after someone who is struggling in deep water; it only means both of you are likely to drown. Their basic impulse is to think: a God who is corruptible cannot save us from corruption, but will only be corrupted along with us. But after the orthodox doctrines of Trinity and incarnation are fully in place, the picture is more complex: for God the Son does truly suffer with us, sharing our corruptibility and even our death. It is as if the Father, standing on the firm ground of his own eternity, throws his Son like a life-preserver into the depths where we are drowning. And the Son of God does indeed drown with us—this immortal one dies—but then the Father pulls him out of the depths by the lifeline of the Holy Spirit, who is the eternal and unbreakable bond of love and unity between the Father and the Son. And when the Son rises out of the depths of death, all who cling to him rise with him.

The Descent of Heaven

Platonism remains of permanent importance for Christian theology because it provided the background assumptions of the orthodox formulations of the doctrines of the Trinity and the incarnation. Maintaining these Platonist assumptions about divine unchangeability, incorruptibility, and impassibility was a way for the church fathers to make absolutely clear, in their cultural and philosophical context, that Christian faith does not assign incarnation, birth and suffering and death, to some subordinate pagan deity, but to the very God who is enthroned above the heavens, beyond all space and time and every created thing, because he is ruler and Creator of all things, and that this same God, the second person of the Trinity, was the man who suffered under Pontius Pilate, who was crucified, died, and was buried, and who was raised from the dead and now is exalted, even in his human flesh, to the throne above the heavens. They included this much Platonist spirituality in their understanding of Trinity and incarnation because in their view, Plato and his followers were right about some things, especially when it came to conceiving of God's transcendence, his being beyond all things.

What was not so essential to Christian orthodoxy, though it was widely shared by the church fathers and was eventually to become firmly entrenched in Christian piety, was the Platonist spirituality of the soul's ascent to God, as in the familiar picture of good souls going to heaven after death. This picture has its roots in Platonism, not in the Gospel. Rather than God raising what is dead into new life, which is the good news of Easter, Platonism envisions a part of us that does not die, the immortal soul. It is immortal because of its spirituality, its kinship with what is eternal, divine, and intelligible, and that is why the ascent to heaven is natural to it.[23] It is certainly possible to combine the concept of the immortal soul with the good news of the resurrection, and most Christian theologians over the centuries have done so—there are passages of the New Testament that leave room for this possibility. Still, it is important to remember the overall shape of the good news, which has often been overshadowed in the practice of Christian piety by the hope of going to heaven. The Gospel of Jesus Christ in the New Testament opens up an eschatology (a view of the last things, the end of the story) in which our hope lies not in ascending to heaven but in heaven descending to us.[24] That is why Paul speaks, as we have seen, not of something immortal escaping its mortal clothing but rather of this mortal putting on immortality (1 Cor. 15:53). What is properly divine, which is to say eternal life in Christ Jesus, must descend from heaven to clothe us.

Our dwelling on earth is a tent, Paul writes, which is to say: our flesh is transient, flimsy, mortal, and corruptible, and we await a heavenly dwelling, "a building from God, a house not made with hands, eternal in the heavens" (2 Cor. 5:1). This does not mean that we trade this earthly tent for a heavenly location, but rather that the heavenly dwelling comes to clothe our flimsy tent with the power of incorruptible and eternal life: "For while we are still in this tent, we groan, being burdened—not that we would be unclothed, but that we would be further clothed, so that what is mortal may be swallowed

23. Plato, Phaedo 79d–80d.

24. This belongs to a larger biblical conception of heaven as the place *from which* divine power comes to earth, rather than the place *to which* we aspire to go; see Morse, *Difference Heaven Makes*. For arguments in favor of returning to New Testament eschatology without Platonist additions, see Wright, *Surprised by Hope*; Middleton, *New Heaven and a New Earth*.

up by life" (v. 4).[25] This follows the movement of the Lord's Prayer, where the kingdom of God comes to be "on earth as it is in heaven" (Matt. 6:10), a movement that is enacted in Christ's glorified flesh when he comes as Lord to judge the living and the dead. Until that day—for which the New Testament, once again calling Jesus by the name of the God of Israel, adopts the Old Testament term "the day of the LORD"[26]—we are to await him in hope, setting our minds on things above, as the apostle says, because that is "where Christ is, seated at the right hand of God" (Col. 3:1). He does not proceed to say that we should hope to join Jesus in heaven when we die. What he says instead is quite startling: we have already died, and therefore our life "is hidden with Christ in God" (v. 3). He is evidently thinking: we have been buried with Christ in baptism as a kind of death, and therefore also raised with Christ in newness of life (Rom. 6:4; cf. Col. 2:12). Our life is already in some measure the eschatological life, the eternal life of the future that belongs now to Christ, a life hidden from us in heaven that will be revealed in his coming, so that "when Christ who is your life appears, then you also will appear with him in glory" (Col. 3:3).

It is this life hidden with Christ in heaven, waiting to be revealed when he comes, that can be pictured, in the interim between death and resurrection, as the life of a disembodied soul—though the New Testament typically avoids the picture. Paul talks about departing (literally, "being set loose") to be with Christ (Phil. 1:23), and in the second letter of Peter, the apostle describes himself as still living "in this tent" but anticipating soon "putting off my tent," an event that he describes as a "departure" (literally an *exodus*).[27] Neither of them uses the word "soul" (*psyche*) to describe what is departing. However, one highly symbolic New Testament passage uses that word to picture the sort of thing they may have had in mind. It is in fact the only text in which the Bible pictures souls in heaven. The souls of the martyrs are depicted as being kept under the altar in heaven, in the safekeeping of the Lamb (Rev. 6:9–11). However, they are not exactly "in heaven," in the usual sense of the

25. One possible image that may have been in Paul's mind is that of the tabernacle, the mobile tent-shrine of the God of Israel, being set up within the inner sanctum of the temple: a tent "clothed" in a much more lasting stone structure. On the likelihood that the tabernacle was set up within the first temple, see Friedman, *Who Wrote the Bible?*, chap. 10 ("The Sacred Tent").

26. See the phrase "the day of our Lord Jesus" in 1 Cor. 1:8 and 2 Cor. 1:14, which is no different from "the day of the Lord" in 1 Cor. 5:5; 1 Thess. 5:2; 2 Pet. 3:10, which is meant by these authors to be equivalent to the phrase "the day of the LORD," which appears frequently in the prophets—e.g., Isa. 13:6; Jer. 46:10; Ezek. 30:3; Amos 5:18; Obad. 15; and, most important for the New Testament, Joel 2:31 (quoted in Acts 2:20).

27. 2 Pet. 1:13–15. I translate literally, as most recent translations prevent readers from seeing the crucial metaphor by rendering the word for tent as "body."

phrase today, because they are not happy. They do not even have life after death, properly speaking, for they are described later as "coming to life" in the resurrection—when they once again have the life that is proper to living, embodied human beings (20:4). In the meantime, in the classic words of the psalms of complaint, they cry out to God, "How long?" (6:10). They are waiting for God to judge the earth, just as we are when we pray, "Thy will be done *on earth* as it is in heaven." As with us, what they hope for has not yet come to pass. Their life, too, is still hidden with Christ in God. Going up to heaven is not what they're looking for, but rather the resurrection of their bodies when heaven comes down to earth.

Heaven does exactly that, according to the picture that inaugurates the final vision in the book of Revelation, when John sees "the holy city Jerusalem coming down out of heaven from God, having the glory of God" (Rev. 21:10–11). Thus is fulfilled the proclamation that comes from the heavenly throne itself: "Behold, the tent of God is with human beings—he will pitch his tent with them, and they will be his people, and God himself will be with them as their God."[28] The picture of God's tent on earth is no doubt a reference to the flesh of Christ, a continuation of the good news that "the Word became flesh and pitched his tent among us."[29] The heavenly dwelling we hope for descends in the tent of Christ's flesh, as it did before, but this time visibly glorious, as "the throne of God and of the Lamb" (22:1) is now on earth as it was in heaven.

So the place in this story for disembodied souls, if that is what you want, lies in the interim between death and resurrection, when we are "away from the body and at home with the Lord" (2 Cor. 5:8), and at least some souls are pictured as being kept safe with the Lamb in heaven while they wait for the kingdom of God to come to earth. The apostles don't actually talk that way in their letters, but the Christian tradition usually has. What such talk of souls departing from the body obscures, and thus the reason why the apostles may be avoiding it, is the startling continuity we caught sight of in Colossians 3:1–3, where the apostle says our life (*zoe*) is already in heaven because we have already died and been raised with Christ. This seems to be the same continuity Paul has in mind when he says, "If we live, we live to the Lord, and if we die, we die to the Lord. So then, whether we live or whether we die, we are the Lord's" (Rom. 14:8). "The Lord" here is clearly the Lord Jesus.

28. Rev. 21:3. Again, I have translated literally so as to restore the metaphor of the tent, which most translations prevent readers from knowing about.
29. John 1:14. Again I translate literally.

One strand of traditional piety catches the shape of this apostolic thinking when it describes death as "going to Jesus." All that needs to be added is that this is something that has already happened to all baptized believers. Dying and going to heaven is an event that is already behind us, just as it is for Jesus, in whom we live. Therefore even while we inhabit this mortal tent, our lives are hidden with him in heaven, like souls kept safe under the altar, awaiting the coming of his kingdom "on earth as it is in heaven." If the picture of souls in heaven is to be generalized, then it must be applied to all the baptized, including those who still "remain in the flesh" (Phil. 1:24). We are all awaiting the same thing. The future we cry and pray for does not consist in going to heaven; it is *the Lord's* future, when he comes again in glory and "we shall be like him, because we shall see him as he is" (1 John 3:2). Then our true life—eternal life in Christ—shall be no longer hidden but revealed in the glory of his own flesh, the tent where God dwells with his people, the eternal house not made with hands, in the holy city that descends from heaven.

Flesh and Spirit

The problem with Platonism is that it is so much more spiritual than Christian faith, focused as it is on human spirituality rather than divine incarnation. It conceives the immortal soul on the basis of its kinship to a realm beyond space and time, the intelligible world that is its proper direction and destiny, whereas the incarnation of Christ directs Christian faith to a particular location in time and space, to a particular story about a particular Jew, in whom is all its hope. Divine incarnation means that there is a particular place to find God, as Christ's body becomes the new temple, the holy place where God is present.[30] This is also the particular location of distinctively Christian spirituality, which is to say the home of the Holy Spirit, who is the Spirit of Christ's body.

"The desires of the Spirit are against the flesh," says Paul (Gal. 5:17), but he clearly is not talking about the flesh of Christ. We are now in a position, at the conclusion of this chapter, to see why this New Testament contrast of flesh and Spirit is saying something different from Platonist spirituality, while also appreciating the important convergences between Christian faith and Platonist philosophy.

---

30. This is the implication of John 2:18–20, as well as of Paul's locating all spiritual gifts of wisdom and knowledge of God within the practice of the body of Christ in Rom. 12:3–8 and in 1 Cor. 12–14.

To begin with the convergences: for both Christian faith and Platonist philosophy, the divine is transcendent, beyond all things and other than all things, over all things in sovereign, formative power and outside all things in virtue of having no dependence on them. The image for this in Scripture is the throne of God above the heavens; the conceptuality for this in Platonism is the omnipresence and immutable eternity of what is divine and intelligible. Both can picture transcendence using imagery of height, which is to say, freedom from dependence on the changing world and power over it. Both conceive of a hope for human life to be united with this transcendent realm in some way, by participation or assimilation, becoming more like what is spiritual and eternal. The difference, as we have seen, is that for Platonist spirituality this means the soul ascending to the transcendent realm, as in the image of climbing out of the cave, whereas in the New Testament this means the divine descending from the transcendent realm, as in the image of the heavenly city descending to earth.

In a Christian context, the word "flesh" signals both the power of divine incarnation and the weakness of human mortality. Human flesh, in New Testament usage, refers to the whole human self, both body and soul, in its corruptibility: both the mortal weakness of the body and the moral diseases of the soul. In Old Testament usage, flesh (Hebrew *basar*) is what can be wounded and needy,[31] and the soul certainly has wounds and needs of its own. As some of the earlier church fathers particularly insisted, the soul does not have eternal life naturally within it, but must await this as a gift from heaven.[32] And as it has no power to free itself from death, it has no power to free itself from bondage to sin.

This need to be freed from sin and death by a divine gift of grace is a point on which Protestant theology is particularly insistent. As we shall see in the next chapter, it is not a thought entirely alien to Platonism, which is quite familiar with the notion that all power for good comes to us from above, descending from the Good itself. What Platonism did not have room for was the notion that such power could come to us incarnate, in the flesh of one particular person. For Platonism, along with the whole ancient world, it was sheer common sense that flesh is not a source of life but of corruption, for it

---

31. See Wolff, *Anthropology of the Old Testament*, chap. 3.

32. See Tatian, *Address to the Greeks*, chap. 13 (written in the mid-second century), and the lengthy argument against immortality of the soul in Arnobius, *Against the Pagans* 2:13–51 (written not long after 300). Even an early Christian Platonist like Justin Martyr (mid-second century) can find reasons to reject the immortality of the soul in Plato himself (*Timaeus* 41b), supporting Justin's argument that nothing that has a beginning can be by nature immortal (*Dialogue with Trypho*, chap. 4) and concluding that the soul "lives not as being life, but as partaker of life" (chap. 5).

is the soul that gives life to the body, not the other way round, and the flesh without the life-giving soul is nothing but a corpse. In this framework, there is no place for a notion of Christ's life-giving flesh, the belief that a particular bodily thing is the holy place where we go to find the grace of God and the power of eternal life. That is the point of deepest contrast between Christian faith and Platonism.

The carnality of the Christian faith means that the Spirit of God must not be confused with human spirituality. The Holy Spirit, the third person of the Trinity, is the Spirit of Christ, inseparably one God with him and with the Father. The Spirit of God is therefore never separate from Christ's flesh, his word, and his body, including the social Body that is the church. The spirituality of Christian faith is properly the work of the Holy Spirit, heard in the word of Christ and operative in the church as the Body of Christ and found in his life-giving flesh.[33] Human spiritualities, of which Platonist philosophy is to my mind the most impressive, offer an alternative to this divine carnality of the Holy Spirit in Christ. Protestant theology is less beholden to Platonist spirituality than are other theologies in the Great Tradition, and this is one of its most important strengths. Yet Protestants too are capable of inventing new kinds of spirituality—distinctively Protestant forms of inwardness or turning to experience as the basis of faith, which can in the end have less integrity and wisdom than Platonist spirituality.[34] There are indeed many ways to forget that Christian spirituality is properly the work of the Holy Spirit, who is one God with Christ in the flesh.

33. For two recent treatments of Christian spirituality from the standpoint of God coming to us in Christ and the activity of the Holy Spirit, see Humphrey, *Ecstasy and Intimacy* (a lovely introduction), and Hughes, *Beloved Dust* (theologically more ambitious), and the extensive discussion of the recent history of spirituality in the latter.

34. The kind of turn to experience I have in mind can be found in both liberal Protestantism and evangelicalism, as described in Cary, *Good News for Anxious Christians*, chap. 10: "How Basing Faith on Christian Experience Leads to a Post-Christian Future."

3

Christ the Mediator in Augustine

T he word "spirituality," when it refers to more than just an incorporeal type of being, typically names a kind of movement, the soul's progress toward what is transcendent, divine, and eternal. In this sense there cannot exactly be a Gospel of spirituality. "Gospel" means good news, and news is about doings other than your own. The good news of the kingdom of God is not about how we come to the kingdom, but about how the kingdom is coming to us (Matt. 4:17). Yet spirituality and the Gospel can be related in a number of ways, for the news does indeed give us something to do. In this chapter we shall examine the most influential proposal in the history of Western Christianity for integrating philosophical spirituality and the Gospel of Christ, in the Christian Platonist project of the great church father Augustine (354–430), who was both Luther's favorite theologian and someone who, it turns out, saw the Gospel rather differently from Luther.

Spirituality and Gospel

The Protestant Reformers joined the whole Christian tradition in affirming that God gives us something to do, for we are "created in Christ Jesus for good works" (Eph. 2:10). Moreover, the Gospel itself comes prefaced with a word of warning, for when Jesus begins preaching the good news of the coming kingdom, his first word is "Repent!" (Matt. 4:17). Hearing such a word can get us afraid or alarmed, for it is when we think about what we have to do that all kinds of performance anxiety kick in. Anything we have to do, even repenting, is something we can do badly, and if you have a strong sense of the reality of sin, this can be a cause for worry and fear. It is because God's word can be worrying and even terrifying that Luther and other Reformers insisted on drawing a clear distinction between two forms of God's word, law and Gospel, which is the difference between God's commandments telling us what to do (often accompanied by warnings and accusations) and the good news that tells us what God does in Christ. Our doings, unlike God's, can always go wrong, and any spirituality that applies to us must deal somehow with what has gone wrong with us.

In particular, if we are moving toward the light, then we must be starting at least partially in the dark, and our spirituality will need to have something to say about the power of darkness. In Platonist spirituality that power is really a lack of power, an inability to retain the form of being over time—the kind of mortal weakness that in previous chapters we learned to call corruptibility, passibility, and changeability (or, to use the older word favored by some great English poets, mutability). It is a feature not just of material things but also of the soul itself, that peculiar being in the middle of things which is not a bodily thing but not pure form either. The human soul has its own kind of corruption: when things go wrong with it, they go morally wrong. The soul is the place of the corruption known as vice or sin—as well as ignorance, which according to the Platonist story of the Fall is a kind of spiritual darkness that always has something to do with vice and sin.

The richest Christian Platonist account of the soul's movement from sin and ignorance to the knowledge and love of God comes to us from Augustine, whose works were, apart from the Bible itself, the most influential theological writings in the West for well over a millennium. His account of the soul's spiritual journey to God is the background for his doctrine of grace, which is the formative matrix for both Catholic and Protestant theology in the sixteenth century, the era of the Reformation. So if we want to understand Protestant theology, we need to understand Augustine's Platonist spirituality and the place it makes for the Gospel. The great disagreement that Protestants should have with Augustine, I will be suggesting, is precisely that he makes room for the Gospel within his spirituality, which means that Platonist spirituality becomes for him the context that gives meaning to what God does in Christ. This is a serious disagreement, but it has its place within a wide field of agreement, because Protestant theologians have from the beginning learned so much from Augustine. So here again, as in the previous chapters, we are in for a critical but also appreciative reading of Platonist spirituality.

Let me illustrate what I mean when I say Augustine makes room in his spirituality for the Gospel of Christ. The illustration will focus on a single passage of Augustine's writing, about two pages long, which is so richly characteristic of Augustine's spirituality that it will be worth our while to spend the rest of this chapter on it. I will proceed sentence by sentence through the whole passage, giving you my own rather literal translation, designed to make key vocabulary and conceptual connections easier to see. But since no translation, however literal, is ever transparent, I will comment on terms that might be misleading.

Strengths and Weaknesses of Platonism

The two chapters are situated at a pivotal point in one of Augustine's most important works, at the beginning of part 2 of his massive treatise, *City of God*. Part 1, consisting of the first ten books of the twenty-two-book treatise, is a critique of the pagan city of Rome, including its politics, ethics, religion, and philosophy. He concludes part 1 with three books (books 8–10) that present a critical discussion of pagan philosophy and its approach to religion, highlighting especially the strengths and weaknesses of Platonism. A brief look at this context will set up our extended illustration.

The strengths of Platonism, for Augustine, are founded on its understanding of the being of God as unchangeable and indivisible. God is indivisible in the very strong sense of being "simple," in the technical language of philosophy, which means God has no parts or inner divisions. In contrast to the being of creatures, therefore, God's being cannot be divided into what he is and what he has. He does not merely *have* life and understanding and happiness, for example; rather, he *is* unchangeable Life itself, Understanding itself, and Happiness itself in inseparable unity, which can never be lost or disrupted, because "for him to be is to live, to understand, to be happy," which means he is also the unfailing source of these good things in the created world: "the author of things, the Light of Truth, the bestower of happiness."[1] He is not only the source but the goal of all things, the highest Good, which all things seek as the cause of their well-being, and which rational beings seek to see with the mind's eye.

---

1. Augustine, *City of God* 8:6; 8:5. The recurrent threefold formulation, which reaches a kind of crescendo in *City of God* 8:10, hints at Augustine's conviction that the philosophers were teaching something analogous to the doctrine of the Trinity—a point that becomes explicit later (11:25). It also illustrates the point that for Augustine, as for Gregory of Nyssa and Pseudo-Dionysius, the simplicity of God does not contradict the doctrine of the Trinity but supports it, by showing that Father, Son, and Holy Spirit, each of whom is God (not *part* of God), are nonetheless only one God: "Each is God and Omnipotent"—but precisely because God is simple and without parts or divisions, "they are not three Gods or three Omnipotents, but one God omnipotent" (11:26).

Thus Augustine endorses in no uncertain terms the Platonist notion of intellectual vision, which he uses to define the ultimate goal of human life and therefore of Christian faith. We all want to be happy, and for Augustine this means that what we ultimately want is not merely bodily pleasure or even personal relationships, but to see the intelligible Light of the mind. This does not mean that the mind takes pleasure merely in its own activity, but rather that it enjoys nothing less than God himself, who is the Light of Truth by which the mind sees. True happiness is therefore "not like the mind enjoying the body or itself, nor is it like a friend enjoying a friend; it is like the eye enjoying the light."[2] Seeing with the mind's eye is more than friendship, or what we would nowadays call a "personal relationship," for the object of vision here is not a changing thing like the soul of your friend but the unchanging Light apprehended only by the intellect, as Plotinus, the great pagan Platonist, explained with particular clarity.[3] Through Augustine, this Platonist conception of intellectual vision becomes the Roman Catholic notion of *beatific vision* (as it was later called), meaning literally "the seeing that makes happy"—referring, of course, to the ultimate happiness found in everlasting life with God.

The great weakness of the pagan Platonists, on which Augustine dwells at length, is that they were willing to countenance and even participate in the worship of beings they knew were not truly God, the highest Good. The Platonists knew perfectly well that the statues in pagan temples were not really gods, but in the centuries after Plato they not only countenanced but even justified pagan worship, contending that there were spiritual messengers, go-betweens who carried the prayers and praises of pagan worshipers from the temples to the abode of living gods on high. The name for these messengers in Greek was *daimones*; for pagan Platonists they were something very much like angels. The word is translated, or rather transliterated, into Latin as *daemones*, from which of course we get the English word "demons." Long before Augustine's time Christian thinkers had already insisted that these *daemones* were in fact demons, which is to say, evil angels who were created by the one true God but had fallen into sin and wickedness and thus become devils. Augustine accordingly insists that the *daemones* are not true messengers, like the blessed angels, but false intermediaries, doing their best to block access to heaven and attract worship and praise to themselves (that's why they hung around pagan temples) rather than to the most high God.[4] They

2. Augustine, *City of God* 8:8.
3. Augustine, *City of God* 10:2, where Augustine quotes Plotinus with approval.
4. This is the issue under discussion throughout Augustine, *City of God*, book 9. See especially the profound contrast between the *daemones* as false intermediaries and Christ as true mediator in 9:15.

were like the kind of "middle men" who get in the way, rather than the kind of mediator who makes peace and reconciliation. Hence the crucial issue in religion, Augustine argues, is how to find a true intermediary or mediator between human beings and the supreme Good. This is the issue he is concerned with as he begins the second part of the *City of God*, starting in book 11.

The Immutable Creator

The second part of the *City of God* turns from the city of Rome to the heavenly city established by God. After a brief introductory chapter, Augustine launches into an explanation of how Christians have come to know, or at least believe, the spiritual things he is about to discuss. He explains the foundations of Christian belief by comparing it to the superior understanding of God achieved by the Platonists.

> It is a great thing, and quite rare, to take the mind's attention beyond the whole bodily and nonbodily creation, having considered it and found it to be changeable, and then arrive at the unchangeable substance of God, and there to learn from him that none but he made every nature that is not what he is.[5]

The great and rare thing is to understand what I have been calling the spirituality of God, his immaterial, incorporeal, incorruptible, and unchangeable being. The word Augustine uses for "being" here is *substantia*, which I have translated literally as "substance." But of course, after what has been said about Platonism in the previous chapters, it should be clear that this does not refer to any kind of material substance. Augustine is not talking the way we now do in a chemistry class, where we call water or salt or some other material "a substance." The "substance of God" is not a material God is made out of, for God is immaterial, not made out of anything. *Substantia* is in fact the standard Latin term used to translate the Greek term for essence or being (*ousia*), which underlies the phrase in the Nicene Creed that says the Son has the same divine being as the Father. So when Augustine speaks of the "substance of God," he is talking about the essence or being of God. It is to this immaterial substance or being of God that the Platonists have directed our "mind's attention" (*mentis intentione*). In Augustine's own life, they succeeded: he tells us in his *Confessions* that it was after reading "the books of the Platonists," which admonished him to turn his attention inward, away from all material things, that he entered his own soul by God's help

5. Augustine, *City of God* 11:2.

and looked above the soul, finally catching sight of the immutable Truth that is God.[6]

The final point in the above sentence, that God alone created every being that does not have God's own mode of being ("every nature that is not what he is"), is a way of stating the doctrine of creation out of nothing, *creatio ex nihilo*. Contrary to what is often said, the "out of nothing" part is not unique to the Judaeo-Christian tradition. It is a notion shared with Neoplatonists since Plotinus. As Augustine explains earlier in the *City of God*, "Because of this unchangeability and simplicity [of God] the Platonists understood that he made all these things, and could be made by none of them."[7] What Augustine means by "all these things" is the whole universe, including all the material of the world, all bodies, as well as all souls, angels, and demons—none of which possesses unchangeable being. He is making the point that other church fathers made by saying: God alone is *uncreated*. The conceptual connection is that an absolutely unchangeable being, one that is above all new beginnings in time, is also above being created—and only God is that kind of being. Augustine is saying that the Platonists (the thinkers we now call "Neoplatonists") knew this. The logical consequence of this point is that matter, too, is not uncreated; it is one of the things God has made (in Neoplatonist vocabulary, it emanates ultimately from the Good). It is not a preexisting material that God had to work with, like a potter making a bowl out of clay. Every material *out of* which things are made originates from God, which means there was nothing already there that God created things out of. That is the sense in which creation comes *out of* nothing, *ex nihilo*. It is a point on which Neoplatonists and Christians were in agreement.

How Immutable Being Speaks

Where Christians disagreed with the Platonists, at least since Nicaea, is over the question of whether God creates the universe by means of a series of intermediaries, a descending gradation of spiritual beings, minds or angels or souls, that eventually ends up at the bottom of the hierarchy forming the material world. The orthodox trinitarian answer to this question, as we saw in chapter 2, is a firm *no*. Augustine sees that this answer has profound implications for the related question of whether we come to know God by ascending through a series of intermediaries. Here too the answer must be a firm *no*.

6. Augustine, *Confessions* 7:10.16. The reference to "the books of the Platonists" that provided this admonition is in 7:9.13.
7. Augustine, *City of God* 8:6.

In the true knowledge of God, no created thing comes between us and God: no spiritual being above us, no angel or superior mind, but also—and here Augustine goes beyond Nicaea—no lower, material being such as words.

> For God does not speak thus with man through some bodily creature, rattling in the ears of the body so that the air in the space between the one making the sound and the one hearing it is made to reverberate . . .[8]

The knowledge of God's being, which the Platonists describe as a kind of vision, can also be described as the result of a kind of divine speech. But of course this cannot mean the same thing as what happens when a human being literally speaks. Augustine here gives a coarsely materialistic description of speaking and hearing in order to emphasize the point: it cannot be that we know God because somebody's tongue has made sound waves reverberate in the air, which then rattle in our ears. So Augustine is excluding the kind of thing that happens when someone preaches the Gospel of Jesus Christ. For Augustine, that's not how we come to know the eternal being of God; the Gospel fits into his spirituality elsewhere, as we shall see.

> nor through something "spiritual" of the sort that is shaped in the likeness of bodies, as in dreams or something else of the sort—for that way too is as if speaking to the ears of the body, because it is as if speaking through a body, as if through an interval in between bodily locations; for such appearances have a great resemblance to bodily things.[9]

Here I put "spiritual" in scare quotes, because Augustine is using the word in a technical sense that is all his own. He is talking about mental images, such as we have in imagination, memory, dreams, or visions, when we "see" something that looks like a body but is (as we say) "only in our minds," or when we hear someone speak in our dreams.[10] What Augustine here calls "spiritual" is closer to what in modern English we would call "mental" or "imaginary," with the proviso that we could be imagining something true, such as when we remember the face of a friend or when the prophets of the Bible are given a vision or a dream by God. Augustine's point is that this is different not only from literally seeing or hearing something with your bodily senses (the kind of sensory experience he has just finished describing in such materialistic terms)

---

8. Augustine, *City of God* 11:2.

9. Augustine, *City of God* 11:2.

10. Augustine discusses this kind of "spiritual" vision extensively in his treatise *Literal Meaning of Genesis* 12:6.15–30.58, distinguishing it sharply from *intellectual* vision, which is how the mind sees God.

but also from the kind of intellectual understanding he is about to describe, which he experienced after reading the books of the Platonists. It is mental rather than physical, as we might now put it, but it consists of mental images resembling physical things, which means it is not in fact as spiritual, in the deeper Platonist sense, as what's coming next:

> Rather, he speaks through the Truth itself, if you're capable of hearing it with the mind, not the body.[11]

Here I capitalize "Truth" because, as usual in Augustine, it is a name for God. When God speaks through the Truth, he speaks through himself, without intermediary. Augustine will often identify this Truth as the eternal Word of God, the second person of the Trinity, whom we inwardly hear or consult (*consulere* is the Latin verb Augustine often uses) because he is the inner teacher.[12] This is not mediated speech (that is to say, it is without intermediary—there is nothing *between* God and us when this happens) because this inward teaching is not given to us by angels or any other created thing, not by dreams or visions or other images, and not by external words—not even the words spoken by Christ himself in the flesh, making sound waves in the air and rattling in human ears. This divine, inward speech is direct and immediate, right there in our inmost mind, where God is the Truth that is present, as Augustine says in the *Confessions*, in a way that is "more inward than my inmost self."[13]

The Soul's Nearness to God

If Truth is to speak directly to us, Augustine thinks, it must do so by addressing what is most inward in us, the mind or reason, which is also what is highest and best in us, the thing in us that is closest to God above. In Augustine's view of the world there is nothing higher than the human mind except for the unchangeable being of God himself. The hierarchy of being in Augustine's Platonism consists of three levels: bodies below and God above and the soul (including angels) in the middle. The crucial distinction between the middle level and the highest is the difference between changeability and unchangeability.[14] This hierarchy is reflected in the natural direction of the various

---

11. Augustine, *City of God* 11:2.

12. Augustine, *Teacher* 11.38.

13. Augustine, *Confessions* 3:6.11; *interior intimo meo* (this striking phrase is found toward the end of this long section).

14. The most succinct statement of this three-level ontology is in Augustine, Letter 18:2 (included in appendix 2 of Cary, *Augustine's Invention*), but it pervades his works and is more fully

powers in our souls: the senses are directed to bodily things, the imagination grasps images within us, and the intellect has the capacity to look above itself to see God.[15] That vision of the intellect is what Augustine himself began to understand when he first read "the books of the Platonists," and that is what he is leading us to in this text.

> For since a human being is most rightly understood as—or if that can't be done, at least believed to be—made "in the image of God," then surely the human is nearer to God above by that part of him which is above his own lower parts, which he has in common with cattle.[16]

Augustine is thinking in his usual hierarchical way, where what is higher in being is also what is more intelligible or spiritual, in the deep Platonist sense of the term. Since seeing and hearing and feeling are powers of the human soul that we share with the beasts of the field, they are clearly too low in the inner hierarchy of the soul to be that by which we ascend to God above. Rather, what makes us higher than the beasts and nearer to God is reason. "Reason" (Latin *ratio*, the plural of which is *rationes*, from which we get our word "rational") is a word that will appear in the next sentence. As Augustine likes to remind his readers, it translates the Greek word *logos* (which, as mentioned in chapter 2, can mean "reason" as well as "word"—it is, after all, the word from which we get our word "logic").[17] Because we are not beasts but rational animals, living creatures with *logos*, we are more like God and his *Logos* than the beasts are, and that is why humans alone in the visible creation are said to be made "in the image of God" (Gen. 1:27). The power of reason and what follows from it make us higher and nearer to God—not literally a nearness in space, of course, but a nearness of resemblance. We are more like God than the beasts are, because our souls have the power of reason.

Augustine is aware that some of the less educated in his audience won't get the point, not because they're unfamiliar with the book of Genesis but because they have no familiarity with that great and rare use of reason that

---

explained in *Eighty-Three Different Questions*, question 54; *Magnitude of the Soul* 34.77–78; *Catholic Way of Life and the Manichean Way of Life* 1:12.20. See also the passages anthologized in Bourke, *Essential Augustine*, chap. 3.

15. Augustine describes this inward ascent in *Confessions* 7:17.23, but he worked out its basic structure earlier, and much more elaborately, in *On Free Choice* 2:3.8–15.39. See Cary, *Augustine's Invention*, 66, 77–78.

16. Augustine, *City of God* 11:2.

17. Most importantly, he points this out in his argument for why Christians ought to believe in Platonic forms as ideas or *rationes* (equivalent to the plural of the Greek *logoi*) in the mind of God. See *Eighty-Three Different Questions*, question 46 (included in appendix 2 of Cary, *Augustine's Invention*).

the Platonists cultivate, the exercise of intellect that he designates here with the verb *intelligere* (which is standardly translated into English as "understand"). So if we can't understand, we should at least believe. That's where the Gospel comes in, as we shall see.

Epistemology as Ethics

Now Augustine turns to the problem of why it is such a rare thing to understand God. For him this is an ethical problem.

> But because of certain dark and ancient vices, the very mind in which reason and understanding [*ratio et intelligentia*] are naturally present is too weak to cling in enjoyment to the unchangeable Light or even to bear it, until it is made capable of such felicity by being renewed and healed from day to day; so it must first be instructed and purified by faith.[18]

A great deal is packed into this sentence, which leads us to the role of faith. To begin with, the "dark and ancient vices" are the impurity of the mind's eye that we inherited from Adam. In other contexts Augustine will give this the more familiar name, "original sin." Here, however, he is concerned not with origins but with our current situation, in which our moral vices bring about an intellectual failure, the inability of minds to enjoy the unchangeable Light—which, like all things unchangeable, is simply God. "Enjoyment" (*fruitio* or *frui*) is a key term in Augustine's ethics, which builds on the notion that we should seek to *enjoy* God alone as the supreme Good who affords us ultimate happiness ("felicity," he calls it here) and should *use* all other things in order to arrive at this enjoyment,[19] rather than clinging to changeable, mortal things as though they could give us the unchangeable happiness of everlasting life.[20]

To clarify the connection between moral vice and intellectual failure, Augustine invokes a set of Platonist metaphors to which he has introduced

18. Augustine, *City of God* 11:2.

19. This contrast between the created things we should *use* and the divine Good we should aim to *enjoy* is the organizing framework of Augustine's ethics in *On Christian Doctrine*, book 1, and thereafter becomes central to many accounts of Christian ethics in the medieval West, mainly through the influence of Peter Lombard.

20. In one of the most breathtaking passages in his writings, this is the lesson Augustine wants us to learn from the torment of his own grief over the death of his best friend in the *Confessions*: "I had spilt out my soul upon the sand, in loving a mortal man as if he were never to die," he says (4:8.13), and he urges us not to seek true happiness in mere human friendship: "Seek what you seek, but it is not where you seek it. You seek happiness of life in the land of death, and it is not there" (4:12.18).

readers in the previous books of the *City of God*. Using the same key metaphor as Plato's allegory of the cave, he pictures the mind as an eye whose natural power is to see the Light of Truth, which is God. To see God in this way is not a supernatural gift, for Augustine is thinking here like an ancient Platonist, not like a medieval Catholic such as Thomas Aquinas. Seeing God, the metaphor implies, is as natural to the human intellect as seeing light is to the human eye.[21] What could be more natural to the mind than to know the Truth? And yet we all fail at this. So something is wrong; it is not a natural limitation of our intelligence but some deep-seated and universal derangement. It is not that the vision of God is beyond our natural capacity, but that our natural capacity is impaired, like an eye that cannot perform its proper function because it has been weakened by disease; so instead of enjoying the light, it is dazzled and pained by the brightness and prone to flee back to the comfort of its accustomed darkness. Elsewhere he suggests, again along the lines of the allegory of the cave, that the disease stems from our inveterate habit of gazing at shadows, as if they were something we could cling to with enjoyment.[22]

Still in this same sentence, Augustine also describes the mind's weakness as a kind of impurity. This metaphor has its roots in Plato's *Phaedo*, where virtue means being purified from bodily attachments, which cling to the soul like a kind of dirt and prevent it from knowing the unchanging truth of things.[23] Augustine finds biblical confirmation for this ethical project of purification in the words of our Lord, "Blessed are the pure in heart, for they shall see God" (Matt. 5:8).[24] What Augustine means by purification has already been exemplified in the previous sentences, where he distinguished true understanding from the perception of the senses and the imaginary kind of

21. For why we should read Augustine in this very un-Thomistic way, see Cary, *Augustine's Invention*, 55–60, 76–71.

22. Augustine, *Soliloquies* 1:6.12; *Catholic Way of Life and the Manichean Way of Life* 1:2.3. Notice how the healing of the mind's eye requires a graded series of exercises in seeing what is brighter than the shadows in *Soliloquies* 2:13.23, and compare Plato, *Republic* 515e–516b (the allegory of the cave).

23. In Plato, *Phaedo* 65c–67a, purity of soul means the soul seeking the truth "by itself," without interference and distraction from the body, so purification means separating the soul as much as possible from the body (67b–69d), with the result that after death the soul lives a disembodied, divine life among the unchanging Platonic forms (79d–81b). Following Plato, Plotinus treats the virtues as purifications for the soul in his treatise "On Virtues," in *Enneads* 1:2.

24. See Augustine's treatment of this verse in *Lord's Sermon on the Mount* 1:2.4–4.12 and, very revealingly, the excerpt from another African Platonist, Fonteius of Carthage (writing while still a pagan, though he died a Christian), who was thinking along similar lines in his treatise "On Purifying the Mind in order to See God," in Augustine, *Eighty-Three Different Questions*, question 12.

"spiritual" vision. To make such a distinction in practice requires a purified mind as well as exercise in philosophy, he says in an earlier work, giving as example the contrast between a pure geometrical figure and the kind of shape our thoughts make up in a mental image.[25] We see the truths in geometry by intellect alone, not by the imagination, which is based ultimately on the senses. Yet in the impurity of our minds we often find it difficult to make the epistemological distinction between intellectual vision and mere imagination, which means (in terms of Plato's allegory of the cave) between the real form of things and the shape of the shadows. This is due to our habit of living in the dark and our attraction to earthly pleasures—not just bodily pleasures like eating, drinking, and sex, but also the deceptive social goods of honor, wealth, and power. Because of our impure hearts we are stuck in a world of phantasms, mental images rather than the eternal Good.[26]

What Augustine adds at the end is that our purification from these things— which he will also call by the Pauline name "justification"—takes place by faith.[27] Through faith we are instructed not to cling to external, changeable things as if they could make us permanently happy, and to learn instead to seek the unchangeable Truth of God as our true Good and ultimate happiness, even though we cannot yet see this with our mind's eye or understand it. Faith thus gets us moving toward an understanding that we do not yet have, by teaching us to love God with all our hearts and to purify ourselves from excessive attachment to lesser goods. For by faith we trust that there is something to see, even though our minds are not yet pure enough to see it.[28] To grasp the role of faith in Augustine's spirituality, therefore, one needs to take seriously his conviction that the purification of the mind is a moral renewal of the soul, because our failure to see clearly with our intellects is due to those "dark and ancient vices" by which we love and seek things other than God as if they could make us truly happy. Like Platonism in general, Augustine is misunderstood if he is read in terms of the modern compartmentalization of

---

25. Augustine, *Soliloquies* 2:20.34; note also the preceding discussion (1:18.32) of how true geometrical figures reside in the unchangeable Truth, as opposed to the figures or shapes we see in bodies, which are mere imitations. These are distinctions discussed at length above, chap. 1, "Intelligible Form and Intellectual Vision."

26. Augustine's attempt to cleanse his mind from phantasms (an ancient term for mental images) is his retrospective explanation of why he needed to become a Platonist in *Confessions* 7:1.1, and this program of purification from phantasms can be seen in his early works, such as *Of True Religion* 10.18. See the discussion of "deceiving appearances" and "the epistemology of evil" in Evans, *Augustine on Evil*, chap. 3.

27. That "justification by faith" is equivalent to "purification by faith" for Augustine is clear from his early exegeses of Paul, especially *Eighty-Three Different Questions*, question 68.3. For further discussion, see Cary, *Inner Grace*, 12–14, 49–50, 75.

28. Augustine, *Soliloquies* 1:6.12.

philosophical disciplines, as if epistemology, the theory of knowledge, were a fundamentally different area of inquiry from ethics, the theory of the good life. If you regard Augustine's discussion of sense, imagination, and intellect in this text as if he were "merely doing epistemology" and not introducing central issues of Christian ethics, then you will fail to see why he insists that faith must come before understanding, and also why he thinks we must be justified by faith.

This is in fact a failing in some modern scholarly readings of Augustine. It leads to the notion that the priority of faith to understanding is an episte-mological thesis about the power of faith to grasp truths that are deeper than the intellect can reach. But that is nearly the opposite of the point Augustine is making here. The ultimate goal or end of human life (as he has already said in explicit agreement with the Platonists earlier in the *City of God*) is to see God inwardly with our intellect, the way the eye of the mind enjoys the light.[29] This inner, intellectual vision means seeing for ourselves, not putting our faith in an external word that rattles in our ears. But until we arrive at this goal we need Christian faith, with its dependence on the authority of the Scriptures and Christian teaching. Faith therefore does not give us a deeper understanding than the intellect; it is what we have in place of deeper under-standing, so long as our intellects are still in the process of being healed and cleansed of our moral vices. Until we are pure of heart and can see God with our own intellects, we need to believe what we are told. That is why Augustine now proceeds to bring another human being into the picture for the first time.

Christ the Way to a Platonist Goal

Faith for Augustine is always centered on Jesus Christ, who is the divine Truth in human flesh.

> In order for us to walk more confidently to the Truth in faith, the Truth itself, God the Son of God, established and founded this faith, having assumed a human being, not consumed God, so that the human being's journey to the God of human beings might be through the human being who is God.[30]

Christ as man is the human way to God. This is not Christ as divine inner teacher, who speaks directly to the mind without using external words. Faith in Christ the man means relying on external things, human words and human

---

29. Augustine, *City of God* 8:8.
30. Augustine, *City of God* 11:2.

flesh, as long as we are far from the full intellectual understanding of God as eternal Truth. We believe in Christ precisely because we still have a long way to go, with a perilous journey ahead of us beset by many dangers and temptations, including many opportunities to seek enjoyment in bodily things rather than in the unchangeable Light of Truth.[31]

So to make straight our path, the unchangeable Truth itself, remaining what he was, assumed what he was not. The way Augustine says this here is by a kind of rhyme: "having assumed a human being, not consumed God" (*homine adsumpto, non Deo consumpto*). This little rhyme is derived from the formula for incarnation that Gregory of Nazianzus taught us in chapter 2: "What he was, he remained; what he was not, he assumed."[32] Augustine echoes this formula in a dozen different ways, always reinforcing the point that God does not change into a man, but rather remains immutably God even as he assumes what is not God, our human flesh, and makes it his own. For example, in one sermon Augustine warns: "Let no one believe that the Son of God was changed and turned into the Son of Man, but rather let us believe both that the divine substance was not *consumed* and that the human substance was fully *assumed*—*remaining* the Son of God, made the Son of Man."[33] Once again Augustine is using the term "substance" to refer to the being or nature of something, not what it is made of. "Human substance" here means human nature, referring to Christ's humanity, just as divine substance means divine nature, referring to Christ's divinity. Augustine's use of the biblical terms "Son of God" and "Son of Man" makes the same point: the Son of God is God, the Son of Man is man. And the Son of God remains God even as he is made man.

A minute later in the sermon Augustine brings in language from Gregory's formula: "For our sake he became *what he was not* . . . not losing the form of God but taking the form of a servant . . . and when he began to be *what he was not*, he was made man, *remaining* God." Then to underline the point: "He was not made *what he was not* in such a way as not to be *what he was*. . . . For he was made man, *remaining* God."[34] Augustine takes the contrast between "the form of God" and "the form of a servant" from Paul's hymn in Philippians 2, discussed in chapter 1. He treats this pair of terms as parallel to the Nicene language of "divine substance" and "human substance," covering the same ground as the terms "divinity" and "humanity," or "divine nature" and

31. See Augustine, *Confessions* 10:28.39, which opens a long discussion of the temptations of this life, taking up most of the second half of book 10.
32. Gregory of Nazianzus, Oration 29:19 (the third "Theological Oration").
33. Augustine, Sermon 187:3, my translation, highlighting the key vocabulary.
34. Augustine, Sermon 187:4, my translation.

"human nature," or "Son of God" and "Son of Man." However you want to say it, Augustine is insisting that God does not change or cease to be fully God when he becomes man. This is not the concept of a changeable, lesser God who changes into God incarnate, as the Arians might have it, but rather of one who has the very same unchangeable divine being or substance as God the Father, who remains unchanged in his divinity as he takes up and assumes— rather than being changed into—our humanity.

This Nicene point about the unchangeability of the Son of God anchors what Augustine has to say next:

> This is the "mediator between God and man, the man Christ Jesus." He is mediator in that he is man, and thus also he is the way.[35]

Augustine takes the biblical quotation, which is from 1 Timothy 2:5, to be reinforcing the key Nicene point that the eternal Son of God is not a subordinate or intermediate deity at a lower level of being than God the Father, as the Arians thought, occupying a place in the hierarchy of being between God and creation, and thus suitable to mediate between them. Rather, it is by taking up our humanity that he becomes the mediator between God and humanity. So he is mediator not in his divinity but in his humanity, which is why the Bible here identifies the one mediator between God and man as the *man* Christ Jesus. As God, he cannot be the mediator, a medium or intermediary, precisely because he is equal to God the Father, not a lesser being at a level *between* the Father and us.[36]

Now Augustine is ready to come to the point of this whole passage. Christ incarnate is our mediator because he is our way, the road we must take in our spiritual journey to God. The way *mediates*, because it is *between* us and our destination. As Christ himself says, he is both the Way and the Truth (John 14:6), and for Augustine this means that as Truth he is our unchanging divine goal, while as Way he is the human path along which we move and through which we are changed. Everything in Christian spirituality is thus an attempt to follow Christ's path, as we draw near to him by becoming more like him. And since the goal to which this path leads is defined in Platonist terms (i.e., as intellectual vision of the Truth), this means that Christian faith, centered on the man Jesus Christ, is the means to attain a Platonist end. For Augustine, in other words, the ultimate meaning of Christ incarnate is defined by

---

35. Augustine, *City of God* 11:2.

36. This is a point to which Augustine frequently returns. In a nutshell: "As God he is not Mediator, but equal to the Father" (Sermon 293:7). For fuller discussion see *City of God* 9:15 and *Confessions* 10:43.68, two of Augustine's most important discussions of Christ the mediator.

Platonism. Christ is our way to the goal Plato describes in the allegory of the cave. This is how the Gospel, and the Nicene doctrine that supports it, fits into Augustine's Platonist spirituality. And this is the point at which, I am suggesting, Augustine's theology goes astray.

God's Way into the Cave

We must be clear about precisely what has gone wrong. Augustine is not saying that the Platonists have some kind of advantage over faithful Christians. Far from it:

> For if there is a way between the one who is traveling and that to which he travels, then there is hope of arriving. But if there is none and you don't know how to go, what good is it to know where you're going?[37]

The pagan Platonists, Augustine tells us more than once, have caught sight of the ultimate goal—indeed, he tells us he caught sight of it himself only after reading their books. But they did not have the humility to follow Christ, the God who humbled himself to become human and thus establish a path that all human beings can follow. They were too proud to admit their need to be purified by faith in this humiliated God.[38] So there can be no real hope for them to arrive at the ultimate Good that they have seen. They have caught sight of the lofty, distant goal, but they have missed the lowly way that could get them there.

What we all need is a way between here and there, literally a *via media* in Augustine's Latin. Christ the mediator is that way, the road that lies between where we are and where we're going. Augustine proceeds to elaborate the metaphor:

> And there is only one road that's really protected against every possibility of going astray, which is for the very same one to be both God and human: God, where we're going, and human, how we go.[39]

God and human are related in Christ as eternal and temporal, goal and movement, destination and journey: as God Christ is the unchangeable Good at which we aim to arrive, but as man he is the path of growth and change we take to get there.

---

37. Augustine, *City of God* 11:2.
38. Such is Augustine's diagnosis of his own spiritual failure after reading "the books of the Platonists" in *Confessions* 7:18.24, which is like the failure of the Platonists themselves in 7:21.27.
39. Augustine, *City of God* 11:2.

The problem with this conception of Christ the mediator is that it makes Christ's humanity our way to God rather than God's way to us. It is about how we change in order to come to God, rather than how God in Christ comes to us, changes us, and makes all things new. It thus misses one of the key insights of Cyril of Alexandria: that Christ's humanity is life-giving flesh. It is the Word's own flesh, given to us so that we may share in his eternal life.[40] The incarnation is God's way to us because it is God's way of giving us nothing less than himself. Because Christ's humanity is God's own flesh, the Eastern Orthodox, following Cyril, call it both deified and deifying, the divine source of eternal life for temporal creatures. To take hold of this man in faith is therefore to take hold of God in person, who gives himself to us precisely in Christ's life-giving flesh.

In Augustine's theology, by contrast, the purity of intellectual vision requires too neat a distinction between Christ's divinity and his humanity, as if we could ultimately direct our mind's attention to the one without the other. The purification of our mind's eye means in the end turning away from all temporal things, even the humanity of Christ, as a traveler turns away from the road when she finally arrives home. Augustine makes this clear in his treatise *On Christian Doctrine*, where he says Christ himself, "insofar as he deigned to become our way, wanted not to detain us but for us to travel onward—not clinging in weakness to temporal things, although they were taken up by him and accomplished for our salvation, but rather running through them eagerly so as to advance and deserve to arrive at himself, who has liberated our nature from temporal things and set it at the right hand of the Father."[41] Augustine thinks we should not cling to Christ's historical life in the flesh, including all the temporal things he took up and accomplished for our salvation (his humanity, his flesh and blood, his suffering), but should pass through it quickly, as Christ himself did in his short life on earth, so as to arrive at the goal above, where Christ himself, still inseparably united to his human nature, sits on the throne of God.

Augustine is not separating the two natures of Christ, which are eternally united in one person, but he is saying that we can direct our attention to the

40. See the eleventh of the twelve anathemas (also known traditionally as "the twelve chapters") and the supporting argument for it in Cyril's third letter to Nestorius, a very important official letter that can be found in many anthologies, including Hardy, *Christology of the Later Fathers*; Stevenson, *Creeds, Councils, and Controversies*; McGuckin, *Saint Cyril of Alexandria*, 266–75. The phrase is based on John 6:51, where Jesus says, "the bread that I will give for the life of the world is my flesh."

41. Augustine, *On Christian Doctrine* 1:34.38, my translation. Cf. also the image of Christ running quickly the race of his life on earth, so as to return to where he came from and call us back to his divine presence by an inward turn: "that we might return to our own heart and find Him." *Confessions* 4:12.19.

one nature rather than the other. This is precisely what purifying the mind amounts to in the end: the possibility of a pure intellectual vision whose gaze is turned away from all sensible and temporal things such as flesh and blood—even Christ's. Indeed, Christ himself is our example in this regard, as his humanity is now liberated from temporal things, free to pay full attention to the divinity he shares with the Father. That is the state to which we also must advance as we travel, not detained on the way to God. Hence the goal of our hope, in this Augustinian picture, is not Christ's coming again in the flesh, descending from heaven to dwell among us, but our ascent to be where he is now, to join him in contemplating the divinity he shares with the Father. We remain embodied and human forever, as he does, but we have everlasting happiness because, like him, we turn our attention away from his humanity to his divinity.

The root of the problem is that for Augustine beatific vision is pure intellectual vision, in the Platonist sense of the term, and therefore it means understanding the unchangeable being of God, not clinging to God in the flesh. The Eastern Orthodox have a better doctrine here, denying that we can ever have such understanding of the being or essence (*ousia*) of God, and affirming that the beatific vision means seeing the glory of God in the human face of Jesus Christ, like the apostles on the Mount of Transfiguration.[42] We must ultimately—even in the end!—find God in the flesh, precisely because we cannot understand the unchangeable being of God. This makes better sense of the fact that the New Testament hope is not that we go to heaven but that Christ returns to earth "in the glory of his Father" (Matt. 16:27), so that the kingdom we pray for comes "on earth, as it is in heaven" (the Lord's Prayer in Matt. 6:10). It means that the ultimate goal of humanity is defined by the Gospel of Jesus Christ rather than by the allegory of the cave.

Yet we can avail ourselves of the allegory of the cave once more, to see how the Platonist conceptual framework cracks when the Nicene Christ of the Gospel gets into the middle of it. Just imagine the Sun itself, remaining what it is, coming down into the cave and becoming one of the dwellers there. It is an astonishing event, unlike anything Plato could have expected, and it would hardly make sense if its purpose were merely to lead us upward, out of the cave.[43] Why would the Sun lower itself, taking on the form of a servant,

---

42. For the Eastern Orthodox conception of beatific vision modeled on the Transfiguration, see Palamas, *Triads* 62–82. This is correlated with the Orthodox teaching that we participate in the uncreated energies, the grace and glory and operation of God, but not in the divine essence or being (*ousia*), as Palamas proceeds to argue in 82–111.

43. Yet this purpose is in effect the gist of the argument about how perfectly Christ fit Plato's expectations in Augustine, *Of True Religion* 3.3, using the imagery of intellectual vision together

to do what other servants could do just as well? Plato himself could imagine a Socratic teacher who leads us up out of the cave, "dragging" us upward by asking us difficult questions that get us turning toward the light. And in Augustine's own estimation there are many examples in Scripture and in Christian tradition of good people who, by the grace of God, turn away from temporal goods or use them properly to arrive at the enjoyment of the eternal Good. If that were all the incarnation of Christ offered us, then it would hardly be indispensable. Surely something more than that must be going on if the Good itself comes down into the cave to "pitch his tent among us," so that "we have beheld his glory . . . full of grace and truth."[44] Surely the cave itself must be a different place than we thought, or must have become a different place than it was, because this One has dwelt there among us, and is even now living in human flesh on the throne of God, and will return to us in glory. And surely our own flesh, our mortality and corruptibility, becomes a new thing because this One has taken it up into his own person.

The good news of the divine incarnation in Christ gives us an alternative to what I have been calling "spirituality." The Good himself has come down to the cave so that we can find him there, not by ascending to him but by recognizing his descent to us, a recognition that requires not intellectual vision but faith in the Gospel of Jesus Christ, preached by prophets and apostles and other ministers of the word and found in the external words of Holy Scripture. "The glory of God in the face of Jesus Christ" (2 Cor. 4:6)—his human face, the head once crowned with thorns—is not just the light that guides us on our way. It is God himself given to us, by God himself, so that he may be ours forever. He has not come to lead us out of the cave but to make the cave a different place—the theater of his glory, as Calvin likes to call it—and to make our own flesh different, as this corruptible body of ours puts on his incorruptibility (1 Cor. 15:54) so that we ourselves, even in our flesh, "shall be like him, because we shall see him as he is" (1 John 3:2). Thus Christ's human life does not merely show us the way to God; it gives us God himself in the flesh.

Faith and Authority

Until the kingdom of God comes to earth and Christ is revealed for all to see, we perceive him by faith alone, believing that he is who the Gospel says he is.

---

with purification and healing of the mind's eye, as well as the notions of faith and authority that we are about to encounter in *City of God*.

44. John 1:14, my literal translation (as in chap. 2).

Thus it is *by faith alone* that we receive the eternal God and know who he is. That is the core of Protestant theology. There are a number of reasons why it does not really fit with Augustine's Platonist spirituality, as we can now see. For one thing, it does not really fit the way Augustine thinks about faith. We can bring this point into focus as Augustine proceeds to the third chapter of *City of God*, book 11, where he situates the role of Scripture in relation to what he has just said about Christ the mediator.

> First by the prophets, then by himself, then by the apostles, he has spoken as much as he judged to be sufficient, and has established the Scriptures that are called "canonical," which are of preeminent authority, in which we put our faith concerning those things of which it would not be good for us to be ignorant, but which we are not capable of becoming acquainted with by ourselves.[45]

Christ incarnate is at the center of the Scriptures, with the Old Testament prophets coming before and the New Testament apostles after him. All of them are speaking literal human words; this is not the direct speaking of divine Truth to the mind that is the source of real knowledge of the unchangeable divine being, as Augustine said at the beginning of our passage. So neither Christ nor the Scriptures are a revelation that makes God known to us; for that we need an intellectual vision that outward words and human flesh cannot supply.

This limitation of the power of words, including the words of the Gospel, is essential to the semiotics or theory of signs that follows from Augustine's Platonism. Words are a type of sign, according to Augustine, and all signs are external things with no power over our inner selves, and especially no power to give an inner gift such as grace, wisdom, or understanding. Hence they cannot reveal God to us, because as Augustine argues elsewhere, "we don't learn anything by these signs called words."[46] The best signs can do is serve as admonitions, reminding us where to look in order to find what we seek. It was in this way that "the books of the Platonists" admonished him to turn inward to see God. Words can function like road signs pointing us in

---

45. Augustine, *City of God* 11:3.

46. Augustine, *Teacher* 10.34. The point is a general one that concerns all signs: "Nothing is learned through its signs" (10.33). In Augustine's semiotics all signs are external things and for that very reason have no power to give us an inner gift of grace or understanding. The usefulness of signs lies not in any power of revelation, but in their use as admonitions or reminders of where to look in order to see things for ourselves (11.36). For the Platonist reasons why Augustine is willing to argue for this startling thesis, and why he persists in holding it throughout his career despite a number of significant modifications in his epistemology, see Cary, *Outward Signs*, chaps. 4–5.

the right direction, but they have no power to move us along the way. They are not fuel or food or an inward energy of grace in our hearts, for they are merely external. They point us in the right direction precisely by pointing away from themselves, like every created thing, whose transitory being says in effect: "Not me! I am not what you seek. You're looking for him who made me."[47] No external word or sign is something we should cling to, as if it had a spiritual gift to give us. Augustine's spirituality thus has no place for the kind of sign that later medieval Catholics call sacraments, which confer an inner gift of grace, nor for the kind of word that Luther calls Gospel, by which God gives us nothing less than himself. Like Christ's own flesh, they are not God's way to us, but our way to God. We are to use them well, not cling to them as if they could give us everlasting happiness.

On the other hand, the directions are well worth using, and Augustine wants us to see why: it is because of the authority of those who give them. This gets us to the heart of his conception of faith. Authority and faith are closely related concepts for Augustine, because faith means believing what you're told by a person who has the right kind of authority, like a teacher who is an authority on her subject or a witness who is telling you what he has seen with his own eyes. This emphasis on authority does not make Augustine an "authoritarian," as moderns typically fear. Authority in Augustine, and also in his medieval followers, is a pedagogical, not a political concept—a characteristic of teachers, not kings. In Augustine's Latin what kings have is *potestas* or *imperium*, "power" or "command," not *auctoritas*, "authority." Faith is based on authority because that is how learning normally begins, for it is the natural order that "authority precedes reason when we learn something."[48] So for example if you're in a math class and you don't quite "get it," then you have to start the process of learning by relying on the authority of your teacher, taking on faith the words she gives you, as well as the formulas and figures she draws on the chalkboard. The goal is to get you to see for yourself, but you have to start by believing what you're told.

This is what is meant by the famous motto "I believe so that I may understand," which for Augustine originally took the form "unless you believe, you will not understand."[49] In the end what we want to understand is nothing less

---

47. Cf. Augustine, *Confessions* 10:6.9.

48. Augustine, *Catholic Way of Life and the Manichean Way of Life* 1:2.3. See also Augustine, *On Order* 2:9.26, on how "authority comes first in time, but reason is first in reality" (*tempore auctoritas, re autem ratio prior est*). For the pervasive importance of the contrast of authority and reason in Augustine, see Cary, *Outward Signs*, 109–20, 176–77.

49. Augustine, *On Free Choice* 1:2.4 and 2:2.6. The original form of the motto ("unless you believe, you will not understand") is a quotation from the old Latin translation of Isa. 7:9. Augustine's later exhortation "Believe, so that you may understand" occurs frequently in his

than God, but to arrive at this end we must start at the beginning, where we put our faith in the authority of our Christian teachers, and especially the preeminent authority of the Scriptures. Scripture thus does not function as revelation, as if it could give us knowledge of God's unchangeable being, but as authority, the first step in a long process of learning that eventuates in our seeing God for ourselves, without the need for anyone else to tell us in words.

> For if, with ourselves as witness, we can know things that are not far removed from our inner or outer senses (and hence these things are designated "present" [*praesentia*], by which we mean they are "before the senses" [*prae sensibus*], just as what is present to the eyes is "before the eyes"), then surely for those things which are far removed from our senses, which we cannot know by our own testimony, we need the witness of others, and we believe people from whose senses we believe they were not far removed.[50]

Christian faith, for Augustine, is not a deeper form of knowledge than reason but a secondhand substitute, making up for what we cannot see for ourselves. This may include historical events we have not witnessed, such as the crucifixion and resurrection of Christ, which are at the heart of what Augustine calls the "temporal dispensation" (his equivalent of the Greek patristic term *oikonomia*, which means the economy or historical plan of divine salvation). But most importantly it includes intellectual vision, the goal toward which the temporal dispensation in Christ is the way. It is a vision we don't yet have but can believe in, based on the testimony of witnesses whose minds have seen more than we have.

Augustine here gets to the heart of the attractiveness of the metaphor of intellectual vision. As we have noticed earlier, he can use metaphors of hearing, consulting, or learning from the inner teacher as a way of describing intellectual understanding. But in the course of the two chapters from *City of God* that we have been examining, he switches effortlessly from metaphors of hearing to metaphors of seeing, because like other Platonists (and like Plato in the allegory of the cave), he is interested in firsthand knowledge—"seeing it for yourself," as we now say, rather than just "hearing about it." This firsthand knowledge is based on a kind of direct inner presence, in which what we know is right there in front of our mind's eye. Augustine finds this presence indicated in the Latin preposition *prae*, used to describe how things are set

---

preaching (e.g., Sermon 43:4; 89:4; 118:1; 212:1; 214:10). The famous formulation "I believe that I may understand" (*credo ut intelligam*) is actually Anselm's version of the motto, in *Proslogion*, chap. 1 (at the end).

50. Augustine, *City of God* 11:3.

before us—right before our eyes or "before the senses" (*prae sensibus*), which Augustine thinks is the root of the very word "presence" (*prae-sentia*). Vision is firsthand because we see what is literally present before us, not far away from us.[51] By contrast, when we believe what we (literally) hear, we are relying on what was once present to others but is not now present to us. That is the sense in which faith is secondhand, inferior to immediate vision. Believing is not seeing but having faith in the word of others telling us what they have seen.

> Therefore, just as for visible things we haven't seen, we believe people who have seen them, and likewise for the rest of the things pertaining to a particular bodily sense, so also for the things that are sensed by the mind or intellect (for it is quite correct to call this also a "sense," which is why it takes the word *sententia*), which is to say that for the invisible things that are far removed from our interior sense, we have to believe people who learned these things as they are set forth in the incorporeal Light or who gaze at them as they abide there.[52]

We now come back to where we began: this is how that great and rare thing happens, when the mind's attention catches sight of the unchangeable being of God and comes to enjoy the unchangeable Light. Faith is what we have when we do not yet have this vision and enjoyment, but must rely on believing others who do—minds that can see what we can't, or at least have caught sight of it once and can tell us about it.

We can use metaphors from any of the five senses to describe this knowledge of theirs, because the mind too has its kind of perception or *sensus*. For between the sensible and the intelligible there is likeness as well as difference, as always in Platonism, where even the shadows participate in the form of the real beings they resemble. Yet our goal remains, in Augustine's spirituality, to rise from the one to the other: from shadows, such as Christ's visible flesh, to the unchangeable divine being that is visible only to the eye of the mind. Thus beatific vision, in the Augustinian tradition, does not look much like the Transfiguration, a vision that sees God in Christ incarnate.

Nor does faith, in Augustine, look much like receiving God himself, given to us in Christ incarnate through the Gospel. For the Gospel consists of external words, signs that cannot give us what they signify. When the Augustinian tradition speaks of "faith seeking understanding" (in Anselm's very Augustinian

---

51. See Augustine, Letter 147:2.7.

52. Augustine, *City of God* 11:3. Augustine remarks parenthetically that the mind has a capacity for *sententia*, which means "judgment," and that this is connected etymologically to *sensus* or sense (as nowadays when a judge gives a sentence, she might say, "my sense is that . . ." or even "I feel that . . ."). This is the language of the senses used to express the rational judgments of the mind.

motto[53]), it is not making faith in the Gospel of Christ the foundation of our knowledge of God. Faith merely puts us on the right road, heeding the signs that point us in the direction of real knowledge of God, which consists in understanding (*intellectus*), in the Platonist sense of intellectual vision. The seeking that moves us along the road to understanding is not faith itself but love, which is always a seeking of what is loved. It is a Protestant misinterpretation to say that it is "my faith itself that summons me to knowledge" and that "the beginning and end are already given in faith."[54] A properly Augustinian interpretation of "faith seeking understanding" must insist on the point that believers seek understanding by love, not by faith alone. For Augustine, "faith alone" could only mean faith at the beginning of the road, devoid of understanding and not yet seeking it. "Love understanding—love it a lot," Augustine urges us.[55] So if we are to grasp the Augustinian spirituality within which Protestant theology first emerged—and from which it diverged—we need to say more about the power of love on the road to understanding God, which will be the task of the next chapter.

53. Anselm, *Proslogion*, prologue.

54. Barth, *Anselm: Fides Quaerens Intellectum*, 18, 25. Barth can be sharply critical of Augustine and especially the Platonist themes in his work (e.g., in *Holy Spirit and the Christian Life*, 3–6, 21–25, and *Church Dogmatics*, II/1, 10–12). But he wants Anselm on his side, and thus furnishes a very un-Augustinian interpretation of Anselm's *Proslogion*, which is an important milestone in Barth's own development but not a reliable guide to the original meaning of Anselm's motto, "faith seeking understanding," which is in fact quite Augustinian.

55. Augustine, Letter 120:3.13; *intellectum vero valde ama*.

4

The Augustinian Journey
and Its Anxieties

F aith alone does not save us, Augustine says quite explicitly.[1] Augustine
teaches justification by faith but not justification by faith *alone*. For
Augustine, faith is only the beginning of the journey to God. Faith sets
us on the right road, but the motive force that moves us along toward our
destination is love. The Protestant disagreement with Augustinian spirituality
is at its most explicit here, because Protestant theology insists on salvation by
faith alone, apart from any works we do, including even the work of love. So
it is important to grasp the fullness of what Protestantism is rejecting here,
in the extraordinary things Augustine has to say about the power of love.[2]
As we shall see in this chapter, Augustine's concept of love is essential to his
doctrine of grace, including many interconnected problems about free will,
predestination, and salvation. The Augustinian doctrine of grace has had a
long life in Western Christianity, both Catholic and Protestant, and more than
a millennium after Augustine it was the framework within which Luther's
theology took shape, as we shall see in part 2.

Intellect and Love

In Augustine's theology, love is the spiritual movement of soul that brings us
from faith to understanding. For many modern readers, this may come as a

1. Augustine, *On Faith and Works* 14.21; 15.25; *Grace and Free Choice* 8.20.
2. For what is still the best full-length study of Augustine on love, see Burnaby, *Amor Dei* (originally 1938).

bit of a surprise. The understanding Augustine is after is an intellectual act (the Latin word for it is *intellectus*), and most of us today are not used to the idea that this could be what love is about—or that a love so intellectual could have anything to do with spirituality. But as before, one of the strengths of Augustine's spirituality is that it is so oblivious to modern expectations and compartmentalizations.[3] Just as epistemology and ethics are really one inquiry for Augustine, so intellect and love are functions of one heart moving in the one direction. It is thus perfectly natural for Augustine to say the heart understands and the intellect loves. The most spiritual love is precisely a movement of the intellect, strengthened by what Augustine often calls mental training or exercise (*exercitatio mentis* or *exercitatio animi*).[4] This is not what is meant in the dismissive modern phrase "merely mental exercise." Rather, it is the heart working hard, in disciplined fashion, to pursue its deepest desire, which is for Truth in all its beauty. For the heart is restless until it attains joy in the Truth, which is its ultimate happiness.[5]

Even those who want to "bring head and heart together," as they say nowadays, are likely to miss the point here. There is no need to bring together what was never separated. To talk about bringing head and heart together is already to compartmentalize, to imagine two parts of our experiential life located in two different places, and then to make a problem of the compartmentalization by trying to overcome the distance between them. Augustine has no such problem because he never compartmentalizes like that in the first place. Like the Bible, he never describes people thinking in their heads. They think in their hearts, in part because the term for "mind" in biblical Hebrew simply is the word for "heart" (*lev* or *levav*). There are not two different things here. Hence it is natural for Augustine to read "blessed are the pure in heart, for they shall see God" (Matt. 5:8) as a reference to intellectual vision, for "intellect" and "heart" in his vocabulary are two ways of talking about the same thing.

Augustine does make a distinction between intellect and will, which are the powers of the heart that are active in understanding and in loving, respectively. But he makes it impossible to separate them as well. Intellect and will go in the same direction, whether in sin, where intellectual error arises from the disordered will and reinforces it, or in righteousness, where both

---

3. This salutary obliviousness, which includes a failure to make any clear distinction between theology and spirituality, is not unique to Augustine but characteristic of the church fathers, and has everything to do with their view of intellect, as shown by A. N. Williams, *Divine Sense*.

4. The idea of mental exercise as contributing to the spiritual health of the soul occurs frequently in Augustine, including for example in *Soliloquies* 1:23; 2:34; *Magnitude of the Soul* 15.25; *Teacher* 8.21; *Usefulness of Belief* 13.29; *Of True Religion* 17.33; *Confessions* 13:11.12; *Trinity* 9:12.17; 13.20.26; 15:6.10.

5. Augustine, *Confessions* 10:23.33.

intellect and will are directed toward God.[6] The intellect desires to see the Truth, and this desire, when it is cleansed of false attachments, is Christian love, the charity by which we love God, who is Truth, with our whole heart, mind, and strength.[7] Or to put the same point in more robustly Platonist terms, the Good that the will desires to possess is none other than the Truth that the intellect aims to see.

To make the Platonism a bit more robust still, we can add: the reason a soul or heart (two words for the same thing) can get so passionate about this very intellectual love is that another name for the Good of Truth is Beauty. This explains why, despite all the effort and the pain of our dazzled eyes, people do like getting up out of Plato's cave: there is nothing more beautiful than what we enjoy when we see the true, unchanging Light. The beauty of it all makes the ascent worthwhile, ultimately a matter not of duty but of delight. Plato's word for this passionate love is *eros*, for he sees in it the secret of all our erotic longing, its madness and joy. When we fall in love, he explains in the *Phaedrus*, it is because something we see in our beloved reminds us of the unchanging Beauty our souls were contemplating before we fell from heaven and came to dwell in physical bodies.[8] That's why it feels like something so much deeper than a mere animal urge for sex or even a longing for another person. Eros is always at root a desire for the eternal.

Another name for this desire, Augustine suggests in his interpretation of Platonism, is philosophy. He often reminds his readers that *philosophia* is a Greek word meaning love of wisdom. For this reason, he says, Plato believed that the true philosopher is a lover of God, because God is eternal Wisdom.[9] In fact there is no place in Plato's texts where this is said, but it certainly does reflect the core of Augustine's Christian Platonism, in which Christ is identified as eternal Wisdom (see 1 Cor. 1:24), and love of true Wisdom is therefore love of Christ, who in his divinity is the goal of all our love. In this view, true philosophy is ultimately the same as Christian charity. In an Augustinian

6. Even the famous analysis of the divided will in book 8 of *Confessions* does not divide will from intellect. The will is divided against *itself*, both desiring to do what's right and wanting to hold on to what's wrong (*Confessions* 8:9.21). This matches the situation of the intellect, which has caught a glimpse of the ultimate Good but is not strong enough to enjoy it and falls back to its accustomed darkness (7:17.23–24). Will and intellect alike are divided; each one is pulled in two opposite directions.

7. A note on old terminology that may now be misleading: the word "charity" (Latin *caritas*) is an Augustinian label for precisely that love which fulfills the twofold command to love God and neighbor. It does not refer to giving money to the poor, which is only one form of charity, the original Christian term for which is "alms."

8. Plato, *Phaedrus* 249d–252b. For *eros* as the motive of spiritual ascent, see Plato's *Symposium* 201d–212b.

9. Augustine, *City of God* 8:1; 8:8; 8:11. Cf. Augustine, *Confessions* 3:4.8.

context, *eros*, charity, philosophy, and spirituality are all terms pointing in the same direction, motives for the same intellectual ascent, climbing out of Plato's cave.

Love as Movement

Augustine's account of love is Platonist not just because it owes something to the Platonist tradition but because it contributes something to that tradition as well. Augustine adds substantially to Platonism's conception of love, for he is a bishop who has to preach the spiritual journey of the soul to ordinary people in such a way that they can grasp what is expected of them, while making clear that this is not literally a movement from place to place. As Plotinus says, in a passage Augustine particularly admires, it is not a journey for the feet, and you can't get there on a chariot or a ship.[10] To get this and other essential points of spirituality across to his largely uneducated congregation, he has to involve their imagination, while also nudging them beyond mere imagination to intellectual understanding. One part of this verbal nudging or admonition is his tendency to picture love as a kind of motive force of the soul, a power of attraction and ultimately of union. We move toward what we love and seek to be one with it, as a thirsty person seeks water, a greedy person seeks money, a lover seeks the beloved, and the true philosopher seeks God. And once we have found what we seek, we stick to it like glue.[11] The thirsty person makes the water she finds part of her body, the greedy person tries to keep money in his possession, lover and beloved become one flesh, friend and friend become one soul, and the true philosopher is united with the eternal Wisdom of God.

To help us imagine how love is a motive force, Augustine compares it to weight, as understood in ancient physics. "My love is my weight: wherever I go, it is my love that takes me there," he says.[12] In the standard version of ancient physics, there are only four basic elements, earth, water, air, and fire, and they are arranged in order of weight. Imagine a lake on a sunny day, and you'll see it: the water rests on top of the earth, with the air above

10. Plotinus, "On Beauty," *Enneads* 1:6.8, using imagery that Augustine combines with the parable of the prodigal son in *Confessions* 1:18.28 and echoes again in 8:8.19 with these words: "The way was not by ship or chariot or on foot."

11. Augustine speaks of the soul united to what it loves by "the glue of care" in *Trinity* 10:5.7 and "the glue of love" in *Confessions* 4:10.15. Unfortunately the metaphor does not come through in every translation.

12. Augustine, *Confessions* 13:9.10. The metaphor recurs elsewhere, though less fully explained; cf., e.g., Augustine, *City of God* 11:28; Letter 55:12.

it and the fire of the sun and stars above it all. And then think about the weight of fire, whose flames always rise upward, never downward, because it is attracted back to its home among the heavenly fires of the sun and the stars, as surely as stones are attracted to their home on earth and fall in that direction whenever we drop them. That's how movement is explained in ancient physics. Each element is directed by an inherent attraction that keeps it moving until it arrives at its natural place of rest. So charity has a weight or motive force like a kind of spiritual fire carrying us upward, while lust and greed are a weight that pulls us downward, drawn to things of earth. As the metaphor develops in the Middle Ages, charity is an ardent desire that does not consume us but burns away impurities and makes us shine with incandescence like glowing iron, in contrast to our evil desires, which are muddy, cold, and filthy. You can see this imagery worked out systematically in Dante's *Divine Comedy*.[13]

For Augustine the real attraction of heaven, which is merely symbolized by its physical height, is its changelessness. The ancients looked up at the same stars year by year and saw an imperishable world of harmonious, regular cycles of movement without corruption or decay. We want to be there, they thought, because we want an incorruptible happiness, which we cannot find anywhere on earth, where the cycles of time make for seasons of birth and death. That is why Augustine says, in the most famous words he ever wrote, "Our hearts are restless till they rest in Thee."[14] Our divinely oriented restlessness is not a moral achievement or a virtue, but the shape of all desire in rational beings living on this changeable earth. Unlike stones at home in the ground or fire at home in the sun, we have no resting place in this world, no place that gives us lasting happiness. So we repeatedly find ourselves dissatisfied with what we thought would make us happy. We all want a happy life, Augustine frequently says (using Cicero's term for happiness, *beata vita*) but since a happiness you can lose is not true, lasting happiness, the happy life we want, whether we realize it or not, must be an everlasting life. (This is Augustine's elegant way of showing why the New Testament term "everlasting life" is the answer to the fundamental question of ancient philosophy, "What is happiness?"[15]) So our deepest desire is constantly being frustrated, as we mistakenly seek happiness among changing things that perish and slip from our grasp. We are

13. See Cary, "Weight of Love."
14. *Confessions* 1:1.1.
15. For the argument that happy life must be everlasting life, see Augustine, *City of God* 14:25, as well as the more extensive discussions in Augustine, *Eighty-Three Different Questions*, question 35.2; Sermon 150:10; *Trinity* 13:8.11. For happiness as the central concern of philosophy, see *City of God* 8:3; 10:1; 19:1.

not at home until, like fire, we find rest in a higher realm above this earth, in the midst of celestial light where there is no death.

In the meantime, we are apt to try everything under the sun, and find none of it makes us happy for long. That is the fundamental form of our restlessness. It results from our misdirected love, which Augustine calls concupiscence (Latin *concupiscentia*). The term is often translated "lust," but it includes every kind of greedy desire that gets us clinging to something other than God as if it could make us truly happy. It becomes a central term in Augustinian ethics,[16] and thus in Catholic theology, in part because it appears in the tenth commandment, "You shall not covet" (Exod. 20:17; cf. Rom. 7:7), which in Latin is *non concupisces*, using the verb that corresponds to the noun *concupiscentia*. This is the love that weighs us down to earth rather than lifting us like fire—or like Plato's *eros*—to heavenly things. It is a wrong desire that also deceives us, seducing us into embracing the illusion that the beautiful and good things in creation are what our heart is really made for, and thus leading us away from their Creator, who alone is our eternal happiness, our true resting place.

This alliance of sinful love and intellectual error moving us in the wrong direction is on display in another famous example of Augustine's imaginative presentation of intellectual truths, when he confesses, "Late have I loved Thee, O Beauty so ancient and so new, late have I loved Thee!"[17] God is eternal Beauty, which has always been present in our inmost self and thus is the most ancient thing in us, but which also encounters us ever afresh, because we always come to it late, delayed by those dark and ancient vices that attract us to everything else but God, getting us stuck to outward beauties that cannot make us happy for long and that cause us grief and torment when we lose them. Our love is wrong because our understanding of things is wrong, and vice versa—intellect and will leading each other astray so that we look for happiness in all the wrong places. Augustine is not denying that these things that God created are beautiful—quite the contrary. The problem is that these beauties are not God, and therefore they are changeable and corruptible; they are goods that we can lose no matter how tightly we cling to them. We are right to find them beautiful, but wrong to think they can make us happy. Yet we keep loving them as if they could. "Thou wert within me, and I outside," Augustine proceeds to explain, still addressing the eternal Beauty and Loveliness of God, "and I sought Thee outside, and in my unloveliness fell upon those lovely things that Thou hast made."[18] God is present in each of us

16. See Nisula, *Augustine and the Functions of Concupiscence.*
17. Augustine, *Confessions* 10:27.38.
18. Augustine, *Confessions* 10:27.38.

as "more inward than my inmost self,"[19] yet that is precisely why we are far from him, for we live outside ourselves, rushing about among all the beautiful things out there. It is as if we have our backs turned to the light within.[20] God himself is our happiness, Augustine has just finished arguing, and can only be found in the inner space of the self.[21] Yet we hardly know where to look, attracted as we are to external things instead.

Persevering in the Church

Even our friends can be loved the wrong way, Augustine teaches, when we seek ultimate happiness in human friendship, "loving a mortal man as if he were never to die."[22] We need to be purified by faith, believing that the unchangeable God is not only better and more beautiful than any created thing, but the source of the only true and lasting happiness—even if we cannot yet see this for ourselves. To sustain such faith we need a different kind of friendship, in which love of neighbor means helping one another on the road to everlasting life in God. The place of this friendship is the church, and the name for it is, once again, charity. For true love of other persons means desiring for them the same Good we desire for ourselves—loving our neighbors as ourselves, as the commandment says.[23]

Because love is a unitive force, it brings communities into being. It is the inner bond of union that brings souls together and makes every community what it is.[24] To use one of Augustine's own examples, even a fan club becomes a kind of community as it is brought together by love for the same actor, uniting their hearts in shared devotion, which each member of the community tries to strengthen and enhance in the others.[25] The church, Augustine is thinking, is like God's fan club, brought together by love of the Good that makes for everlasting life, of the Beauty that gives lasting delight, and of the Truth that

19. *interior intimo meo*, in Augustine, *Confessions* 3:6.11.

20. Cf. the metaphor in Augustine, *Confessions* 7:7.11: "That light was within, I looking outward."

21. Augustine, *Confessions* 10:20.29–24.35.

22. Augustine, *Confessions* 4:8.13.

23. For this interpretation of love of neighbor, see Augustine, *Of True Religion* 46.87, where the rule of love is to will that your friend have the same good you will for yourself, and *Confessions* 4:18, where Augustine urges us: "If souls please you, then love them in God, because they are mutable in themselves but in him firmly established . . . and draw as many souls with you to Him as you can, saying to them, 'Him let us love.'" See also the interpretation of the twofold love commandment in Augustine, *City of God* 10:3 and 19:14.

24. For this view of community in Augustine, see Cary, "United Inwardly by Love."

25. Augustine, *On Christian Doctrine* 1:29.30.

every mind by nature desires to know. And all the members of the church, insofar as they truly belong to its unity of love, strengthen and enhance in each other the love for God, which is the first part of charity, and thus aid each other on their spiritual journey, which is the second part of charity, the love for neighbor. Even those in the church who are not yet fully spiritual in their manner of life have a hope of arriving at the ultimate goal, because this is a community traveling together along the one road that, as we saw Augustine put it in the *City of God*, is truly safe from all straying and error, since it is based on faith in the supreme authority of Jesus Christ, the man who is God.

The crucial question for all who want to be saved is whether they belong to this community, which is the social Body of Christ. Augustine has a great deal to say about this because it was a topic of intense controversy in the African church at the time, which was split by a schism between two fiercely opposed communities. The flashpoint of the debate was the practice of baptism, the rite that marks a person's membership in the church. The Donatists, Augustine's opponents in the controversy, thought of baptism as the act of a holy bishop who made others holy. This meant that baptism was not valid if the bishop failed to be holy. Augustine treated baptism instead as the outward sign of an inward community, a sign that has no power of its own but signifies the power of love that unites a whole people to God in holiness. Neither the bishop nor the mere external rite itself can make people holy—especially not the Donatist bishops who baptized people in schism, separated from the community of the true church and refusing to share in its love and unity. (Augustine frequently pointed out that the Donatists were an African splinter group, not in communion with the rest of the church worldwide.) In Augustine's view, the salvific effect of baptism—its "sacramental efficacy," to use a later term—depends on the inner unity of the church, outside which there is no salvation. So for Augustine the sacrament of baptism is salvific not because it has the power to save—it is not, to use the later language, an efficacious external means of grace—but only in that it is an outward mark of the real inward power of salvation, which consists in the soul's participation in this community and the inner grace given to it by God. For an adult, this means willingly sharing in the church's life of love. For a baptized infant, this means being consecrated by the prayers of the whole church—not just the local congregation, but the whole inward communion of Christ's body, which is the genuinely efficacious means of grace in the sacrament.[26]

Baptism is salvific in the sense that if we hold on to the inner gift it signifies, we will be saved in the end. But that does not mean that everyone who is

---

26. For more details on Augustine's theology of baptism and the inward, communal source of its efficacy, see Cary, *Outward Signs*, 168–77, 193–217.

properly baptized is sure to be saved. In fact we are not yet saved, Augustine insists,[27] which means that in baptism we are saved, as he puts it, "in hope" but not yet "in reality" (*in spe* but not *in re*, in the Latin formulation that was still influential in Luther's time).[28] Baptism marks our sharing in the community that is on the right road, but contains no guarantee that we will remain within that community for the rest of our lives. Only those who persevere to the end shall be saved,[29] and this perseverance is a gift of God's grace that we cannot know in advance we shall receive. In contrast to later Protestant understandings of conversion, therefore, Augustine and the ancient church knew of no irreversible event of coming to faith, no experience you can undergo that guarantees that you will continue to believe in Christ until the end of your days and thus assures you of eternal salvation. Augustine takes it as obvious that nothing you decide today can prevent you from changing your mind tomorrow. No one has that kind of control over their own future, and therefore "no one can be secure about life eternal."[30] There is therefore no such thing as "eternal security," as some Protestants call it. Only God can give the gift of perseverance, and he does not ordinarily tell us to whom he is giving it.[31]

This Augustinian view of perseverance, with its implication that no one knows whether they are ultimately saved, prevailed in Western Christianity until the rise of Calvinism, and is still the Roman Catholic view. It results in a profoundly different set of anxieties than most Protestants are used to. To set these anxieties in context, we need to turn to the Augustinian concept of grace, which is the framework for the theological debate between Catholics and Protestants in the sixteenth century.

Grace and Free Will

The gift of perseverance is a gift of unearned grace, and not the only one. "Grace," for Augustine, is a word to describe how God helps us inwardly along our whole journey to him, giving us not only the gift of persevering to

27. We are not yet saved (*nondum salvos*), according to Augustine, *City of God* 19:4 (at the bottom of p. 854 in the translation by Bettenson, where it is rendered simply "not saved").

28. The contrast between salvation *in spe* and *in re* is pervasive in Augustine; some important examples are found in *Punishment and Forgiveness of Sins* 2:8.10; *Spirit and the Letter* 29.51; Letter 140:6.17. The language is based on Paul saying that we are "saved by hope" in Rom. 8:24.

29. This thought, based on Matt. 24:13, becomes a keynote of Augustine's thinking about baptism and salvation, for instance in *On Baptism against the Donatists* 1:10.14; 4:14.22.

30. Augustine, *Gift of Perseverance* 22.62.

31. This account of perseverance underlies Augustine, *Gift of Perseverance*, although the most lucid explication of it is in Augustine, *Rebuke and Grace* 6.10–9.25. On the uncertainty of perseverance see also Augustine, *City of God* 11:12.

the end but also the initial gift of faith in Christ that gets us started on the path, and then working with us all along the way to keep our hearts turned in the right direction and moving us along on the road of Christian love. The initial gift of faith comes before any choice we make to believe, and therefore is called *prevenient*, from the Latin word for "coming before," *prae-venire*. Over the course of his career, as Augustine thinks through the logic of grace, he comes to the conclusion that if grace is to be fully gracious, which is to say a free and unmerited gift, then prevenient grace must do more than simply make an offer of salvation that it is up to us to accept. Grace must mean that God *causes* us to come to Christ in faith and accept him.[32] Huge controversies have swirled around this teaching, so we need to spend some time with it. It is an Augustinian doctrine embraced most famously by the Calvinist tradition, but it is Luther's teaching as well, and is taught also by the strand of Roman Catholic thought that follows Thomas Aquinas (associated especially with the Dominican tradition, as opposed to the Jesuit tradition). These three forms of Augustinian theology disagree about a great deal, but on prevenient grace they teach substantially the same doctrine.

Augustine's notion is that God can *cause* us to accept his grace in faith without *forcing* us to do so, and thus without depriving us of free will. This is because grace is an inner gift, not a form of external coercion. It comes to us from the inner presence of God, which is more inward than our inmost selves. So it is nothing like being compelled to do what we do not want to do. When grace moves us, it is precisely our inmost will that is moved in a new direction, with the result that we willingly, indeed delightedly, come to believe in Christ and love God and neighbor. Grace is God in action. It is the Holy Spirit at work in our hearts to give us the gift of *freely* choosing what is good. God's grace thus causes us to accept his grace, using our own free will.

Indeed, it is precisely grace that frees the will from bondage to sin so that we can freely choose as we ought. The Spirit of God moves the will by giving it a delight in what is good and thus making it easy to turn away from carnal desires, because now there is something else that attracts us more. It is like falling in love, which makes you glad to do anything that pleases your beloved. The good deeds that had before been difficult or impossible to do are now a sweet joy to perform, even if they are hard work. Who would not gladly climb a mountain or cross a desert for love? "Everything, of course, is

---

32. Augustine's most elaborate discussion of the initial gift of faith (*initium fidei*) is in his late treatise *The Predestination of the Saints*. For the development of his theology of grace leading up to this point see Burns, *Augustine's Doctrine of Operative Grace*; Cary, *Inner Grace*. For the key philosophical and theological issues this raises, see Cary, "Augustinian Compatibilism and the Doctrine of Election."

easy for love," as Augustine puts it.[33] Thus in describing the outcome of his own most remarkable experience of grace, he says he was no longer captive to earthly desires because he found God to be sweeter than the attraction of money or power or sex.[34]

It is a famous episode, coming at the end of book 8 of his *Confessions*, after a long description of the paralysis of his divided will. He desires both chastity and sexual gratification, unable to attain the one because he is afraid to give up the other. His divided will is reflected in his famous half-hearted prayer, "Grant me chastity and continence, but not yet."[35] He wills to give up sex for the sake of chastity and continence, but he also wills not to give it up, and the one will is in conflict with the other, tearing his soul apart. He wills chastity and continence—or more precisely, he wants to will them, which is to say, in his extraordinary language, he wills to will them—but he finds that he is unable to will wholeheartedly what he wills to will, because the contrary will for sexual gratification keeps part of his soul in thrall. This conflict of wills intensifies until he hears a child's voice nearby chanting, "Take and read, take and read."[36] So he takes a copy of the letters of Paul, reads the first words he lays eyes on, and finds his heart is suddenly different, his desires changed, his will whole, because now it is chastity, not sexual gratification, that wholly attracts and delights him. That is how grace feels.

The episode is misunderstood, however, if it is confused with Protestant conversion narratives. This is not a story about how Augustine got saved or how he accepted Christ into his life. This misunderstanding persists despite Augustine's best efforts, for he tells us in the previous book of the *Confessions* that he already had firm faith in Christ as savior.[37] The narrative in book 8 is about the gift of grace, but not specifically about the prevenient gift of faith. It is a story about how, in response to his prayers, God's grace came to him and gave him the ability to love as he ought, putting the journey to God ahead of all the desires of this world. This is the way grace most commonly shows up in Augustine's theology: as an inner gift of delight, weakening

33. Augustine, *Nature and Grace* 69.83.
34. Augustine, *Confessions* 9:1.1.
35. Augustine, *Confessions* 8:7.17.
36. Augustine, *Confessions* 8:12.29.
37. See Augustine, *Confessions* 7:5.7 (at the end) and 7:7.11 (near the beginning), both of which insist that Augustine had faith in Christ the Savior *before* the episode narrated in book 8. For this episode as an illustration of Augustine's doctrine of grace, see Cary, *Inner Grace*, 63–65. For the quite different elements in Augustine's later doctrine of prevenient grace that led to Protestant notions of conversion, see Cary, *Inner Grace*, 101–16. Read properly in context, the episode in *Confessions* 8 is not the story of how Augustine came to faith but how he finally gave in and decided to be baptized; or so I argue in Cary, *Outward Signs*, 169–77.

concupiscence and strengthening charity, which is given to us when we pray in faith for God's help.

The fact that we're praying, even if halfheartedly, means that this particular grace is not prevenient, for none of us prays at all unless we already have some degree of faith, which is always a gift of grace. The prayer for grace is in fact a crucial link connecting faith and love: because we pray in faith for the grace of Christ, we receive the inner gift of delight that strengthens our love for God. The key point is that this strength of delight comes after we already have a good will—but one that is not strong enough to accomplish what it wills against the opposition of the old, sinful will and its desires. In Augustine's earlier writings, and also in some parts of the later Augustinian tradition, such grace can also be said to be merited by our praying in faith. (This concept of "congruent merit," as it was called by late medieval theologians, was vehemently rejected by Luther, which meant he had to find some other means of getting the grace of God—a means that he called the Gospel.)

As Augustine's theology of grace develops, he eventually gets rid of every hint of such merit, every possibility that some act of our good will precedes and earns the gift of faith. This is what laid the foundation for later Protestant notions of conversion, in which the crucial experience of grace takes place when the will is brought to accept Christ for the first time. Yet unlike some later versions of Protestantism, Augustine does not call this, "being saved." Coming to faith is just the beginning of the journey, and perseverance in faith to the end is necessary for salvation. So for Augustine we must continue lifelong to pray in faith for the gift of grace that makes us able to love God and do good works. Not only the initial gift of faith but also all the subsequent merits of our good works are therefore due to God's grace. (Protestants drew the conclusion that Augustine agrees with them that grace alone saves us; whereas Catholics replied that merits resulting from grace are still genuine merits and are required for salvation.[38]) Everlasting life is thus the reward promised for the merit of righteousness (called *condign* merit by later medieval theologians), which is a gift of divine grace, so that everlasting life is really God's grace crowning his own prior gift, "grace for grace" as Augustine puts it.[39] (Again, Protestants drew the conclusion that all is grace; Catholics replied that you can't eliminate the requirement of merit.) Like the reward of

---

38. See, for example, Calvin's reading of Augustine on merit in *Institutes* 2:5.2 and 3:18.5, and contrast the Council of Trent's affirmation of the necessity of merit in the decree of Session 5, chap. 16, in Schaff, *Creeds of Christendom* 2:107–10.

39. Augustine, *Grace and Free Choice* 8.20; *Rebuke and Grace* 13.41; *Enchiridion* 107. See also two of Augustine's most important writings on the topic of grace, Letter 186:3.10; Letter 194:5.21.

everlasting life, the grace of charity is not prevenient, because it is preceded by the good will of faith. But the initial gift of faith is something that, by the very logic of the case, we cannot pray for in faith, and therefore it is absolutely unmerited as well as fully prevenient. The person who is given the initial gift of faith is not just a sinner but an unbeliever. Yet God, who created the will, can work inwardly in the depths of the human heart to turn or redirect the will, causing the unbeliever to choose—freely—to believe.

There have always been theologians after Augustine who think this is simply impossible. They take it for granted that a truly free will must be self-determining, which means its choices can be influenced but not determined by God's grace. It is important to see that Augustine (like Aquinas and Luther and Calvin after him) rejects what these theologians take for granted. In his view our will is genuinely free even when it is moved by God's grace and determined by God's will to choose faith in Christ. Augustine sees no opposition between grace and free will, as if giving more power to the one meant giving less power to the other. On the contrary, the power of free will to do what it was made for, which is to choose the good, is from the beginning a gift of God who created it, which his grace restores and strengthens, never opposes or destroys. The real enemy of free will, by Augustine's reckoning, is not grace but sin. It is sin, not grace, that opposes free will and corrupts it, bringing the soul into a kind of bondage to its own wayward desires. Of course this does mean that Augustine has a different conception of free will from his opponents. As his doctrine of prevenient grace develops over the course of his career, his conception of free will becomes more and more clearly a version of what philosophers today call "compatibilist" rather than "libertarian" free will. The mature Augustine is a theological compatibilist, in that he sees free will as compatible with God's power to determine what we freely will. (If you think this is not really a concept of free will at all—that he is actually denying free will, despite what he says—then your conception of free will is probably libertarian.)

Election and Predestination

Whatever you make of Augustine's views on the compatibility of grace and free will, it leads to a recurrent set of pastoral problems, which are closely bound up with Augustine's spirituality. The nature of the problems is clearest when we think about the end rather than the beginning of the spiritual journey. Since no choice we make today can prevent us from choosing differently tomorrow, none of our choices—not even our conversion—can guarantee that we will persevere in faith tomorrow and the next day and at the end of our lives. So believers remain dependent on the grace of God for their salvation, because only God can choose that we shall persevere to the end and be saved. This divine choice to save us has been given the name "election" (from the Latin word *electio*, which simply means "choice"). For Augustine, it amounts to the same thing as predestination.

In an Augustinian framework, predestination does not mean our choices are made for us in advance. The "pre" in predestination refers to causal, not temporal priority. That is to say, God does not make a choice at one time that results in our salvation later; rather, divine election is an eternal choice, which means it is not something in the past, over and done with, but is always present. For the eternity of God means he is beyond all times, past and future, yet present at all times, just as the omnipresence of God means he is beyond any location or restriction of space, yet present in all places. That being said, however, the issue is much the same whether you call it "election" or "predestination": Does God have the power to choose what our free choices will be—causing us to choose freely, throughout the road of our life, the good that will lead us to salvation and everlasting life? Augustine in his later works answers with a clear "yes." It is an answer that Luther and Calvin love, but which many others, both Protestant and Catholic, find unsettling, unacceptable, or appalling.

For purposes of understanding the anxieties generated by Augustinian spirituality, the important question is not the philosophical problem of how predestination can be compatible with free will but the pastoral problem of how it relates to the knowledge of our salvation and everlasting life. It is a problem with an intensely first-person focus: Can I ever know whether I am one of the elect, chosen by God for salvation? I can presumably know that I believe in Christ (though this will actually become a major problem in Protestantism, as we shall see), but even if I do have such faith, that does not mean, on Augustine's reckoning, that I will be given the gift of persevering in faith to the end of my days. The problem with Augustine's doctrine of election, from this first-person perspective, is that God's choice is so inscrutable and deeply hidden that I can never be certain that his will is for my ultimate salvation and happiness. It is this problem of uncertainty—or rather, the anxious need for certainty—that Protestant theology took up with a vengeance.

There are distinctively Augustinian reasons why God's choice must be so deeply hidden. Prevenient grace comes to sinners when they deserve nothing but punishment, so there is no merit in human beings to explain why God should choose to give grace to one person rather than another. It is not as if those who are least unworthy are the most likely to receive grace. On the contrary, greater unworthiness can be an occasion for greater grace, as Augustine finds in the case of Saul the persecutor of the faith, who was converted by God's grace and became Paul the apostle and preacher of the faith.[40] Or consider a case of perfect equality: twins born in sin like all the children of Adam and equally deserving of damnation. So it is with Jacob and Esau, together in their mother's womb, "having done nothing either good or bad," when God announced that he chose Jacob over Esau, as the prophet later put it: "Jacob have I loved and Esau have I hated" (Rom. 9:10–13, quoting Gen. 25:23 and Mal. 1:2–3). In Augustine's reading of this story, which is really a reading of Paul's reading in Romans 9, this means Jacob is chosen for salvation, destined to be the recipient of undeserved grace, while Esau is left in his sins, receiving the damnation he deserves.

And why is this? Since it has nothing to do with any difference in their merits (not even merits God foresees in their future life, which in Augustine's view are the result, not the cause of his gift of grace), we cannot possibly identify any reason for God's choice of Jacob over Esau. Augustine assures us that there *is* a reason, but it is hidden deep in God's wisdom. So if we press the question—Why is one chosen rather than the other? Why Jacob rather than Esau?—the answer Augustine gives will be another reading of Paul, from two chapters further on:

> Oh, the depth of the riches and wisdom and knowledge of God! How unsearchable are his judgments and how inscrutable his ways! (Rom. 11:33).

In Latin the passage begins, "*O altitudo*," using a word that means both height and depth. This becomes Augustine's standard answer to the question why God chooses to save some but not others. This *altitudo* is the kind of depth that makes you shudder with fright when you look into it. Since the word for shuddering in Latin is *horror*, Augustine will speak of our minds being struck with horror as we try to look into the depth of God's choices. Calvin picks up on this language when he says God's hidden decree of election is indeed *horribile*, a cause for shuddering.[41] Here the Augustinian project of arriving at an intellectual understanding of God runs up against an insurmountable limit.

A More Jewish Doctrine of Election

At this point Augustine, despite his best efforts in earlier writings, has traveled very far from Platonism. Think how different this is from the picture of

---

40. For Augustine on Paul's conversion see Cary, *Inner Grace*, 101–10.
41. Augustine, *Punishment and Forgiveness of Sins* 1:21.29; *"Answer to the Two Letters of the Pelagians"* 2:7.15; Calvin, *Institutes* 3:23.7.

God as the Good in the allegory of the cave, shining like the sun equally for all. Early in his career, Augustine followed the logic of this picture. If some of us do not see the light as clearly as others, the difference must come from our own bad choices: we have turned our backs more resolutely to the light, have grown more accustomed to the darkness, more attracted to the shadows, more diseased and impure in our mind's eye.[42] In this picture the choices are all ours, not God's, because in Plato's allegory the divine Good is not at all like a person, someone who makes choices. The Good may be said to have a kind of will by which it loves its own being and goodness and is good for all,[43] but it does not make choices favoring one person over another, and it certainly does not have one person in particular who could be called its beloved son, or one nation who could be its chosen people. It is the ultimate source of justice, and it is the same justice for all, treating equal cases equally, not making the kind of difference that the God of Israel makes between Jacob and Esau.[44] It is the inward source of grace and power for souls to do what is right and choose what is good and fall in love with divine beauty, just as Augustine says,[45] but it does not make choices to give grace to some people rather than others, when all are equally undeserving. In some sense it can be said that the Good loves, but it does not choose. Hence Platonism can be the basis of a doctrine of grace but not a doctrine of election.

This is because the concept of divine election is not Platonist but Jewish. More than any other concept, election marks the difference between God as the Beauty we love and God as the person who loves us. This personal conception of God has a price, which is particularity. It is related to the key difference between the concept of will and the concept of choice. One can *will* generalities, like beauty and happiness and the good, but one must *choose*

42. See *Teacher* 11.38; *Lord's Sermon on the Mount* 2:3.14; *On Free Choice* 2:16.43. For Augustine's notion of will in this early stage in his doctrine of grace, see Cary, *Inner Grace*, 38–40.

43. Cf. also Plotinus, *Enneads* 6:8.13–21.

44. The deepest problem in Augustine's doctrine of predestination, as Augustine himself realized, is the notion that God differentiates between people without any concern for desert or merit, as summed up in his interpretation of Paul's reading of Mal. 1:2–3: "Jacob have I loved, but Esau I hated" (Rom. 9:13). See Cary, *Inner Grace*, 48–52, 87–91, 100–101, 121–26, as well as Cary, "Augustinian Compatibilism."

45. Contrary to an oft-repeated but seldom-examined scholarly opinion, Augustine's notion of grace is not a departure from Platonism. Augustinian grace is rooted in a Platonist ontology in which all power for goodness flows from the divine Good, as is particularly clear in his earliest treatise on grace, the long letter to which he gave the title "On the Grace of the New Testament" (Letter 140; see discussion in Cary, *Inner Grace*, 72–77). Augustine specifically identifies grace as a doctrine Platonists share with Christianity in *City of God* 11:29. This is why developments in the doctrine of grace are not the place to find a fundamental break or discontinuity in Augustine's theology, as Carol Harrison rightly argues in *Rethinking Augustine's Early Theology*.

particulars, like Jacob rather than Esau, or Israel rather than other nations. For *election* is inevitably *selection*: you choose this good thing rather than that one, or this bad person rather than that one. That is why divine election inevitably starts to look like favoritism. It is not like a just judge applying one and the same law to all, treating equal cases equally, but like a lover who chooses one particular person and, forsaking all others, cleaves lifelong to her alone. In the biblical account, God is that kind of lover in his covenant with Israel. He has a favorite, a beloved, the apple of his eye,[46] and his choice to make covenant with her makes all the difference in the world. Most of us are Platonist enough to find this troubling, even offensive. It was certainly a conclusion that Augustine tried to avoid for many years, as he worked hard to trace the difference that divine election makes back to some antecedent difference in the people God chooses—as if somehow Jacob were better than Esau, despite what Paul says. But it is a doctrine that would not be so troubling, I think, if it were understood in a more thoroughly Jewish way.

In a more Jewish understanding of election, it is a good thing for the Gentiles that God has chosen the Jews as his own people. For in the Bible, God always chooses some for the blessing of others. Abraham is chosen for the blessing of all nations, like his son Isaac and also his grandson Jacob, whose name is changed to Israel, the father of the chosen people.[47] We would not be so offended by the biblical doctrine of election, I think, if we recognized that it has this structure: some are *chosen for the blessing of others*. And Christians would not be so inclined to persecute Jews if they recognized that it is a good thing for the Gentiles that the Jews are the chosen people. Jews are not fully safe from Christian persecution until Christians are glad that the Jews are the chosen people. But recognizing this requires us to see the doctrine of election very differently from the way Augustine sees it. The structure of election is not God choosing some to the exclusion of others, but God choosing some *for the sake of* others. The key example of this for Christian theology, as Karl Barth realized, is Jesus Christ himself, the Jew who is God's beloved Son—his favorite son, we could well say—who is chosen to suffer for the redemption of the world. As the Jews are chosen to bless the nations, Christ is chosen to save the world. This realization by Barth is in effect a rediscovery of the original structure of the doctrine of election, so that once again, as in the Bible, it is the basis of good news—indeed the foundation of the Gospel

46. God's love for Israel is in fact the origin of this famous phrase; cf. Deut. 32:10; Lam. 2:18; Zech. 2:8.

47. On the blessing of all nations through God's chosen people see Gen. 12:3, 18:18, and 22:18 (Abraham); 26:4 (Isaac); and 28:14 (Jacob); as well as Gal. 3:8, 14, where Paul identifies this blessing as the Gospel fulfilled in Christ. Jacob is renamed Israel in Gen. 32:28.

itself.[48] For what the doctrine of election really means is that God gave the Jewish people to the world because he intended all along to give us his own Son, the King of the Jews.

The Augustinian doctrine of election has, over the course of long centuries, been a serious disaster, but this is not all Augustine's fault. The root of the problem is that by Augustine's time the Christian church could no longer hear of the election of Israel as good news, unless "Israel" became a name for Christians (the true and spiritual Israel) rather than a name for the Jews, the children of Jacob according to the flesh. This doctrine of supercessionism (as it is called), according to which the church supercedes the Jews as the chosen people, resulted in a doctrine of election in which God chooses some for salvation instead of others (us rather than them, Christians rather than Jews) instead of choosing some for the benefit of others (Israel for the blessing of all nations, Christ for the salvation of the world). And when this anti-Jewish doctrine of election is combined with Augustine's concept of the divine inner gift of grace, it is something to make one shudder.[49] The "O altitudo!" which in Paul is the beginning of a doxology, an utterance of glory and praise, becomes in the Augustinian tradition an expression of horror, not celebration.

The Protestant doctrine of the Gospel is a partial recovery of biblical ways of thinking about God's choices and how they are revealed through his good word. It is only a partial recovery, however, because until Karl Barth in the twentieth century, the underlying doctrine of election in Protestantism remained Augustinian, which means that God's eternal choices are not seen to be revealed in the word of the Gospel but concealed from us in what Calvin calls "the hidden decree" or what Luther calls "the hidden God." Still, it is a giant step in the right direction, because it gives us good news about God's will and reminds us that in Scripture, God's word reveals God's choices. That, after all, is precisely why we know about God's choice concerning Jacob and Esau, not to mention the eternal election of Jesus Christ. Despite Augustinian talk about the hiddenness of election, the choices of God that Scripture tells us about are those that it reveals to us. Thus a properly Christian doctrine of election will be more Jewish than Augustine's doctrine, in that it finds the deepest choice of God in what the Gospel reveals about Christ, the particular individual chosen to be the light of all nations and the glory of his beloved people Israel (Luke 2:32). Eternal election is nothing other than God's decision that the story of Jesus Christ told in the Gospel shall be the true story of the whole world.

48. See Barth, *Church Dogmatics*, II/2, 3–93.
49. See Cary, *Inner Grace*, chap. 4.

PART 2

The Gospel and the Power of God

5

Young Luther

Justification as Penitential Process

The word "Gospel" has a distinctive meaning for Martin Luther. It means more than just the four documents by that name in the New Testament.[1] Any preaching of good news that gives us Christ is the Gospel, including the prophecies in the Old Testament, such as Isaiah's announcement, "For to us a child is born, to us a son is given" (Isa. 9:6), and including the witness of the apostles in the New Testament, such as Paul's announcement of "the Gospel of God" at the very beginning of the letter to the Romans. The Gospel is thus not a set of documents but a preaching of good news. For Luther it is essentially oral and only secondarily written down.[2]

Luther's doctrine of justification by faith alone, which becomes the distinctive doctrine of Protestantism, is based on his conception of the Gospel as the word that gives Christ to all who believe it. The doctrine is in one sense new, in another sense not. The church has not always had a doctrine of justification by faith alone, but it has always had faith in the Gospel of Jesus Christ. Luther's doctrine of justification is therefore best understood as a new explanation of how faith in the Gospel has always functioned to justify and save those who believe it. Always this good news has given to those who believe it nothing less than God in the flesh, who saves and justifies us. What happened in the

---

1. Luther, *A Brief Instruction What to Look for and Expect in the Gospels*, LW 35:117.
2. Luther, *Brief Instruction*, LW 35:123. For further discussion see Althaus, *Theology of Martin Luther*, 73.

sixteenth century is that this function of the Gospel needed to be articulated much more fully and explicitly, for urgent pastoral reasons that are strikingly illustrated by Luther's own struggles. To this sixteenth-century setting we now turn, with the aim of seeing eventually (in chaps. 7 and 8) how the Protestant concept of the Gospel arises out of the medieval concept of sacraments. But first we shall look at the shape of Luther's theology before he had his mature concept of the Gospel, when justification had to proceed without good news that gave Christ to sinners. In Luther's early theology justification was a kind of spiritual masochism, an incessant penitential process of self-accusation and self-hatred meant to anticipate and thus prevent the judgment of God.

A More Fearful Journey

The pastoral need was urgent in the sixteenth century because something fundamental about the Augustinian spiritual journey had changed by the time of the late Middle Ages. A new anxiety had come to pervade the journey, or rather a very old anxiety had grown to huge proportions. The God to whom the soul is journeying, who for Augustine is fundamentally an object of desire, had become by the late Middle Ages fundamentally an object of fear. He appears less like the Truth the soul desires to see than like the judge who speaks the truth about us—a terrifying truth that may well amount to everlasting damnation. The one to whom we journey may turn out to be the one who judges us worthy of nothing but unending torment.

Of course the thought that God is our judge is hardly new to the Middle Ages. But it can be strikingly absent from classic statements of the Augustinian journey. Augustine's own *Confessions*, for example, has a great deal to say about the misery of wandering far from God, but very little to say about fear of damnation. It is Augustine's unphilosophical mother who has that fear, worrying that her son may die young while he is still a heretic and therefore suffer the death of his very soul in hell.[3] Augustine himself thinks of his sins rather differently, as a disordered love that seeks happiness in all the wrong places and therefore finds no rest. He does not deny there is a hell, but he directs his readers' sense of horror elsewhere, to the darkness of heart that keeps us far from God in this life.[4] The misery he feels and wants to escape

---

3. Augustine, *Confessions* 3:11.19; 5:9.16.

4. See for example *Confessions* 1:18.28, where Augustine's imagery about being far from God combines language from the parable of the prodigal son (Luke 15:13) with language from Plotinus about a nonspatial journey of the soul, which is not by chariots or ships and certainly "not for the feet" (Plotinus, *Enneads* 1:6.8).

is not a future punishment but the darkness of ignorance and false delights that overshadow life on earth.

Nearly seven hundred years later, this same sense of misery can still be felt in the *Proslogion*, a very Augustinian book written late in the eleventh century. Its author, Anselm, begins the book with a prayer, which includes these words of anguish:

> I have never seen thee, O Lord my God; I do not know thy face . . . what shall this exile do so far from thee? What shall thy servant do, tormented by love of thee, and cast so far from thy face? He pants for the sight of thee, and thy face is too far from him. . . . He longs to find thee, and does not know thy dwelling place. . . . I was made in order to see thee, and I have not yet done that for which I was made. O pitiful lot of man, who has lost that for which he was made![5]

This is a prayer that would be quite at home in the *Confessions*. It displays an intense awareness of sin but not a great fear of divine judgment. Anselm's sense of misery is deep, but not because he is afraid to face God. He feels far from the light of God's face and wants to draw near. Like Augustine, he pictures his life in a way that resembles a soul trying to climb into the light from the darkness of Plato's cave, rather than an offender being brought before a great Judge who sees all our misdeeds.

Probing for Mortal Sins

The journey to God looks different by the time Martin Luther is learning to be a theologian, four centuries after Anselm. It is a more fearful prospect, not only because there is a judge to meet at the end of the road but because of a new intensity of introspection that has taken hold of the late medieval conscience. Penitential practices that did not exist in Augustine's day and had not developed fully even in Anselm's time have generated a deep kind of performance anxiety, a worry about whether one is doing well enough to escape everlasting punishment. For the late medieval penitent it is always possible, and often necessary, to look into one's own soul and ask whether it really does have a strong enough love for God to move it along the road toward eternal happiness rather than damnation. And as a matter of theological principle it is impossible to be certain of the answer.

The one thing sinners can be sure of is that they are not perfect until they reach the end of the road. Every day in this mortal life, as Augustine often

5. Anselm, *Proslogion*, chap. 1.

reminded his congregation, a Christian should be praying, "Forgive us our debts" (Matt. 6:12). To pray this way is to confess that you do not love God with your whole heart, mind, and strength, or your neighbor as yourself. Not loving as fully as you should is, at the very least, a venial sin. That's a technical term in medieval theology for what Augustine usually called a "daily sin," because it is the debt we pray to be forgiven every day when we say the Lord's Prayer.[6] We must pray like this because we never love perfectly in this life. Yet we may hope that we are making progress, drawn toward God by a love that is ever more pure, full, and deep.

The problem that grew upon medieval Christians was the uncertainty about whether their sins were not merely venial but mortal—which is to say, sins that are deadly in that they kill the life of grace and charity in the soul. In mortal sin the will deliberately chooses to violate the law of God by setting some created thing before life with God, because it loves that thing more than it loves God himself.[7] This happens, for example, when a Christian chooses to commit adultery or murder, knowing full well that this offends God. But it might also be happening in the little hidden moments of lust and anger and greed in daily life—looking the wrong way at an attractive woman, or a man you resent, or something you want—which, by an inward act of consent, might amount to the same kind of sin in the depth of your heart, where the true nature of your will may be hidden even from yourself. Jesus had warned about this kind of sin in the Sermon on the Mount (Matt. 5:21–30), and for the Christians of the late Middle Ages there was no telling for sure when what is outwardly a venial sin might be, at its inner root, a mortal sin—a deliberate turning away from the love of God tantamount to adultery or murder, and every bit as deserving of God's wrath and damnation.[8] This turning of the will does not just impede but reverses our journey to God. As a consequence, the soul is no longer in a state of grace but in a state of mortal sin. This is something to worry about, for while it is often quite clear when you are in a state of mortal sin, you can never be fully certain that you are in a state of grace. In the inmost depths of your heart it could be that the imperfection still separating you from the journey's end is not just slowing your progress,

6. For Augustine on venial and mortal sins see Augustine, Sermon 278:9–14, as well as Augustine, *City of God* 21:27, which includes a discussion of why it can be difficult to tell the difference.

7. To cite one influential account, Thomas Aquinas says venial sin occurs when someone "is excessively attached to some temporal thing, but does not will to offend God for it" (*ST* I-II, 87.5), whereas a mortal sin occurs when "the soul is disordered by sin so much as to turn away from its ultimate end, which is God" (*ST* I-II, 72.5).

8. For the difficulty of distinguishing venial from mortal sin, see Tentler, *Sin and Confession*, 144–56.

as venial sin does, but moving you in the opposite direction, toward unending torment and eternal separation from God.

This is why, as a medieval Catholic, you go to confession. You turn to the sacrament of penance, which is the surest means of getting rid of the mortal sins that would otherwise result in your damnation. You go, even though it can be a harrowing experience. By the time Luther was growing up, many confessors (that's the technical term for the priest to whom you make your confession) were trained to probe deeply into the sinner's conscience. They were supposed to ask not just about what you did but about your inner motivations. So the sacrament of penance could mean being subjected to an interrogation such as this:

> Are your prayers, alms and religious activities done more to hide your sins and impress others than to please God? Have you loved relatives, friends or other creatures [i.e., any created thing] more than God? Have you had doubts about Scripture, the sacraments, hell, the afterlife. . . . Have you practiced or believed in magic?—These are sins against the first commandment.
>
> Have you muttered against God because of bad weather, illness, poverty, the death of a child or a friend? . . .—These are sins against the second commandment.
>
> Have you skipped mass on Sundays and holidays without a good excuse? Have you conducted business on Sundays rather than reflecting on your sins, seeking indulgence, counting your blessings, meditating on death, hell and its penalties, and heaven and its joys? Have you dressed proudly, sung and danced lustily . . . girl-watched, or exchanged adulterous glances in church or while walking on Sundays?—These are sins against the third commandment.[9]

And on it goes, through all ten commandments. Other lines of inquiry might examine the seven deadly sins or the five senses—anything that might make a complete sweep of *all* the mortal sins that could be hiding in your heart. This private inquisition, pursued thoroughly and mercilessly enough, could generate an experience that Luther described as a kind of torture of conscience. It was quite different from anything we hear about in Augustine, who never encountered the sacrament of penance in this deeply interiorized form. The practice of regular private confession simply didn't exist in his time, so nobody then had confessors probing the depths of their conscience. In Luther's day, this relatively new practice was generating a new type of inner life. The effect was to bring a kind of monastic rigor into the conscience of ordinary Christians, and it was terrifying.

9. These are excerpts from a much longer set of questions from a fifteenth-century manual for confessors, a sample of which is given by Ozment, *Reformation in the Cities*, 24.

The Terrified Conscience

When Luther was aware of his sins, which was often, the word he typically used for the feeling in his conscience was not "guilty" but "terrified." It seems everybody at the time knew what he meant. Christians in his day did not seem to have felt much in the way of what we now call "guilt." They certainly were made aware of their guilt in God's sight (their objective guilt, we could call it), but the emotional result of this awareness was not guilt feelings but terror. It is not hard to see why. Just imagine God asking you on judgment day the kind of questions the confessors were trained to ask you in the sacrament of penance. The practice of private confession was designed to get you asking those questions before God does, internalizing them so that your conscience can always accuse you when you sin and thus drive you to repentance.

Now imagine coming to your deathbed with such a conscience to accuse you. A long, drawn-out illness would allow you time to grow deeply terrified of what comes after death, as you try to recall every sin you ever committed that might turn out to be mortal, serious enough to deserve everlasting punishment. If you are the kind of person who is easily plagued by recurrent, nagging thoughts that you can't stop thinking about (in modern psychological terms, if you are prone to "perseverate"), then your conscience could become a kind of torture chamber filled with endless accusations. The medieval description of this torture goes back to the desert fathers of the church, who identified persistent, unwanted, evil thoughts (*dialogismoi*) as the workings of the devil. We have medieval woodcuts illustrating this situation, with people on their deathbed surrounded by devils whispering in their ears the names of their sins.[10] The word for this kind of temptation was "assault" (*Anfechtung* in Luther's German[11]) because it meant the demons were attacking your conscience, trying to drive you to terror and despair, so that you would give up all hope of salvation. It was an experience Luther knew well: he was a terrific perseverator and a lifelong insomniac, easily woken up by accusing

10. Examples can be found in Bainton, *Here I Stand*, 21, and Duffy, *Stripping of the Altars*, plate 117; for a discussion of the scene, see Duffy, *Stripping of the Altars*, 317.

11. One sometimes hears that the term is untranslatable, but that is nonsense. It is an ordinary German word for "assault," equivalent to the Latin term *impugnatio*, which medieval theologians like Thomas Aquinas use to describe the assaults of the demons (e.g., *ST* I, 114). Luther often uses it as a translation of *tentatio*, the Latin term for "temptation"; he makes the equivalence explicit in the preface to his collected German writings, *WA* 50:660 (= *LW* 34:286). The connection is a familiar one in medieval theology, where temptation often takes the form of demonic assault. Far from being unique or distinctively Lutheran, the term is used by Luther in the confidence that his sixteenth-century readers are quite familiar with the experience he is talking about.

thoughts that tormented him.[12] For Luther himself, these *Anfechtungen* involved nothing as crude or literalistic as fearing the flames of hell, which is imagery that scarcely ever appears in his writings or his preaching. Fire and brimstone are not very fearsome compared to God himself, whom the sin-laden conscience feels to be an enemy and accuser rather than a savior. It is the most terrifying thing in the universe to stand under a divine judge whose knowledge penetrates to the inmost depth of your own soul—just like your confessor except omniscient and almighty—whom you can never escape, try as hard as you may. Imagine the word of accusation and condemnation from this judge reaching to the bottom of your heart and becoming the only truth about who you are, the only thing you ever hear, forever. That seems to have been the shape of Luther's terrified conscience.

As an overly scrupulous monk, young Luther lived at the social epicenter of this kind of anxiety, and in his early theological work he did a great deal to make it worse, as we shall see. One reason his writings later became important to so many people is that he had been there: he knew the depth of terror and all the religious countermeasures that failed to help, both the more external, superstitious practices and the more inward, spiritual disciplines of penitence. He became a monk in the first place in order to escape a classic moment of medieval terror. The story is that he was originally going to be a lawyer, as his father intended, but one day when he was on his way back to start a new term at law school he was caught outside in a thunderstorm. He cried out in terror, "St. Anne, help me! I will become a monk!"[13] This is a characteristically medieval prayer in the face of a characteristically medieval fear. Young Luther was pleading for a patron saint to rescue him from sudden death. A sky raging with thunderbolts puts you in a position of utter helplessness much like a gun held to your head—will the next moment be your death?—except that in the Middle Ages what you had to fear was much worse than death. Being struck by lightning could mean not just the end of your life but the beginning of everlasting torture. Everyone faced with this prospect wanted at least "short shrift," meaning a chance to make at least a brief confession of their worst sins, because dying in a state of mortal sin meant the soul went straight to hell, with no second chances. Young Luther was begging St. Anne, as his patron in the heavenly court, to get him a second chance before it was too late. And he was offering her his life in exchange, a whole lifetime devoted to the penitence that he had no time for in this one brief, terrifying instant.

12. For how this affects Luther's notorious familiarity with the devil, see appendix 1.

13. See Bainton, *Here I Stand*, chap. 1. Luther ended up joining the Order of St. Augustine (Hermits), making him technically a friar rather than a monk, but neither Luther nor his contemporaries were especially fussy about the distinction.

There were other things he could have tried. At a less total level of commitment, he could have promised to go on pilgrimage to some saint's shrine far away, such as Santiago de Compostela in Spain. He could have kept vigils, lit candles, paid for masses to be said. Such acts of devotion could serve as payment in fulfillment of a sacred vow, because they were works of gratitude but also of penitence and prayer, asking forgiveness or indulgence. All these works later came to seem horribly insufficient to Luther, and completely uncertain in their effect. Many years afterward, he tells us that in his one trip to Rome, back when he was still a devout monk, he climbed up a famous set of sacred stairs on his knees, following the approved ritual of saying a prayer at each step, so as to release the soul of his grandfather from purgatory. Yet when he reached the top, he thought, "Who knows whether it is so?"[14] He was expressing a doubt that could have plagued late medieval Christians engaged in any number of penitential practices designed to keep souls out of hell or free them from purgatory (which in most popular depictions was a great deal like hell, the only difference being that it was temporary—lasting only a few thousand years rather than forever). What made the Gospel he preached in his mature theology so powerful is that it leaves no room for such doubts. It contains God's own promise of salvation, which no one has a right to be uncertain of. Unlike every work of penitence, spirituality, and devotion, God's word alone is strong enough to overcome the doubts and fears of the terrified conscience.

Justification as Process

Luther seems to have been a very intense young man, always the smartest and also the most serious person in the room. If you imagine a hard-charging future lawyer who must suddenly channel all his ambition into becoming the most deeply penitent monk in the monastery, you get a picture that would explain the emphasis of his early theology. Rather than engaging in an anguished quest for a gracious God, which is how his spiritual life is often portrayed nowadays, his primary aim at first was to undermine the tepid complacency that he thought was the besetting sin of his era.[15] In Germany at the time, the Order of St. Augustine, which he joined, was riven by arguments between stricter and more lax monasteries, the former calling themselves "Observants" because they were more scrupulous about observing the rules of the order.

14. Bainton, *Here I Stand*, 38.
15. For this as Luther's earliest diagnosis of the problems of his era, see Wicks, *Man Yearning for Grace*, 56–57, 61–64, 98–99, 217–18.

Luther sided with the Observants, but he was more serious than most about the *inner* work of penance, and was frequently critical of the kind of monks who thought they could purify their hearts simply by a rigid observance of the outward regulations of monastic life. In other words, he was a critic of works righteousness from the very beginning, which he saw as superficial and, what was worse, a form of self-deception; it soothed a monk's conscience and thus made him lazy about the arduous, ongoing work of inner, heartfelt repentance.

After finishing his monastic training, Luther was sent by his superiors for advanced academic study that eventually qualified him to become a professor lecturing on the Bible at the University of Wittenberg in Northern Germany. We have the extensive notes he made for his lectures on the Psalms beginning in 1513 and on the letter to the Romans beginning in 1515, which are his first substantial theological writings, composed while he was still a monk but not published until centuries after his death. A major aim of these lectures was to accentuate the awareness of sin and thus to intensify the experience of repentance. To put it in terms of later Lutheran theology, at this stage in his career Luther was intent on preaching law rather than Gospel. But precisely for that reason, this early theology gives us the context for grasping why Luther's mature notion of Gospel was so powerful when it did come on the scene.

To understand Luther's earliest writings, we have to imagine bringing an education rooted in a late medieval version of Aristotelian philosophy to a study of the Bible informed by a growing knowledge and love of Augustine's writings on sin and grace. Luther was required to study Aristotelian philosophy in school, where it had long been the foundation of the curriculum in higher education, but Augustine's theology was something he learned largely on his own, by reading extensively in the first printed edition of Augustine's collected works, which had been published only a decade earlier.[16] The result was that Luther began working out his thinking on the Augustinian spiritual journey in terms of an Aristotelian theory of process. This theory is one of Aristotle's most important modifications of the philosophy of his teacher Plato. Aristotle in effect brought Plato's forms down to earth, making them part of the world of time and change. Instead of thinking of justice, for example, as if it belonged in the same unchanging realm of eternal truth as mathematics,

---

16. For an account of how Luther "stumbled upon" Augustine's books, most importantly the anti-Pelagian writings contained "in the eighth volume of his works," see Luther, letter to George Spalatin, Oct. 19, 1516, *LW* 48:24. He does not need to mention which edition of Augustine's works he's referring to, because at that point there was only one, published by Amerbach in 1506. For the fascinating history of printed editions of Augustine in the Reformation era, see Visser, *Reading Augustine in the Reformation*.

Aristotelian philosophy sees it as the goal or endpoint (*telos*) of a process on earth, like the full-grown form of a living thing that has finished growing up or the completed structure of a house that is done being built. The form is the good that governs what happens on earth, because the completion of the form—its being full grown or fully built—is what the process of growing or building is all about.

Luther situated his account of the Augustinian spiritual journey in the context of the doctrine of *justification*—a Pauline term that Augustine used in his thinking about grace, but which became a great deal more important in later strands of Augustinianism than in Augustine himself. Justification means the process of becoming just or righteous, which in Aristotelian terms means attaining the complete or perfected form of justice or righteousness. To say this much, however, already calls for several words of warning about technical terminology—three in fact. First of all, it is important for readers not to miss the connection between *justification* and *justice*. The verbal relationship should seem obvious, but it has often been obscured by the fact that for several centuries the standard English word for justice was "righteousness." Hence to this day most discussions of the doctrine of justification in English focus on the word "righteousness," which is used as equivalent to the Latin word for justice, *justitia*, as well as the Greek word for justice, *dikaiosune*, and the Hebrew word for justice, *tsedeqah*, and the German word for justice, *Gerechtigkeit*. All these languages have only one word where English has two. So it is important to realize, as you read about the doctrine of justification, that "righteousness" is just another way of saying "justice." They are not even two words for the same thing; in translations of Luther or Augustine or Paul, they are two words for the same *word*.

It is unfortunate, though perhaps historically inevitable, that these two words have drifted apart, with the result that nowadays they have very different shades of meaning. Often when we call people "righteous" today, we're saying they're self-righteous. Strikingly, we never use the words "just" and "justice" in this way. This is a change in the meaning of the word "righteousness" that we have to be aware of when we step into the long history of discussions of the doctrine of justification in English, where "righteousness" has been the standard term in use since the sixteenth century. In translations of Luther and every other theologian discussing justification, "righteousness" always means justice, never self-righteousness. How the meaning of the word came to drift toward something that is nearly its opposite—exactly the kind of thing the doctrine of justification was trying to avoid, in fact—is an interesting story that no doubt has a great deal to do with anxious Protestants trying to find that they are truly and inwardly righteous, as I shall suggest in chapter 10.

Whether we call it "justice" or "righteousness," what we are talking about is the end state of the process of justification, the completed form toward which the process is headed. To be in that state—to have the form of justice or righteousness in our souls—is to be in right relation with God, according to the doctrine of justification as stated in Aristotelian terms. Those who are justified are acceptable to God, because they are just or righteous in his sight, not sinners deserving of damnation. The process of justification that gets us to this end state is thus equivalent to the whole Augustinian journey toward God. As Augustine insists, this is a journey of love as well as righteousness. Indeed there is no great difference between love and righteousness, because Christian righteousness for Augustine means obeying the law of God, which means, most fundamentally, loving God and neighbor. Hence while love is the keynote of Augustine's ethics, righteousness or justice is also an important concept, because it plays such a prominent role in the Bible as well as classical philosophy and is at root equivalent to love for God and neighbor.

But now a second word of warning: despite prevailing opinion to the contrary, I will be arguing that throughout Luther's career "justification" remains a term for a process—in contrast to the way the term "justification" is used by later Protestant theologians who, for reasons we will get to in chapter 10, tend to equate it with a once-in-a-lifetime event, the moment when you are converted and saved. No such event can be equivalent to Luther's notion of justification, which is an ongoing process, not something that happens only once in your life. In particular, the event or experience of conversion, or the choice to accept Christ, is not the starting point of faith, because for Luther no experience or decision of ours is the starting point of faith. There is indeed a once-in-a-lifetime event at the beginning of Christian life, but it is baptism, when the promise of God is given to each one of us in particular, as the basis for our faith.

Third, while Luther's doctrine of justification by faith alone amounts in the end to a doctrine of *salvation* by faith alone, which is the key notion in many later forms of Protestantism, the terms "justification" and "salvation" are not simply interchangeable. For Luther salvation is the end or completion of the process, which does not take place until the process of justification is all done. You can be justified by faith today, but that means you are still in process, on a journey that has not yet reached its destination, so your salvation is not yet a present reality. Hence in contrast to much of later Protestantism, Luther's theology is not about how to "get saved," as if salvation were something that happened at a particular moment in your life. Like Augustine, he thinks that as long we live on earth we are not yet saved. Until we arrive at eternal salvation in the next life, we are still in the process of justification, having salvation only in hope, not in reality—*in spe*, not *in re*, to use Augustine's terms.

Luther applies these terms to righteousness as well: "We are sinners in fact [*in re*] but righteous in hope [*in spe*]."[17] Because we are still in the process of justification, Luther can say—in a famous and contentious formulation—that every Christian is "at the same time both a sinner and righteous man" (*simul peccator et justus*).[18] "The *simul*," as theologians have taken to calling it, may sound like something paradoxical or contradictory, but Luther is simply talking the way an Aristotelian philosopher does when describing a process of movement from one state to another: you can describe the process in terms of both its starting point and its endpoint. Because this way of talking has caused a great deal of confusion since Luther's day, it will be worth our while to say a bit more about how medieval Aristotelians thought about processes.

In Aristotelian philosophy the term for process is "movement" or "motion" (*motus* in Luther's Latin), which is used to describe not just movement in space but any process that moves from a starting point to an endpoint as its goal. A growing plant moves from being a seed to being a sprout to being a full-grown life-form, a house in the process of being built moves from being a pile of materials to being a completed structure, a student being educated moves from ignorance to knowledge, a cloth being cleaned moves from dirty to clean, a sick person being healed moves from illness to health, and a soul in the process of justification moves from sin to righteousness.

One of the most important features of any Aristotelian process is that so long as it is still going on it is not completed. Here is cause for yet another warning about words, because the term for "completed" in Latin is *perfectus* (from *per-factus*, "thoroughly done," in the sense of the common English phrase, "all done"). Therefore the English word "perfect," when used to translate medieval and Reformation theology, has to be understood as a process term, designating the completion of a process, when you come to the end and have no more growing or building or cleaning to do. The root meaning of the term is not so much like getting everything right on a test (getting 100 out of 100, a "perfect score," as we now say) as it is like *completing* the test,

---

17. Luther, Romans Lectures, on Rom. 4:7, *LW* 25:258 (= *WA* 56:269).

18. Luther, Romans Lectures, on Rom. 4:7, *LW* 25:260 (= *WA* 56:272). Nearly the same formulation is found twenty years later in Luther, 1535 Galatians Commentary, on Gal. 3:6: "A Christian is righteous and a sinner at the same time" (*simul justus et peccator*) (*LW* 26:232 [= *WA* 40/1:368]). It is rooted in the same Augustinian process of justification, according to which "we are justified and nonetheless not yet justified. . . . What remains is for us to be perfectly justified, and this is what we hope for. Thus our righteousness is not yet in reality [*in re*] but is so far in hope [*in spe*]" (Luther, 1535 Galatians Commentary, on Gal. 5:5, *WA* 40/2:24 [= *LW* 27:21]).

getting it all done. Any completed task is, in this original sense of the term, "perfect." This is why Schubert's unfinished symphony is labeled an *opus imperfectum* in Latin; the label does not mean the symphony is flawed but that it is an unfinished work.

The English word "perfect" was still being used in this original sense when the translators of the King James Bible wrote of becoming "a perfect man," meaning not someone who was morally blameless (there are other terms for that) but a full-grown adult in the faith, attaining "the measure of the stature of the fullness of Christ" (Eph. 4:13 KJV). Likewise, when medieval theologians say God is eternally perfect, they are not praising his moral character but indicating that he is always, as it were, full grown—with no room for growth or improvement, no unactualized potential, because every possible good is already fully complete and actualized in him. The basic idea is that it can only be a joke to talk about "back when God was a boy." This original sense of perfection is also involved when the New Testament tells us of Christ on the cross saying, "It is finished" (John 19:30), using the Greek word for perfection, derived from the word for the endpoint of a process, its *telos*. He did not simply mean that he was about to die and his suffering would at last come to an end; he meant he had completed the work his Father sent him to do. This is why theologians often speak of the "finished work" of the cross. It is all done, not an unfinished work or *opus imperfectum*.

Always in Motion

When describing the process of justification, Luther can sound paradoxical when he is merely being philosophical. This is especially true of "the *simul*," which is often misunderstood as if it were a denial that we make progress in justification. In fact it is a description of what our progress looks like so long as it is still in process. Drawing on a standard Aristotelian example, Luther illustrates the point by describing a house in the process of being built: "Because it is under construction, the same house is properly said both *to be* and *to be becoming* a house, but because of its incompleteness [*imperfectionem*] it is at the same time [*simul*] said *not yet to be* and to *be lacking* the attributes of a house."[19] It's like a riddle: When is something both a house and not a house,

19. Luther, Romans Lectures, on Rom. 7:17, WA 56:352 (= LW 25:341). The carefully contrasted technical terms don't come across fully in translation: "to be" (*esse*) is in contrast to "not yet to be" (*nondum esse*), and "to be becoming" (*proficere*) is in contrast to "to be lacking" (*deficere*). The latter pair are the source of our words "proficient" and "deficient" (as well as "defect") and refer to the process moving forward and falling short, respectively.

at the same time? The answer: When it's a house in the process of being built. You can look at it and tell someone, "I don't have a house yet," but you can just as well say, the next moment: "*There is the house* I'm building." This is no paradox but a very ordinary and sensible way of talking, which corresponds to the in-between character of every incomplete process, which can be described both in terms of its completion ("There's the house I'm building") and its incompletion ("I don't have a house yet"). Aristotelian philosophers merely noticed that in this ordinary and sensible way of talking, one and the same process can be described in terms of both its end and its beginning.

In a similar vein, we can ask: When are people both sinners and righteous at the same time? The answer: When they are in the process of being justified. For in Luther's doctrine of justification we are always in process, *semper in motu*, as he explains, again using Aristotelian terminology:

> This is the way Aristotle philosophizes about these things—and well, although people don't understand him this way. A man is always in *not being*, in *becoming*, in *being*; always in *privation*, in *potential*, in *actuality*; always in sin, in justification, in righteousness, i.e., always a sinner, always repenting, always righteous. For repenting makes the unrighteous righteous. Therefore repentance is in the middle, between unrighteousness and righteousness. And thus he is in sin as a starting point and in righteousness as an endpoint.[20]

Luther wants us to think in terms of the three fundamental aspects of any process: the starting point (*terminus a quo*), the endpoint (*terminus ad quem*), and the middle (*medium*), which is the road leading from one to the other. We are both in sin and in righteousness at the same time, precisely because we are in the middle of the process of becoming righteous, progressing from the one to the other on the road of repentance. The process of justification is the middle or mean because it lies between the starting point and the endpoint, between privation (i.e., sheer lack or deprivation of righteousness) and the full actuality of perfection, when righteousness is no longer merely a potential achievement toward which we are moving but an actual, completed accomplishment at which we have arrived. Luther calls this process "repentance" as well as justification, because at this early stage in his career he thinks of justification as essentially a penitential process, driven forward by ever deeper hatred of one's own sin. Thus there are two names for the same process: "repentance" describes it in terms of its starting point, the sin we are leaving behind, whereas "justification" describes it by looking forward to the goal, the perfected righteousness we have not yet attained.

20. Luther, Romans Lectures, on Rom. 12:1, *WA* 56:442 (= *LW* 25:434).

Likewise, both the starting point and the endpoint can be used to designate where we are in the process while it is still going on, and that is why we can quite properly be called sinners and righteous at the same time:

> So if we are always repenting, then we are always sinners, and yet by the same token we are also righteous and justified, partly [*partim*] sinners, partly righteous, i.e., nothing but penitents.[21]

There has been a great deal of fruitless discussion about whether "the *simul*" should be qualified with the words "partly" or "wholly" (*partim* or *totus*). Often the notion is that Catholics like Augustine get by with thinking we are only partly sinners and partly righteous, while Lutherans bite the bullet and accept the paradox of our being wholly sinners and wholly justified at the same time. The contrast is misdrawn, however, because there is no paradox in either way of speaking, and Luther himself speaks both ways, for good Aristotelian reasons. On the one hand, we are partly sinners and partly righteous because so long as we are in motion we are always partly at the starting point and partly at the goal (like the half-built house that is partly built and partly not-yet-built). Yet on the other hand, we are still wholly sinful in the sense that our whole being is affected by the sin we still have. It is like a fever that affects our whole body, even as we are being gradually healed and getting better every day: it makes good sense to say both that we are partly healed and that we are still wholly sick, feverish from head to toe—for it is not as if the sickness is only in part of us. Thus, just before the passage about the process of building a house, Luther describes our sinful flesh as "an infirmity or a wound of the whole man [*totius hominis*] who by grace is beginning to be healed."[22]

The "partly" language is inherent in the notion of moving from one point to another, in a passage of Aristotle that Luther quotes in one of his earliest sermons:

> For "all motion is partly [*partim*] in the starting point and partly in the end point," just as a sick man being healed is in the sickness he's leaving behind but also in the health he's heading toward [*in aegritudine recedendo, sed in sanitate accedendo*]. So also the righteous man is always in sin with his left foot and old man, but in grace with his right foot, i.e., the new man.[23]

---

21. Luther, Romans Lectures, on Rom. 12:1, *WA* 56:442 (= *LW* 25:434).

22. Luther, Romans Lectures, on Rom. 7:17, *LW* 25:340–41 (= *WA* 56:352). Cf. the similar analogy in Luther, Romans Lectures, on Rom. 5:12, *LW* 25:300, comparing the sinner to a sick man whose illness is "a lack of health in all his members, the weakness of all of his senses and powers."

23. Luther, sermon on Dec. 27, 1514, *WA* 1:42. The quotation is Luther's version of Aristotle, *Physics* 6:4.234b15: "part of that which is changing must be at the starting-point and part at the goal" (McKeon, 323).

It is a superb metaphor: at every step you have one foot in the place you're leaving behind, even as you move forward to a new place with the other foot. So the process of justification includes (in Pauline terms) both the old man and the new man, flesh and spirit, which are with us at every step along the road to our destination. We are always leaving the old man behind, precisely because he is with us at every step; he is what we are always pushing away from with our back foot, even as we step forward toward the new person we are becoming. We are righteous and sinner at the same time because we are always partly the old Adam and partly the new person we are becoming in Christ—and thus (again in Pauline terms) partly flesh and partly spirit.

The conceptual point here could also be illustrated by imagining a white cloth that is thoroughly drenched in some kind of filth: while it's in the process of being cleaned, the color goes from dark to gray, then closer and closer to pure white, but it never covers less than the whole extent of the cloth.[24] Thus at every stage in the process the cloth is wholly stained yet partly cleaned, until it arrives at the point where it is completely and perfectly clean. Sin is such a stain in those who are in the process of being justified, who find themselves partway along the road to perfect righteousness but still wholly sinners.

This Aristotelian theory of motion helps Luther say something that is vastly more important to him than anything in Aristotle: sin is where we begin and it remains in us, staining every part of our being, so long as we remain on the journey of this life. Luther accentuates this point by insisting that we must always keep moving forward, taking the next step rather than standing still, because every present moment is sin by comparison to the righteousness we must get to next. This goes further than anything Aristotle says, but Luther can still use the language of Aristotelian philosophy to say it:

> It is not enough to have done and to rest, but according to philosophy a process [*motus*] is an uncompleted actuality [*actus imperfectus*], always in part acquired and in part to be acquired, *always in the midst of opposites*, and standing at the same time [*simul*] at the starting point and at the goal.[25]

Since a process is incomplete so long as it's still going on, it can always be described in terms of where it's coming from as well as where it's going, which means that every stage in the life of penitence partakes of its starting point in sin. In that sense we are always starting afresh, and every step puts us once again at square one. For we must always be pushing away from the

---

24. This illustration is drawn from Dieter, *Der junge Luther und Aristoteles*, chap. 4, to which my overall interpretation of Luther's theory of motion is much indebted.

25. Luther, First Psalms Lectures, on Ps. 119:121, LW 11:494 (= WA 4:362).

past with our back foot as we stride forward with our front foot to the next step in the process of justification. Or to use the other analogy, at every moment in our lives we have the same dirty garment to clean, even though it's always getting cleaner.

Because we are always still morally unclean, we can never sit still and rest on our present achievements but must always regard ourselves as sinners still needing to repent and be made righteous. As Luther explains, in an important passage that reveals much of his thinking about the journey of this life:

> We are always in motion [*semper . . . in motu*], and we who are righteous need always to be made righteous. From this it comes about that every righteousness for the present moment is sin with regard to that which must be added in the next moment. For blessed Bernard says truly, "When you begin not to want to become better, you stop being good. For there is no stopping place on God's way. Delay itself is sin." Hence he who in the present moment trusts that he is righteous and stands in that opinion has already lost righteousness, as is clear likewise in motion: That which is the goal in the present moment is the starting point in the next moment. But the starting point is sin, *from* which we must always be going; and the goal is righteousness, *to* which we must always be going. Therefore I have correctly said that the preceding righteousness is always wickedness with regard to the next.[26]

To be always in motion toward the goal of righteousness is to be always presently in sin. Thus the Aristotelian philosophy of motion or process supports Luther's lifelong conviction that we must never trust in any righteousness of our own or believe that we have earned any kind of merit in God's sight.

Habitus and Elicited Acts

Reinforcing the conviction that we must always keep moving is Luther's criticism of a different part of Aristotle's philosophy, the theory of *habitus*. This is a Latin term for intelligent habits of the heart such as skills and virtues—not merely mechanical or rote repetition, like modern notions of mere habit. A *habitus* gives shape to people's thinking and perceiving and feeling as well as their actions. Aristotle thinks of these intelligent habits as qualities in the soul, forming it and giving its activities a definite shape, as we saw in chapter 1. The usefulness of the concept of *habitus* has much to do with its two-sided relationship to our actions. On the one hand, you acquire a *habitus* by

---

26. Luther, First Psalms Lectures, on Ps. 119:122, *LW* 11:496 (= *WA* 4:364). The quotation is from Bernard of Clairvaux, Letter 91:3.

doing the same thing repeatedly, like learning to play a musical instrument by practice. On the other hand, once you have acquired a *habitus*, the actions that flow from it are both easier to do and better done, like a skilled musician playing her instrument more easily and accurately, with more joy and confidence and artistry, than someone still trying to master the basics. So you become a good musician by practice, but only a good musician does a good job playing music. The same two-sided relationship between *habitus* and action is operative in human virtues; for as Aristotle puts it, on the one hand, "a person comes to be just from doing just actions and temperate from doing temperate actions," whereas on the other hand, "if we do what is just or temperate, we must already be just or temperate."[27] Luther will insist on the latter point, but fiercely reject the former. In his parlance, a person must be good and righteous before he can do good works, as a tree must be sound and healthy before it can bear good fruit—not vice versa.

A purely Aristotelian doctrine of justification would have us getting better at being good people by practice, just like the way we get better at playing a musical instrument. In the process of habituation a multitude of good deeds accumulates, as it were, and becomes a firm possession of goodness in the soul. The philosophical difficulty of Luther's theology—the sense in which, as he often insists, it is an offense to reason—stems from his emphatic rejection of this rather commonsense model of moral progress. To say we acquire the virtue or *habitus* of justice by performing just actions is precisely to say that we are justified by good works. There is nothing Luther hates more, in all of philosophy, than this notion that "we become just by doing just actions."[28] He has many harsh words for Aristotle on this score: "that rancid philosopher,"[29] the "chief of all charlatans,"[30] that "damned, conceited, rascally heathen," whose book on ethics is "the worst of all books"[31] and "the worst enemy of grace."[32] Over and over, this is what he finds to disagree with in the philosopher: "We are not, as Aristotle believes, made righteous by the doing of righteous deeds,"[33] and "The righteousness of God is not acquired by means of acts

---

27. Aristotle, *Nicomachean Ethics* 2:4.1105b10; 2:4.1105a21 (Irwin and Fine, 370).

28. Aristotle, *Nicomachean Ethics* 2:1.1103b1 (Irwin and Fine, 366).

29. WA 9:43. From Luther's marginalia on Peter Lombard's *Sentences*, ca. 1510, approving Lombard's disagreement with theologians who use *habitus* theory to interpret Augustine's notion of charity, in Lombard, *Sententiae* 1:17.4. For discussion see Dieter, *Der junge Luther und Aristoteles*, 243–50.

30. Luther, letter to John Lang, Feb. 18, 1517, LW 48:37.

31. Luther, *To the Christian Nobility of the German Nation*, LW 44:201.

32. Luther, Theses on Nature and Grace, 1517 (commonly known since the eighteenth century as *Disputation against Scholastic Theology*), thesis 41 (LW 31:12).

33. Luther, letter to George Spalatin, Oct. 19, 1516, LW 48:25.

frequently repeated, as Aristotle taught."[34] Yet he is willing to concede that Aristotle is right about ordinary human justice, which Luther calls civil righteousness or righteousness before human beings (*justitia coram hominibus*), contrasting it sharply with righteousness before God (*justitia coram Deo*). The former is "the righteousness of man, which comes from works, as Aristotle describes it very clearly in Book III of his *Ethics*."[35]

So Luther is not denying that we can acquire habits and skills and virtues. Even the most rascally heathen knows that. What he is saying is that none of these count as righteousness *before God*. If we could acquire a *habitus* that made us righteous in God's sight, we would not have to be always in motion, always on the move toward righteousness. There would be such a thing as a righteousness in our souls that we could rest on. For a *habitus* is a stable and enduring possession of our souls (the word comes from Latin *habere*, which is cognate to English "have"). We have it in us even when it is inactive and not being used, the way a courageous person is still in possession of the virtue of courage even when she's sleeping, or a musician still has the skill of musicianship even when he's doing something besides making music. Luther often scoffs at these inert "idle qualities," as he calls them, which can slumber inactively in the soul, and he insists that the grace of God "is never present in such a way that it is inactive, but it is a living, active, and operative spirit,"[36] and Christ himself is present in us in a way that is never idle but always "supremely active" (*actuosissimus*).[37] So also the righteousness of faith that results from the grace of Christ in us is "a living thing that cannot be idle,"[38] and faith itself "is not a *habitus* residing in the soul and snoring there."[39] As we shall see in chapter 8, this helps explain the complexity of Luther's view of faith, which on the one hand is not an action or work we do to justify

34. Luther, *Heidelberg Disputation*, 1518, proof of thesis 25, LW 31:55.

35. Luther, Romans Lectures, on Rom. 1:17, LW 25:152. Luther is probably thinking of *Nicomachean Ethics* 3:5, where Aristotle explains how virtue and vice are "up to us." See also Luther, 1519 Galatians Commentary, on Gal. 2:16, LW 27:219, describing how "human righteousnesses [*sic*] . . . are acquired by practice (as it is said) and by habit. This is the kind of righteousness Aristotle and other philosophers describe." See also Luther's affirmation that Aristotle is right about civil righteousness in the 1535 Galatians Commentary, on Gal. 3:10, LW 26:256: "In civil life the situation is different; here one becomes a doer on the basis of deeds, just as one becomes a lutenist by often playing the lute, as Aristotle says." Hence the general contrast: "In theology those who have been made righteous do righteous things, not as in philosophy, where those who do righteous things are made righteous" (1535 Galatians Commentary, on Gal. 3:10, LW 26:260).

36. Luther, Theses on Nature and Grace, thesis 55, LW 31:13.

37. Luther, sermon on Feb. 24, 1517, LW 51:29 (= WA 1:140).

38. Luther, sermon on Jan. 1, 1517, WA 1:119.

39. Luther, Second Psalms Lectures (1519–21 *Operationes in Psalmos*), on Ps. 16:8, WA 5:460.

ourselves, but on the other hand is not an inert quality but is always actively taking hold of Christ as well as doing good works.

It also helps explain what is unusual about Luther's concept of free will, or rather his rejection of the concept. For Luther the will is never inert, but is always an active, eager willingness, "a cheerful and spontaneous readiness . . . and willing good pleasure."[40] Luther sees this described in Psalm 1:2, where the standard Latin translation, which Luther used in his teaching, renders the notion that a righteous man has a "delight in the law of the Lord" with the word for will (*voluntas*). Hence the first text on which Luther lectured in his course on the Psalms in 1513 (which is to say, the first major work of his that we have in writing) describes the righteous person by saying, in effect, "His *will* is in the law of the Lord." In thinking of will as if it meant something like delight, Luther is focusing on the aspect of our moral lives that, as Augustine realized long before, was the least in our will's control.[41] The problem with us, Luther thinks, is that the sinful will is so willful: it wants its own way and takes no delight in anything else, including God's law or God himself.

That is why Luther insists so emphatically—and not just in his early works—that our will is in bondage to sin. This does not mean it is forced or coerced into sinning, but rather that it acts freely only when it does what it really wants to do—and what it really wants to do is to sin. Hence when it sins, it does so freely and willingly, indeed with great eagerness and gusto and delight, and because it does so it has no capacity to change itself or turn its willingness in a better direction.[42] Sinning has become a kind of second nature in our will, because our nature is vitiated by original sin, our inheritance from Adam—the old man in us, as Paul calls it (Rom. 6:6; Eph. 4:22; Col. 3:9). This forms, or rather deforms, our souls in such inveterate sinfulness that any attempt we make to change ourselves is met with inner resistance, from the depths of our souls, because we are trying to coerce ourselves into doing what we aren't really willing to do.

We can try to practice doing what is good, but it will accomplish nothing, Luther thinks. We can make the effort of forcing ourselves to delight in God's law, for example, by inwardly forming a good intention to love God above all things, which is what late medieval theologians called *eliciting* an act of the will. But Luther is deeply unimpressed with such efforts, because "anyone can forcibly elicit an act of willing in the law of the Lord, and yet

40. Luther, First Psalms Lectures, on Ps. 1:6, *LW* 10:32.
41. Peter Brown highlights the importance of Augustine's realization that delight is not in our control in Brown, *Augustine of Hippo*, 148–49, 163–64. I take this realization to be central to Augustine's doctrine of grace in Cary, *Inner Grace*, 15–16, 57–62, 108–13.
42. Luther, *Bondage of the Will*, LW 33:39, 64–65.

his will would not be in it."[43] This act of will is not free at all, but unwilling, "forcibly extorted and tyrannically elicited."[44] It is the will forcing itself to do something against its own will. Thus a notion that lies at the core of free will for Luther's late medieval predecessors, the ability to elicit an inner act of love when we choose, looks to Luther like coercion rather than freedom. (This is why, in his later work, he can speak of "that miserable bondage of free choice."[45] The effort to be good by our own free choice is precisely the slavery from which he wants to escape.) When he says the act is elicited "forcibly," he is using a technical term in Aristotelian philosophy that describes the kind of motion you produce when you force a stone to go upward by throwing it high in the air. This is movement in a direction that is unnatural for a stone, and it cannot last. Nature soon wins out over force—which means that inevitably, what goes up must come down.

In terms of the Augustinian metaphor of love as weight, the point is that after original sin vitiates human nature, our wills are like stone, not fire; they are drawn to things of earth, not heaven. So people can elicit an act of will, a feeble little wish to love God above all things, but "once the act is past, they will fall back into their customary state, and there is no perseverance."[46] It is like trying to get a stone to fly by throwing it up in the air over and over again—as if the stone could develop a habit of flying by sheer repetition.[47] And yet it is precisely this sort of act, forcibly elicited and frequently repeated, that is supposed to turn into a *habitus*, a virtuous habit! Luther's point is that elicited acts of love for God have no lasting effect on us, because they are diametrically opposed to what our sinful wills are really willing to do. Augustine is certainly right to say that "a large part of righteousness is *willing* to be righteous," Luther admits, but we delude ourselves if we equate this willing with "the tiniest little elicited act, which soon falls back again and doesn't start anything."[48] Our elicited acts of love for God get us nowhere.

43. Luther, First Psalms Lectures, on Ps. 1:6, *LW* 10:32.
44. Luther, First Psalms Lectures, on Ps. 1:6, *LW* 10:32 (= WA 3:30). This could be translated, somewhat more precisely: "extorted by violence [*violenter*] and elicited by command [*imperiose*]."
45. Luther, *Bondage of the Will*, LW 33:144.
46. Luther, First Psalms Lectures, on Ps. 1:6, *LW* 10:32.
47. Luther may be thinking of Aristotle, *Nicomachean Ethics* 2:1.1103a21: "A stone, for instance, by nature moves downward, and habituation could not make it move upward, not even if you threw it up ten thousand times to habituate it" (Irwin and Fine, 366).
48. Luther, Romans Lectures, on Rom. 4:7, WA 56:280 (= *LW* 25:267). *LW* leaves out the important technical term "elicited." The quotation on which Luther is commenting is Augustine, Letter 127:5.

The Counterfactual Test

To think our sinful will is free to love and obey God is an illusion that Luther tries to expose with help from Augustine. In one vivid illustration, he pictures a bored, complacent monk in church, fretting and turning over the pages in his prayer book while he wishes for the service to be over with. The monk tries to reassure himself that he is righteous by forming the good intention to love God.[49] He might even have been taught, using the technical terminology of late medieval theology, that by "doing what is in him" (*facere quod in se est*), using nothing but his natural ability (*ex puris naturalibus*), he is capable of "eliciting" from his will the act of loving God above all things, through which he can deserve to obtain the grace of God by "the merit of congruity."[50] But he should examine himself, Luther warns, and ask whether he would really rather be doing something else if he were free to do so. That would show him what is really going on with his supposedly free will. Think of it as a kind of counterfactual test: imagine, contrary to the actual fact of the matter, that there were no law of God, no monastic rule, no compulsion, nothing to fear by way of punishment and no reward for being righteous. What would you do then, you bored, wretched monk? The answer to that question reveals what your will is really willing to do, and that is also what God sees in the depth of your heart and holds you accountable for. What the counterfactual test reveals is that your inmost will does not delight in the law of the Lord but resents every righteous thing you're trying to do. And it is by your inmost will that God judges you. Recognizing that, you now have reason to fear all your supposedly good works and repent of them rather than continue in your complacency.

We catch sight here of young Luther's campaign to reform and renew the monastic life of his community, uprooting smug security and promoting a more serious penitential life. The counterfactual test, which is one of his most powerful weapons in this campaign, is something he learned from Augustine's treatise *The Spirit and the Letter*, where it supports Augustine's argument for the necessity of an inner gift of divine grace. Without grace, Augustine argues, we obey God only the way a slave obeys a master he fears, rather than the way a son obeys the father he loves. You can tell the difference using the counterfactual test, which distinguishes the true inward will from

---

49. Luther, Romans Lectures, on Rom. 14:1, *LW* 25:494.

50. The notion of *facere quod in se est* appears two pages later, Luther, Romans Lectures, on Rom. 14:1, *LW* 25:496 (= *WA* 56:502), rendered "doing what is in their power." Luther gives an explanation of these concepts in the 1535 Galatians Commentary, on Gal. 2:16 and 2:20, *LW* 26:124–29, 172–73.

external slavish obedience. Luther quotes Augustine's key formulation of the counterfactual test in his early lectures on Romans:

> Even those who did what the law commanded, without help from the Spirit of grace, did it from fear of punishment and not from love of righteousness, and hence there was not in the will before God [*coram Deo*] what appeared in the works before human beings [and conversely, what did not appear in the works, was nonetheless before God in the will], and they were held guilty of committing what God knew they would rather have done, if it could have been done with impunity.[51]

What we can learn from Augustine's counterfactual test is that our supposed love of God is actually fear of punishment. Far from our will and delight being in the law of the Lord, the fact is—as Luther puts it a few years later—that "if the law were not there, you would prefer to act otherwise," which shows that "from the bottom of your heart you hate the law."[52] Or as he would put it many years later, all the law of God achieves when sinners try to obey it is that "they would rather that there were no law, no punishment, no hell and finally no God."[53] Thus in the end, far from causing us to love God, "the Law produces extreme hate toward God."[54]

The Terrors of a Personal God

The theology of the young Luther is piling up troubles for people on the road to God, of a kind that Augustine had not anticipated. In Augustine's Platonist spirituality, the good things we must love, such as inward Beauty, eternal Truth, and supreme Justice, all of which are names for God, are inherently attractive to the soul. Although we sinners are often more attracted to lower goods, Augustine conceives of the grace of God turning us around to catch sight of these higher and more inward things with our mind's eye, so that we are powerfully moved to delight in them, which means to love and seek God. As we saw in chapter 3, for Augustine our highest goal is not a kind of personal encounter but like the eye enjoying the light.[55] We may find it too

---

51. Augustine, *Spirit and the Letter* 8.13, translated from Luther, Romans Lectures, on Rom. 2:13, WA 56:200 (= LW 25:184). The bracketed insertion in English is Luther's addition. Earlier, on Rom. 2:4, LW 25:174, Luther gives a paraphrase of the same passage, which is very much on his mind throughout the lectures. For fuller discussion, see Cary, "Augustine and Luther," 153–55.
52. Luther, 1522 Preface to Romans, LW 35:267.
53. Luther, 1535 Galatians Commentary, on Gal. 3:23, LW 26:337.
54. Luther, 1535 Galatians Commentary, on Gal. 3:19, LW 26:314.
55. Augustine, *City of God* 8:8. See above, chap. 3, "Strengths and Weaknesses of Platonism."

bright at first and resist what the light of Truth reveals about us,[56] but the whole journey is about strengthening the eye of our heart to see the light in its fullness, so that we may attain the happiness of what Catholics came to call beatific vision. Luther, by contrast, who is no Platonist, is not teaching us how to come to the vision of God as intelligible Truth or Beauty or Justice, but how to hear a God whose word may be against us, a word of accusation and condemnation. In short, Luther is thinking of God as a person, not a Platonic form. For Luther our spiritual journey brings us into the presence of a great and fearsome king who is our judge and will have the final word about the meaning of our lives, for good or ill. There are surely many things you would rather do than journey to such a king—your will is not in it, as Luther would say—and your attempts to get yourself cleaned up and dressed properly for the occasion are likely to seem fake and forced, even to yourself. How can you ever learn to love this terrifying judge with your whole heart, mind, and strength?

The mature Luther's answer to this question is that what God has to say to us is not merely accusation, judgment, and condemnation, but includes a kind word of grace that reveals his friendly heart. This word is the Gospel of Jesus Christ, by which the king gives us his own Son as our bridegroom and beloved. The striking thing about Luther's theological development is how absent this kind word is at the beginning of his career. In Luther's early theology, as we are about to see, the word of God always comes to us as an adversary, accusing and condemning us. No wonder our will is not in it! But this is the road to justification, according to the young Luther. In the next chapter we will look at this teaching in more detail, in order to understand, beginning in chapter 7, what happens when his mature concept of the Gospel comes into the picture, producing the theology that we now know as Protestant.

56. Augustine, *Confessions* 10:3.3.

6

Young Luther

Justification without Gospel

Luther's early theology is a moving target, not easy to pin down.[1] In the first decade for which we have much of his writing—stretching about five years on either side of the famous 95 Theses in 1517—he goes through enormous changes, and not just in his thinking. In 1513 he is an obscure monk preparing lectures for his Bible courses at the University of Wittenberg. By 1522 he is the leader of a new reformation of the church, condemned by both pope and emperor, and author of the earliest works of Protestant theology. What we shall examine in this chapter is his theology of justification in the early period up to the time of the 95 Theses.

Through all the changes, some things stay the same. Never does Luther believe we are, in ourselves, righteous before God. Always he looks to the truth and power of God's word as the source of our justification. Always, belief in God's word is at the center of his account of justification. What we need to examine in this chapter, in order to understand the shape of his theological

---

1. There is a large and contentious scholarly literature trying to keep track of how Luther changes his mind, especially in his early period. My approach here is much indebted to one trajectory in this scholarship, represented by Ernst Bizer and Oswald Bayer, which focuses on the development of the notion of Gospel as efficacious promise—a word that not only promises grace but has the power to give it to whoever believes. However, I agree with Berndt Hamm that there are many "Reformation turns" in Luther's early development, not just one "Reformation breakthrough" that makes the difference between the Catholic and the Protestant Luther. My focus on the concept of Gospel is because of its theological importance, not because it has a uniquely decisive place in Luther's development.

development, is what justification looks like for him when God's word contains no Gospel, as he was later to understand the term—no promise of grace in Christ that gives what it promises. For the obscure monk working on his first lecture course on the Psalms in 1513, the word of God is fundamentally a word of judgment and accusation, driving us forward in the work of penance. Faith in this word means agreeing that God's judgment is true and internalizing the divine accusation against us, by accusing ourselves in humble confession of sin. We make progress only as we overcome our tendency to talk back, our desire to defend ourselves and insist that there is some corner of our souls that is righteous and holy.[2]

Gospel as Judgment

"Judgment" (*judicium*) is a key term in Luther's first lectures on the Psalms because it sums up the notion of penitence as young Luther understands it from his predecessors, the scholastic theologians of the late Middle Ages. It designates "what our scholastics theologically call the act of penance, which means to be displeased with oneself, to detest, condemn, accuse, desire to take vengeance and punish oneself, to chastise and seriously hate evil and be angry with oneself."[3] Penance is thus the human activity of internalizing the divine judgment of condemnation. The striking thing is that young Luther calls this judgment "Gospel." He is thinking that God's grace moves us forward in the process of repentance and justification precisely by the power of a word of judgment that causes us to accuse, condemn, and hate ourselves.

> Therefore the judgments of God are punishment and crucifixion of the flesh and the condemnation of everyone in the world—which he brings about in his own people *through judgment, that is, through the Gospel and his grace.* And thus righteousness comes into being. For God gives his grace to him who is unrighteous to himself and thus humble before God.[4]

This is how Luther connects faith with the grace and righteousness of God in his early writings. God "judges and justifies the one who believes in him,"

2. That the prohibition of back talk, though often violated, is a fundamental issue in Luther's own personality is an important insight of the psycho-biography by Erikson, *Young Man Luther*, 66. Though Erikson is not a reliable guide to Luther's theology, he is right to focus on Luther's extraordinary relationship with *words*, including his intense awareness of our inner resistance to any word spoken against us, even if it is God's word.
3. Luther, First Psalms Lectures, on Ps. 1:6, WA 3:31 (= LW 10:33).
4. Luther, First Psalms Lectures, on Ps. 72:1, WA 3:462 (= LW 10:404).

Luther explains, because "any word of God whatever is judgment."[5] But the specific judgment that justifies us, which Luther identifies with the Gospel (in the italicized passage above), is a word that drives us to condemn ourselves:

> By this judgment God condemns and makes us condemn whatever we have of ourselves, the whole old man with his actions. This is properly humility, indeed humiliation. For it is not the one who *thinks* he's humble who is righteous, but the one who regards himself as detestable and damnable in his own eyes—there's the righteous man.[6]

This is quite a different theology from what we see in Luther's mature thinking. The judgment by which we are justified here functions as what the mature Luther calls law rather than Gospel.[7] It justifies us by humiliating us to the point where we detest ourselves and join God when he condemns us. It will take some effort, in this chapter, to understand how this startlingly un-Lutheran doctrine of justification works. It is worth the effort, however, because it will illuminate the framework within which Luther's mature conception of Gospel first arose and will show us what it originally meant for him. It is a framework that desperately needs—and lacks—a concept of Gospel as *good* news.

Luther's early writings do not present us with a cheerful theology. As we saw in the last chapter, he was trying to confront what he saw, at this stage in his career, as the besetting sins of his era, which he describes as tepid, smug, and self-righteous. He was not looking for a gracious God but for ways to become more deeply, inwardly penitent. His pastoral concern was focused not, as later, on the terrified conscience of the laity but on the complacency of his fellow monks, especially those who thought it was easy to become righteous just by following their monastic rule strictly enough. He wanted these people to hear the word of condemnation in all seriousness and judge themselves by God's judgment, stripping them of any confidence in their own works and driving them to sincere penitence and humble confession of sin.

The message is grim, but it does avert a kind of performance anxiety that Luther himself always found hard to bear. He never wanted to be in a position where he had to claim to be righteous. The presumptuousness of such a claim, as well as its uncertainty and the likelihood that he was deceiving himself, were

---

5. Luther, First Psalms Lectures, on Ps. 72:1, WA 3:462 (= LW 10:404).

6. Luther, First Psalms Lectures, on Ps. 72:1, WA 3:465 (= LW 10:406). Note likewise Luther, First Psalms Lectures, on Ps. 72:1, LW 10:404: "Whoever clings to Him by faith necessarily becomes vile and nothing, abominable and damnable, to himself. And that is true humility."

7. E.g., "When a man is taught this way *by the Law* . . . he justifies God in His Word and confesses that he deserves death and eternal damnation" (Luther, 1535 Galatians Commentary, on Gal. 2:16, LW 26:126).

always intolerable to him. When you look at your imperfect righteousness with your flawed self-knowledge, how can you possibly be confident that the righteousness you have is sufficient to please God? Luther's answer is always clear: you should know, indeed be quite certain, that it never is. As we saw in the last chapter, he explains that whatever righteousness we do have at present is unrighteousness by comparison to what is demanded of us in the next step of our lives. So the imperfect righteousness in us is always actually sin, something to be repented of. This is why we must be always in motion, always repenting, always beginning again. It means there can be no end of self-accusation, self-condemnation, and the humble confession of sin in this life. If you're not convinced of this, Luther thinks, all you have to do is pay attention to the word of God as it passes judgment on you. The telltale mark of an evil heart is that it talks back against this word; it grumbles and resents being called a sinner and tries to justify itself.

Justification as Self-Condemnation

Luther takes as a motto for his early doctrine of justification the proverb "The just man is from the beginning his own accuser."[8] Righteousness is in effect the opposite of back talk, for "as the righteous man is from the beginning his own accuser, the ungodly man is from the beginning his own defender."[9] Luther is thinking: you make progress in justification by realizing you always have to begin at the beginning, confessing the unrighteousness that is your starting point and hating it. When you accuse yourself, you agree with God's word as it accuses you, and thus you can "be in agreement with your adversary," as our Lord commands (Matt. 5:25).[10] For the word of God, young Luther believes, always comes to us as an adversary and an enemy, contrary to our thinking and our desires, as it works to break down our self-will. "Since we are liars," he explains, "the truth can never come to us except as an apparent adversary to what we are thinking."[11] The word of God is intended ultimately to justify

8. This motto, which I have translated a bit more literally than *LW*, stands near the beginning of Luther's First Psalms Lectures in 1513, *WA* 3:29 (= *LW* 10:31) and his Romans Lectures in 1516, *LW* 25:15. It is a quotation of Prov. 18:17, varying slightly from the standard Latin version of the time, Jerome's Vulgate, which is in turn quite different from modern translations. Luther's just man accuses himself "from the beginning" (*in principio*), while Jerome's just man accuses himself before others do (*prior*).

9. Luther, First Psalms Lectures, on Ps. 1:6, *WA* 3:29 (= *LW* 10:31).

10. Luther, Romans Lectures, on Rom. 12:2, *WA* 56:447 (= *LW* 25:439).

11. Luther, Romans Lectures, on Rom. 3:20, *LW* 25:236. See likewise Luther, Romans Lectures, on Rom. 10:14, *LW* 25:415: "If the Word of God comes, it comes contrary to our thinking and our will."

us, but it can only achieve this by humbling us, contradicting the lies that we tell ourselves in our willfulness. In a telltale little vignette, Luther dramatizes how this adversarial relationship ends up justifying us:

> It is similar to a situation in which two men are fighting over something, and one of them humbly gives in and says, "I freely admit that you are right and truthful. I am willing to be the one who was wrong . . . [so] that you might be the one who did right . . . ." Will not the other man say, "I have wronged you. You are right"? For thus they will be of one mind.[12]

Young Luther seems inadvertently to be telling us what he wants to hear from God: "I have wronged you. You are right." But to get to that point, where God finally gives up accusing him, he is convinced he must begin by thoroughly agreeing with the accusation. So he seeks justification by condemning himself.

For the early Luther our progress in righteousness consists in continually renewing our agreement with God as he continually accuses us. In this way we take on the very form of the word of God, the righteousness that condemns sinners.[13] That is how the righteousness of God (*justitia Dei*) becomes ours— simply because we believe his word as it judges, accuses, and condemns us. This is the original version of Luther's doctrine of justification by faith alone, as we can see from the following passage:

> *By faith alone* we must believe we are sinners. . . . Therefore, we have to stand under the judgment of God and believe His word with which He says that we are unrighteous, because He Himself cannot lie. . . . We must strenuously accuse, judge and condemn ourselves and confess that we are sinful, so that God may be justified in us.[14]

Here, strikingly, we have a doctrine of justification by faith alone without a Lutheran concept of Gospel. The word of God in which we must believe is not a word of grace but of accusation, and justification by faith alone is therefore a process of ongoing self-accusation.

12. Luther, Romans Lectures, on Rom. 3:7, *LW* 25:217.
13. Luther, Romans Lectures, on Rom. 3:7, *LW* 25:211. The language of form here is once again Aristotelian, stemming from Aristotle's theory of perception, where the same form is in the perceiver as in the thing perceived. Thus for Luther, to agree with what we hear in the word of God is to have the same form in our hearts that is also in the word.
14. Luther, Romans Lectures, on Rom. 3:7, *LW* 25:215. This is the culmination of a long series of corollaries explaining how "the justification of God in His words is actually our justification" (*LW* 25:198). The passage that has caught Luther's attention is Rom. 3:4: "God is true, though every man a liar, as it is written: 'that You may be justified in your words'" (quoting Ps. 51:4).

Without a concept of Gospel, justification by faith alone means that we become righteous by believing God's word when it says we are unrighteous. This results in a paradoxical "joining of opposites" (*coincidentia oppositorum*, a favorite designation for paradox in Luther's day), in which we become righteous precisely by believing we are not. The process of justification thus instills in us an ever-deepening sense of being *un*justified. As Luther often puts it, righteousness for us is hidden under our sins, as the mercy of God is hidden under his wrath, our salvation is hidden under his word of condemnation, and every good thing for us is hidden under its opposite.[15]

The overall result is what I would describe as a kind of hopeful spiritual masochism, in which progress in righteousness consists in an ever more sincere self-accusation, leading to deep self-hatred. Luther wants us to be serious about this, not just playing around:

> We need to flee good things and take on evil things. Not by words alone or in pretense of heart, but in full feeling we must confess and *wish ourselves to be destroyed and damned*. We need to act toward ourselves like someone who hates someone else. He doesn't just pretend to hate him, but seriously desires to destroy and kill and damn the person he hates. So if we also in a true and heartfelt way destroy and persecute ourselves, and offer ourselves to hell for God's sake and his righteousness, then we have truly made satisfaction to his justice, and he will have mercy and deliver us.[16]

Once again, Luther is saying we are justified by agreeing with our adversary, thinking about ourselves as an enemy would. But now we can see how far he wants to take this: we should not merely condemn ourselves but sincerely desire for God himself to condemn us to hell, wanting him to be our enemy and internalizing his hatred for us. After that, it seems, there is nothing more for God himself to condemn—we've already done it all. It is like loving your neighbor as yourself, except upside down and backwards: hating yourself as your own worst enemy, or rather, wanting God to hate you for eternity, as you wish you could hate your own worst enemy. It is as if you were to become the devil to yourself—for how could any demon, even Satan the prince of all accusers, want anything worse for you than what this theology teaches you to want for yourself? Yet this is how, in the view of young Luther, you get God to justify you.

---

15. For a few samples of this pervasive notion that what is good for us is hidden under its opposite (*sub contrario*) see Luther, Romans Lectures, on Rom. 8:28; 9:3; 12:2, *LW* 25:370, 382–83, 439.

16. Luther, Romans Lectures, on Rom. 9:3, *WA* 56:393 (= *LW* 25:383–84).

Evil Goods

Lacking a word of God that forgives us, young Luther insists we put our faith in a word of God that condemns us. For we misuse every good thing that comes our way, Luther argues, and therefore everything that is truly good for us must be hidden under its opposite: we can only be justified by agreeing that we are unrighteous, we can only seek salvation by desiring damnation, and we can only love ourselves properly by hating ourselves. This masochistic faith takes young Luther in the opposite direction from Augustine, who affirms that the desire for happiness means seeking the highest good and that our sin lies in clinging to lower goods that cannot give us true and lasting happiness. For Augustine, we're looking for happiness in all the wrong places. For young Luther, on the contrary, our desire for happiness is itself the root of the problem. Every good thing that we desire has become evil for us because of our selfishness. Luther admits that God created all things good, but for us sinners they are "evilly good" (*male bona*) because our perverted human reason "seeks itself and its own in all things."[17]

Our self-centeredness in effect reverses the teleological ethics of ancient philosophy and medieval theology, which is to say the kind of ethics that is based on some variant of Aristotle's notion of an end or *telos* of human life—not a mere objective that we happen to pursue but the innate goal of human nature, the highest good, which is the ultimate source of desire as well as moral obligation.

To explain the failure of teleological ethics, Luther introduces the famous image of man "curved in on himself" (*incurvatus in se*). Because of original sin, which is the old Adam still dwelling in us, each one of us uses even the best spiritual goods only for his own satisfaction and "bends them to himself" (*sibi inflectat*).[18] This picture of human selfishness goes well beyond Augustine's notion of sin, and in a quite precise way. As we saw in chapter 3, Augustine contrasts using and enjoying (*uti* and *frui*) and teaches that we should not seek to *enjoy* temporal goods but rather *use* them so as to arrive at enjoyment of the eternal Good, which is God. Young Luther, by contrast, teaches in his lectures on Romans that even our desire for God amounts to an attempt to use God for our own enjoyment. The bottomless iniquity of the "old man," which represents everything in ourselves that we must try to kill, is at work not just in obvious sins of the flesh but most deeply in the kind of spiritual works to which a monk dedicates his life, as "he acts righteously, practices wisdom and exercises himself in all spiritual good works, even to the point

---

17. Luther, Romans Lectures, on Rom. 8:3, WA 56:354 (= LW 25:344).
18. Luther, Romans Lectures, on Rom. 8:3, WA 56:356 (= LW 25:345).

of loving and worshiping God. The reason for this is that in all these things he 'enjoys' the gifts of God and 'uses' God."[19]

Young Luther is using Augustine's language to turn Augustine's ethics upside down, introducing an idea that is entirely foreign to the church father: that for us sinners even the love of God is wrong. Because we are so curved in on ourselves, our love for God as the highest Good is a sin; for we are seeking God only for our own sake. Thus Luther in these early lectures puts us in an extremely nasty bind: the very fact that we desire what is good for us makes us evil, because desiring what is good *for us* means we are curved in on ourselves. The practical effect is to make it wrong to desire what is good—even the supreme Good, which is God. I think this is deeply perverse, turning good into evil and evil into good. It lies at the root of young Luther's spiritual masochism, his insistence that we ought to hate and condemn ourselves.[20]

The mature Luther, I am happy to say, thinks quite differently. In a catechism written more than a decade later, for the benefit of anxious lay people rather than complacent monks, he teaches that knowing God *requires* us to seek what is good. For as he famously says in the opening words of his exposition of the Ten Commandments, "A god is that to which we look for all good."[21] This means that the first of all the commandments, which is, "You shall have no other gods besides me" (Exod. 20:3), cannot be obeyed unless we desire good things from the true God. It is as if God himself were saying: "Whatever good thing you lack, look to me for it and seek it from me."[22] There is no trace here of the notion that we must find these good things hidden under their opposites, or that seeking them from God is a kind of selfishness in which we merely use God. On the contrary, the "unselfish" attitude is what Luther now condemns. It's complacent monks, insisting on a life of pure self-giving, who cut themselves off from the one true God, the giver of all good things. Even in their prayers, "not one of them thinks of asking for the least thing" because in relation to God they are "not willing to receive

19. Luther, Romans Lectures, on Rom. 6:6, *LW* 25:313. See likewise Luther, Romans Lectures, on Rom. 5:4, *LW* 25:291–92. For Augustine on using and enjoying, see above, chap. 3, "Epistemology as Ethics."

20. In one of the most influential twentieth-century treatments of both Augustine and Luther, Anders Nygren, *Agape and Eros*, uses Luther's attack on self-centeredness to critique Augustine's teleological ethics. Nygren's scholarship is often first rate, but I think his ethical judgments are profoundly off kilter.

21. Luther, *Large Catechism*, discussion of the first of the Ten Commandments, in Tappert, *Book of Concord*, 365.

22. Luther, *Large Catechism*, discussion of the first of the Ten Commandments, in Tappert, *Book of Concord*, 365.

anything from him, but only to give him something."[23] If we want to obey the first commandment, then we will have to have the humility of desiring to receive what is good. We will have to get over our perverse and arrogant desire to be totally unselfish.

Gospel as Good Word

In order for the Gospel to function as good news, it must give us something good—something other than condemnation. Hence in his mature teaching Luther famously insists on distinguishing law from Gospel, God's word of accusation and condemnation from God's word of grace and forgiveness. To understand how he came to make this crucial distinction, we need to trace how the term "Gospel" (*Evangelium*) acquired a new meaning for him. It happened by stages—through an accumulation of insights that, despite the efforts of a multitude of scholars, cannot readily be reduced to one datable event or experience. We have a number of reminiscences from Luther's later years in which he describes his excitement at these insights,[24] but for purposes of understanding the meaning of Protestant theology we need not investigate which experiences got him so excited, but can focus instead on the texts written by Luther in which key concepts first appear.

To see where he is starting from, we should notice how far his early texts are from his later insistence on distinguishing Gospel from law. Near the beginning of his first Psalms lectures in 1513, he describes the Gospel as a kind of law, speaking of "the Gospel, the law of God," and "the law of the Gospel."[25] A bit later he treats "the law of Christ, the law of peace, the law of grace, the Gospel" as equivalent terms.[26] Behind this identification of law and Gospel is the medieval notion that in the Gospel Christ gives us a "new

23. Luther, *Large Catechism*, discussion of the Lord's Prayer, in Tappert, *Book of Concord*, 423.

24. The most famous is a reminiscence late in Luther's life about his discovery of the meaning of "the righteousness of God," in Luther's preface to the first collected edition of his Latin writings, *LW* 34:336–37. A great deal of scholarly effort has gone into trying to fix the date of this discovery, which is often identified as "the Reformation breakthrough." I think these efforts are mistaken for two reasons: (1) the insight about the righteousness of God is not distinctive of the Reformation but is already prominent in Augustine, *Spirit and the Letter* 11.18, which is well known to Luther and quoted in his Romans Lectures (*LW* 25:151), and (2) when Luther first deploys this Augustinian notion of the righteousness of God, he incorporates it into his project of justification by self-accusation, which is quite contrary to his later theology.

25. Luther, First Psalms Lectures, on Ps. 1:6, *LW* 10:28; on Ps. 2:9, *LW* 10:37.

26. Luther, First Psalms Lectures, on Ps. 72:1, *LW* 10:403.

law" different from the "old law" of Moses. When Luther wants to work out
the relation between law and Gospel in detail, however, he goes back beyond
medieval theology to Augustine's distinction between letter and Spirit, where
"letter" means an outward word and the Spirit is an inward gift of grace.
This explains how Luther can identify the Gospel with a certain kind of law,
when it is grasped inwardly and understood by faith: "The Law *spiritually
understood* is the same as the Gospel."[27] Gospel and law are not two different kinds of word, as in Luther's mature theology, but two different ways of
relating to the same word. Law is to Gospel as letter is to Spirit, and these
two in turn are related as outer is to inner. Hence the term "Gospel" does
not really refer to a kind of word at all, because it does not refer to anything
spoken externally. It is a label for what happens when the Spirit writes the
law of Christ on our hearts, through faith:

> The Gospel is not the law of Christ unless it be grasped by faith. Now, the law
> of the Lord [i.e., of Christ] is "living and active" [Heb. 4:12]; hence it is not a
> matter of letters and words. But otherwise *faith in words is always under the
> Law*, as long as one does not have the faith of the Gospel. . . . So Christ says . . .
> that he will write His law on their hearts.[28]

The Gospel is simply the law of Christ taken inwardly to heart by faith and
thus active in the heart, through the power of the Spirit. It is not the letter
of the law, and because it is not the letter it is not an external word—and
thus is not a word at all in the literal sense. For at this stage in his career,
Luther is Augustinian enough to think that no external thing can have power
to save us.

The way the law of the Gospel is inwardly active, as we have seen, is by
getting us to accuse and condemn ourselves. This is tied to Luther's early view
of Christ, whose cross means that we can find justification only by sharing
in Christ's suffering, in which righteousness is hidden deeply underneath the
experience of condemnation. The cross is the paradigm of the "coincidence
of opposites" in which all believers must participate, with the result that being
justified by faith in Christ means embracing evil for ourselves:

> Thus he who gives up God, creatures, and himself too, and freely and willingly
> goes into nothingness and death, and of his own accord confesses his damna-
> tion . . . has surely satisfied God and is righteous. . . . He does this by faith, by
> which a man takes captive his own thoughts by the word of the cross and denies

---

27. Luther, First Psalms Lectures, from a gloss on Ps. 11(12):7, *WA* 3:96, not translated in *LW*.
28. Luther, First Psalms Lectures, on Ps 1:6, *LW* 10:30.

himself and is dead to all things. . . . And thus alone does he live to God, "to whom all are alive," even the dead.[29]

This interpretation of faith in the cross as a coincidence of opposites is given the label "theology of the cross" (*theologia crucis*) in some of Luther's more famous writings in 1518, a year or two later.[30] It represents the pinnacle of his project of spiritual masochism, which a surprising number of scholars actually admire. For my part, however, I am glad that it quickly disappears from view as Luther learns to make a clear distinction between law and Gospel.

The basis of the distinction is a conception of Gospel that looks at Christ differently, as one in whom grace and righteousness are openly preached and given, not hidden under condemnation. By 1520, Luther's early and innovative "theology of the cross," with all its spiritual masochism, is replaced by the ancient and traditional notion of Christ taking on our evils and giving us all his goods. In 1521, Luther sums up the import of this "wondrous exchange" (*admirabile commercium*) for the doctrine of justification by saying: "Our sins are no longer ours but Christ's, and the righteousness of Christ is not Christ's, but ours."[31] This theme is not wholly absent from his earlier work, however. In his lectures on Romans, for example, Luther turns for a moment from his concern to undermine the complacency of his fellow monks and gives pastoral consideration to the conscience that is burdened by a sense of inward accusation. If a believer in Christ finds his heart accusing him, Luther says, "he will immediately turn away and turn to Christ, saying, 'But He has made satisfaction, He is righteous, He is my defense, He died for me. He has made His righteousness mine, and my sin His. If He has made my sin His, then I have it no longer—I am free. And if He has made His righteousness mine, then I *am righteous now* with the same righteousness as He. My sin cannot absorb Him, but is absorbed in the infinite depths of His righteousness.'"[32] We can be righteous, even now, because by faith Christ's righteousness is ours, while our sins are no longer ours but his. That we are righteous already in this life is an implication of Luther's conviction, which we examined in chapter 5, that a believer is "at the same time righteous and a sinner" (*simul justus et peccator*). Yet it is not an implication he says much about in his early

29. Luther, Romans Lectures, on Rom. 10:12, *WA* 56:419 (= *LW* 25:411). The quotation is from Luke 20:38. Cf. the development of the same theme a little earlier in the Romans Lectures, on Rom. 9:3, *LW* 25:382–83.

30. Key examples are in Luther, *Heidelberg Disputation*, discussion of theses 20–24, *LW* 31:52–55, and Luther, *Explanations of the 95 Theses*, near the end of the long discussion of thesis 58, *LW* 31:225–27.

31. Luther, Second Psalms Lectures (1519–21 *Operationes in Psalmos*), on Ps. 22:2, *WA* 5:608.

32. Luther, Romans Lectures, on Rom. 2:15, *WA* 56:204 (= *LW* 25:188).

works. It is a Christological theme that will later become fundamental for his thinking about what makes the Gospel good news. But notice that at this stage the notion that we are righteous *now*—even in this life—comes to us only as one of our own thoughts, not through the proclamation of the Gospel or any other word spoken to us.[33] At this point the Christological theme of wondrous exchange sits in uneasy contradiction with the overall direction of Luther's thought, where the theology of the cross aims at self-hatred and condemnation, not comfort and joy.

Luther begins to distinguish Gospel from law late in 1516 when he starts speaking of the Gospel as a word of consolation and peace for troubled consciences. Commenting on Paul's quotation from Isaiah, "How beautiful are the feet of those who preach the Gospel of peace" (Rom. 10:15), he describes the Gospel as beautiful, lovely, desirable, and sweet to the ear, because it announces the forgiveness of sins and fulfillment of the law by Christ. Now he says, quite starkly, that "the Law is evil, and the Gospel good," because "the Law oppresses the conscience with sins, but the Gospel frees the conscience and brings peace through faith in Christ."[34] This sounds more like Luther's later teaching, except that there is no notion that we should believe we are justified by faith in this good word. Indeed, the good things this word brings to us, including the peace it announces, are hidden, "not exhibited to feeling but announced by the Word and . . . perceived only by faith, which is to say, without experience, until the future life comes."[35] It is a good and beautiful word that we ought to believe, but it evidently remains external, not affecting our feeling or experience—not comforting or consoling us, as Luther later insists that the Gospel must do. It makes no inward impression on our hearts, where all good things must remain hidden under their opposites.

Luther had presented a less stark contrast between law and Gospel just a little earlier in the Romans Lectures. Recalling the opening of the letter to the Romans, where Paul says that the Gospel of Christ was promised by the prophets of the Old Testament, he adds now that the Old Testament law makes the same promise: Christ is the one "whom the Law promised and the Gospel exhibits."[36] Although the Gospel can, as before, be a word of

33. See likewise the appearance of this theme in Luther, letter to George Spenlein, Apr. 8, 1516, *LW* 48:12–13, where again there is no proclamation of good news, but just a thought we should think about Christ.

34. Luther, Romans Lectures, on Rom. 10:15, *LW* 25:416.

35. Luther, Romans Lectures, *WA* 56:425 (= *LW* 25:416).

36. Luther, Romans Lectures, on Rom. 7:6, *WA* 56:338 (= *LW* 25:326). Cf. the promises of the OT prophets discussed in Luther's comments on Rom. 1:1–4, *LW* 25:145–48.

judgment that rebukes and condemns, "properly speaking it is Gospel when it preaches Christ."[37] In a remark that comes close to his mature teaching, Luther distinguishes law and Gospel as two kinds of external word: "The Law commands us to have charity and Jesus Christ, but the Gospel offers and exhibits them both."[38] But this is not quite the mature teaching, because the Gospel here only offers and exhibits but does not *give* us Christ. Luther does not yet have the notion of an external word with the power to give us, in the present, what it promises. Yet at this point he does have a conceptual framework in which there is space, indeed a great gaping hole, that is waiting to be filled with such a notion.

Promise and Prayer

To complete our sketch of Luther's early theology, we need to say more about the hopeful side of his hopeful spiritual masochism. As we saw in the last chapter, young Luther can designate the process of justification either by its starting point or by its endpoint. Looked at from the starting point, which is sin and unrighteousness, the process can be called penitence, because it consists of humble confession of sin, self-accusation, and self-condemnation. But when we look toward the endpoint, which we have yet to reach, we call it a process of justification or being made righteous. In between, we remain in fact unrighteous for as long as the process continues, but we can be called "righteous in hope," because we can describe ourselves in terms of the endpoint as well as the starting point. That is the sense in which each one of us is both righteous and a sinner at the same time (*simul justus et peccator*): we are still sinners but we are headed toward righteousness, and our current state can be described in terms of either point of the process, its beginning or its end. But even to say we are righteous in hope requires some ground of hope, some assurance of our arrival at the endpoint—which is not an assurance we can find in ourselves. And that's where a crucial role is played by the notion of a divine *promise*, which will later become an indispensable component in Luther's mature conception of the Gospel.

37. Luther, Romans Lectures, *LW* 25:326. Luther also speaks of the proper work of the Gospel in a sermon on Dec. 21, 1516 (*WA* 1:112–13), where he contrasts it with the "alien work" of the Gospel, which is to show that we are all sinners. In this sermon the operative contrast is not between law and Gospel but between the alien and proper work of the Gospel, based on Luther's reading of Isa. 28:21. The key shift in Luther's theology takes place when these two different ways of God's working are connected to two different forms of God's word, law and Gospel. For a summary of this sermon, see Wicks, *Man Yearning for Grace*, 155–58.

38. Luther, Romans Lectures, on Rom. 7:6, *WA* 56:338 (= *LW* 25:326).

In the Romans Lectures Luther compares the promise of God to the word of a doctor who assures a sick man he will recover, so long as he follows the doctor's orders.[39] The implication is that he must continue to take his medicine, swallowing the bitter pill of self-accusation according to the doctor's word.[40] The patient is still sick, but he is regarded as already cured—reckoned or counted healthy. All these verbs ("regarded," "reckoned," and "counted," along with "imputed") can be used to render the Latin verbs *imputare* and *reputare*, which Luther uses here. Thus a man in the process of justification is "a sinner in fact but a righteous man by the sure imputation and promise of God."[41] The promise is essential to the process—it's the only way to be sure you're really heading toward the goal—but it does not give you what is promised. At present you are only counted as cured, not actually cured, for the promise will not actually be fulfilled until you reach the end of the process and are fully healed of sin. By contrast, Luther's mature theology will treat the Gospel as the promise of God that actually gives us Christ and his righteousness in this present life. It does not bring us to the end of the process right away, but it does more than simply reckon us to be what we are not. As a gift of Christ's righteousness, which is the very righteousness of God, it replaces works of penitence as the driving force in the process of justification in Luther's mature theology.

Since we lack a promise that can give us the righteousness God requires of us, we must seek it by our own words: we must pray for grace and justification. When we see that God commands us to have the virtue of continence, for example, and yet we know that no one can have continence unless God gives it, then we must pray, in words that Augustine made famous in the *Confessions*: "Give what you command, and then command whatever you want."[42] Augustine explains this prayer for grace in his treatise *The Spirit and the Letter*, which had an enormous impact on Luther's thinking in the Romans Lectures. Prayer is the way we flee for refuge to the Spirit of grace after being humbled and terrified by the letter of the law. In a passage Luther quotes twice in the Romans Lectures, Augustine writes:

> What the law of works requires by threatening, the law of faith acquires by believing. . . . By the law of works God says, "Do what I command." By the

39. Luther, Romans Lectures, on Rom. 4:7, *LW* 25:260–61, one of the most important passages in the Romans Lectures.

40. The implication is made explicit in Luther, Romans Lectures, Rom. 3:7, *LW* 25:202–3.

41. Luther, Romans Lectures, on Rom. 4:7, *LW* 25:260 (= *WA* 56:272). The phrase "in fact" here is *re vera*, a variation of *in re*.

42. Augustine, *Confessions* 10:29.40. Augustine is thinking of Wisdom of Solomon 8:21, which in the Latin reads: "For I knew I could not be continent unless God gave it" (cf. *Confessions* 6:11.20).

law of faith what is said to God [that is, by humble prayer] is, "Give what you command."[43]

Faith here does not mean believing in a divine word of grace but praying for grace. The process of justification, as it looks forward to righteousness rather than back to our sin, means we are continually seeking grace by humble prayer.

This posed no problem for Augustine, because he conceived of prayer as a form of love, part of the longing that continually pulled us upward on our journey to God. The admonition "Pray without ceasing" (1 Thess. 5:17) means for Augustine, "Desire without ceasing the happy life, which can only be eternal, from him who alone can give it."[44] As I have argued elsewhere, the experience of grace in Augustine is not like the kind of Protestant conversion experience that happens only once in lifetime, but like the ongoing experience of monks at prayer, drawn ever deeper into love and contemplation as they pray and receive grace upon grace.[45] Luther's early theology, however, aimed to create a different kind of monk, one who was drawn ever deeper into self-hatred and awareness of sin. In that context, the continual prayer for grace means that believers "spend their whole life seeking justification."[46] They are "always begging, seeking, asking to be justified by the groans of their heart, the voice of their works, the works of their bodies, never standing still, never apprehending, with none of their works putting an end to obtaining righteousness but waiting for it as something always still outside of them, while they still live and are always in their sins."[47]

The work of our prayers for grace never ends in this life, for "we must always be praying and working [*orandum et operandum*] that grace and the Spirit may grow."[48] Justification by faith alone thus means a lifetime of working at prayer as well as self-accusation. Luther hastens to add that he is not speaking of works by which we are justified but rather "works which are performed in order that we may seek justification," which means they are "no longer works of the law but of grace and faith."[49] This distinction between

43. Luther, Romans Lectures, on Rom. 3:21, WA 56:256–57 (= LW 25:243), where Luther is quoting Augustine, *Spirit and the Letter* 13.22, which in turn is explaining Paul's phrase "the law of faith" (Rom. 3:27). The bracketed insertion is Luther's. Luther quotes the passage again, Romans Lectures, on Rom. 3:27, LW 25:251. For more in-depth discussion of Luther's use of Augustine's treatise *Spirit and the Letter*, see Cary, "Augustine and Luther."

44. Augustine, Letter 130:9.18. The whole of this long letter could be designated Augustine's treatise on prayer.

45. Cary, *Inner Grace*, 110.

46. Luther, Romans Lectures, on Rom. 3:27, LW 25:252.

47. Luther, Romans Lectures, on Rom. 3:27, WA 56:264 (= LW 25:251–52).

48. Luther, Romans Lectures, on Rom. 3:21, WA 56:258 (= LW 25:245).

49. Luther, Romans Lectures, on Rom. 3:27, LW 25:252.

works of the law and works of grace and faith, which makes it possible to combine works with justification by faith alone, is not one that Luther maintains in his mature theology. But because at this point he recognizes the Augustinian prayer for grace as a kind of spiritual work, he is willing to say things that he will later vehemently repudiate. He even affirms that because our justification is incomplete, we are "always under the works of the law."[50]

We must keep working because the prayer for grace is never quite answered in this life. As Luther puts it, "We all pray, 'Give what You command,' and yet we do not receive."[51] Hence, although we are justified only by faith, faith is not sufficient to justify us, not even when accompanied by the works of grace and faith. "*We all believe* and speak, confess and work," Luther explains, "and yet *we are not all justified*."[52] So we can believe and yet not be justified. This follows from Luther's early understanding of the process of justification: "For God has not justified us"—another thing the mature Luther would not say!—"that is, He has not made us perfectly righteous or completed our righteousness, but he has begun, in order to perfect it."[53]

Fear and Love

Since we remain always unjustified and unrighteous in this life, we must be always in fear, young Luther teaches his monks.[54] He wants them to keep examining themselves using tools such as Augustine's counterfactual test, described in the last chapter, so that they remain uncertain whether their good works are any good at all. The result will be that "they who truly do good works, do nothing without always considering, Who knows that the grace of God is acting with me in this work? Who lets me know that my good intention is from God? How do I know that what I have done . . . is acceptable to God?"[55]

The motto for this aspect of Luther's doctrine comes from the Latin (Vulgate) translation of Job 9:28, "I feared all my works."[56] This fear of our works humbles us and drives us to pray for grace, so that "grace is found through

---

50. Luther, Romans Lectures, on Rom. 3:22, *LW* 25:239.

51. Luther, Romans Lectures, on Rom. 3:21, *WA* 56:257 (= *LW* 25:244).

52. Luther, Romans Lectures, on Rom. 3:21, *WA* 56:257 (= *LW* 25:244).

53. Luther, Romans Lectures, on Rom. 3:21, *WA* 56:258 (= *LW* 25:245). *LW* has "not *yet* justified us" with no basis in the text.

54. For this recurrent theme of being "always in fear" see Luther, Romans Lectures, on Rom. 4:7; 4:13; 9:6; 14:1, *LW* 25:268, 278, 385, 497–98.

55. Luther, Romans Lectures, on Rom. 14:1, *LW* 25:497.

56. *Verebar omnia opera mea.* Luther quotes or refers to this passage when commenting on Rom. 3:10; 3:22; 4:13; 14:1, *LW* 25:222 (where *LW* mistranslates, substituting "suffering" for "works"), 239, 278, and 497.

fear."[57] This is a dubious teaching, especially when Luther immediately adds that through this grace, "a man is made willing for good works," implicitly contrasting it with the elicited acts of the will which he has just finished criticizing.[58] Here Luther is swimming upstream against a strong Augustinian current, which identifies true willingness for good works with love, not fear. What grace gives us, Augustine teaches, is precisely a delight in God and his will rather than a fearful and slavish submission to it. Luther is well aware of this teaching, and agrees that there are no truly good works except those that are done out of a will that is not slavish but "free and cheerful toward the works of the law."[59] Yet he also wants to make sure that we never know whether we have such a will. Going beyond Augustine, he insists that "those who are truly righteous not only sigh and plead for the grace of God . . . they see that they can never see fully how deep is the evil of their will and how far it extends, as if the depth of their evil will were infinite."[60] If we diligently apply something like Augustine's counterfactual test, he suggests once again, then "who knows or who can know, even if it seems to him he is doing good and avoiding evil according to that will [i.e., one that is free and cheerful toward the works of the law], whether it is really so?"[61]

I call this a dubious teaching because it is hard to see how such a free and cheerful will could arise in a person who is working as hard as he can to (a) agree with a word of God that condemns him, (b) seek a justification that he never believes he has, and (c) cultivate the fear that all his works are the result of the bottomless iniquity of his own self-will. How does someone who believes these things ever come to love God rather than fear him? Where in this teaching is there any ground for a will that is free, cheerful, and delighted with God? How do you delight in a God whose word toward you is always condemnation, and who moreover demands that you love him with a free and cheerful will, which you must never believe you actually have? It seems much more likely that a monk who adopts such a theology will end up hating the God whom he must regard as his adversary and accuser. Or he will be driven to anguish and despair by a kind of vicious circle, in which fear drives out love, resulting in a slavish and resentful obedience, for which he has every reason to accuse himself and anticipate God's further condemnation, which

57. Luther, Romans Lectures, on Rom. 4:13, LW 25:498.
58. Luther, Romans Lectures, on Rom. 4:13, LW 25:498. This is four pages after the vignette about the bored monk and his "elicited act" of loving God (LW 25:494), discussed in the previous chapter.
59. Luther, Romans Lectures, on Rom. 3:9, LW 25:220.
60. Luther, Romans Lectures, on Rom. 3:10, LW 25:220–21.
61. Luther, Romans Lectures, on Rom. 3:10, WA 56:236 (= LW 25:221). LW misleadingly translates *voluntas* as "frame of mind" here.

gives him yet more reason to fear rather than love God, resulting in a yet more slavish and resentful obedience, and so on.

This may help explain why, when he looked back many years later, Luther regularly described the monastic life as a kind of torture for the conscience. His own theology at the time made the torture impossible to escape. He recalls how he wearied his confessors with his unending self-accusations, until one of them aptly diagnosed his problem: "Man, God is not angry with you. You are angry with God!"[62]

What alternative did he have? Being no Platonist, he did not think of God as what we aim to see in intellectual vision.[63] He never imagined seeing God but only hearing his word, and in this early period of his career he was convinced that all the power in God's word lay in its ability to accuse, judge, and condemn. It is quite extraordinary, in fact, how little visual imagery there is anywhere in Luther's writings—how overwhelmingly verbal and auditory his imagination is, filled with imaginary dialogues, songs and sighs, whispers and groans, words spoken and heard, with occasionally a tactile metaphor such as taking hold of Christ, clinging to his promise or groping where the word is. One wonders if he was severely near-sighted, in those days before glasses. At any rate, Luther is a theologian who insists on hearing God, not seeing him, and in his early works the word of God that he insisted on hearing could speak in the present tense only of condemnation. There is no way out of the trap he has set for himself until he is forced to hear a different kind of word, one that is kind and comforting as well as strong to save, because it gives him in the present a gracious God he can love. He needs a promise that can bestow on him the delight and love of God that the commandment requires of him. When he finally recognizes that such a promise has already been given to him, he has found the truth for which he will fight the rest of his life.

---

62. Bainton, *Here I Stand*, 41, based on Luther's table talk #122, *LW* 54:15.

63. One of Luther's few sharp disagreements with Augustine stemmed from Luther's rejection of the concept of intellectual vision, as we shall see in chap. 11, "Against Augustine: Where to Find God."

7

Luther the Reformer

Gospel as Sacramental Promise

According to Luther and a great deal of Protestant theology after him, the Gospel is a saving word of promise that gives us everlasting life in Christ. This makes it look very much like a Catholic sacrament, which is an efficacious means of grace that confers the grace it signifies. The similarity turns out not to be accidental. A sacramental conception of the Gospel is essential to Luther's mature theology as it develops in 1518–20, replacing his earlier theology of justification by self-accusation and self-hatred. What is new and distinctive about Luther's view of the power of faith, as we shall see in detail in this chapter, stems from his sacramental conception of the Gospel.

Sacramental Signs

"Word and sacrament" is a favorite cliché among Lutherans, and for good reason. It aptly indicates a fundamental parallel in Luther's mature theology: both the word of the Gospel and the sacraments instituted by Christ are outward means by which God gives us Christ and all that is his, including his righteousness, holiness, blessing, salvation, and everlasting life. Word and sacrament go together because every true sacrament is based on the word of God, a Scriptural promise of Christ from which it derives its truth and power. Moreover, when the sacrament is actually performed, the word of God is addressed to its hearers in person, as when Christ says through the mouth of a minister: "This is my body, given for you." On a Lutheran view, this is Christ giving himself through his word, according to his Scriptural promise, to those who are present to hear and believe. To have faith in this sacramental word is not only to believe it's true, but also to realize that when Christ says "you," he means *me*. Since Christ is God, this means God is giving himself to me in his own flesh, so that I may be united with him in person.

The parallel between word and sacrament has a conceptual structure that goes back to Augustine, who treats both words and sacraments as signs.[1] In Augustinian semiotics, words are outward signs that signify an inner thought of the heart, while sacraments are outward signs that signify an inner grace of God in the heart. Hence in medieval thinking both word and sacrament are understood in terms of the relationship between an outward *sign* and the inward *thing signified*: the *signum* and the *res significata*—or simply *signum* and *res*, for short. Every word that comes out of our mouths, sacred or profane, has an inner *res* in our minds that it properly signifies. A sacrament, on the other hand, is a very specific sacred sign, consecrated by the word of God. Strictly speaking, the sacrament (*sacramentum*) is simply the *signum* itself, precisely because the term "sacrament" refers by definition to a type of sign. But of course to understand any sign, one must identify the thing it signifies, so any account of the nature of a sacrament will refer to both *signum* and *res*, both the outward sacramental sign, such as immersion in the water of baptism, and the particular grace it signifies, such as death and rebirth in Christ.

In the twelfth century a key point was added to the Augustinian tradition when the sacraments of the Gospel were treated as signs that not only signify but also confer a gift of grace upon those who properly receive them. Thus in the first chapter of Peter Lombard's *Sentences*, which was the primary textbook of theology from the twelfth century up to the time of Luther's education, he writes: "There are some signs whose whole use is in signifying, not justifying, i.e., which are used merely to signify grace, such as some legal sacraments, but other signs which not only signify but confer what inwardly helps, such as the Gospel sacraments."[2] Lombard's distinction between legal sacraments and Gospel sacraments is a precursor to Luther's distinction between law and Gospel, though it is not quite the same thing. The "legal sacraments" Lombard is thinking of are the ceremonies and sacrifices of the Old Testament (which he elsewhere calls the "Old Law"), and the "Gospel

---

1. For this Augustinian conception of the sacraments, as well as the medieval development that makes them efficacious means of conferring grace, see Cary, *Outward Signs*, chap. 6.

2. Lombard, *Sententiae* 1:1.1.

sacraments" are those of the New Testament (which he calls the "New Law"), whereas Luther thinks that any word that effectually gives us Christ is not law but Gospel, even if it is found in the Old Testament. Thus Luther finds the Gospel in the psalms and prophets when they prophesy the coming of Christ. The Lutheran law/Gospel distinction is not the difference between Old Testament and New Testament but the difference between any word of God that tells us what to do and any word of God that gives us Christ.

The law/Gospel distinction began to take its mature form as Luther came to think of the sacraments as efficacious means of grace with the power to bestow Christ and all his benefits on those who have faith in the sacrament (*fides sacramenti*). Always what gives the sacraments this power is the word of God, which has its gracious effect in us only when it is believed. This line of sacramental thinking begins to develop in Luther's writing only after his famous 95 Theses kindled the great controversy that led to the Reformation. Since the theses were about the sale of indulgences, the controversy initially centered on the sacrament of penance, which is the practical context for the theology of indulgences. Judging from Luther's previous writings, this seems to have been the first time that he had to think seriously about the nature of a sacrament. It is thinking that opened the door to changes far more profound than he had anticipated when he first wrote against indulgences.

Believing the Word of Absolution

Before the 95 Theses made Luther famous throughout Europe as a Reformer of the church, he was a reformer in a more local way. As a professor at the University of Wittenberg, he was working to reform the curriculum and move its center of gravity away from Aristotle and Lombard and toward Augustine and the Bible.[3] He also preached at his monastery and in the town church, which meant he had pastoral responsibilities for both monks and laity. It was evidently these pastoral responsibilities that led him to compose his 95 Theses on the theology of indulgences late in 1517. His reforming efforts started taking a much wider scope after the theses were published. With the new media of printing, the theses went viral—probably the first text in history to do so—as printers in various towns, acting independently of Luther, reprinted them in numerous editions throughout Germany. As a result they were spreading far beyond Wittenberg by the time they were forwarded to the pope in early 1518.

3. See Luther, letter to John Lang, May 18, 1517, *LW* 48:41–42.

Luther was soon very busy defending the theses from attacks, which required him to think about the penitential life in a new way: in the context of the sacrament of penance. As the opening theses make clear, his focus at the time he composed the 95 Theses was still on inward penitence, the lifelong struggle of seeking justification through self-hatred. Hence the first two theses assert that when the Lord Jesus said "Repent," it was this lifelong struggle that he had in mind, not the sacrament of penance.[4] Still, the sacrament had its place in the life of the church, and within it there was a place for indulgences, as Luther acknowledged. He did not yet altogether reject the legitimacy of indulgences, though he was deeply skeptical of the indulgence-sellers' claims that they could shorten someone's time in purgatory. Above all, he questioned the *usefulness* of indulgences, because he thought they were likely to be harmful to people's spiritual lives, leading them to be complacent and to neglect the inward penitential work of self-hatred. In his concluding theses he claimed that relying on indulgences is like saying "Peace, peace" when there is no peace.[5] It is clear that his main pastoral concern at this time was still to undermine false security rather than to comfort terrified consciences.

What evidently changed the focus of Luther's concern was an aspect of the sacrament of penance that he had not discussed before in any of his writings. This was the word of absolution, in which the confessor (i.e., the priest) says to the penitent: "I absolve you of your sins in the name of the Father, of the Son, and of the Holy Spirit." The word of absolution mimics the words of baptism ("I baptize you in the name of the Father, and of the Son, and of the Holy Spirit") and, like baptism, is based on the word of Christ. In this case the word of Christ is his promise to Peter, "Whatever you loose on earth shall be loosed in heaven" (Matt. 16:19). The connection is clearer in Latin than in English, because the Latin for "absolve" (*absolvere*) is derived from the Latin for "loose" (*solvere*). The confessor's word of absolution is thus based on Christ's promise, and that is why the penitent must believe it. To doubt that your sins are forgiven after hearing this word is in effect to call Christ a liar. This is the conviction that grows on Luther in the year 1518, which results in a reworking of the doctrine of justification by faith alone and the emergence of his mature conception of the Gospel.

4. Luther, 95 Theses, *LW* 31:25–26.

5. Luther, 95 Theses, thesis 92, *LW* 31:33, quoting Jer. 6:14. This overarching concern about how indulgences might promote complacency is also the concluding note in the much less well-known but more clearly argued treatise on indulgences (*Tractatus de Indulgentiis*), which he wrote at the same time as the 95 Theses. The whole treatise is translated, with commentary, in Wicks, *Man Yearning for Grace*, 238–61.

The sacrament of penance gives Luther a word of God requiring him to believe not that he is a damned sinner who should hate himself but that he is a forgiven sinner who must be at peace with God, comforted and consoled, because his sins are loosed and absolved according to the promise of Christ. All the considerable resources of Luther's vehement repudiation of back talk, his sense that we must never contradict the word of God when it comes as an adversary to our own thinking, now require him to stop accusing and condemning himself. For if Christ himself promises that his sins are forgiven, who is Luther to say otherwise? It is therefore no longer presumptuous to believe he is actually justified. In fact it is required—unless he wants to say God himself is lying to him.

This is a line of thought we can see developing, in fits and starts, in key texts of 1518, where it eventually replaces the spiritual masochism of his so-called theology of the cross, in which we receive grace only by hating ourselves.[6] The clearest way to trace the development in readily available English translations is through Luther's first book-length publication, the *Explanations of the 95 Theses*. His explanation of thesis 7, for example, tries to incorporate the word of absolution into his long-standing program of spiritual masochism, but doesn't quite succeed. He tries repeating his teaching that justification is hidden under its opposite, maintaining that "when God begins to justify a man, he first of all condemns him."[7] This is the "alien work" of God, by which "sinners are turned to hell."[8] He describes what this means a few pages later, in what is probably his most vivid description of his own experience of *Anfechtung*, the temptation that comes when the conscience is assaulted by the thought of one's own guilt in God's sight. The experience involves no fire or brimstone (which in fact never played an important role in how Luther imagined damnation) but only terror at a word, when God seems horribly angry, together with all creation, and "there is no flight, no comfort, within or without, but *all things accuse*."[9] Hell for Luther is like hearing everything

---

6. The key discussion of these texts is by Oswald Bayer, *Promissio*, chap. 4. I focus here on texts readily available in English, passing over two important little documents: the 1518 *Sermo de poenitentia* (WA 1:329–34), whose conclusion presents ideas that are developed in the explanation of thesis 38 (discussed below), and also, most importantly, a little-known set of disputation theses composed in 1518, *Pro veritate inquirenda et timoratis conscientiis consolandis* ("For investigating the truth and comforting frightened consciences"), which Bayer identifies as the first fully Reformational document. These theses are translated in *Lutheran Forum* 44/4 (Winter 2010): 34–35. Many of the theses are incorporated into Luther's 1519 sermon *The Sacrament of Penance*, LW 35:9–22, discussed below.

7. Luther, *Explanations of the 95 Theses*, on thesis 7, LW 31:99.

8. Luther, *Explanations of the 95 Theses*, on thesis 7, LW 31:99.

9. Luther, *Explanations of the 95 Theses*, on thesis 15, LW 31:129. Luther is describing the experience of purgatory in this life, which he believes is very near the experience of hell itself.

in the world condemn you, speaking a word of accusation you can never escape. The soul experiencing this is reduced to sheer helplessness, a "stark naked desire for help" that goes unanswered.[10] And yet this is the state of one who is justified by grace, according to his explanation of thesis 7, which follows the familiar path of Luther's early doctrine in which we are justified by agreeing with God's judgment against us. Precisely in this experience of condemnation and terror, the infused grace of justification is already present, "hidden under the form of wrath."[11]

Only afterward comes the new element in Luther's thinking: the word of absolution that assures the terrified sinner that his sins are forgiven, giving him peace of conscience. The stark naked desire for help now receives help, for there is one word at least that does not condemn him, and it is backed by the promise of Christ himself. Still, the absolution is only the priest's remission, an external word that comforts the terrified heart, not the hidden inner grace that brings about true penitence of heart, contrition, and justification. The order is therefore: "God's remission effects grace," and then "the priest's remission brings peace."[12] At this brief and unstable point in the development of his theology, Luther does not think the word of absolution actually absolves sins. Rather, it declares that they have already been absolved through the grace of justification present in hidden fashion in a heart that feels nothing but damnation.

The project of justification by self-condemnation is about to be cut short, however, because the penitent is required to believe the word of absolution. Suddenly Luther seems to realize that unrelenting self-hatred is not a good way to progress in righteousness. He writes, "Conscience, already justified by grace, would by its own anxiety cast out grace if it had not been aided by faith in the presence of grace, through the ministry of the priest."[13] What the priest's absolution gives the sinner is a kind word from another human being, an external word rather than the internalized self-accusation that Luther had earlier called "Gospel." And because it is not merely a human word but based on the promise of God, the penitent must believe it, or else lose the inner grace and remission of sins he has gained by his self-condemnation: "Indeed the sin would have remained if he had not believed that it was remitted. For the remission of sin and the gift of grace are not enough; one must also believe that one's sin has been remitted." The result is an odd and deeply inconsistent

10. Luther, *Explanations of the 95 Theses*, on thesis 15, LW 31:129.
11. Luther, *Explanations of the 95 Theses*, on thesis 7, LW 31:101.
12. Luther, *Explanations of the 95 Theses*, on thesis 7, LW 31:102.
13. All quotations in this paragraph are from Luther, *Explanations of the 95 Theses*, on thesis 7, LW 31:104.

picture: the penitent has succeeded in obtaining remission of sins by believing he is condemned, but now he must do an about-face and believe in the absolution and remission of his sins instead, which means the whole project of obtaining a justification hidden under its opposite must be given up as soon as it is accomplished, and he must trade terror for peace of conscience. Luther does not seem to realize it yet, but the whole masochistic project of the so-called theology of the cross has just been overturned. Now instead of having grace and remission of sins by believing in a word of condemnation, he has them only to the extent that he believes he has them, based on the word of absolution. "You have it because you believe you have it," he writes, and then adds: "You have only as much as you believe according to the promise of Christ."

This was not the first time that Luther had warned that you have only as much as you believe.[14] But now, along with the reversal of the project of justification by self-condemnation, faith itself is about to mean something different. It is not just agreeing with our adversary and repressing back talk; it is the power of salvation, because it is based on the truth of God's promise of grace. By the time he comes to the explanation of thesis 38, Luther has dropped the notion of justification by self-condemnation altogether and replaced it with justification by faith in the gracious promise of Christ. The picture that results is much more straightforward and consistent. Now the depth and sincerity of one's inward penitence or contrition cease to be decisive. Someone who is not sufficiently contrite, or doesn't think he is, should simply believe the word of absolution and trust that "you have as much as you believe."[15] This faith, Luther goes on to explain, is why sacraments are efficacious signs of grace. The absolution does not merely declare or announce a remission of sins that has already taken place. It is efficacious, which is to say, it really and effectively absolves and remits sins—and not because of the sincerity of our contrition but simply because we believe it. Indeed, it is only this faith, not our contrition or inward penitence, that justifies us, for "we ought to place our hope in Christ's word, not in our penitence [*contritionem*]."[16]

---

14. The precursor to the famous motto "Believe it and you have it" (*Glaubst du, so hast du*) from Luther, *Holy Sacrament of Baptism* (sermon, 1519), WA 2:733 (= LW 35:38), served originally as a warning against unbelief and back talk rather than an assurance of grace. This is an important point on which Gyllenkrok, *Rechtfertigung und Heiligung*, 30 and 74, corrects the influential view of Holl, "Die Rechtfertigungslehre in Luthers Vorlesung über den Römerbrief," in Holl, *Gesammelte Aufsätze*, 134.

15. Luther, *Explanations of the 95 Theses*, on thesis 38, WA 1:595 (= LW 31:193).

16. Luther, *Explanations of the 95 Theses*, on thesis 38, LW 31:194 (= WA 1:595). LW frequently renders *contritio* with "penitence."

At this point justification by faith alone, which in the lectures on Romans had meant submitting to a word of condemnation, requires us to believe in a word of grace instead. The turn toward inward penitence and self-accusation has been replaced by an outward turn, toward the external word of absolution, a sacramental word based on Christ's promise in Scripture. Now we hear something that sounds like the Luther whose preaching would soon console anxious consciences throughout the Christian world: "Take care, therefore, that you do not in any manner trust in your own contrition but completely and only in the word of your kindest and most faithful Savior, Jesus Christ! Your heart may deceive you, but he will not deceive you."[17] The word of God is no longer the accusation of an adversary but the kind word of a friend.

The Double Structure of God's Word

This new development in Luther's notion of faith was put to the test almost immediately.[18] In October 1518 he traveled to the Diet, a kind of parliament of the Holy Roman Empire, which was held that year in Augsburg (not to be confused with the later Diet of Augsburg in 1530, when the Augsburg Confession was composed), and there he had a series of private discussions with Thomas de Vio Cajetan, a cardinal who was the papal legate, the pope's official representative at the Diet. Cajetan was the most accomplished theologian of his time, who wrote a complete commentary on Thomas Aquinas's massive *Summa Theologica*.[19] He prepared carefully for the discussions by reading all the works of Luther he could find at Augsburg, including the *Explanations of the 95 Theses* as well as Luther's 1518 sermon on penance (the Latin *Sermo de poenitentia*), whose concluding section presents the same themes we have seen in the explanation of thesis 38. We know what Cajetan thought about these writings, because as part of his preparations he wrote a series of short treatises on the issues Luther raised.[20] While questions about the nature of indulgences and the power of the pope were major issues, Cajetan also objected to Luther's insistence that faith in the sacrament of penance must be certain and undoubting. When Cajetan raised this issue in his discussions with Luther, it was the first time that the doctrine of justification by faith alone became a

17. Luther, *Explanations of the 95 Theses*, on thesis 38, LW 31:195.
18. The connection between Luther's writings in the first half of 1518 and his encounter with Cajetan is most helpfully discussed by Wicks, "*Fides sacramenti—fides specialis.*"
19. For a brief but very informative biography, see Wicks's introduction to Cajetan, *Cajetan Responds*, 1–46.
20. Collected under the title of "Augsburg Treatises, 1518," in Cajetan, *Cajetan Responds*, 47–98.

matter of controversy in the church. Luther amplified the importance of the controversy a month later, when he published an account of the discussions in a little book, *Acta Augustana* or *Proceedings at Augsburg.*

Cajetan, whose job was to reconcile Luther with Rome if possible, was struck by the novelty of Luther's view that faith in God's word requires us to be certain our sins are forgiven when we hear the word of absolution in the sacrament of penance. This was contrary to the long-standing teaching of the medieval church. In one of his preparatory treatises, Cajetan criticized Luther's view by making a distinction between two kinds of faith: infused faith and acquired faith.[21] Infused faith (from a Latin word meaning "poured into," because it is poured into our hearts by the grace of the Holy Spirit, as in Rom. 5:5) is Christian faith in the strict and proper sense of the term, which is always certain because it is based on what God has revealed. This is not a certainty about *me*, however, but only about the truth of Christian doctrine in general. As for me and my state of grace, that is a matter of acquired faith, which can and must be uncertain. For example, it is a matter of infused faith to believe that Christ instituted holy baptism, as revealed in Scripture, but it is a matter of acquired faith to believe that I was properly baptized and therefore came to be in a state of grace. For those baptized in infancy, the latter belief will be based on the witness of parents and godparents or a baptismal certificate, not on divine revelation. Likewise, it is a matter of acquired faith to believe that I have properly received the sacrament of penance, which requires me to have sufficient contrition or hatred of my sin. Because I cannot be certain about the state of my own heart, I can have no certainty about whether the word of absolution, which is efficacious only for those who are properly contrite, has actually absolved me of sin and restored me to a state of grace, which is what it means to be justified.

This turned out to be a point on which Luther could not possibly back down. He could not in good conscience doubt what he believed was the word of God. In his discussions with Cajetan he insisted that faith was all that was needed to secure the grace of forgiveness and justification, for the proper way to receive the sacramental word of absolution is simply by believing it. This is how "faith alone" ended up becoming a focal point in the controversies set off by the 95 Theses—although, as we have seen, the phrase itself had appeared earlier, in Luther's lectures on Romans, when he taught that we are justified solely by faith in the word of condemnation. By the time he confronts Cajetan, however, "faith alone" is closely connected to his conviction that doubting the word of absolution is tantamount to rejecting the grace of God and calling

21. In the second of the "Augsburg Treatises," in Cajetan, *Cajetan Responds*, 49–55.

Christ a liar when he promised that whatever is loosed on earth is loosed in heaven.[22] Luther clearly thinks this is Christian faith in the strict and proper sense, not just an uncertain "acquired faith."

On this point Luther's faith is indeed novel, in that it differs from the long-standing teaching of the medieval Catholic church.[23] However, it is far from rejecting Catholic sacramental faith, as would happen in many later forms of Protestantism, but rather is a striking intensification of faith in the sacrament (*fides sacramenti*). The logic of Luther's sacramental faith, which goes beyond what Cajetan was willing to call properly Christian faith, depends on a kind of double structure of God's word. First there is Christ's promise in Scripture, which Cajetan agrees we must believe without doubt or uncertainty, but secondly there is the sacramental word of absolution which it authorizes, so that in Luther's view it is as if Christ himself were saying, through the mouth of the priest, "I absolve you of your sins in the name of the Father, of the Son, and of the Holy Spirit." In this sacramental word, unlike the Scriptures themselves, God says "you" and means me in particular. One can scarcely get the point across without using the first-person singular pronoun (which is indeed characteristic of Luther's expositions of this point, and will often be necessary in the expositions of Luther's theology in this book). Whereas for Cajetan anything I believe about myself in particular is not in the strict sense Christian faith but only an uncertain "acquired faith," for Luther it is God himself who tells me in the sacramental word that my sins are forgiven, so that proper Christian faith includes my confidence that God is gracious and forgiving not only in general but to me in particular.

We need to bear this double structure of God's word in mind when we hear Luther saying that Christian faith is "nothing else but believing what God promises and says."[24] This agrees with standard medieval theology, which teaches that Christian faith means believing what God has revealed.

---

22. See Luther, *Proceedings at Augsburg*, LW 31:271.

23. Such is Cajetan's conclusion in *Cajetan Responds*, 55. See for example Aquinas, *ST* I-II, 112.5, where Aquinas denies that it is even *possible* for believers, under ordinary circumstances, to be certain they have grace. Later, the Council of Trent (Session 6, chap. 9, in Schaff, *Creeds of Christendom* 2:98) evidently aims to reaffirm this teaching when it denies the *necessity* of being certain one has grace in order to be justified. This does not aptly characterize Luther's view, however, in which (I shall argue below) the requirement of certainty is best thought of not as instrumental (in order to be justified) but as absolute (it is simply commanded). Cajetan himself seems to have reconsidered and for a brief time after the Augsburg interview thought that Luther's view of sacramental faith might be interpreted in a way that does not contradict church teaching; see Wicks, "*Fides sacramenti—fides specialis*," 134. But the reconsideration was evidently not permanent (138).

24. Luther, *Proceedings at Augsburg*, WA 2:13 (= LW 31:270–71).

But because Luther conceives of what God reveals in terms of this twofold word—not just Christ's Scriptural promise but also the sacramental word it authorizes—the logic of Luther's faith is different from anything Cajetan had encountered before. It means hearing a gracious word of God that says "you" and means me. Luther's first-person faith is based on a second-person address from God himself. That is why doubting that my sins are forgiven amounts to calling God a liar. As Luther puts it a year later in a German sermon on the sacrament of penance: "By such disbelief you make your God to be a liar when, through his priest, he says to you, 'You are absolved of your sins.'"[25]

Cajetan rejects Luther's view of faith because he does not accept Luther's view of the word of God. In Cajetan's view the sacramental word of absolution is not the word of God but merely the word of the priest, based not on Christ's promise alone but also on the priest's judgment that the penitent is sufficiently contrite. This judgment, like the penitent's own belief about the extent of his contrition, is uncertain. Hence Cajetan concludes that the penitent's belief that his sins are forgiven does not have the certainty of Christian faith, but only the probability of an acquired faith about his particular situation, based on his own conscience and reflective knowledge of the state of his heart, reinforced by the quite fallible judgment of his confessor.

The Certainty of Unreflective Faith

Luther's sacramental faith differs from Cajetan's "acquired faith" because it is not reflective. It looks away from the self even when it is about myself and the forgiveness of my own sins. This unreflective faith about myself is logically distinctive and easy to misunderstand. The logic of faith in a sacramental word permits me to ignore the deceitfulness of my own heart and simply believe that what God says about me is true. That is what makes justification *by faith alone* possible for the mature Luther. "Faith alone" means that I need know nothing about myself other than what God has said about me in the sacramental word. So Luther's faith is both profoundly unreflective and yet focused on the first-person singular. As Luther often insists, it is *pro me* (Latin for "for me"), but that is not because I am reflecting on the state of my own heart or conscience or even my own act of believing, but rather because the word I am required to believe has something to say about me in particular. To say the word of God is *pro me* is thus very different from saying

25. Luther, *Sacrament of Penance* (sermon, 1519), *LW* 35:13 (not to be confused with the 1518 Latin sermon on penance, the *Sermo de poenitentia*).

"I believe."[26] It is the difference between speaking of myself as subject (I or *ego*) and hearing about myself in a word addressed to me (when God himself says "you" and means *me*). Unlike reflective faith, the word of address gets me thinking about myself as the object of God's love and grace; for the Gospel truth is that Christ died for *me*, to forgive *me*, a sinner. The grammar itself illustrates how Luther's faith is about being the *object* of divine forgiveness and grace, the one whom God loves and addresses and justifies, rather than the *subject* of faith, the one who believes. For the sacramental word that I must receive with certainty is not "I believe" but rather "I absolve you" and "I baptize you," where the "I" is Christ's, not mine—precisely so that the "you" can mean *me*. To be justified by faith alone, in Luther's theology, is therefore to focus my attention on the word of Christ alone, and not on anything I do about it—not on the depth of my contrition nor even on the firmness of my faith when I say, "I believe."

In later writings we can see Luther working out this sacramental logic of faith in contrast to Protestants, not just Roman Catholics. About a decade after his encounter with Cajetan, for example, he was writing about Christians who refused to baptize their babies, on the ground that infants have no faith and only believers should be baptized. The reasoning of these "Anabaptists," as they were called,[27] seems to catch Luther by surprise: as if the first thing to know is whether I have faith, and only then can I receive the sacramental word. This is an exact reversal of Luther's view of faith, where the truth of the sacramental word comes first and I have no right to doubt it, to talk back

---

26. Hence I find Paul Hacker's account of the "'I' of faith" and his comparison of Luther to Descartes in *Ego in Faith* to be deeply mistaken. Descartes wants us to acquire a reflective certainty about our own existence, knowing that "I think, therefore I am." Luther believes that God commands an unreflective certainty that Christ died for me, because I know God can't be lying when he says, "I baptize you in the name of the Father, and of the Son, and of the Holy Spirit." These are two entirely different sources of certainty, one based on the subject of knowledge (the knower, the "I"), the other on the object of knowledge (the *Deus verax* and his promise). And they have two very different results: Descartes thinks he has found in his own consciousness a certainty that he can build on as a kind of foundation, whereas Luther has no foundation but the external word of God, which is external in precisely the sense that it is not found in the self, its consciousness or experience. Hence when Luther reflects on his own faith, he finds that it is a weak and imperfect thing, not a foundation to build on but a goal that will never be perfectly accomplished in this life. He does not build on his faith but on the word of Christ, for that is what faith builds on.

27. At this point Luther is only hearing secondhand about "rebaptizers" (*Anabaptistae* in Latin, *widderteuffer* in Luther's German), mainly those in Switzerland associated with Balthasar Hubmaier (cf. *LW* 40:229, the opening page of Luther's 1528 treatise *Concerning Rebaptism*). The term Anabaptist came to be applied to many later groups, including most importantly the Mennonites. In the seventeenth century, English and American Baptists take up the same fundamental position on baptism as the continental Anabaptists, though in a different social setting.

or say otherwise—and thus no right to defy our Lord's command to believe and be baptized. Those who come to be baptized should indeed say, "Yes sir, I do believe," Luther writes, but they should immediately add, "but I do not build on this my faith. It might be too weak or uncertain. I want to be baptized because it is God's command that I should be, and on the strength of this command I dare to be baptized."[28] We must get baptized not because we believe, but because the word of God demands it—the word to which alone faith must cling, not heeding anything in the human heart (including faith) but only the truth of God's word. Word and faith require each other, but they do not have equal footing, for "faith builds and is founded on the Word of God rather than God's Word on faith."[29]

The Anabaptist reasoning is exactly the opposite of that which led Luther to insist on "faith alone" against Cajetan. To make knowledge of our own faith a prerequisite for receiving the sacrament of baptism is like making contrition a prerequisite for believing that my sins are absolved in the sacrament of penance—as if the truth of the word of absolution were dependent on my ability to be contrite rather than on the truthfulness of God. Similarly, the Anabaptists were basing faith not on the word of God but on something I believe about myself, an "acquired faith" in precisely Cajetan's sense. This makes baptism dependent on the belief that "I believe," which is no more certain than the belief that "I am contrite."

The key logical point is that reflective faith—the belief that I believe in Christ—is necessarily uncertain because it is based not on God's word but on what I can find out about my own deceitful heart. Because "all men are liars and God alone knows the heart," Luther argues, "whoever bases baptism on the faith of the one to be baptized can never baptize anyone."[30] He is thinking of a favorite passage from Paul: "God is true [Deus verax] but every man a liar" (Rom. 3:4).[31] This Deus verax theme, which is always near at hand whenever Luther discusses the doctrine of justification, means that we should gladly trust in the truth of God's word alone, and not any human truthfulness or faithfulness—including our own. For "every man a liar" certainly includes myself. Because I have a lying heart and am prone to deceive even myself, I am in no position to be certain, introspectively, that I have true faith. So if knowing that I have faith is a prerequisite for baptism, then I cannot be

28. Luther, *Concerning Rebaptism*, LW 40:253.
29. Luther, *Concerning Rebaptism*, LW 40:260.
30. Luther, *Concerning Rebaptism*, LW 40:240.
31. A proper translation from the Greek is "Let God be true . . . ," but Luther is typically thinking of the Latin rendition of the Vulgate, where the mood is indicative and declarative: *est autem Deus verax, omnis autem homo mendax.*

baptized at all; for "the baptized one who receives or grounds his baptism on his faith . . . is not sure of his own faith."[32]

Weak Faith

It would therefore be misleading to say that Luther wants us to rely on faith. Rather, he wants us to rely solely on the word of God, which is what faith does. For "there is quite a difference between having faith, on the one hand, and depending on one's faith and making baptism depend on faith, on the other."[33] We should put no faith in our own faith but only in God keeping his promises, for properly Christian faith is based on the certainty that God will be true to his word, not on the very uncertain belief that I have faith. While on my good days I may have reason to believe that I have true Christian faith (and thus may reasonably attain what Cajetan would call an "acquired faith" in my own faith), this is not essential or necessary to a properly Christian faith. And that is a very good thing to remember on my bad days, when I feel my own sin and unbelief, and am tempted to believe that I am nothing but an unbeliever. Experience confirms that every believer is also an unbeliever, just as every believer is *simul justus et peccator*, both righteous and a sinner at the same time—righteous by faith alone and a sinner because of continuing unbelief, which is at the root of all sin.[34] Hence on my bad days I must turn away from my heartfelt experience of my own unbelief, and believe instead what the word of God, including my baptism, has to say about me. "For it happens," as Luther explains, "indeed it is so in this matter of faith, that often he who claims to believe does not at all believe; and on the other hand, he who doesn't think he believes, but is in despair, has the greatest faith."[35]

Luther's theology is thus a great comfort for those who know what it is like to be weak in faith. The faith of those who don't believe that they believe is characteristic of the times of trial, or *Anfechtung*, when it seems "that all creatures are threatening us with evil, and that hell is opening up in order to swallow us."[36] As Luther goes on to insist in his great Galatians commentary

32. Luther, *Concerning Rebaptism*, LW 40:240.
33. Luther, *Concerning Rebaptism*, LW 40:252.
34. That "unbelief alone commits sin" (Luther, 1522 Preface to Romans, LW 35:369) is a fundamental conviction of Luther's, found repeatedly, for example, in Luther, *Freedom of a Christian*, LW 31:347, 350, 361, 362. Cf. also his sermon on the Gospel for the fourth Sunday after Easter, where "sin is unbelief; righteousness is faith" (Luther, *Sermons* 3:121). Hence I draw the conclusion: "righteous and sinner at the same time" amounts to the same thing as "believer and unbeliever at the same time."
35. Luther, *Concerning Rebaptism*, LW 40:241.
36. Luther, 1535 Galatians Commentary, on Gal. 4:6, LW 26:382.

in 1535, this is the time when it is especially important "to turn your eyes away . . . from your own feelings and conscience, to lay hold of the Gospel, and to depend solely on the promise of God."[37] Only thus can we strengthen our faith, which "must take hold of nothing but Christ alone," whom we find in the Gospel alone.[38] Any reflective turn to look at the self undermines faith, for "by paying attention to myself and considering what my condition is or should be . . . I lose sight of Christ . . . therefore, we must form the habit of leaving ourselves behind."[39]

Not that this is easy. In the struggle for certainty we find that faith is the hardest work of all. When all creatures are accusing us and we have nothing to cling to but the bare word of Christ, then "it is effort and labor to cling firmly to this in the midst of trial and conflict, when Christ does not become visible to any of our senses. We do not see him, and in the trial our heart does not feel his presence."[40] Hence the faith of Christians is typically weak and uncertain, often lacking the experience of Christ's presence, and not the sort of thing to build our hopes on. But we are nonetheless commanded to be certain that God is gracious to us in his good word, and precisely for that reason we are permitted to be confident that he is present with us in his grace even when we feel weak in faith. The commandment to believe grants us permission to believe. In effect, it is a *must* in service of a *may*. Because we must believe and not doubt, we may rejoice in the certainty of God's grace, even when we do not feel at all certain, have no experience of his presence, and are not in fact doing a very good job of believing it. For the basis of our faith is not our success in believing—that would be one more form of works righteousness—but the truth of the word we are commanded to believe.

The certainty of faith is therefore an unconditional requirement, not a prerequisite condition. It is not as if I have no right to believe my sins are forgiven until I am certain I believe the word of absolution. Logically, that gets things entirely backwards: it's tantamount to saying I have no right to believe the word of absolution until I am certain I believe it. The requirement of certainty implies, on the contrary, that if I want to know whether my sins are forgiven, the uncertainty of my heart is irrelevant, because all that matters is whether God's word is true—for that alone is what I am commanded to be certain of. The command to believe God's word with certainty is therefore always in force, despite my sinful uncertainty. As a consequence, I always have permission to believe I am absolved and justified by the grace of Christ,

37. Luther, 1535 Galatians Commentary, on Gal. 4:6, *LW* 26:389.
38. Luther, 1535 Galatians Commentary, on Gal. 2:4–5, *LW* 26:88.
39. Luther, 1535 Galatians Commentary, on Gal. 2:20, *LW* 26:166.
40. Luther, 1535 Galatians Commentary, on Gal. 4:6, *LW* 26:380–81.

precisely because I am commanded to believe it despite my unbelief. It would be logically perverse to insist on being certain about my faith *before* believing I was justified. That would be saying I had no right to obey the commandment of God until I was certain I had already obeyed it.

This same *must* in service of a *may* is also operative when Christ promises that "whoever believes and is baptized will be saved" (Mark 16:16). As Luther puts it in his criticism of the Anabaptists, "One must believe, but we neither should nor can know it for certain."[41] The uncertainty we *should* have is about *whether* we actually believe, not about *what* we must believe. On the basis of this *must*—what God commands us to believe—we are to be baptized, not claiming we have sufficient faith but submitting in faith to Christ's word. Faith is thus not a prerequisite condition we must meet before getting baptized; rather, believing the promise of God that institutes baptism is something we are simply commanded to do, just like baptism itself. Each of us therefore *may* get baptized—we are permitted to do so, despite our sinful doubts and uncertainties—precisely because we *must* believe and be baptized, according to God's commandment.

Faith as Work

Luther's distinction between good works and faith, closely related to his distinction between law and Gospel, does not mean that faith is not a work. Quite the contrary: Luther takes faith to be "the most excellent and difficult of all works"[42] and "the chief work,"[43] because "no other work makes a Christian."[44] He regularly identifies faith as the first work required of us in the Ten Commandments, which begin with "You shall have no other gods besides me" (Exod. 20:3). To "have a god," Luther explains in his *Large Catechism*, "is nothing else than to trust and believe him with our whole heart."[45] Having a god means having wholehearted faith in your god, so obedience to the first commandment consists in Christian faith, a wholehearted trust in the one true God that excludes doubt and uncertainty. We are quite simply commanded to believe in the one true God, which is to say: Christian faith

41. Luther, *Concerning Rebaptism*, LW 40:241.

42. Luther, *Babylonian Captivity*, LW 36:62.

43. Luther, *Treatise on Good Works*, LW 44:60. Cf. earlier in the same treatise: "The first, highest and most precious of all good works is faith in Christ" (*LW* 44:23).

44. Luther, *Freedom of a Christian*, LW 31:347.

45. Luther, *Large Catechism*, in Tappert, *Book of Concord*, 365. For purposes of understanding my exposition it is important to be aware that German, like Latin, has no equivalent to the difference between "belief" and "faith" in English. Hence I am using the two terms interchangeably; likewise "to believe" and "to have faith in."

is required by the law of God. But a commandment *to believe and be certain* is not a commandment *to believe we are certain.* On the contrary, we should believe that, like all our works, our faith does not amount to perfect obedience; it is quite inadequate and insufficient to save us. As Luther points out elsewhere, "There is not a man living who does not have a full share in breaking the first and greatest commandment, i.e., the commandment to believe."[46] For as he puts it many years later, "In the heart of the godly, too, there remains a lack of trust. . . . Pure faith that truly trusts in Christ is not there."[47] Thus the commandment to believe, like all commandments, is one we do not adequately fulfill in this life. This is indeed the fundamental respect in which we are righteous and sinners at the same time (*simul justus et peccator*): righteous by faith alone, but sinners because of the unbelief that remains in us, the imperfection of our faith that still harbors doubts and uncertainties and refuses to honor fully the truth of God in his word.

Thus faith is derived from both law and Gospel, but in different ways, due to the logically unique relationship faith has to the truth of God's word. On the one hand, like other good works, believing God's word is something we are commanded to do and don't do very well—certainly not well enough to earn our salvation. On the other hand, this same belief has the power to save us, not because our work of faith is perfect, sufficient, or even adequate, but because God is true to his promise. For the proper way to receive a promise, as Luther often insists, is simply by believing it is true—which is to say, by faith alone.[48] This is what makes faith unique among all the things we have and do in our hearts: it is the nature of faith alone to be defined not by how well we do it, but by the truth of what we believe.

I think we can see this in the distinctive logic of the verb "to believe," when its subject is in the first-person singular. If I want to know what I believe, I do not look at myself, examining my heart to see if faith is present there. I look at the object, not the subject of the verb "to believe."[49] For example, if I want

46. Luther, *Treatise on Good Works, LW* 44:60.

47. Luther, Commentary on Psalm 45, 1532, *LW* 12:243–44.

48. Perhaps most importantly in his discussion of the second "great power of faith" in Luther, *Freedom of a Christian, LW* 31:350–51.

49. For those who like modern vocabulary, we can call this the "objectivity" of faith. But I think the concept of truth is far more helpful and precise than the concept of objectivity—which, ever since it was introduced by the philosopher Immanuel Kant in the eighteenth century, turns out to be in fact a form of subjectivity. Objectivity is based on transcendental subjectivity, in Kant's terms. Similarly, in modern science, the concept of "objectivity" tends to mean following the right method, which means scientific objectivity actually amounts to methodological subjectivity: the subject of knowledge, the knower, must conduct herself in the appropriately methodological way in order to produce objective scientific knowledge. To import this modern concept in place of the ancient concept of truth does not really capture Luther's point, I think.

to know whether I believe it's raining outside, I do not search the depths of my heart to find out if I really, truly believe it; I look outside and see if it's raining. Once I know whether *it's true* that it's raining, I know what I believe. Likewise, the logic of Luther's faith is that if I want to know whether I believe in Christ, I do not examine my heart, but rather look at the truth I am commanded to believe. That way I learn what I must believe, which implies also what I *may* believe. I am not at all certain of the truth of God's word, and that is my sin. But I am commanded to believe it, and therefore I am permitted to rejoice and believe that it actually is true that God is gracious to me because of Christ my savior. For in Christian faith what I believe is not determined by the truth of my word when I say, "I believe," but by the truth of God's word when he says such things as "I baptize you in the name of the Father, and of the Son, and of the Holy Spirit." On the basis of such a word alone I can say: "I am a Christian" and therefore "I am a believer."[50]

Efficacious Sacramental Faith

The unreflective logic of Luther's faith starts with the word of absolution in the sacrament of penance and expands rapidly from there. Already in his 1518 writings on penance he sees the implication that it is faith that makes a sacrament efficacious, and he soon draws this conclusion for baptism and the Lord's Supper as well. Since Luther's notion of sacramental efficacy is another momentous and easily misunderstood point, it is worth looking at more closely. It has to be understood in terms of the Augustinian concept of sacraments as signs of grace. A sacrament is efficacious to the extent that it effectively confers the grace it signifies. So the question of sacramental efficacy is a question about the relation of *signum* and *res*, the sign and the thing signified. This is how Luther sets up the question in his 1519 trilogy of German sermons on the sacraments of penance, baptism, and supper. For each sacrament he identifies what is the external sign and what is the thing it signifies, then points to the necessity of faith for bringing the two together in the life of the believer.[51] Without faith, one receives a sacrament but not the thing it signifies, a *signum* but not its *res*.

Like the Bible and Aristotle, Luther can get along quite well without the concept of objectivity, precisely because he has the concept of truth.

50. On the first-person logic that connects baptism with the belief that I am a Christian, see below, chap. 10, "Lutheran Syllogisms."

51. Luther is explicit about this general structure of every sacrament at the beginning of the 1519 sermon on the Supper, *The Blessed Sacrament of the Holy and True Body of Christ, and the Brotherhoods,* LW 35:49.

Baptism is the most straightforward example. Here the sign is the act of immersing a person in water and drawing her up out of it, which signifies death and rebirth in Christ. Luther says this sacrament establishes a covenant in which "God allies himself with you and becomes one with you."[52] Faith in this sacrament means "you give yourself up to the sacrament of baptism and to what it signifies."[53] The language of process that we saw in earlier chapters remains prominent: the baptized person "*has begun* to grow into purity and innocence," but "because all is *not yet completed* and he still lives in sinful flesh, he is not without sin."[54] As before, the process looks both backward and forward: back to the death of sin that it leaves behind and ahead to the eternal life toward which it is moving. Your baptism is at work in this process precisely as you believe in it, confident that the sacrament "not only signifies death and the resurrection at the Last Day . . . but also that it assuredly begins and achieves this."[55] Sin can hinder the work of baptism, but "only through unbelief in its work does it come to nothing."[56] Thus faith in the efficacy of baptism makes baptism efficacious, just as faith in the word of absolution has the effect that you are actually absolved of your sins. Luther can therefore say, famously, "Believe, and you have it."[57]

In the 1519 sermon on the sacrament of penance, the point about efficacy is put this way: "Faith . . . alone makes the sacraments accomplish that which they signify," with the result that "as you believe, so it is done for you."[58] The underlying principle is one that appears numerous times in his 1518 writings on penance: "Not the sacrament, but the faith that believes the sacrament is what removes sin."[59] In other words, the sheer performance of the

---

52. Luther, *Holy and Blessed Sacrament of Baptism* (sermon, 1519), LW 35:33.

53. Luther, *Holy and Blessed Sacrament of Baptism* (sermon, 1519), LW 35:33.

54. Luther, *Holy and Blessed Sacrament of Baptism* (sermon, 1519), LW 35:33.

55. Luther, *Holy and Blessed Sacrament of Baptism* (sermon, 1519), LW 35:35.

56. Luther, *Holy and Blessed Sacrament of Baptism* (sermon, 1519), WA 2:733 (= LW 35:38).

57. Luther, *Holy and Blessed Sacrament of Baptism* (sermon, 1519), LW 35:38. The phrase here has become famous—in modern German: *Glaubst du, so hast du* (= WA 2:733).

58. Luther, *Sacrament of Penance* (sermon, 1519), LW 35:11.

59. Luther, *Sacrament of Penance* (sermon, 1519), LW 35:11. The formulation of this principle that Luther uses most often is that faith in the sacrament (*fides sacramenti*), not the sacrament itself, is what *justifies*. Versions of this principle appear in the 1518 *Sermo de poenitentia* (WA 1:324), the theses *Pro veritate*, thesis 10 (WA 1:631), the *Explanations of the 95 Theses* on thesis 7 (LW 31:107), and the 1519 Hebrews Commentary, on Heb. 5:19 (in *Luther: Early Theological Works*, 106), as well as *Babylonian Captivity*, LW 36:66. Note also the formulation in the explanation of thesis 38, which addresses the question of efficacy explicitly: "You receive as much as you believe. And this is what I understand it to mean when our teachers say that the sacraments are efficacious signs of grace, not because of the mere fact that the sacrament is performed but because it is believed. . . . So also here. Absolution is efficacious, not by the mere fact that it takes place . . . but because it is believed" (LW 31:193). On the importance of

sacrament—which in this case means especially the priest's act of uttering the word of absolution—does not release me from my sins if I don't believe the word is true. Hence I am justified not by the sacrament alone (what medieval theologians called *sacramentum tantum*, which is the same as saying "the mere sign") but by faith in the sacrament (*fides sacramenti*). The issue of efficacy is particularly clear here because Luther identifies the word of absolution itself as the sign in this sacrament.[60] The thing signified by this verbal sign is, of course, absolution—which is to say, the forgiveness of my sins and justification. Faith alone connects the sign and the thing signified, *signum* and *res* (or equivalently, *sacramentum* and *res*), so that I receive not only the word of absolution in my ears but the absolution itself in my heart and conscience, taking away all my sin and guilt in God's sight. I have God's forgiveness because I believe I have it—a faith that is properly certain because it is based on nothing but God's own word.

In the sacrament of penance, therefore, justification by faith alone means that my sins are absolved for no other reason than that I believe the word that says they are absolved. In this respect faith has great power, but it is important to recognize that the power of faith is not due to its own strength but is completely dependent on the outward sign, without which it has nothing to believe and therefore no power at all. So faith alone makes the sacrament efficacious, but faith alone has no efficacy without the sacrament, the external sign to which it clings. It is precisely faith *in the sacrament*, which is to say, believing *the outward sign*, that justifies. As before, this is an intensification rather than a rejection of Catholic sacramental faith, extending it beyond its previous boundaries by way of a distinctively Lutheran outward turn.

And once again, the double structure of the word of God is essential. Faith in the sacrament is grounded on the promise of Christ, who said, "Whatever you loose on earth will be loosed in heaven" (Matt. 16:19), which is a promise we can rely on despite all our unworthiness and inadequate contrition, since "Christ, your God, will not lie to you."[61] Because God's truth, the honor of the *Deus verax*, is at stake here, the promise implies a command: "He not only promises us forgiveness of sins," Luther says, "but also commands us, on pain of committing the most grievous sin of all, to believe that they are

---

this principle for Luther's thinking in 1518 and afterward, see Wicks, "*Fides sacramenti—fides specialis.*"

60. "This is why it [penance] is called a sacrament, a holy sign, because in it one hears the words externally that signify spiritual gifts within" (*Sacrament of Penance* [sermon, 1519], *LW* 35:11).

61. Luther, *Sacrament of Penance* (sermon, 1519), *LW* 35:12.

forgiven."[62] This command is a *must* in service of a *may*: "With this same command he constrains us to have a joyful conscience."[63]

A True Inheritance

It is worth asking, then, what happens to the truth of the word of absolution when it is not believed. The priest says, "I absolve you . . . ," and this is God's word, yet whoever hears it without believing it has no absolution or forgiveness of sins, but is an even worse sinner than before. Does that mean the word is not true? Luther insists, on the contrary, that "the forgiveness is truthful, as true as if God had spoken it, whether it is grasped by faith or not."[64] What he is thinking here is perhaps best explained in a treatise he wrote in 1530 on the gift of the keys. The treatise is concerned with the passage in which Christ makes the promise to Peter and the whole church that grounds the word of absolution: "I will give you the keys of the kingdom of heaven . . . and whatever you loose on earth shall be loosed in heaven" (Matt. 16:18–19). What happens when this promise of the keys and the word of absolution that is based on it are not believed? Luther answers: "He who does not accept what the keys give receives, of course, nothing. But this is not the keys' fault. Many do not believe the gospel, but this does not mean that the gospel is not true or effective. A king gives you a castle. If you do not accept it, then it is not the king's fault, nor is he guilty of a lie. But you have deceived yourself and the fault is yours. The king certainly gave it."[65] Luther is evidently thinking here of something like an inheritance. If the king in his last will and testament gives his daughter a castle, then when he dies his daughter has truly been given a castle, even if she refuses to believe her father's testament and therefore never takes ownership and never benefits from what she has been given. It is like a bank account established in your name which you do not believe in and therefore never use; it makes you none the richer. Or as Luther puts it in the context of the sacrament of baptism: "The treasure is opened and placed at everyone's door, yes, upon everyone's table, but it is also your responsibility to take it and confidently believe that it is just as the words tell you."[66]

---

62. Luther, *Sacrament of Penance* (sermon, 1519), LW 35:14.

63. Luther, *Sacrament of Penance* (sermon, 1519), LW 35:14.

64. Luther, *Sacrament of Penance* (sermon, 1519), WA 2:722 (= LW 35:22). The crucial connection between *wahrhaftig* and *wahr* ("truthful " and "true") is lost in LW.

65. Luther, *The Keys*, LW 40:367.

66. Luther, *Large Catechism*, on the sacrament of the altar, in Tappert, *Book of Concord*, 450.

The concept of inheritance in fact becomes prominent in Luther's writing on the sacraments in 1520, culminating in the epochal treatise he writes on all the sacraments, the *Babylonian Captivity of the Church*. There he treats Christ's words at the Last Supper as a promise that is in effect a last will and testament, giving us an inheritance so great that it is hard to believe it could be ours. We are like a wicked and unworthy servant who is bequeathed a huge fortune by a great lord. If the servant has any conscience at all, he will have a hard time believing that the inheritance could really be his. But if someone challenges him on this point (like the devil tempting us not to believe Christ's promise of forgiveness), then he should reply: "What is that to you? What I accept, I accept not on my merits. . . . I claim what I claim by the right of a bequest and of another's goodness. If to him it was not an unworthy thing to bequeath so great a sum to an unworthy person, why should I refuse to accept it because of my unworthiness?"[67] In a similar way, the worthy reception of the sacrament is not based on our own worthiness; it requires nothing but "a faith that relies confidently on this promise, believes Christ to be true in these words of his, and does not doubt that these infinite blessings have been bestowed upon it."[68]

Returning to Baptism

One peculiar development in the *Babylonian Captivity* is worth briefly noting here, because it shows how the sacramental word of absolution remains important in Lutheranism, even though the Lutheran church no longer recognizes a sacrament of penance. In the introduction to the treatise, Luther denies that there are seven sacraments, as the Roman church teaches, and affirms only three: baptism, penance, and the Supper. The title of the treatise comes from his efforts to rescue these three from their "miserable captivity to the Roman curia."[69] Yet at the end of the treatise he changes his mind and argues that, strictly speaking, there are only two sacraments, because the term "sacrament" should be used to designate only those promises of Christ to which he adds a visible sign, and penance has no visible sign added to the word of absolution.[70] Yet this is not a consequential change of mind, and it certainly does not mean Luther is

---

67. Luther, *Babylonian Captivity*, LW 36:46. The same analogy was developed at greater length a few months earlier in Luther's 1520 *Treatise on the New Testament, That Is, the Holy Mass*, LW 35:87–90.

68. Luther, *Babylonian Captivity*, LW 36:40.

69. Luther, *Babylonian Captivity*, LW 36:18.

70. Luther, *Babylonian Captivity*, LW 36:124.

getting rid of sacramental penance. Rather, he includes it under the sacrament of baptism, because penance is "nothing but a way and a return to baptism."[71] This was already his view of the sacrament of penance in the body of the treatise, where penance means "returning to the power and the faith of baptism from which we fell, and finding our way back to the promise then made to us, which we deserted when we sinned."[72] This view becomes standard Lutheran doctrine after it is incorporated ten years later into the *Large Catechism*, which teaches that "repentance . . . is nothing else than a return and approach to Baptism, to resume and practice what had earlier been begun but abandoned."[73]

If the notion of "return to baptism" sounds strange, think of how a repentant woman, seeking to be reconciled with her husband after abandoning him and committing adultery, returns to the promises they both made in their exchange of wedding vows. The promises remain in force throughout the time of her adultery: that is to say, she's still married, and that is precisely why her deeds are adultery. Hence if her husband receives her back and is reconciled with her, the two of them do not need to get married again, but rather begin once more to live according to the promises that established their marriage in the first place. In much the same way, Christian repentance is a return to the divine promise in baptism that established a person's Christian life. For in Christ we have a bridegroom who is eager to be reconciled with his wayward bride, and "the truth of the promise once made remains steadfast, always ready to receive us back with open arms when we return."[74]

Therefore penance, in Luther's mature teaching, "is nothing else than the practice and power of baptism";[75] indeed, it is "really nothing else than baptism."[76] In effect, it is still a sacrament, but not a different sacrament from baptism. Hence Luther is not being inconsistent when throughout his career he sees himself as defending the sacrament of penance against the papists, who "have completely abolished it."[77] In fact he has no qualms about maintaining that it is a sacrament in his arguments against the pope a year after the *Babylonian Captivity*.[78] In a similar vein, the Lutheran tradition continues to

---

71. Luther, *Babylonian Captivity*, LW 36:124.
72. Luther, *Babylonian Captivity*, LW 36:59.
73. Luther, *Large Catechism*, on baptism, in Tappert, *Book of Concord*, 446.
74. Luther, *Babylonian Captivity*, LW 36:59.
75. Luther, 1528 *Confession concerning Christ's Supper*, LW 37:370.
76. Luther, *Large Catechism*, on baptism, in Tappert, *Book of Concord*, 445.
77. Luther, *Babylonian Captivity*, LW 36:81.
78. Luther, 1521 *Defense and Explanation of All the Articles*, LW 32:16, a passage evidently based on *Babylonian Captivity*, LW 36:82–83.

treasure the word of absolution as "the true voice of the Gospel"[79] and even on occasion identifies absolution as a third sacrament.[80]

Union with Christ and Wondrous Exchange

The third sermon in the 1519 trilogy on the sacraments, *The Blessed Sacrament of the Holy and True Body of Christ, and the Brotherhoods*, brings together two key themes of Luther's theology for the first time: sacramental efficacy and the wondrous exchange. In the previous chapter we have seen the latter theme adumbrated in the Romans Lectures; here it is connected with several other themes that came together in the *Explanations of the 95 Theses*. Just before the explanation of thesis 38, in which his mature view of the word of absolution emerges, Luther presents the wondrous exchange as rooted in our union with Christ by faith. Every Christian possesses Christ, Luther says, which means "he possesses at the same time all that is Christ's."[81] Thus faith unites us with Christ and with all Christ has. This connection between who Christ is and what he has becomes central to Luther's mature doctrine of justification. Because faith unites us with Christ himself, what he has becomes ours and in exchange what we have becomes his. Thus Christ takes on all that is evil in us, and we receive all that is good in him. What makes the exchange so wondrous is that we get all the benefit and blessing and he gets all the pain and penalty. The implication for the doctrine of justification is that "by means of faith our sins become no longer ours but Christ's," while in exchange, "righteousness, strength, patience, humility, even all the merits of Christ" are ours "through the unity of the Spirit by faith in him."[82]

The sermon on *The Blessed Sacrament of the Holy and True Body of Christ, and the Brotherhoods*, which becomes Luther's first treatise on the Eucharist, makes this wondrous exchange central to the thing signified by the sacrament, its *res significata*. But that is not all. In what has long been the standard Augustinian conception, the body of Christ signified by this sacrament is identified as Christ's spiritual or ecclesial Body, the social body of which he is head.[83]

---

79. Philip Melanchthon, *Apology of the Augsburg Confession*, article 12, in Tappert, *Book of Concord*, 187.

80. Melanchthon, *Apology of the Augsburg Confession*, article 13, in Tappert, *Book of Concord*, 211.

81. Luther, *Explanations of the 95 Theses*, on thesis 37, WA 1:593 (= LW 31:190).

82. Luther, *Explanations of the 95 Theses*, on thesis 37, WA 1:593 (= LW 31:190).

83. In the sacrament of the altar, says Augustine, "the whole redeemed community . . . is offered to God" (*City of God* 10:6; cf. also 10:20). This understanding of the eucharistic offering is based on Augustine's conception of the church as an inner unity of souls bound together by common love of God; see Cary, *Outward Signs*, 164–71.

Luther describes this as the fellowship or communion (*Gemeinschaft*) of Christ and his saints. Here "saints" means everyone who is holy (*sanctus* in Latin or *heilige* in German), which includes the angels and "the blessed in heaven and all pious men on earth."[84] The sacrament tells me I belong with them in a holy fellowship, or *communio sanctorum*, a phrase from the Apostles' Creed usually translated "the communion of saints," but which in Latin can mean both a fellowship of holy people and a sharing of holy things. Luther dwells on both meanings. In this communion of the holy, all good things are shared, and likewise everyone bears each other's sufferings and ills. Thus in sum:

> This holy sacrament is nothing else than a divine sign, in which are pledged, granted, and imparted Christ and all saints together with all their works, suffering, merits, mercies and possession, for the comfort and strengthening of all who are in anxiety and sorrow. . . . And to receive the sacrament is nothing else than to desire all this and firmly to believe that it is done.[85]

Thus to state the thing signified by this sacrament, its *res*, we have to connect three themes: union with Christ, wondrous exchange, and *communio sanctorum*, in that order. For by faith in this sacrament we are first united with Christ, which then brings about the wondrous exchange between Christ and us, which in turn brings us all together in a holy fellowship through which we share all things.

This account of Christ and believers develops in two directions in Luther's later work. First, the theme of *communio sanctorum* becomes central to Luther's thinking about love and good works, by which we are to bear one another's burdens and ills and share all our goods with our neighbors.[86] Second, and more fundamental, the theme of wondrous exchange becomes central to Luther's doctrine of justification, according to which we share by faith alone in Christ's righteousness, and he bears the burden of all our sins. The two themes are intimately connected here in what Luther calls "a fellowship and a gracious exchange or intermingling of our sins and suffering with the righteousness of Christ and his saints."[87] As Luther's thought

---

84. Luther, *Blessed Sacrament of the Holy and True Body of Christ* (sermon, 1519), *LW* 35:54.

85. Luther, *Blessed Sacrament of the Holy and True Body of Christ* (sermon, 1519), *LW* 35:60.

86. For a survey of the theme of *communio sanctorum* in Luther, see Althaus, *Theology of Martin Luther*, chap. 22. For a brief and powerful introduction to the theme, see Luther, *Fourteen Consolations* (1519), *LW* 42:160–63.

87. Luther, *Blessed Sacrament of the Holy and True Body of Christ* (sermon, 1519), *LW* 35:60.

develops, the two themes are distinguished more clearly but also connected more powerfully—in that faith, as cause, is distinguished from love and good works, as effects. Receiving the good things of Christ by faith causes us to love him, so that we gladly share the sufferings of Christ and his saints, while we are also comforted as they share our struggles and sufferings. The interiorized masochism of Luther's old "theology of the cross" is replaced by a new and far healthier view of human suffering, in which we gladly share in the suffering of others, not in order to be justified, but because we are eager to obey the command to love them and bear their burdens. For love means taking on others' weaknesses "as if they were your own" and offering them your strength "as if it were their own." To do this is to do "just as Christ does for you in the sacrament."[88] And what Christian would not want to do as Christ does?

The Promise of Faith

The conceptual structure of what the mature Luther calls "Gospel" is now in place. The Gospel is the promise of God at the basis of justification by faith alone, because promise and faith require each other. As Luther puts it in the 1520 *Babylonian Captivity of the Church*, one of the first great treatises of the Reformation:

> Wherever there is a divine promise, there faith is required. . . . These two are so necessary to each other that neither can be efficacious apart from the other. For it is not possible to believe unless there is a promise, and the promise is not established unless it is believed.[89]

The conceptual connection between promise and faith gives form to the personal connection between God and the believer, as faith "clings to the word of the promising God."[90] This is clearly how God intends to relate personally to human beings, because "God does not deal, nor has he ever dealt, with man otherwise than through a word of promise."[91]

---

88. Luther, *Blessed Sacrament of the Holy and True Body of Christ* (sermon, 1519), *LW* 35:61–62.

89. Luther, *Babylonian Captivity*, WA 6:533 (= *LW* 36:67).

90. Luther, *Babylonian Captivity*, *LW* 36:39.

91. Luther, *Babylonian Captivity*, *LW* 36:42. Luther explains this claim in a brief survey of biblical history that sketches a very early version of what Reformed theologians call "covenant theology" (Luther, *Babylonian Captivity*, *LW* 36:39–40). He makes essentially the same point in sacramental terms in his response to the pope's condemnation of his teaching: "God deals with us in no other way than by his holy word and sacraments" (Luther, 1521 *Defense and Explanation of All the Articles*, on article 1, *LW* 32:15).

The implication is mutual: not only is faith nothing without the promise of God, but the promise of God accomplishes nothing if it is not received in faith. The latter point might seem to make the efficacy of God's promise depend on us, but not if Luther's view of faith is properly understood. Luther is adamant that it is an illusion when people "get busy and by their own powers create an idea in their heart which says, 'I believe'"; for the fact is that "no one can give himself faith."[92] My belief that Christ died for me is not a result of my own free will or choice or activity or experience, but only of the word of God instilled in me by the Holy Spirit, who alone is "the Author who inscribes it in my heart."[93] As Luther makes abundantly clear in his 1525 treatise *On the Bondage of the Will*, he abhors the very notion of human free will in connection with justification and salvation. God does not make Christian faith depend on human choice, as if he left it up to me to decide whether or not to believe that Christ died for me. On the contrary, he commands me to believe this truth and forbids me to doubt it.

Luther therefore never evangelizes people by urging them to make a decision to believe in Christ, as if this were a choice they needed to make. Everyone who hears the Gospel is commanded to believe and be baptized, and once we are baptized we are offered no choice but to believe that God has already given us the gift of faith through the Holy Spirit that is promised to us. Hence the teaching that Luther wants every child to learn about the Holy Spirit is first, "*I believe that* by my own reason or strength *I cannot believe* in Jesus Christ my Lord or come to him," but then, "the Holy Spirit has called me through the Gospel, enlightened me with his gifts, and sanctified and *preserved me in the true faith*."[94] The immense logical subtlety of these words from Luther's *Small Catechism* should not be passed over. The reason Christian faith is never something to make a decision about is that it is always something that I should believe I already have, because I have received it from the Holy Spirit, who is promised to all the baptized—and I have no right not to believe God's promise. If I am a child growing up in a good Lutheran household, baptized as an infant and learning my catechism, I will not be told to make a decision for Christ but taught, in the words of the catechism, to "believe that . . . I cannot believe" as well as to believe the words that follow, which are in the present perfect tense, signifying what has already been done: "But the Holy Spirit has . . . preserved me in the true faith." I have no decision to make, because I have no right to deny what the

92. Luther, 1522 Preface to Romans, *LW* 35:370–71.
93. Luther, *Sermons on the Gospel of John*, on John 3:5, *LW* 22:286.
94. Luther, *Small Catechism*, on the third article of the Creed, in Tappert, *Book of Concord*, 345.

Holy Spirit has already done in me and for me, just as Christ promised. Of course in my heart and in my deeds I often do deny it, and that is my sin. But that is just one more reason to "believe that . . . I cannot believe" and believe instead in the promised Holy Spirit and his gift of faith. The logic is: I should always believe that I already believe, because of what the Holy Spirit has already done, which I know he has done because of the promise of Christ, which I have no right not to believe. And when I do fail to believe, which will happen daily, then I should repent of my unbelief.

Making Progress by Beginning Again

Thus I make progress in faith by always going back to what has already been done and given to me by God, like a child learning and relearning my catechism. Luther insists on this in his own case: "I must still read and study the Catechism daily," he says, meaning not the catechism he has written but the ancient texts on which it is based: the Ten Commandments, the Creed, and the Lord's Prayer. These are texts he has never finished mastering: "I . . . must remain a child and pupil of the Catechism, and I do it gladly."[95] It is in fact characteristic of Luther to describe himself as "glad that I still remain a pupil with those who are just beginning to learn."[96] This is how it is with all who really know the Gospel, no matter how learned they are, for "all men, be they ever so illumined by the Holy Spirit, still remain pupils of the Word."[97] The word of God therefore "is our perpetual school, from which we never graduate as perfect masters, neither we nor the Apostles nor the Prophets. We all remain students here . . . as long as we live."[98]

It sounds like another paradox: "No matter how much progress we make, we remain still at the beginning."[99] But once more (as we saw in chap. 5) this is just Luther's distinctive version of the Aristotelian theory of process, where we are always at the starting point and the endpoint at the same time, precisely because we are always moving forward (*semper in motu*). The difference is that in his mature theology, we move forward not by self-condemnation but by faith in the Gospel giving us Christ. We make progress precisely by returning over and over again to this beginning, which is to say by taking hold of Christ once again by faith alone, so that our hearts are increasingly formed in his image.

95. Luther, Longer Preface to the *Large Catechism*, in Tappert, *Book of Concord*, 359.
96. Luther, sermon on the Gospel for the 19th Sunday after Trinity, in Luther, *Sermons* 5:217.
97. Luther, Commentary on Psalm 51, 1532, *LW* 12:305.
98. Luther, Commentary on Psalm 51, 1532, *LW* 12:331.
99. Luther, Preface to the Disputation on Justification, 1536, *LW* 34:157.

Thus Luther continues throughout his career to speak of faith in process terms, as something that "must grow from day to day even to the future life."[100] This is precisely why in this life we have only "that weak faith or the first fruits of faith by which we have begun to take hold of Christ."[101] Our faith is always inadequate in itself, apart from Christ as its object, because it is only "coming to be [*in fieri*], but it is not done [*in facto*]."[102] Here Luther once again uses Aristotelian terminology for process, as he explicitly tells us in the previous paragraph: "As the Aristotelians say, we are coming to be holy [*sumus in fieri sancti*], and not done yet [*et non in facto esse*]."[103] The verbal distinction between *in fieri* and *in facto* marks the difference between what is in process of becoming and what is all done, and Luther's use of it here makes the same contrast that Augustine makes by the distinction between *in spe* and *in re*. In this life we are never done building on what God has already done in Christ, and therefore we are fully righteous and holy only in hope, not yet in reality. What is different from Augustine is Luther's conviction that faith is not just the beginning of the process of building and growth but the heart of the progress we make throughout our lives. Faith makes progress by always coming back to the beginning, its foundation in the word of God. Our movement toward perfection—toward "all done"—is therefore not a journey in which love has the power to bring us closer to God but a process in which faith alone forms our hearts in the image of the Beloved, as we shall see in the next chapter.

The fact that this is still a process means that Luther is not immune to the anxieties of the Augustinian spiritual journey that distressed people in the sixteenth century. Because believers are always also unbelievers, and neither free will nor reason can do anything to overcome our deep-seated unbelief, Luther has a distinctive anxiety about faith, which we encounter in his talk of temptation, or *Anfechtung*. My experience of faith is always an experience of my own inability and my utter dependence on the truth of God's word.[104]

100. Luther, *Freedom of a Christian*, LW 31:358.
101. Luther, 1535 Galatians Commentary, LW 26:234.
102. Luther, Commentary on Psalm 45, 1532, WA 40/2:533 (= LW 12:244). LW translates *in facto* suggestively but anachronistically as "in fact." Latin *factum* means "thing done," which is why it can be used, as here, as equivalent to *perfectum*, "thing completed." It only metamorphoses into our notion of "fact" when the meaning of the Latin is gradually forgotten.
103. Luther, Commentary on Psalm 45, 1532, WA 40/2:532 (= LW 12:243).
104. Luther's talk of the experience of faith is complex, involving at least three elements: (1) faith must always be based on the word, not on experience, as we have seen above in the 1535 Galatians Commentary, on Gal. 4:6, LW 26:387; (2) I cannot learn the power of the Gospel except by experience (cf., e.g., Luther's *Sermons on the Gospel of John*, on John 14:14, in LW 24:99); for (3) what I learn by experience, i.e., in *Anfechtung*, is how weak and powerless I am without the word of the Gospel. Hence it is *Anfechtung* that teaches a person "not only to know

Hence I can always ask: How can I be certain God will give grace and salvation to one as uncertain and weak in faith as I am? When that question grips me, I am plunged into the hard struggle for faith—a struggle I would always lose if the Spirit did not help me in my weakness with sighs that are too deep for words (Rom. 8:26).[105] Victory in the struggle always takes the same form, which becomes central to Luther's thinking about pastoral care: peace and consolation return to me when I remember, yet again, that God's word to me can never be a lie. My faith is unworthy and uncertain, but his promise is not. Hence it is precisely through such trials and temptations that my faith is renewed and strengthened and always increasing, for they drive me back again and again to the truth of God's promise, which is both the beginning of faith and the cause of its continual growth. I keep finding myself at square one, returning to the promise given to me in my baptism, precisely so that I may once again move forward. In that sense I must remain, as in Luther's early doctrine of justification, always in motion (*semper in motu*): whenever I try to rest on the faith I currently have, I find it inadequate. This leaves Luther with a different kind of anxiety as well as a different kind of assurance from most other Protestants, as we will see in chapter 10.

---

and understand, but also to experience [*erfahren*] how right, how true, how sweet, how lovely, how mighty, how comforting God's word is" (Luther's preface to his collected German writings, *LW* 34:287). Luther's concept of the experience of faith can therefore never be separated from his emphasis on the word of God.

105. Cf. Luther's beautiful exegesis of the sigh of the Spirit, which is too weak for us to hear or experience in ourselves in our times of doubt and *Anfechtung*, but which is nonetheless a loud cry for mercy in the ears of God, in the 1535 Galatians Commentary, on Gal. 4:6, *LW* 26:380–89.

8

Luther the Reformer

Gospel as Story That Gives Us Christ

uther's distinction between law and Gospel is a variation of Augustine's distinction between law and grace. It adds a kind of Lutheran codicil to the Augustinian heritage. The codicil is about the Gospel: it tells you where to go to find the grace of God when you're fleeing from the terror of the law. Instead of seeking grace by prayer, which is a human word, you find grace in the Gospel, which is a divine word. This dependence on God's word affords Luther's faith a kind of certainty lacking in Augustine and his medieval heirs, an assurance that the grace of God is for you in particular.

But the Gospel gives you more than grace or forgiveness of sins. Most fundamentally, it gives you Jesus Christ himself, God in the flesh. For Luther, it is by giving you Christ that the Gospel also gives you all good things and divine gifts in him, as we have seen in the previous chapter. Hence the crucial thing to understand in Luther's theology is how the Gospel can be a word that gives you a person. The Gospel is a promise like the wedding vow by which a Bridegroom gives himself to his beloved, but it is also the story of Christ in which that promise is found. The focus of the present chapter is on how Luther came to the conviction that the story of Christ not only tells us who he is but gives him to us in person, so that we are united with him in a kind of spiritual marriage that makes us inwardly new persons, formed in his image.

Gospel Story as Sacrament

Luther's theology requires an outward turn, because the Gospel is an external word, like the sacramental word in which Christ says "I baptize *you* . . ." and means, in each particular circumstance of utterance, one particular believer or another. Yet the outward turn does not imply that the Gospel remains outside us. Like music,[1] the word gets into our hearts through our ears. The result is that Jesus Christ dwells within us, because "this God, who becomes man, who suffers, dies and rises from the dead, is proclaimed to me, enters my ears, and by way of my ears enters my heart."[2] Because the word has a sacramental kind of efficacy, it brings with it into the believing heart the things it speaks of, including righteousness, all the gifts of grace, and Christ himself. Hence the outward turn in Luther's shift to a law/Gospel framework does not mean that God merely says we are righteous outwardly, as if the Gospel were a kind of declaration or announcement that made no inward change in us. Rather, what it signifies outwardly becomes inwardly ours through faith.

Luther's teaching must therefore be distinguished from the later Protestant doctrine of forensic justification—called "forensic" because it uses the language and concepts of the courtroom (one of the meanings of the Latin word *forum*, from which we get the word "forensic"). In the forensic doctrine of justification, the word of grace is essentially a verdict in the divine courtroom from God our judge, who for Christ's sake forgives the sin of believers, not imputing it to them but counting or reckoning them to be righteous even though they are in themselves still sinners. As we shall see later in this chapter, Luther has a place for such language, but it is not nearly the whole of his account of justification—as it might have been if his concept of the Gospel were confined to its initial focus on the word of absolution, which we examined in the previous chapter. What the word of absolution signifies is of course the forgiveness of sins, but what the Gospel came to signify for Luther is Christ himself and everything that belongs to him, including the righteousness of God. Because Christ enters our hearts through the Gospel, Luther takes union with Christ to be the basis of justification. Unlike the purely forensic doctrine, he thinks of justification as something that makes us inwardly new persons, precisely because faith in the Gospel brings Christ into our hearts.

Luther's focus on union with Christ is especially evident in his sermons on the theme of Christmas, which seems to have had a special place in his

---

1. The parallel is explicit in Luther's extravagant praise of music "next to the Word of God" (*LW* 53:323); cf. Bainton, *Here I Stand*, 266–67.

2. Luther, *Sermons on the Gospel of John*, on John 3:32, LW 22:471.

theological imagination because it is the story of how Christ comes to us. "Behold, your king *is coming* to you!" says the prophet (Zech. 9:9), and the gospel writer sees this as a prophecy of how Christ comes to us in the triumphal entry into Jerusalem (Matt. 21:5). This passage is also the text for Luther's sermon on the first Sunday of Advent, which begins his Church Postil, the book of sermons he composed for church use in 1521. This is the season leading up to Christmas, called "Advent" (from *adventus*, Latin for "coming") because it is the time when the church awaits the coming of Christ both at Christmas and at the end of the age. The Gospel proclamation that our king is coming to us gives Luther his version of the Augustinian concept of prevenient grace (from *prae-venire*, to come before), the grace that begins every good work in us, including our faith, because it *comes before* any good thing we can will or do.[3]

As usual, Luther is thinking of a process of justification in which we are always at square one, always having to begin again no matter how far we have already come, and therefore always in need of the grace that begins the process in us. "Everything that *you* begin . . . remains sin," Luther says in this sermon, which is why there can be "no other beginning than that *your king comes to you* and begins to work in you."[4] So he must come to us, because we cannot even begin to come to him. Luther is clear on this point: "You do not come to him and bring him to you,"[5] and likewise, "You do not seek him, but he seeks you. You do not find him, but he finds you. . . . Your faith comes from him, not from you."[6] The preaching of the Gospel thus meets us in our helplessness, when we are stuck at square one, and moves us forward with a grace we are never capable of finding unless our king first comes to us. As Luther puts it in his instruction on how to hear the Gospel, with which he prefaces his book of sermons, "The preaching of the Gospel is nothing else than *Christ coming to us*, or we being brought to him."[7]

If the preaching of the Gospel is how Christ comes to us, giving us Christ in person just like the sacramental word, then Luther must be thinking of the Gospel story itself as if it were a kind of sacrament. And in fact he tells us just this in a striking sermon on Christmas Day 1519, when he says that "all the Gospel stories are sacraments of a sort, i.e., sacred signs through which God brings about, in those who believe, whatever the story

3. For Augustine on the prevenience of grace, see chap. 4, "Grace and Free Will."
4. Luther, *Sermons* 1:25–26.
5. Luther, *Sermons* 1:25.
6. Luther, *Sermons* 1:26.
7. Luther, *Brief Instruction on What to Look for and Expect in the Gospels*, LW 35:121.

designates."[8] He makes the parallel with the sacraments of the church quite explicit:

> Just as baptism is a kind of sacrament through which God makes a person new, and as absolution is a sacrament through which God remits sins, so the words of Christ are sacraments through which he works our salvation. Thus the Gospel is to be regarded sacramentally, i.e., the words of Christ are to be meditated on as symbols through which is given the same righteousness, virtue, and salvation that the words themselves set forth.[9]

Like the sacraments, the words of the Gospel give us comfort and joy by presenting Christ to us as God in the flesh, a divinity who is utterly human, a baby boy in his mother's lap on Christmas Day, who belongs not just to her but to all of us because it was for us that she bore him, as the prophet says ("for *to us* a child is born," Isa. 9:6). Hence we must recognize that the words of the story are not just about people long ago, but are meant for each one of us in particular, all who hear the story and believe it:

> That is, if I hear the story of Christ and don't think that it all pertains to me, so that it is for me that Christ is born, suffered, and died, then the preaching or knowledge of the story isn't worth a thing. . . . No matter how sweet or good Christ is, he is not recognized, he will not cheer us up, unless I believe that *to me* he is sweet and good—unless I say, "*Mother, this baby is mine!*"[10]

Once again, it is faith that makes the word efficacious, so that it brings about what it signifies in those who believe.

This makes the Gospel a very unusual kind of story. Other stories give us examples of virtue to imitate, but cannot give us the virtues they tell us about. The Gospel narratives themselves give us examples of virtuous behavior in the apostles, Luther says, but their virtues are not ours and cannot make us

8. Luther, sermon on Dec. 25, 1519, WA 9:440. To my knowledge this important sermon has not appeared in English except for two paragraphs in Bainton, *Martin Luther Christmas Book*, 39–40. I provide a complete translation in appendix 2.

9. Luther, sermon on Dec. 25, 1519, WA 9:440. Though Luther does not end up counting the Gospel as a sacrament in the strict sense of the term, he continues to think of a broad sense of the word "sacrament" in which it includes "all those things to which a divine promise has been given, such as prayer, the Word, and the cross" (Luther, *Babylonian Captivity*, LW 36:123). The fact that there had always been a broad sense of the term *sacramentum* is familiar from Augustine and medieval theology, and indeed could hardly be missed by any reader of the Latin Bible (Vulgate), where the term *sacramentum* is frequently used in a broad sense; see Cary, *Outward Signs*, 158–61.

10. Luther, sermon on Dec. 25, 1519, WA 9:440. With the italicized words at the end Luther breaks into German, in this otherwise Latin sermon.

righteous. Only Christ, taken hold of by faith, can give us the righteousness and goodness that we read of and hear in the story. For only Christ is presented to us—to use a resonant pair of terms Luther takes from Augustine—as both a sacrament and an example.[11] Thus Luther begins his Christmas sermon by saying, "We must treat the whole life of Christ, all of Christ's deeds, in two ways: both as sacrament and as example."[12] To speak of a sacrament here means that we are dealing with an external means of grace that gives what it signifies. Hence in later explanations of the meaning of the word "Gospel," Luther can drop the technical term "sacrament" (which might confuse a lay audience when used of something other than a church ceremony) and speak instead of Christ as *gift*. To read the New Testament gospels and see Christ as a lawgiver like Moses or an example to follow like the apostles is to miss the point of the Gospel, whose purpose is to give us Christ as a gift, not just an example. To hear the one Gospel in the four New Testament gospels therefore means that

> before you take Christ as an *example*, you accept and recognize him as a *gift*, as a present that God has given you and that is your own. This means that when you see or hear of Christ doing or suffering something, you do not doubt that Christ himself, with his deeds and suffering, belongs to you. On this you may depend as surely as if you had done it yourself; indeed as if you were Christ himself.[13]

Once again faith does not doubt that this word gives what it signifies. And what is signified and given here is not merely absolution or forgiveness of sins but Christ himself and all that is his. This is what "Gospel" means for the mature Luther, as he explains in his oft-reprinted Preface to the New Testament (included originally in his German translation of the Bible): you are hearing the Gospel when you hear that "Christ is your own with his life,

---

11. The pair of terms appears in an influential passage in Augustine, *Trinity* 4:3.6, which played an important role in Luther's earlier thinking (e.g., Luther, Romans Lectures, on Rom. 4:25 and 6:3, *LW* 25:284 and 309–10). Augustine's original point was rather narrowly focused and different from Luther's. Augustine took Christ's bodily death and resurrection to be an *example* for our death and resurrection, but noted that our inward death in sin and inward resurrection in righteousness cannot be exemplified by Christ, because he did not sin and therefore had no inward death to overcome. Hence his outward, bodily death and resurrection is a *sacrament*, an external sign of the inner death and resurrection of our souls. The crucial step beyond this that Luther takes is to assume, in agreement with later medieval theology, that a sacrament is efficacious in giving what it signifies.

12. Luther, sermon on Dec. 25, 1519, *WA* 9:439.

13. Luther, *Brief Instruction on What to Look for and Expect in the Gospels*, *LW* 35:119. The distinction between Christ as gift and example recurs in a somewhat different context more than a decade later in Luther, 1535 Galatians Commentary, on Gal. 5:8, *LW* 27:34.

teaching, works, death, resurrection, and all that he is, has, does and can do."[14] Through faith in the Gospel Christ becomes emphatically our possession, making a deep inward change in us, because "this is the great fire of the love of God for us, whereby the heart and conscience become happy, secure and content. This is what preaching the Christian faith means."[15]

What the Gospel Gives

Combining story and promise in the concept of Gospel is easy to do, because it is in the Gospel story that Christ makes his promises to us. The crucial result is that the story does the same thing as the promise: it gives us Christ and all that is his, including the righteousness of God for our justification. So when the concept of Gospel embraces story as well as promise, telling us what Christ is and does becomes a way of giving us what Christ is and does. With this conception of Gospel, the mature form of Luther's famous contrast between law and Gospel comes into focus. Law and Gospel are both forms of the Word of God, but the one is about what we do, the other about what Christ does. In literary terms, they are two different genres of discourse: one is God telling us what to do, and the other is God telling a story about what he has done for us in Christ, including promises about what he will do for us in Christ. It is all about God's doing, not ours. In what I think is his most illuminating explanation of the law/Gospel contrast, Luther puts it this way:

> The law commands and requires us to do certain things. . . . The gospel, however, does not preach what we are to do or avoid. It sets up no requirements but reverses the approach of the law, does the very opposite, and says, "This is what God has done for you; he has let his Son be made flesh for you, has let him be put to death for your sake."[16]

In an important sense the difference between law and Gospel is rhetorical (insofar as rhetoric is the art of speaking effectively to an audience), because they are two different ways God has of talking, which have two different kinds of effect on those who hear. As Augustine explained long ago, God's law tells us what to do but cannot give us the power to do it—at least, not the power to do it gladly and with true love in the heart—with the effect that it humbles and terrifies sinners.[17] To this Luther adds, as a kind of codicil to the

---

14. Luther, Preface to the New Testament, *LW* 35:361.
15. Luther, *Brief Instruction*, *LW* 35:119.
16. Luther, 1525 Sermon, *How Christians Should Regard Moses*, *LW* 35:162.
17. Augustine, *Spirit and the Letter* 10.16.

Augustinian heritage: the Gospel is God speaking so as to give us the grace to obey the law, with the effect that we are comforted, cheered, and consoled. For it tells us Christ's story, including the promises he makes to us, and when we believe the words of the story that tell us this is *for us*, then we have taken hold of nothing less than Christ himself and made him our own. And that, rather than a discourse that tells us what to do, makes us new and different people, capable of obeying the law of God willingly, with love and delight.

Thus according to the Lutheran codicil, the Gospel is how God answers the Augustinian prayer for grace, "Give what you command, and then command whatever you want."[18] As Luther puts it in the great 1520 treatise *The Freedom of a Christian*: "The promises of God give what the commandments of God demand."[19] This is a formulation of the Lutheran codicil that seems deliberately to echo Augustine's prayer for grace, but replaces human prayer with divine promise. Talking about "promises" here is another way of saying *Gospel*, and talking about "commandments" is another way of saying *law*. Luther's point is that instead of *seeking* grace by prayer, we *find* it in the Gospel. This shows how Luther's law/Gospel contrast steps into the conceptual space of Augustine's law/grace contrast, and what difference it makes. He agrees with Augustine that the law humbles and frightens us so that we flee to grace by faith, but then adds, in effect: faith finds what it seeks not by asking God to give us grace, but by believing that God has given us grace and righteousness and all good things in Christ, as the Gospel promises. This makes a radical change in the spiritual journey envisioned in Augustine's theology. Christ's humanity is not how we get to God; it is how God gives himself to us. It is how God comes in his own flesh to save us, just like at Christmas.

In *The Freedom of a Christian* Luther's doctrine of justification reaches its mature form, based on a Gospel promise that gives us Christ, to be received by faith alone. The result, Luther says, using a biblical image that recurs throughout the Christian tradition, is like a marriage, in which "the wife owns whatever belongs to the husband."[20] Marriage illustrates the way union with Christ results in the wondrous exchange by which sinners come to possess Christ's righteousness and Christ takes ownership of all our sins:

> Here this rich and divine bridegroom Christ marries this poor wicked harlot, redeems her from all evil, and adorns her with all his goodness. Her sins cannot now destroy her, since they are laid upon Christ and swallowed up by him.

18. Augustine, *Confessions* 10:29.40. Cf. above, chap. 6, "Promise and Prayer," for discussion of Luther's use of this saying in his early works.

19. Luther, *The Freedom of a Christian*, LW 31:349.

20. Luther, *Freedom of a Christian*, LW 31:354.

And she has that righteousness in Christ, her husband, of which she may boast as of her own.[21]

The swallowing-up of sins, as Luther explains, means that Christ defeats them in a kind of "mighty duel" on the cross, where he is victor over sin, death, and hell because "his righteousness is greater than the sins of all men, his life stronger than death, and his salvation more invincible than hell."[22] This is a divine bridegroom, with all the power of God, so his sufferings in the flesh overcome all suffering, as well as every evil. This is the good news of the cross that replaces the spiritual masochism of Luther's early "theology of the cross." Instead of teaching us to hate ourselves and desire suffering, it gives us a Beloved who suffered not because he hates himself but because he loves us.

And it gives us the wherewithal to go and do likewise. To extend Luther's metaphor: we could think of a once-filthy harlot who is now dressed like a queen, because that is what she now is. She is married to the king of kings and possesses all the wealth of his heavenly kingdom. What is she to do with this infinite treasury of righteousness, grace, and blessing? To hoard it as a private possession would mean going back to thinking like a harlot, not a queen. So instead, she does what the king does, sharing his kingdom's riches with her neighbors. In this way faith overflows in good works, like a cup filled up to the brim with an inexhaustible supply of living water pouring down from above—and she cannot put a lid on it, so that the water of life keeps spilling over and spreading all around. In Luther's words, "From Christ the good things have flowed and are flowing into us. . . . From us they flow on to those who have need of them."[23] Less metaphorically, the Christian is one who, realizing that she already has "all the riches of righteousness and salvation" and needs "nothing except faith which believes this is true," freely and gladly resolves that "I will therefore give myself as a Christ to my neighbor, just as Christ offered himself to me."[24] This is how faith leads to love and therefore to good works, which are always works of love.

Person and Work

The good works we do, of course, should not be confused with the real righteousness in us, which we receive from our bridegroom alone. We must

21. Luther, *Freedom of a Christian*, LW 31:352.
22. Luther, *Freedom of a Christian*, LW 31:352. The mighty duel remains a theme of Luther's work, for example in Luther, 1535 Galatians Commentary, on Gal. 3:13, LW 26:281–82.
23. Luther, *Freedom of a Christian*, LW 31:371.
24. Luther, *Freedom of a Christian*, LW 31:367.

already possess the riches of divine righteousness and grace and blessing in Christ before we can do anything to share these good things with others. Thus when Luther says the promises give what the commandment demands, this implies that "the commandment must be fulfilled before any works can be done."[25] He explains this startling claim by making a distinction between person and works: "Good works do not make a good man, but a good man does good works," he says, because "it is always necessary that the substance or person himself be good before there can be any good works."[26] The good works are the fruits of faith, which are possible only because faith has already made the person into a good tree capable of bearing good fruit—for as Christ says, "a good tree cannot bear evil fruit, nor can a bad tree bear good fruit."[27]

This analogy of tree and fruit, parallel to person and work (or doer and deed), is used by Luther to explain why, contrary to Aristotle, we cannot acquire a *habitus* or virtue of righteousness in God's sight by practicing repeated acts of righteousness. As he put it years earlier, in the Romans Lectures: "The tree does not come from the fruit but the fruit from the tree. And virtue does not come from acts and works, as Aristotle teaches, but acts come from virtues, as Christ teaches."[28] He makes the same point (minus the learned reference to Aristotle) in *The Freedom of a Christian*: because the fruits do not bear the tree but the other way round, it follows that "the fruits do not make the trees either good or bad, but rather as the trees are, so are the fruits they bear."[29]

So faith must make the person good before her works can be any good. In the great Galatians commentary a decade and a half later, which contains his most elaborate defense of his doctrine of justification, Luther puts the point even more strongly, saying faith makes a new person. Before faith, the person who can do good works isn't there at all: "Faith first makes the person, who afterward performs works," which is to say, "faith takes the doer himself and makes him into a tree and his deeds become fruit."[30] Thus when Paul says it is the doer of the law who is justified (Rom. 2:13), this means there is no doer of good things until there is faith, for "the 'doer of the Law' is not one

25. Luther, *Freedom of a Christian*, LW 31:353.
26. Luther, *Freedom of a Christian*, LW 31:361. The use of the technical term *substantia* here is a hint at the Aristotelian principle that being (i.e., substance) precedes working or operation, which we will find Luther using to interpret the tree-fruit analogy in the 1535 Galatians Commentary, below.
27. Luther, *Freedom of a Christian*, LW 31:361, quoting Matt. 7:18.
28. Luther, Romans Lectures, on Rom. 8:7, LW 25:354.
29. Luther, *Freedom of a Christian*, LW 31:361.
30. Luther, 1535 Galatians Commentary, 3:10, LW 26:255.

who becomes a doer on the basis of his deeds; he is one who, *having already become a person through faith*, then becomes a doer."[31]

Thus Luther does not make the kind of distinction between justification and sanctification that is common in the forensic doctrine of later Protestantism, where righteousness is merely imputed to us, and a real inward transformation takes place in us only as we cooperate with the Holy Spirit, turning our hearts from love of sin to a genuine love of righteousness and good works. Such a doctrine would mean that adding real righteousness to merely imputed righteousness requires our work. Luther, on the contrary, never assigns good works any role in making us better persons. This is an offense to reason and to Aristotle, as Luther likes to point out, but it is essential to the effect of the Gospel in us. To say that good works—even with the help of grace and the Holy Spirit—make us inwardly better persons would be like trying to make a tree good by getting it to grow good fruit, which is exactly backward. The tree must be good before the fruit can be any good, which is to say the person must be good—really and truly good—before his work can be good. And that good tree comes into being only by faith, for the new person comes into being only in Christ. Nothing we do makes us more righteous or holy than we already are simply by believing in the Gospel; for there is no righteousness that improves upon Christ himself, who dwells in our hearts by faith alone.

Writings by Luther that might seem to make a distinction between justification and sanctification[32] are really doing something else, as we can see by looking at the often-anthologized sermon *Two Kinds of Righteousness*. Here Luther famously distinguishes between "alien righteousness" and "proper righteousness." Readers without Latin might reasonably expect that "alien righteousness" would remain outside us, as in the later Protestant notion of justification, and that "proper righteousness" would mean the real righteousness in us, produced by sanctification. But Luther's point is nearly the exact opposite. The alien righteousness is what makes us inwardly new persons; it is called "alien" because it is the righteousness of another person (Latin *alieni*), for it is Christ's righteousness. To suppose that this righteousness remains outside us and alien to us would be to miss the whole point of faith, which makes the righteousness of Christ our own, so that we can say, "Mine are Christ's living, doing, and speaking, his suffering and dying, mine as much as if I had lived, done, spoken and died as he did."[33] This is the result of the

---

31. Luther, 1535 Galatians Commentary, 3:10, *LW* 26:260.

32. Here my focus is on what Luther means by the terms "justification" and "righteousness." For what he means by the terms "sanctification" and "holiness," see chap. 10, "Sanctification as Evidence."

33. Luther, *Two Kinds of Righteousness* (sermon, 1519), *LW* 31:297.

wondrous exchange, which is like a marriage in that "a bridegroom possesses all that is his bride's and she all that is his."[34]

On the same page, Luther uses the scholastic term for a grace that inwardly forms our soul, when he says the alien righteousness is infused (*infusa*), Latin for "poured in." This was a central technical term in the medieval theology of grace, indebted to Augustine's reading of Romans 5:5, where the love of God is poured out (*diffusa*) into our hearts by the Holy Spirit.[35] Introducing the concept of alien righteousness at the beginning of the sermon, Luther says it is "infused from without" (*infusa ab extra*), a point that is obscured in most English editions, which render the phrase "instilled from without."[36] What this means is that the alien righteousness does the work of an infused virtue, in the medieval Augustinian sense: it is a divine gift that comes to us from outside our own soul and its powers but makes its home deep within us and changes us from the inside out, so that we have true faith, hope, and love.

Thus the alien righteousness, like Christ himself and the external word of the Gospel, comes to us from outside but doesn't stay there. Faith takes them all in. The alien righteousness thereby becomes the core of a believer's being, as Christ dwells in her heart by faith,[37] making her a new person, the good tree that is capable of bearing good fruit, a doer of the law who does good works. These works are her *proper* righteousness because they are her own (Latin *propria*). However, because she lives in Christ, not in herself, her own righteousness is a superficial thing compared to the alien righteousness of Christ that is poured into her. She has no need of this "proper righteousness" to make her really righteous, for she already has true righteousness in Christ. But as Luther emphasizes in *Freedom of a Christian*,[38] her neighbors have need of her righteousness and good works, which is why God commands the tree to bear fruit, so that she might serve her neighbor in works of love. So "proper righteousness" is an external and relatively superficial thing, the outward good works that are useful indeed to her neighbor but make no real change in the depth of her heart, where it is Christ who dwells within her by faith alone and changes everything.

The righteousness of God is thus not merely imputed to us but becomes our very own, in a way deeper than our own righteousness. Our most fundamental

34. Luther, *Two Kinds of Righteousness* (sermon, 1519), LW 31:297.

35. For particularly influential examples of this pervasive Augustinian reading of Rom. 5:5 as describing the inner effects of divine grace, see Augustine, *Spirit and the Letter* 5.3; 14.25; 17.29; 25.42; 26.46; 28.49; and (specifically in connection with "the righteousness of God") 32.57.

36. Luther, *Two Kinds of Righteousness* (sermon, 1519), WA 2:145 (= LW 31:297).

37. Cf. Eph. 3:17, quoted in this sermon at LW 31:299.

38. Luther, *Freedom of a Christian*, LW 31:365.

possessions, which make us the persons we are, are never our own except as gifts, which we receive and then give again. For by faith we possess Christ as a gift, together with all he possesses, whereas by works of love we are given to our neighbors and become their possession, together with all we possess. Because "faith possesses nothing of its own, only the deeds and life of Christ,"[39] we possess all things, including the righteousness of God. Good works, on the other hand, are a possession that is our own in a more superficial sense. There is "something of your own in them," but in such a way that "they should not belong to you but to your neighbor."[40] Thus the alien righteousness of Christ is related to our own proper righteousness as faith is related to works of love: "Faith brings and gives Christ to you with all his possessions. Love gives you to your neighbor with all your possessions."[41]

Yet there is a concept that is even more helpful than "possession" for Luther when he needs to present his most technical and detailed account of the doctrine of justification, and that is the Aristotelian concept of form, as we are about to see.

The Word Forms Persons

The tree-fruit analogy helps Luther get across what is philosophically the most counterintuitive point in his teaching: that we do not become more righteous by practice, getting better at justice by doing what is just. Yet justification is still a process in which we do get better and more righteous, for the alien righteousness of Christ grows in us; it "is not infused all at once, but it begins, makes progress and is finally perfected at the end through death."[42] To see how this is possible we need to turn once more to Aristotle, but to his theory of perception rather than his concept of *habitus*. What perception and *habitus* have in common is the fundamental concept of a form in the soul, or we could say, the formation of the soul—the way that the soul or mind or heart (Luther uses these terms interchangeably) takes on a definite shape that characterizes its actions, thoughts, and emotions, like a just man whose deeds and thinking and feelings are just. For Aristotle, justice is a form in the soul that takes shape by practice, like learning to be a builder or an athlete. For Luther, it is more like learning a favorite song, getting it written on our hearts as we hear it over and over again. For faith comes by hearing

39. Luther, *Brief Instruction*, LW 35:120.
40. Luther, *Brief Instruction*, LW 35:120.
41. Luther, *Sermons* 1:34.
42. Luther, *Two Kinds of Righteousness* (sermon, 1519), WA 2:146 (= LW 31:299).

(Rom. 10:17), which means that in this regard our heart is formed not by our actions but by our perceptions. We keep hearing the word of Christ, which is the Gospel, and as we believe it our heart takes on the form of the word, which is the form of Christ himself. For according to the Aristotelian theory of perception, the mind takes on the form of the external thing it perceives. It is shaped by what it knows.[43] Accordingly, Luther conceives faith as the act of perception in which we take on the form of Christ by knowing him, through hearing the Gospel with faith.

This is what Luther has in mind, I think, in the great Galatians Commentary of 1535 when he says that faith is "the formal righteousness on account of which a man is justified" because Christ is "the form of our faith."[44] Formal righteousness is a concept about which Luther usually has very critical things to say, because in medieval theology it means a *habitus*, the virtue of justice that gives form to the soul of a righteous person.[45] But if it's another name for Christ dwelling in us by faith, then Luther is happy to affirm that we have a formal righteousness. Our true formal righteousness is the form of Christ himself, which Luther equates with what Paul calls "the new man who is being renewed in knowledge after the image of the one who created him" (Col. 3:10).[46] This is another way of talking about the alien righteousness infused or poured into us, making us new persons and doers of the law, the good trees that can bear good fruit. It means that Christ is present in our hearts by being present in faith itself as its form, which is an Aristotelian way of saying that Christ is what makes Christian faith what it essentially is. Thus faith makes us truly and inwardly righteous, because by faith our hearts take on the form of Christ himself.

Luther explains how this happens in his comment on Galatians 4:19, where Paul compares himself to a mother who is in labor "until Christ be formed

43. Thus the Finnish tradition of Luther interpretation is appropriately combined with an appreciation of Luther's Aristotelianism; for the way faith takes hold of Christ "is to be understood in terms of Aristotelian epistemology, which Luther uses when he speaks about Christ as the form of faith. Aristotle claimed that in the act of knowing, the form of the object of knowledge is transferred into the knower" (Vainio, *Justification and Participation in Christ*, 31).

44. Luther, 1535 Galatians Commentary, on Gal. 2:16, LW 26:130. This is part of a passage that is very important for the Finnish school of Luther interpretation inaugurated by Tuomo Mannermaa with the volume now translated as *Christ Present in Faith* (cf. also Mannermaa's essays in Braaten and Jenson, *Union with Christ*). I am very much in agreement with the Finnish approach in general, and what I am doing here is identifying the Aristotelian thread in this complex knot of thought. See also Vainio, *Justification and Participation in Christ*, 19–36.

45. Luther, 1535 Galatians Commentary, on Gal. 2:16, LW 26:127.

46. As quoted in Luther, 1535 Galatians Commentary, on Gal. 4:19, WA 40:650 (= LW 26:431). Luther is commenting on Gal. 4:19, where Paul writes, "I am again in the labor of childbirth until Christ be formed in you," WA 40:649 (= LW 26:430).

in" the Galatians,[47] which reminds Luther of how Paul describes himself also as a father who begets believers "through the Gospel" (1 Cor. 4:15), which is to say "in the Spirit"[48] (as Luther adds, in a typical Reformation pairing of word and Spirit). For Paul is a teacher of the faith, and every teacher is like a parent, giving birth to the form of a mind as a parent gives birth to the form of a body. The form of the Christian mind is faith, Luther explains, because the heart which has faith has "the true form of Christ, which is provided by the ministry of the word."[49] Thus it is that word and Spirit work together, in the ministry of the church and its preaching, to form Christ in the hearts and minds of believers. The word proceeds from the teacher, who is the minister of the word, to the heart of the hearer, where "the Holy Spirit is present and impresses the word on the heart."[50] This is hardly what Aristotle had in mind, to be sure, but it does make use of Aristotelian concepts. The Holy Spirit is the divine power that brings Christ into our hearts—a thoroughly biblical teaching—but the language about the "form of Christ" picks up on Aristotelian explanations of how the soul is inwardly formed by the external forms it takes in through perception. After all, this is the only theory of perception actually available to Luther if he wants to articulate what happens when hearing an external word changes the heart.

That Luther actually is using Aristotelian philosophy is clear from remarks he makes in his early works, where he uses the Aristotelian theory of perception to articulate the way the wondrous exchange is based on the incarnation. The key text to consider on this point is a sermon he preaches on Christmas Day 1514, one of the earliest texts we have from him. The sermon uses Aristotelian philosophy to articulate one of the most striking themes of the church fathers, usually thought to be foreign to Protestantism, but which Luther clearly finds both true and beautiful: the concept of deification, whereby believers can be said to be gods because they are sons and daughters of God, not by nature (which is true only of Christ, the eternally begotten Son of God) but by grace of adoption (cf. Rom. 8:15), as they receive the immortality of everlasting life and thus "become partakers of the divine nature" (2 Pet. 1:4). Therefore the purpose of the incarnation, according to church fathers like Irenaeus and Athanasius, can be formulated thus: "God became man so that man might become God."[51] Luther repeats

47. Luther, 1535 Galatians Commentary, on Gal. 4:19, WA 40:649 (= LW 26:430).
48. Luther, 1535 Galatians Commentary, on Gal. 4:19, LW 26:430.
49. Luther, 1535 Galatians Commentary, on Gal. 4:19, LW 26:430.
50. Luther, 1535 Galatians Commentary, on Gal. 4:19, LW 26:430.
51. Luther, sermon on Dec. 25, 1514, WA 1:28. Cf. Irenaeus, *Against Heresies*, the end of the preface to book 5; Athanasius, *The Incarnation of the Word* 54:3; Gregory of Nazianzus,

this formula, and adds another way of making the same point, taking off from the language of John 1:14: "The Word became flesh so that the flesh might become the Word."[52] That is to say that Christ, the eternal Word of God, takes on the form of human flesh so that human flesh—that is, ourselves—may take on the form of the Word, participating in his reality as the eternal Son of God.

So what Luther needs to explain at this point is how it is that "just as the Word of God became flesh, it certainly must be that the flesh will become Word."[53] We creatures of flesh, who have a beginning in time, cannot simply be transformed into the eternal Word, which has no beginning in time. Our participation in the divine life must work differently. Here is where Luther finds Aristotle's theory of perception helpful.

> It's not surprising that we must be said to become the Word, when even the philosophers say that intellect *is* the intelligible through actual [i.e., the act of] understanding, and sense *is* the sensible through actual sensation—how much more is this true in the Spirit and the Word! For Aristotle says that the possibility of understanding is in actuality none of the things it understands, but it is all of them in potentiality, and thus is in a certain sense all things. . . . This is fine philosophy but few understand it.[54]

The technical Aristotelian language here means: the soul's intellectual ability, which is the power or possibility of understanding in us (*intellectus possibilis*), moves from potentiality to actuality as it is actualized in the act of understanding (*actualem intellectionem*). This actualization takes place, according to Aristotelian theory, as the intellect takes on the intelligible form of what it understands, just as the senses take on the sensible form or image of what they perceive. That is why the intellect, the possibility of understanding in us, "is in a certain sense all things": it can potentially understand anything, and when it does actually understand, it takes on the form and thus the reality of whatever it understands. For example, color is the form of visibility according to Aristotelian philosophy (for without it there is nothing to see), and to perceive the color that gives visible form to a wall is to have that form—the reality of the color—in your mind, analogous to the way that the same color

---

Oration 29:19 (the third "Theological Oration"). For adoption as sons and daughters of God making us gods by grace, see Irenaeus, *Against the Heretics* 3:6.1 (end) and the end of the preface to book 4.

52. Luther, sermon on Dec. 25, 1514, WA 1:28.

53. Luther, sermon on Dec. 25, 1514, WA 1:28.

54. Luther, sermon on Dec. 25, 1514, WA 1:29, accepting the emendations suggested by Dieter, *Der junge Luther und Aristoteles*, 261.

is present in the jelly of your eye that is also present externally on the wall.[55] Or to use an illustration that is closer to Luther's own heart: the form of a favorite song gets into our ears and then into our minds as the musical form we perceive in sound becomes the form of our souls. That is what we mean when we say we've learned the song "by heart."

Luther applies this set of conceptual connections to the doctrine of justification in the Romans Lectures the next year, where he repeats the point that the Word became flesh "so that we might be made the Word."[56] Combining two key biblical passages on the incarnation, he teaches that the Word became flesh (John 1:14) and took on the form of a servant (Phil. 2:7) so that "flesh might become the Word and man become the form of the Word."[57] This requires our flesh (which in the biblical sense means the whole of our human existence in this world, body and soul) to "give up its form and take on the form of the Word."[58] Luther compares this giving up of form to the famous Aristotelian notion of the mind as *tabula rasa*, a blank slate or, literally, "erased tablet." The underlying metaphor is of a tablet for writing, which must be erased and cleaned off before new forms can be inscribed in it (think of erasing a chalkboard). Thus in order to take on the form of the Word we must expel all previous forms, including our belief in our own righteousness—by confessing that everything in us is sin, which means the form of righteousness is something we utterly lack. We must confess that our souls are, in the technical Aristotelian sense, in a state of privation.

> For as the philosophers say: the form is not brought in except where there is privation of form and the expulsion of the previous form. Also, the possibility of understanding does not receive a form unless in its beginning it is stripped of all form like a *tabula rasa*.[59]

Luther feels free to use Aristotelian philosophy here because it is only saying, in abstract conceptual form, what "all creatures proclaim": that it is only the empty who are filled, only the sick who are healed, only the lowly who are lifted up, and so on.[60]

---

55. Cf. the comparison of Christ as form in the soul to the color as form in a wall in Luther, 1535 Galatians Commentary, on Gal. 2:16; 2:20, LW 26:129, 167.

56. Luther, Romans Lectures, glosses, Luther's note on Rom. 6:17, LW 25:54.

57. Luther, Romans Lectures, on Rom. 6:17, WA 56:330 (= LW 25:317).

58. Luther, Romans Lectures, on Rom. 6:17, WA 56:330 (= LW 25:317).

59. Luther, Romans Lectures, on Rom. 3:7, WA 56:218–19 (= LW 25:204). Here, as in the sermon on Christmas 1514 above, I translate *intellectus possibilis* as "possibility of understanding." The full technical meaning is more elaborate than a brief translation can suggest: it is the soul's innate power or faculty of intellect in its potential rather than actualized state.

60. Luther, Romans Lectures, on Rom. 3:7, WA 56:218–19 (= LW 25:204).

The crucial connection between incarnation and the wondrous exchange is made in the midst of Luther's most elaborate account of justification in the Romans Lectures, when he says that God justifies us "when He makes us to be like His Word, that is, righteous, true, wise, etc."[61] This is clearly a deep and real change in the believer:

> He thus changes us into His Word. . . . He makes us such when we believe His Word is such, that is, righteous and true. *For then there is a similar form of the Word and the believer*, that is, truth and righteousness."[62]

Here, as the context of the Romans Lectures makes clear, the similarity of form between Word and believer is our heart's agreement with God's word when it accuses and condemns us, in accordance with Luther's early program of spiritual masochism. What we see twenty years later, however, in the 1535 Galatians Commentary, is the same Aristotelian conceptuality applied to the Gospel word of grace, where we take on the form of the word by believing that God is gracious to us in Jesus Christ.

Those who believe the Gospel, according to the Galatians Commentary, take on the form of Christ. This is another way of talking about the renewed image of God in us, Paul's "new man," which for Luther means that we "feel, think, and want exactly what God does, whose thought and will is that we obtain the forgiveness of sins and eternal life through Jesus Christ."[63] We think as God thinks, feel as God feels, and will what God wills, insofar as we agree with the word that gives us Christ. Thus we have the same form in us that is in Christ our God, because the form of Christ himself is in us through faith in his word. For those who believe the word of Christ "are like God; that is they think of God altogether as he feels in His heart, and they have the same form in their mind that God or Christ has."[64] This form in us is what Luther is thinking of when he affirms that we do have a "formal righteousness," which consists not of our works but of our faith.[65] To call it "formal," in the context of medieval Aristotelianism in which Luther is arguing, means that it is real and makes a real change in us—in Pauline terms, that it makes us a new man, or in Jesus' metaphor, that we are a good tree that can bear good fruit.

61. Luther, Romans Lectures, on Rom. 3:7, *LW* 25:211.
62. Luther, Romans Lectures, on Rom. 3:7, *LW* 25:211.
63. Luther, 1535 Galatians Commentary, on Gal. 4:19, *LW* 26:431.
64. Luther, 1535 Galatians Commentary, on Gal. 4:19, *LW* 26:431.
65. Luther, 1535 Galatians Commentary, on Gal. 2:16; 3:6, *LW* 26:130, 229 (cf. also *LW* 26:132).

In the Galatians Commentary Luther even elaborates the tree-fruit analogy in an Aristotelian way. To try to become righteous by doing the works of the law, he says, "is to make apples without a tree, out of wood or soil, which is not to make apples but to make sheer fantasies."[66] The conceptual contrast in this illustration is between material and form, which is the difference between what something is made out of and what it essentially is (like our example in chapter 1 of a bowl made out of stone, whose essence is to be a bowl, not merely unformed stone). In Luther's illustration, wood and soil are the material, since the tree is made out of wood composed of material drawn from the soil, but these materials are inert and inoperative, so far as bearing fruit is concerned, until they are formed into an active, living tree. As he puts the point a few pages later, using technical Aristotelian terminology: "being precedes working."[67] The implication is: the tree has to be formed and come into being before there can be any activity that bears fruit. In the same way, the good person must be formed and come into being as a good person, one who is truly good and righteous, before she can do good works. The material to be formed in us is our human will, thoughts, and feelings. What gives this material form and being as a good person is the form of Christ in us, which means that we will and think and feel just as Christ does, who wills and thinks and feels just as God does. Our souls thus take on a real or formal righteousness not because we follow Christ's commandments (his *law*) or practice living like Christ (imitating him as an *example*) but because we receive him as a *gift*, perceiving who he is, his real form, through the hearing of faith, as we take hold of him in the external word of the Gospel.

Perceiving Who We Are

Because Luther thinks of perception and understanding in Aristotelian terms, it is a mistake to assimilate his talk of Christ dwelling in us to modern concepts of consciousness, in which the world of conscious experience becomes a kind of inner space where we may turn and look inward to find what is within. Luther never looks inside himself to find Christ. It is precisely by taking hold of Christ outside us, in the external word of the Gospel, that faith brings Christ into the heart.

This might seem paradoxical, but once again from an Aristotelian perspective it is just common sense. The form of external things gets into our minds

66. Luther, 1535 Galatians Commentary, on Gal. 3:10, WA 40/1:402 (= LW 26:255).
67. Luther, 1535 Galatians Commentary, on Gal. 3:10, LW 26:261 (= WA 40/1:410). The Latin is *esse praecedere operari*.

precisely as we perceive and pay attention to things outside us. If you want to learn a song by heart, you don't listen to your heart but to the song, as the sound of it reverberates in the air and in your ears. Listen often enough, and (to put it in Aristotelian terms) the *form* of the song will come to be in you without the *material*. That is to say, the sound waves are not in your heart, but their musical structure is. It is written on your heart (to use that biblical metaphor again) as truly and really as it is written on an electronic disc or translated into radio waves—and the proof is that any of these media make it possible to reproduce the music in the medium of sound waves, by singing or playing the stereo or the radio. So there is a very real sense in which the form of the music is in you. And this is much more than just an idea you have about the music: it is the music itself, the form that makes it what it is. Likewise, if you want to be united with Christ, Luther thinks, you must listen to the Gospel as it comes to you from outside, through your ears and into your heart. When you receive this word by faith, the form of Christ becomes your own, like the music of your heart. But if you want to know the form of your own heart—to know who you really are—you must not look at your heart but call to mind the words spoken to you when you were baptized and when you hear the Gospel preached. That is how the bride knows she is a bride—how the queen knows she is a queen, the beloved of the Son of God. She lives like a queen and does what a queen does only because she knows who she is, and she knows who she is only because of the promise of her bridegroom by which he gives himself to her, so that she shares his life, his thinking, his feelings, and his deeds. So it is for Luther a fundamental point of pastoral theology that faith means directing our attention not inwardly to our conscious experience but outwardly to the truth of God's word.

This helps explain the startling language Luther uses to locate our own existence outside ourselves in Christ. It is a matter of where we look and direct our attention:

> The Gospel commands us to look, not at our own good deeds or perfection but at God Himself as He promises, and at Christ himself. . . . And this is why our theology is certain: it snatches us away from ourselves and *places us outside ourselves* so that we do not depend on our own strength, conscience, *experience*, person or works, but depend on that which is outside ourselves, that is, on the promise and truth of God, which cannot deceive.[68]

What we have here, once again, is the certainty of unreflective faith, grounded on the external word rather than anything I see in myself. For if Christ is being

---

68. Luther, 1535 Galatians Commentary, on Gal. 4:6, *LW* 26:387.

formed in me by faith, then the only way I can know who I am in the depths
of my soul is to look away from my soul at the form of Christ in the Gospel.
Therefore "faith is a constant gaze that looks at nothing except Christ,"[69] and
its effect is that I am "pulled out of my own skin and transferred into Christ."[70]

The Activity of Faith

Another peculiar feature of Luther's language follows from his thinking in
terms of the Aristotelian theory of perception rather than the Aristotelian
theory of *habitus*: he treats faith as passive in one sense but active in another.
On the one hand, faith is a "passive righteousness,"[71] because it receives Christ
and his righteousness not by doing anything about it but simply by believing
what is heard in the Gospel. On the other hand, believing the Gospel does not
mean merely to have a positive opinion of it; it means actively "taking hold of
Christ" (*apprehendere Christum*) in what is often a strenuous battle against
temptation, anxiety, and doubt.[72] Elsewhere he says that faith is always "a
living, busy, active, mighty thing."[73] These oft-quoted words are not just vague
praise of the power of faith. They are telling us that faith is not a *habitus*, a
disposition of the soul that could possibly be inactive or asleep like "an idle
quality."[74] This in turn means, as Luther puts it in the startling opening lines
of *The Freedom of a Christian*, that faith is not a virtue,[75] for a virtue is by
medieval reckoning a type of *habitus*.

So also the righteousness of faith, which is the form of Christ in us, cannot be thought of as a *habitus* or inert quality of the soul. Or we could
say: insofar as it does become a *habitus*, it is no longer Christian faith, but
merely our idle thoughts about Christ rather than the active taking hold
of Christ in the Gospel. For the form of Christ in us is not a mere idea or
opinion about him. It is Christ living and acting in us through the power of
the Holy Spirit, precisely to the extent that we pay attention to the external

---

69. Luther, 1535 Galatians Commentary, on Gal. 3:38, *LW* 26:356.

70. Luther, 1535 Galatians Commentary, on Gal. 2:20, *LW* 26:167.

71. A key point dwelt upon at length in Luther, 1535 Galatians Commentary, Preface, *LW*
26:4–12.

72. *Apprehendere Christum*, "taking hold of Christ," is a characteristic way of talking about
faith in the 1535 Galatians Commentary; e.g., *LW* 26:87–88, 130, 132, 287, 357. Note also the
1535 Theses on Faith, thesis 12, where Luther describes true faith as *fides apprehensiva Christi*,
WA 39/2:45 (= *LW* 34:110).

73. Luther, Preface to Romans, *LW* 35:370.

74. As Luther puts it twice in the 1535 Galatians Commentary, on Gal. 2:16; 2:20, *LW* 26:129,
168. See above, chap. 5, "*Habitus* and Elicited Acts."

75. Luther, *Freedom of a Christian*, *LW* 31:343.

word of the Gospel.[76] This same form of Christ in us makes us true doers of the law, as faith becomes the "do-all" or *factotum* of good works.[77] It is not as if the works themselves merit anything, but only faith itself, which is "the divinity in the work, in the person and the members of the body, as the one and only cause of justification."[78] This is true, of course, only to the extent that Christ himself is present in faith (which contains Christ like a ring that contains a gem, Luther says[79]) because no matter how active faith is, if it is judged apart from Christ, it is as sinful as everything else we do. As we have seen, in the process of justification faith begins and grows in us but does not reach perfection in this life.[80] The imperfection of the process is the reason Luther adds a forensic component to his doctrine of justification, teaching that God does not impute or count the sins of believers against them. Once again, this is something he learns from Augustine.

The Nonimputation of Sin

Though he is not an Aristotelian, Augustine knows quite well that any process is imperfect so long as it is still under way. Rather than using the Aristotelian theory of motion, however, Augustine includes the process of justification in his overall picture of the Christian life as a pilgrimage, a journey of our souls on the road to their heavenly home. And he makes it quite clear that until we reach home, our righteousness is imperfect. He belabors the point in his treatise on *The Perfection of Human Righteousness*, where he observes that in this life we are saved only in hope (*in spe*) because we are still being healed of sin and "there is full righteousness only when there is full health."[81]

Yet those who are not fully righteous may be counted righteous by God's grace. Turning to Psalm 32:2 ("Blessed is the one to whom the Lord will not impute sin"), Augustine teaches that God does not impute sin to those who

---

76. As might be expected, Luther has an especially powerful exegesis of Paul's striking formulation in Gal. 2:20—"I live, yet not I, but Christ lives in me"—in the 1535 Galatians Commentary, LW 26:167–72. This includes the claim, "Christ is my form," LW 26:167.

77. Luther, 1535 Galatians Commentary, on Gal. 3:16, LW 26:266 (= WA 40/1:417).

78. Luther, 1535 Galatians Commentary, on Gal. 3:16, LW 26:266 (= WA 40/1:417).

79. Luther, 1535 Galatians Commentary, on Gal. 2:16, LW 26:132.

80. Cf. Luther's use of Augustinian language (*in spe* / *in re*) together with Aristotelian language about the beginning and perfection of a process, to make this point in the 1535 Galatians Commentary: "We have indeed *begun* to be justified by faith. . . . But we are not yet *perfectly* righteous. . . . Thus our righteousness does not yet exist in fact [*in re*] but it still exists in hope [*in spe*]" (LW 27:21 [= WA 40/2:24]).

81. Augustine, *The Perfection of Human Righteousness* 3.8.

pray in faith for forgiveness.[82] This explains why Scripture can say that believers, despite their imperfection, may walk unblemished (*immaculati*) in the way of righteousness. How can those who are merely on the way (*in via*) toward righteousness be walking without blemish? The answer is that a sin that isn't imputed to us doesn't count, and what doesn't count makes no blemish:

> It's not absurd to say that someone is walking without blemish who is not yet perfect, but running toward that perfection blamelessly, *lacking damnable crimes* and not neglecting to cleanse even *venial sins*. . . . For our walk, which is to say our journey toward perfection, is cleansed by clean prayer . . . so that, as long as *what is not imputed is not blamed*, our path to perfection may be taken without blame, which is to say without blemish.[83]

"Damnable crimes" is a term that covers what medieval theology calls mortal sins, as opposed to venial sins, which (as we saw in chap. 5) are cleansed by daily prayer. Luther eventually rejects this distinction between mortal and venial sin, as we shall see. But this should not obscure the fact that Luther's use of forensic language, and especially his talk of the nonimputation of sin, conforms to Augustine's usage here. The nonimputation of sin is not justification, nor is it the righteousness of God by which we are made truly righteous. Rather, it is a stopgap, making up for the imperfection that is an inevitable feature of any incomplete process. In a passage Luther likes to quote, Augustine explains, "All the commandments are counted as done [*facta deputantur*] when whatever is not done is excused [*ignoscitur*]."[84] Thus for Luther, the forensic element in justification is not the merits of Christ imputed to us or a declaration that we are righteous, but simply God excusing our ongoing failure to keep all his commandments, because he knows that Christ is in us by faith bringing us to a perfection that is not yet.

Augustine is also one of the inspirations for Luther's conviction (which we first examined in chap. 5) that in the process of justification we are always at square one, needing to depart from the sin that is our *terminus a quo*

---

82. Augustine, *Perfection of Human Righteousness* 6.15; I translate the psalm verse from Augustine's Latin: *Beatus cui non imputabit Dominus peccatum.*

83. Augustine, *Perfection of Human Righteousness* 9.20. Augustine is commenting on Ps. 119:1: *Beati immaculati in via, qui ambulant in lege Domini.* At this point in the treatise he has just finished quoting a series of passages where God commands people to be perfect, followed by a series of passages where the people of God are described as *immaculati.*

84. Augustine, *Retractations* 1.19.3. Luther twice gives a close but not exact quotation of this passage: in *Explanations of the 95 Theses*, on thesis 58 (LW 31:214), and in *Against Latomus* (LW 32:189). He also alludes to it as one of the two most important passages from Augustine in his table talk #347 (LW 54:49). The other is the passage about sin not being imputed in *On Marriage and Desire* 1:25.28, discussed below.

in order to move toward the righteousness that is our *terminus ad quem*. In one of his letters Augustine writes that the virtue of charity is never present in us "to the fullest extent, which cannot be increased; but as long as it can be increased, *that which is less than it should be actually comes from vice. . . .* And because of this vice, no matter how much we progress, we must always pray, 'forgive us our debts.'"[85] The Augustinian prayer for grace must always therefore include a prayer for forgiveness, because the imperfection of the virtue we have so far achieved is always sin. Luther quotes this passage in his Romans Lectures to support his view that all our sins are mortal and none of our works are meritorious, because "in doing good works, we sin—unless God through Christ covers this imperfection and does not impute it to us."[86]

Luther succinctly explains the connection between the Augustinian journey and the forensic component in justification in his first Galatians Commentary, published in 1519. Describing the process in the Augustinian terms we encountered in chapter 5, he says: "Everyone who believes in Christ is righteous, not yet fully in reality [*in re*] but in hope [*in spe*]. For he has begun to be justified and healed."[87] Because the believer has begun to be but is not yet completely righteous in reality, "the sin that remains in his flesh is not imputed to him. This is because Christ, who is entirely without sin, has now become one with His Christian."[88] Hence union with Christ is the basis of the forensic element in justification—not the other way round, as is frequently the case in later Protestant doctrines of justification.

In his second Galatians Commentary, published in 1535, Luther spells out more fully the relation between the forensic component of justification and the real righteousness that faith begins in us. His most elaborate discussion of the relation is in his long comment on Galatians 3:6,[89] the passage where Paul quotes Genesis 15:6, "Abraham believed God, and it was imputed to him as righteousness."[90] The backbone of Luther's discussion here is a distinction he makes between faith and imputation, which together compose what

---

85. Augustine, Letter 167:4.15, as quoted in Luther, Romans Lectures, on Rom. 4:7, *WA* 56:289 (= *LW* 25:276). Luther identifies this as Letter 29, but that is not the numbering in modern editions.

86. Luther, Romans Lectures, on Rom 4:7, *WA* 56:289 (= *LW* 25:276).

87. Luther, 1519 Galatians Commentary, *WA* 2:495 (= *LW* 27:227).

88. Luther, 1519 Galatians Commentary, *WA* 2:495 (= *LW* 27:227).

89. Luther, 1535 Galatians Commentary, on Gal. 3:6, *LW* 26:229–35.

90. Luther, 1535 Galatians Commentary, on Gal. 3:6, *WA* 40:358 (= *LW* 26:226). The verb in the quotation, *reputare* in the translation Luther is using in his commentary, is along with *imputare* one of two Latin verbs commonly translated "impute." Other common, less technical translations are "reckon" and "count," which I used also for Augustine's term *deputantur* above.

he calls "Christian righteousness." The faith in our hearts, says Luther, "is indeed a formal righteousness,"[91] which means—in the standard Aristotelian vocabulary he is using in his dispute with medieval theologians—that it is a real righteousness, belonging to a process that aims at a completed or perfect form analogous (as we saw in Luther's Romans Lectures in chap. 5) to the process of building a completed house or completely healing a sick person. This real but incomplete righteousness is not sufficient to justify us because sin still remains in us, so "the second part of righteousness has to be added, which perfects it in us, namely, divine imputation."[92] (In this discussion, as in chap. 5, it is particularly important to bear in mind that *perfectus*, which I am translating "perfect," is simply the Latin word for "completed.") Imputation is needed to complete our righteousness precisely because the real righteousness of faith is not perfected in this life. In explaining this point, Luther continues to use the Aristotelian vocabulary: "Faith does not give enough to God formally, because it is imperfect."[93] Hence, in sum, "faith begins righteousness, but imputation perfects it."[94]

Precisely because imputation perfects or completes what faith begins, it does not lay the foundation. It is (I suggest) like the tarpaulin spread over a building site to keep it from being damaged by the weather until the structure is completed; there is no point to the tarpaulin without the ongoing process through which the structure moves toward its completed form. The foundation of the structure is union with Christ by faith, and the process of building the structure progresses through the wondrous exchange, which Luther here expresses succinctly: "His righteousness is yours; your sin is His."[95] On the one side of the exchange, a real formal righteousness begins to take shape in us, as we learn to think and feel and will as Christ does, thus taking on the form of Christ. On the other side, the nonimputation of sin follows, because our sin now belongs to Christ, not us. Thus Luther says it is because of "the faith by which I begin to take hold of Christ" that on account of Christ, "God reckons imperfect righteousness as perfect righteousness and sin as not sin, even though it really is sin."[96] So the sin is real, but so is the incomplete but real righteousness that Luther speaks of when he says, once again, that "a Christian man is righteous and a sinner at the same time."[97]

---

91. Luther, 1535 Galatians Commentary, on Gal. 3:6, *LW* 26:229.
92. Luther, 1535 Galatians Commentary, *LW* 26:229.
93. Luther, 1535 Galatians Commentary, *LW* 26:229–30.
94. Luther, 1535 Galatians Commentary, *LW* 26:230.
95. Luther, 1535 Galatians Commentary, *LW* 26:233.
96. Luther, 1535 Galatians Commentary, *LW* 26:232.
97. Luther, 1535 Galatians Commentary, *LW* 26:232.

The point about the sin being real goes back to a crucial bone of contention between Luther and the pope in 1520, when Luther insisted that the sin remaining in all who are baptized is really and truly sin. Yet it does not lead to our condemnation, because as Augustine says, in an important passage that Luther quotes, "Sin is forgiven in baptism, not that it is no longer present, but it is not imputed."[98] Because the sin that remains is real, Luther can reformulate the point about believers being righteous and sinners at the same time by saying, "A righteous man sins in all his good works." And what is more, the sin is not just venial, the sort of sin that is not really worthy of damnation, but rather "all our good works are mortal sins" if they were judged strictly, apart from the mercy of Christ.[99] This point, on which Luther departs from Augustine, is so scandalous that Luther must come back to it in the next year, in his treatise *Against Latomus*, where he defends at great length the thesis that "every good work of the saints while pilgrims in this world is sin,"[100] quoting the same passage from Augustine to explain why this sin that is really in us does not cause our damnation because God does not impute it to us.[101]

Luther's quotations from Augustine may hide the extent to which Luther departs from Augustine on the gravity of our sin. Luther's point about the sin that remains after baptism really being sin is something that Augustine explicitly denies, saying that "by a certain manner of speech it is called sin . . . even though in the regenerate [i.e., the baptized] it is not actually sin."[102] This is just a couple chapters before the passage we have seen Luther quote twice, against the pope and against Latomus, about how the sin that remains after baptism is not imputed to us. Luther emphasizes Augustine's point that the sin really remains but overlooks Augustine's point that what remains is not really sin.

Despite the differences, however, recognizing the Augustinian roots of Luther's doctrine helps us understand its meaning. Like Augustine but unlike later Protestants, Luther does not speak of Christ's merits being imputed to us. The

---

98. Luther, *Defense and Explanation of All the Articles*, 1521, on article 2, *LW* 32:28. This is the German version of a 1520 treatise in Latin (*Assertio Omnium Articulorum*) against the papal bull condemning Luther in 1520. The quotation is from Augustine, *Marriage and Desire* 1:25.28. Luther had quoted it once before, in the Romans Lectures, on Rom. 4:7 (*LW* 25:261). He will quote it again in *Against Latomus* (later in this paragraph). He identifies it, together with *Retractations* 1:19.3 (above), as one of the two permanently important passages in Augustine's works, in table talk #347 (*LW* 54:49).

99. Luther, *Defense and Explanation*, on articles 31 and 35, *LW* 32:83 and 91; cf. also on article 32, *LW* 32:86.

100. Luther, *Against Latomus*, *LW* 32:159.

101. Luther, *Against Latomus*, *LW* 32:209.

102. Augustine, *Marriage and Desire* 1:23.25.

language of imputation in Luther is overwhelmingly negative: it is the *non*imputation of sins,[103] not the imputation of Christ's merits. The reason for this difference is clear from the place of the forensic component in Luther's doctrine of justification: it is the third element after union with Christ and the wondrous exchange. In other words, by faith we first receive Christ himself, and then secondly all that Christ has, including his righteousness, and finally the forgiveness or nonimputation of our sins. "All that Christ has" is a phrase that regularly leads Luther to make lists of divine attributes, including holiness and blessedness and salvation and eternal life, as well as the righteousness of God (*justitia Dei*), which is the key term in his doctrine of justification. This divine righteousness or justice is what Luther means when he speaks of "the righteousness of Christ" and "the righteousness of faith." It differs from the *merits* of Christ, which are not divine but human—a result of his sinless human life. The righteousness *of God* must be something different from the merits of Christ because God is not subjected to the responsibility of earning merits. Christ earns merit, just as he is born and dies, only insofar as he lives a human life. When Luther does discuss the merits of Christ, it is typically by contrast to Roman Catholic notions of merit, such as the treasury of merits applied by indulgences[104] or the scholastic notions of merit of condignity and congruity.[105] He does not use Christ's merit as an important concept in his own doctrine of justification, nor does he connect it in any systematic way with the language of imputation.

For many later Protestant theologians, a purely forensic doctrine of justification looks like the only alternative to the Roman Catholic notion of righteousness as a quality or *habitus* of the soul, which is righteous and therefore meritorious. But Luther's doctrine is a third alternative, neither purely forensic nor dependent on the notion of quality or *habitus*. In place of imputed merits or a quality of the soul Luther puts Christ himself, received by faith alone and united to the soul or heart. This is what he means by saying Christ is our formal righteousness, the real justice which is our possession like the baby on his mother's lap at Christmas, who is present in our hearts as the form of our faith. Later Protestant theology does have a place for union with Christ, either as the basis of the imputation of Christ's merits or its consequence, but in either case not as the very meaning of justification itself.

Luther's notion of Christ as the form of our faith is conceptually innovative and requires him to revise some standard Augustinian categories, which

---

103. In his Romans Lectures Luther even uses the ungainly Latin term *non-imputatio* (WA 56:291; cf. *LW* 25:278), which I suspect is his coinage.

104. E.g., Luther, *Explanations of the 95 Theses*, on thesis 58, *LW* 31:216, 224; *Proceedings at Augsburg*, *LW* 31:282–84.

105. E.g., Luther, 1535 Galatians Commentary, *LW* 26:132, 153–54, 374–75.

may be easily misunderstood. Perhaps the most important example is an oft-noticed revision of the language of grace in *Against Latomus*, where Luther makes a distinction between *grace* and *gift*. Having no place for the standard medieval notion of grace as a *habitus* or quality in the soul, Luther speaks instead of grace as "an outward good, God's favor, the opposite of wrath."[106] But this does not mean the righteousness of Christ is an outward good, merely imputed to us and not really in us. For here too, as in the Galatians Commentary, faith in Christ is a real righteousness, "the true righteousness which is the *gift* of God."[107] This is clearly another name for the alien righteousness we encountered in the sermon *Two Kinds of Righteousness*, for this righteousness is "an innermost root whose fruits are good works"[108]—a variation on the theme of the good tree that bears good fruit. Again like the alien righteousness, "the gift has been *infused*,"[109] and it is at work in a lifelong process, fighting against the sin that remains in us. Grace has the effect that this remaining sin is not imputed to us, for the believer in Christ "has a gracious God on his side who does not impute this sin."[110] Hence the distinction between grace and gift in this text runs parallel to the distinction between imputation and faith in the 1535 Galatians Commentary, for "everything is forgiven through grace," which implies the nonimputation of sin, "but as yet not everything is healed through the gift," which is the imperfect righteousness that is begun in faith, in the process of justification.[111]

From Anxiety to Love

Luther's law/Gospel distinction modifies the Augustinian spiritual journey in two fundamental respects: it tell us our life on the road to God is both better and worse than Augustine thought. It is worse, because the law shows us that the sin remaining in us is real and all of it is mortal. It is better, because the Gospel gives us already, in the very beginning of our journey, what for Augustine is the ultimate goal, which is union with God. The one point leads to the other: the law must teach us that even our most pious actions are mortal sins so that we may realize there is no hope for us but in the Gospel of Jesus Christ. The purpose of the law, we could say, is to rid us of performance anxiety by eliminating the expectations of good performance

---

106. Luther, *Against Latomus*, LW 32:227.
107. Luther, *Against Latomus*, LW 32:227.
108. Luther, *Against Latomus*, LW 32:227.
109. Luther, *Against Latomus*, LW 32:229: *donum . . . infusum est* (= WA 8:107).
110. Luther, *Against Latomus*, LW 32:230.
111. Luther, *Against Latomus*, LW 32:229.

that make the anxiety possible. Anxious efforts to tell which of your sins are mortal have no point when it's a foregone conclusion that they all are. Thus Luther's frighteningly severe view of sin is not some unaccountable form of pessimism. It should be evaluated not according to whatever roots it may have in his unusual personality, but according to the rhetorical purpose for which he uses it, which is to urge us all to despair of our good works, give up our performance anxiety, and turn for hope and salvation to Christ alone, given by the Gospel alone, to be received by faith alone.

To despair of our good works means to recognize that nothing we do moves us along the way to God. So if there is to be hope for us, it must be that God has made a way to come to us. That way, of course, is the flesh of Christ. It is not our way to God but God's way to us, precisely because Christ comes to us as God in person, and it is he who does all that needs to be done to unite us to God. There is a way for us to travel as we grow in the righteousness of Christ, becoming more and more like him, but it is not a way of growth in love, as Augustine depicts it, but of growth in faith. For it is a way of growth *in Christ*, who is united to us by faith alone. The growth in love that results from faith in Christ is also God's gift to us, but it is not a way to God or a power that draws us near to him. The drawing near must be done by God alone.

From an Augustinian perspective, the crucial change that Luther's theology makes is epistemological: the concept of intellectual vision, which gave point to the spiritual journey because it was the goal of the whole thing, drops out of the story. We know God in a different way, according to Luther. Instead of hoping to see God with the eye of the mind, we hear God in the word of the Gospel. Of course, like Augustine's seeing, Luther's hearing is metaphorical. Deaf people can hear the Gospel, in Luther's sense. For the crucial feature of hearing a word is epistemological: the knowledge that comes from it is dependent on the testimony of the person who speaks or writes or gives the word. It is secondhand knowledge, rather than something you see for yourself with your own eyes or figure out for yourself with your own reason and understanding. This is precisely what makes it the appropriate way to know another person, as I have argued elsewhere.[112] It makes our knowledge of others dependent on what they have to say about themselves, on how they choose to give themselves to be known in their words. It may be that we can "see through" a liar sometimes and know him against his will, but this should not be the model for how we know people we love and respect, and it certainly can't be the way we know God. Respect for persons means acknowledging their authority to speak for themselves, with the result that our knowledge of

112. Cary, "Believing the Word."

them is founded not on the astuteness of our understanding but on their testimony about themselves, the word by which they give themselves to be known.

Protestant theology thus inhabits the Augustinian tradition but with modifications, the most crucial of which is that it replaces a Platonist notion of intellectual vision with a biblical notion of hearing the word of God as the highest and ultimate source of the knowledge of God. There is no beatific vision of the essence of God at the end of the road for Luther, but only the perfection of our union with Christ incarnate through faith in his word. That union is from first to last the knowledge of a human being who is God in person, known by believing the Gospel that tells us the story of who he is, in which he promises to give himself to us as our Beloved.

As we saw in chapter 7, Luther's concept of the Gospel word could not have developed without the medieval Catholic notion of a sacrament as an outward sign that confers the inner gift it signifies. The Protestant Gospel is to that extent a Catholic sacramental notion. Or we could put it more broadly: the Gospel is an external means of grace, and in that regard it is like an Orthodox icon as well as a Catholic sacrament. It is not merely the kind of sign we found in Augustine's semiotics in chapter 3, which points away from itself to something that is deeper and more fundamental. Rather, it calls attention to itself as a particular thing at a particular time and place where we may find the power of salvation in Christ. Unlike an Augustinian sign, it does not admonish us to look in a more inward direction, saying "It's not me you want!"[113] but like an Orthodox icon it says, in effect, "Look here! Here you can find what you're seeking!" It gives us something to cling to because, like a medieval Catholic sacrament rather than an Augustinian sacrament, it is a sign that gives what it signifies. And what it signifies is Christ in the flesh, who is at the basis of every external means of grace.

The point of Luther's unreflective faith in the Gospel is that Christ alone is enough, that nothing else in creation is needed to save us from the powers of sin, hell, death, the devil, and our own conscience. We need pay attention to nothing else, not even the quality of our own faith, in order to be drawn effectually into the life of God through the body of Christ in the power of the Holy Spirit. But of course the result of this new life in God will be that we pay attention to our neighbors, our world, and our own life in a new way, bearing fruit and doing the work of love that comes from Christ's presence in us.

This is the purpose of the Gospel: to make Christians, formed in the image of Christ, given to their neighbors in a love that anticipates the kingdom that is to come. To do this the Gospel must give Christians what Luther calls peace

---

113. Cf. Augustine, *Confessions* 10:6.9.

of conscience, freedom from the terror of recognizing our own sinful inadequacy. We are no longer in the sixteenth century, and the terrified conscience is not as common among us as it used to be, but we too have our performance anxieties, which keep leading us to ask the wrong questions about whether we're doing a good enough job at being Christians—whether we have true saving faith (the Calvinist question) or are really true Christians (the pietist question). The great insight behind Luther's law/Gospel distinction is that we need the freedom to answer such questions in the negative, simply repenting and saying: nothing I do or am is good enough to make me a true Christian with saving faith. For it is Christ alone who is good enough, thank God. So now I can stop looking for evidence in my life that I am in a state of grace or have a strong enough faith or am a true Christian or am making progress in my spiritual journey. Instead of trying to find something good in myself to rely on, I am free simply to confess my sin and start again at square one, taking hold of Christ once more in the Gospel. That is precisely how I grow in grace, faith, and love.

Faith opens up the life of love because it means I can ask better questions than the ones that arise from my performance anxieties. Instead of worrying whether what I'm doing is good enough to show I'm really Christian, I can worry about whether what I'm doing is really good for my neighbor. That is the question that love asks, after all. And while my works of love are never good enough to save me or make me a true Christian, they can be good enough to be a real help to my neighbor. In that way the Gospel frees me to live in love, concerned for the good of my neighbor rather than wrapped up in my spiritual anxieties about myself. It is precisely because I am justified by faith alone that I am free to love.

PART 3

Christian Teaching and the Knowledge of God

9

Scripture

Demanding the Wrong Kind of Certainty

L uther's insistence on the certainty of Christian faith stirred up all kinds
of trouble. It promoted a fierce contentiousness that is an ongoing
legacy of many forms of Protestantism today. Over the centuries it
solidified in institutionalized claims of theological certainty that fared very
badly against the rise of modern biblical scholarship in the research universities of nineteenth-century Germany. And in Luther's own writing it resulted
in inexcusably harsh polemics against a whole range of opponents, Catholic,
Protestant, and Jewish. Anyone concerned with the future of Protestantism
needs to think hard about why this happened. So in this chapter we shall
survey some of the misadventures of Protestant certainty and consider where
exactly Luther himself went wrong in this regard.

Controversial Certainties

Luther's teaching that the Christian faith is and must be certain is something
startling for readers today, who are used to thinking that faith is not knowledge
and that believers should be modest in their claims, epistemically humble and
aware of their doubts. As we have seen in the previous two chapters, Luther
is vividly aware of the doubt that lurks in a believer's heart, but he does not
hesitate to call it unbelief and sin, not humility, for it means dishonoring
God by doubting that he is true to his word. What greater wickedness can

there be, Luther asks, and "what greater contempt of God is there than not believing his promise? For what is this but to make God a liar or to doubt that he is truthful?"[1]

In this regard Luther is unmodern but not at all unusual. He agrees with the whole Augustinian tradition up to his time, which associates humility not with doubt but with submitting in faith to the authority of Christian teaching.[2] It is reason, not faith, that needs to learn humility, because "knowledge puffs up," as Scripture says (1 Cor. 8:1), meaning that those who have knowledge easily become swollen with pride, which is the besetting sin of the pagan philosophers, according to Augustine.[3] It is no surprise, therefore, that in Luther's confrontation with Cajetan the two agreed that Christian faith was certain. Both saw faith as firmly based on the authority of divine revelation, derived from the certainty of God's own knowledge. Their disagreement was about the content of Christian faith and whether it included certainty of God's grace toward me in particular. What is distinctive about Luther's concept of faith is based on his conviction that the Gospel is an external word of promise that can address each one of us where we are, saying "you" and meaning me in particular. Hence the certainty of faith, for Luther, includes the certainty that Christ is mine, together with his righteousness and salvation, because the Gospel has given him to me.

The trouble is that Luther's certainty about the Gospel was born in controversy, so that it seemed to need another kind of certainty to back it up: the certainty that the Gospel actually means and promises what Luther says it does, despite what the pope or other theologians like Cajetan might say. Thus from the very beginning of Protestant theology, disputes about the Gospel turned into disputes about the interpretation of Scripture, and the certainty of believers appeared to require the certainty of theologians. Protestant theologians in fact undertook to prove that the Bible and its promises could not possibly be read contrary to the way Protestants read it—as if faith in God's promises were not possible until the theologians on *our* side proved without a doubt that the theologians on *their* side misunderstood the meaning of Scripture. This is a subtle but terrible mistake, for it meant putting faith not in the word of God alone but also in the correctness of our interpretation, and it had very

---

1. Luther, *The Freedom of a Christian*, LW 31:350, in the discussion of "the second great power of faith."

2. The humility, indeed humiliation, needed to submit to the teaching authority of the church is the central moral issue in Augustine, *Confessions*, book 8; see Cary, *Outward Signs*, 171–77.

3. The Augustinian critique of intellectual pride has its roots in the "anti-Porphyrian theme" identified by J. J. O'Meara in *Young Augustine*, chap. 10. For examples, see Augustine, *Of True Religion* 4.7; *City of God* 10:24; Letter 118:3.17; and *Trinity* 4:15.20.

bad consequences in the long run. In a world of ferocious polemics, the need for interpretive certainty became a driving force in Protestant theology, producing a number of unintended consequences as the Reformation proceeded into the modern world in the seventeenth and eighteenth centuries, including a fateful refocusing of attention as Protestant preaching and teaching came to be less about giving people Christ in the Gospel than about proving that Protestants—and indeed one's own particular kind of Protestant, Lutheran or Reformed or Baptist—have the only correct interpretation of Scripture.

A renewal of the meaning of Protestant theology today requires bringing the focus back to the Gospel promise that gives us Christ, which also means returning to the shared authorities of the Christian tradition and giving up the kind of claims to theological certainty that emerged in the course of sixteenth-century polemics and marked the history of Protestantism in the centuries thereafter. As we shall see in the course of this chapter, belief in the wrong kind of certainty not only left Protestant theology particularly unprepared for new developments in biblical scholarship in the nineteenth century; it resulted in a stunning lack of charity in Luther's own writing, which is most horrifyingly evident in his attacks on the Jews. A proper return to the Gospel must give us hope for a different way of doing theology.

The Meaning of "Scripture Alone"

Luther's claims to certainty originate in a long Augustinian tradition of putting faith in authority (introduced at the end of chap. 3), which had for several centuries been combined with a conception of theology as a science. "Authority," by the time of the Middle Ages, was a term that could be used in the plural. It could refer to any text that was deserving of belief, including the works of the church fathers in theology as well as Aristotle and Cicero in philosophy—all of which were labeled "authorities" (*auctoritates*). But of course there were gradations of authority, ranging from certain to probable,[4] because the church fathers themselves acknowledge the supreme authority of Scripture, and Aristotle was no authority at all on Christian doctrine. But one thing Aristotle was an authority on is the nature of science. Science, according to Aristotle, means knowledge that is certain, not subject to revision or

---

4. In fact "probable" originally meant something like "worthy of approval" ("probable" and "approve" come from the same root, the Latin verb *probare*), which in medieval thought was applied to the teaching of esteemed authorities like the church fathers, which was worthy of approval or belief but not certain or infallible. For this history, see Hacking, *Emergence of Probability*.

change. It therefore requires premises or axioms that are certain and unrevisable, so that it may proceed like geometry, using deductive proofs to produce conclusions that are also certain, because what the proofs are designed to show is that things could not be otherwise.[5] Accordingly, Thomas Aquinas argues that Christian doctrine is a science because its conclusions are based on the most certain premises of all, the articles of faith that are derived from God's own knowledge revealed in Holy Scripture.[6] The medieval notion of theological certainty based on Scripture is thus common ground for Luther and Cajetan and other Christian disputants of the sixteenth century.

However, in Luther's estimation Cajetan was at a severe disadvantage in their confrontation, because it was Cajetan's job to defend the value of indulgences based on a papal decretal, an official document whose claims were not supported by the supreme authority of Scripture but only by the inferior authority of a pope. This was not sufficient authority to make Luther back down. "I am not so extraordinarily rash," he writes, "that I would pull back from so many great and very obvious testimonies in the divine scriptures on account of a single decretal of a human pope, which is so ambiguous and obscure."[7] Aquinas would have had no trouble seeing the point Luther is making: papal decretals do not give us the kind of certainty needed for premises in theological science or Christian doctrine. If you're in a tight spot that calls for certainty about what to believe (like a conscientious young monk being grilled by an experienced theologian on matters that could get you arrested for heresy), then what your conscience really needs is the authority of Scripture.

Here we can see why the Protestant principle that Scripture alone is the source of Christian doctrine came to be so important. In the midst of a dispute where not only life and death but salvation and damnation were at stake, Scripture alone gave the young monk Martin Luther a word he could cling to in good conscience, no matter what the pope or his minions might say. Hence under pressure from Cajetan, he is willing to back down on his interpretation of the papal decretal (despite his evident feeling that it is teaching nonsense, he admits that perhaps there is some interpretation that can make sense of it), but he will not retract his insistence that we are justified by faith alone, which is supported by a whole long string of passages he quotes from the Bible.[8]

---

5. Aristotle, *Posterior Analytics* 1:2; 1:6, in *Basic Works*, 111–13, 119–21. The key Greek term in these chapters, *episteme*, is now often translated "knowledge," but the standard Latin rendering of the term is *scientia*, the source of our word "science," and medieval readers took Aristotle to be giving an account of the nature of scientific knowledge.

6. Aquinas, *ST* I, 1.2.

7. Luther, *Proceedings at Augsburg*, WA 2:10 (= LW 31:266).

8. Luther, *Proceedings at Augsburg*, LW 31:264–77.

Luther's certainty in his encounter with Cajetan is twofold, corresponding to the double structure of the word of God discussed in chapter 7. The key example, once again, is the sacrament of penance, where the peace that consoles the terrified conscience is based on the requirement of certainty, for after hearing the word of absolution "it is necessary to believe with certain faith that one is justified."[9] Luther insists on this requirement despite Cajetan's objections, because he is convinced it is based on the prior Scriptural certainty of the promise of Christ, "Whatever you loose on earth is loosed in heaven" (Matt. 16:19). It is a sin to doubt or be uncertain that the word of absolution justifies you, because "with your doubt you make of Christ a liar."[10] The forgiveness of your sins is certain because the Scriptural word of Christ is certain.

Although the phrase "Scripture alone" does not appear in the dispute with Cajetan, we can already see the underlying principle (often stated in Latin: *sola scriptura*) at work in Luther's theology. It is an ecclesiological principle, concerned not with individual belief but with the teaching of the church. As Luther puts it many years later: "The holy church . . . must teach nothing except what is holy and true, that is, God's word alone."[11] There are other truths in other areas of science or history, but the truths the church teaches must be the holy truths to which Christian faith clings: the articles of the faith, as they came to be called in the Middle Ages. The critical implication of the principle is clear: the church has no authority to invent new doctrines or articles of faith and impose them on people as if they were necessary for Christians to believe. We can in good conscience reject the pope's teaching because papal decretals and the like have no authority to lay down the law for Christian faith apart from Scripture. We are freed from such papal tyranny because "the Word of God shall establish articles of faith and no one else."[12] Half a century later the English Reformation offered a classic formulation of this *sola scriptura* principle:

> Holy Scripture containeth all things necessary to salvation: so that whatsoever is not read therein, nor may be proved thereby, is not to be required of any man, that it should be believed as an article of the faith, or be thought requisite or necessary to salvation.[13]

Faith in the word of God alone is sufficient for salvation, and all the authorities in the church are no more than ministers of the word. They serve God

---

9. Luther, *Proceedings at Augsburg*, WA 2:13 (= LW 31:270).
10. Luther, *Proceedings at Augsburg*, LW 31:271.
11. Luther, *Against Hanswurst*, LW 41:214.
12. Luther, *Smalcald Articles* 2:2.15, in Tappert, *Book of Concord*, 295.
13. Thirty-Nine Articles, article 6, in Schaff, *Creeds of Christendom* 3:489.

by serving his word, not by claiming an independent authority for their own words.

The ecclesiological principle of "Scripture alone" should not be confused with the notion of private judgment that developed in some later versions of Protestantism, which assumed that individuals should read the Bible on their own, apart from the life of the church and its long tradition of interpreting and teaching the Scriptures. In practice, *sola scriptura* meant that Reformers like Luther and Calvin accepted a version of the traditional gradation of authorities, with Scripture alone as the source of certainty and the church fathers as indispensable but not infallible guides to sound interpretation of Scripture. One of the reasons Luther found the pope's intervention in the indulgence controversy unconvincing, for example, is that the pope failed to cite Scripture, the church fathers, or even canon law.[14] Protestant theologians after Luther were in fact eager to claim the church fathers as allies on their side of the debate, and they were happy also to quote favorite medieval theologians such as Bernard of Clairvaux in their favor. Hence while papal decretals soon carried no weight for Protestants in the debate, Augustine and other ancient teachers of the church kept being quoted by all sides.[15] To put the point in medieval terms, the great writings of the Christian tradition, and especially the church fathers, were treated as authorities but not as revelation.

The Most Up-to-Date Scholarship

But there is also a relatively new note in Luther's dispute with Cajetan, which we hear when he complains about the ambiguity and obscurity of the decretal. This is the kind of complaint that Renaissance humanists made about medieval Latin, which they found grammatically and stylistically inferior to the eloquence of ancient, classical Latin. Like other Reformers, Luther was a staunch supporter of the humanist project of restoring the knowledge of ancient languages, including not just classical Latin but also Hebrew and Greek, the original languages of Scripture. When Luther complains that papal decretals are "extremely verbose and pompous, which detracts from any faith in them, so crammed are they with ignorance,"[16] he is speaking

14. Luther, letter to Elector Frederick, Jan. 1519, *LW* 48:105. Luther is criticizing the recent papal bull, *Cum Postquam.*

15. For example, see the long section of patristic argument by Luther in his contention against other Protestants on the Lord's Supper, *That These Words of Christ, "This Is My Body," Etc. Still Stand Firm against the Fanatics*, *LW* 37:104–24. The principle of *sola scriptura* does not mean for Luther that the church fathers have no place as authorities in theological argument.

16. Luther, *Proceedings at Augsburg*, *WA* 2:8 (= *LW* 31:262).

like a humanist. He is also illustrating an important feature of the sixteenth-century intellectual landscape: the humanists' new linguistic knowledge typically favored Protestants rather than Catholics. The most famous example of this is when the humanist Lorenzo Valla exposed as a fraud the so-called donation of Constantine, a document in which the first Christian emperor of Rome supposedly gave the pope Western Europe to govern. Valla showed that it was an eighth-century forgery, written in a barbarous Latin style that did not exist until four centuries after Constantine.[17] Humanist scholarship could be deployed by the Reformers to make the papacy's reading of Scripture look as barbarous as its use of Latin, thus overturning faulty biblical interpretations as well as ignorant decretals. Luther is speaking in terms a humanist like Erasmus could appreciate when Luther describes himself, in his disputation with Cajetan, as "seeking nothing but the unadulterated meaning of Scripture, which in many places the so-called sacred decretals either corrupt for us, or else cover them up like a cloud obscuring the purest sunlight with twisted words and inept discussion."[18] The same humanist scholarship could also be applied to overturn inaccurate interpretations of the church fathers such as Augustine.

Far from rejecting the ancient Christian tradition, therefore, Protestant theologians were convinced that they had a more accurate grasp of its revered teachings than the papists did. In effect, they got used to the idea that the most up-to-date historical scholarship supported their interpretation of both Scripture and tradition. Though this hardly persuaded all their Catholic opponents, it was enough to convince Protestant theologians that both modernity and antiquity were on their side, supporting their claims to interpretive certainty. Thus it was a severe shock to the Protestant system when, almost three centuries later, the new historical-critical scholarship on the Bible took shape in Germany and began undermining traditional Christian understandings of Scripture. This was scholarship that claimed to be science in a new and un-Aristotelian sense. It was *Wissenschaft*, a German term that is broader than what most Americans mean by "science," since its most characteristic forms are not the natural sciences but historical disciplines. The term can be used of any academic discipline that follows a rigorous method. Hence biblical scholarship was regarded as "scientific" (*wissenschaftlich*) not because it was demonstratively certain like an Aristotelian science but because

---

17. Coleman's edition of Valla, *The Treatise of Lorenzo Valla on the Donation of Constantine*, includes Latin text, English translation, and a helpful introduction.

18. Luther, *Proceedings at Augsburg*, WA 2:18 (= LW 31:278). For a taste of the humanists' quest for purity of sources and its influence on the Reformation, see Eire, *Reformations*, chaps. 4 and 5.

it followed a rigorous method of critically evaluating all historical documents, including the Scriptures themselves. This historical-critical approach came to dominate biblical scholarship in the German universities, which became the leading research centers of the nineteenth century. By the end of the century, understanding the Scriptures scientifically meant, for German scholars, treating them critically, like any other set of ancient documents: liable to errors, inconsistency, and historical development—not the "purest sunlight" of unshakable certainty that Luther assumed.

The social context of this new biblical scholarship, as well as its epistemological implications for Protestant theology, can be illustrated by considering the historical place of a famous little article by the great German philosopher Immanuel Kant. His "Answer to the Question, What Is Enlightenment?" (1784) helped define a whole period of Western history, solidifying the label "Enlightenment" for the key intellectual developments of the eighteenth century. The article is well known for questioning traditional authorities and announcing a kind of coming-of-age that freed people to think for themselves, as intellectual adults, in accordance with the motto "Dare to Know!"[19] It was a kind of declaration of independence for German intellectuals, many of whom had been working under regimes of academic censorship in the interest of state churches. In fact it heralded the end of the "confessional" era, the period in Germany when claims of theological certainty were defended fiercely, interminably, and in Latin, by scholars at state-supported universities who were required to teach in accordance with the Augsburg Confession, the official formulation of Lutheran doctrine, or one of the Reformed confessions—depending on which of the many independent territories of Germany they were teaching in, and which confession it adhered to and enforced. Likewise pastors, who were also paid functionaries of the state, serving in the state church, were bound by oath and civic duty to teach according to the confessional commitments of their territorial government. Kant's declaration of independence meant that when pastors or professors were publishing research rather than teaching in the church, they must be free to follow their scholarly conscience rather than have the church or the state tell them what they were allowed to think and say. Kant drew a parallel with an army officer who must obey orders from his commanding officer in the field, but should have complete freedom to publish his opinions about how to reform the army in scholarly or political journals.

Over the course of the nineteenth century, as the Protestant confessional universities of Germany gave way to secular research universities, this kind

19. Kant, *Perpetual Peace, and Other Essays*, 41.

of academic freedom became an essential presupposition of the new biblical scholarship.[20] By the end of the century, a hundred years after Kant, the balance of power between church and academy had shifted decisively. The church's theologians no longer supervised the university's biblical scholars, as they had up to the eighteenth century, but the other way round. Now the professors, not the pastors, determined what counted as real knowledge of the Bible. The state-supported research universities were in charge of "scientific" biblical interpretation, which owed no allegiance to the traditional "confessional" teaching of the churches. Quite the contrary: scientific biblical scholarship aimed, in service to both the state and civic unity, to overcome the endless bickering between rival forms of confessional theology. For the academic, intellectual, and political elite, the word "confessional" came to sound like the word "fundamentalist" in upscale America today: it meant an ideology that was out of date, irrational, and socially disruptive.

A Brief Narrative of Modernity

Clearly, by the nineteenth century the most advanced scholarship in Europe no longer served the kind of theological certainty that Luther insisted on. When historical-critical scholarship came on the scene, it was as if Protestant theology didn't know what hit it, and never fully recovered. To explain what hit it is to tell a story that is central to the narrative of modern thought. It is a complicated story, but the plotline that interests us can be summarized in three episodes, century by century.

In the first episode, in the seventeenth century, religious pluralism undermined theological certainty.[21] The proliferation of fiercely contending claims to certainty on all sides, including more than one variety of Protestantism, resulted in growing uncertainty and skepticism. How was an ordinary Christian to judge which of the contending theologies advocated by learned scholars was really biblical? Each country or territory in Europe subscribed to its own religion or confession, in accordance with the political principle *cujus regio, ejus religio*, which meant that the ruler of a territory determined its religion (the phrase literally means: "whoever's region—his religion"). Universities were state-supported institutions that trained theologians and pastors how to prove that only their religion or confession represented the truth of the Scriptures,

20. Howard, *Modern German University*, tells this story in illuminating detail.

21. The historical connection between post-Reformation pluralism and the felt need for a new kind of scientific certainty is a story that has been told many times, but a particularly impressive recent telling is Gregory, *Unintended Revolution*, chaps. 1, 2, and 6.

and such proofs became central to their preaching. Ordinary Europeans were not in a position to sift through the contending arguments, though often they got a steady diet of them from the pulpit. Meanwhile, people who did much traveling could easily find decent Christian people from other countries who held contrary religious beliefs. Hence the more cosmopolitan a gentleman was, the more likely he was to be skeptical of claims to theological certainty.

It was the gentlemen, not the university professors, who did the most to invent modern science in this period: people like René Descartes, Gottfried Leibniz, Robert Boyle, and the members of the Royal Society of London and the Académie Royal des Sciences of Paris. (Sir Isaac Newton was an exception, being both a gentleman and a professor at Cambridge University.) In the scientific revolution of the seventeenth century, these gentlemen developed new sources of knowledge in physics, chemistry, and mathematics that seemed much more certain than theology, because over the course of time they tended to produce converging rather than conflicting results. The gentlemen who created early modern science were mostly pious Christians who had no intention of setting science against religion, but they ultimately changed the religious landscape of Europe by establishing not only new forms of knowledge but also a new ground of social consensus. Many of them followed Descartes in thinking that the philosophical basis of the modern sciences could provide foundations of certain knowledge that were quite different from the claims of the endlessly squabbling theologians in the universities.[22] For those impressed by the new sciences, the word "reason" came to stand for a kind of secular judgment of what's true, providing a neutral common ground shared by all and not beholden to any particular religion.

In the second episode, in the eighteenth century, this neutral, secularized conception of "reason" precipitated the most important conceptual development in the Enlightenment's philosophy of religion. This was the contrast between "natural religion," which was the universal religion of reason accessible to all, and "revealed religions," which included Christianity, Judaism, and Islam, all based on claims of divine revelation in sacred texts such as the Bible and the Qur'an, which were not accepted or even known by all. The Deists were the people in the eighteenth century who thought that natural religion was sufficient: that any revealed religion was at best a supplemental and unnecessary addition to what was already known about God and morality through reason alone, and at worst a distortion or perversion of true religion, a form of superstition and fanaticism promulgated by self-interested priests

22. Descartes, *"Meditations on First Philosophy"* and *"Discourse on Method,"* in *Selected Philosophical Writings.*

and pastors. This generated a distinctive new crisis for Protestantism, as the Deists turned many of the standard Protestant attacks on Catholicism (as "superstition," "dogma," "fanaticism," and "priestcraft") against Protestantism and eventually against Christianity itself.[23]

The defenders of revealed religion, of course, did not think that believing in revelation is contrary to reason. But with "reason" increasingly conceived as a secular form of judgment exemplified by the modern sciences, their task was to support revelation by arguments that appealed to common ground independent of the assumptions of any specific religious tradition. John Locke, one of the founding figures of the Enlightenment, though not himself a Deist, stated the task clearly near the beginning of the eighteenth century. "Whatever God has revealed is certainly true," he wrote, "but whether it is a divine revelation or not, reason must judge."[24] On what basis then does reason judge that the Christian Scriptures really are a divine revelation? Locke's recourse was to use miracles to authenticate claims of revelation. They are the credentials God gives to those who deliver his message, and thus serve as "the foundation on which the believers of any divine revelation must ultimately base their faith."[25] The miracles of Jesus and the apostles, for example, could be cited as evidence that the New Testament is a proper basis for revealed religion.

It was an ill-fated recourse. There is nothing the Deists were more eager to cast doubt on than reports of miracles, and they largely succeeded in making such reports look suspect, even superstitious—a far cry from the proper basis of religious belief, much less of certainty. The most influential argument along these lines came from David Hume, a philosophical skeptic who relied on the recently invented modern concept of probability as a quantifiable likelihood modeled on throws of the dice. (When we use a phrase like "90 percent probability," we are using the word "probability" in a sense that did not exist before 1650.)[26] Which is more probable, Hume asked: that a miracle occurred or that there is some mistake made by the witnesses who claim to have observed it or the historical documents that report it? If we were

23. For a brief introduction to the early Deist writers, see Gay, *Deism*. For a rich and nuanced account of their place in Western intellectual history, see Stephen, *English Thought in the Eighteenth Century*, vol. 1.

24. Locke, *Essay concerning Human Understanding*, 4:18.10 (English modernized).

25. Locke, "Discourse of Miracles," 86 (English modernized). Cf. also Locke, "Discourse of Miracles," 80, as well as Locke, *Essay concerning Human Understanding*, 4:16.13–14; 4:19.15.

26. Hume, "Of Miracles" (section 10 of Hume, *An Enquiry concerning Human Understanding*). For the new conception of probability, first published in the *Port Royal Logic* (1662), see Hacking, *Emergence of Probability*. Hume's argument has been influential but has not always impressed philosophers of religion. See for example Evans, *The Historical Christ and the Jesus of Faith*, chap. 7, and Earman, *Hume's Abject Failure*.

acting as unbiased judges, considering some religion other than our own, we would be inclined to say that it is far more probable that the witnesses or the documents are somehow in error. And for good reason, in Hume's view. In the eighteenth-century context, a miracle was understood to be a violation of the laws of nature as established by modern science, which means (according to Hume's philosophy of science) that it is contrary to universally shared human experience, and so is surely less probable than witnesses being mistaken or documents being inaccurate—especially given what the Deists had been arguing about the human tendency toward credulousness and superstition. (One major inconsistency of Hume's argument emerges here: it turns out that "universal human experience" conforms to the expectations of eighteenth-century gentlemen and does not really include the experience of people whom the gentlemen regarded as primitive, savage, credulous, or superstitious.)

Even on its own terms, Hume's argument did not prove that miracles couldn't happen; his approach was more subtle than that. He was not arguing that miracles were impossible but rather that no miracle report could be believed by rational people—because it is always more reasonable (based on the probabilities involved) to believe that something unmiraculous happened instead, such as superstitious people telling stories about imaginary miracles. The immediate effect of the argument was to show why Locke's recourse to miracles was ill considered: if you're looking for arguments that are acceptable in the light of secular reason judging in accordance with modern science, then reports of miracles in ancient documents such as the New Testament are about as unconvincing a piece of evidence as you could possibly imagine. Scriptural miracles may have happened (Hume's skeptical philosophy does not allow him to exclude that possibility), but they are not suited to be the secular basis on which to prove that the Scriptures really are divine revelation, as Locke had argued. Reports of ancient miracles are too easily doubted to furnish the grounds of certainty for Christian faith in the modern era.

In the third episode, in the nineteenth century, biblical scholarship incorporated Hume's point. For the really important implication of Hume's argument concerns historiographical method. If Hume is right, no historian who takes modern science for granted as the summation of universal human experience can accept miracle reports. This is not because miracles are impossible or have been disproved, but because scientific historians must judge according to probabilities, and miracles are by definition vastly improbable events. Such is the assumption under which biblical scholarship continues to operate in the "historical-critical" method, which is so called because it regularly makes critical judgments about the reliability of historical documents, making no special exception for the Bible and its supernatural claims. The result is a severe challenge to any account of the certainty of Scriptural revelation, not only John Locke's but also Martin Luther's.

The problem this posed for Protestant theology was larger than simply the issue of whether biblical reports of miracles were believable (though when it came to the miracle of Christ's resurrection, this issue loomed very large indeed). The biblical critics of the nineteenth century were heirs of the Deists of the eighteenth century in a way that undermined traditional Protestant readings on many fronts. The Deists directed scathing attacks against the Bible by drawing attention to things in it that offended a gentleman's moral sensibilities, such as the violence and polygamy of Old Testament Israelites. The historical critics a century later transformed this moral critique into evidence of historical distance. They saw that there was a great gap between the morality and culture of our day and those of ancient Israel, but instead of using this insight to attack the Bible they made it into a hermeneutical principle of historical consciousness, establishing a vast distance between the Bible and the modern world. It became difficult if not impossible to read the biblical authors as straightforwardly as Luther did, as if they had something directly to say to us that did not require much effort of interpretation to cross the historical distance between us and them. For the biblical critics, the Bible needed to be translated not just from its original languages but from its original cultures and historical settings.

The effect was not so much to refute traditional readings of the Bible as to show that they were traditional. What had seemed transparent and perspicuous in the sixteenth century came to seem opaque and obscure in the nineteenth century, requiring a different kind of interpretation from that practiced in the church. Ever since Luther, Protestant theologians aiming for certainty had tried to make their interpretations so clear that they disappeared *as* interpretations, like transparent glass that you could see right through. Now the tradition of Protestant interpretation was exposed as belonging to a tradition, making it opaque and visible as one ecclesial tradition of interpretation among others. This was a serious problem for Protestant theologians, who were not used to thinking of themselves as belonging to a tradition of interpretation. It became very difficult to sustain the sense of transparency in their reading of Scripture that could once have been taken for granted—their sense that they were simply explaining what Scripture said without adding any interpretation of their own.

The new biblical criticism of the nineteenth century was based on a social transformation that had epistemological consequences. In contrast to traditional, doctrinal or confessional readings of Scripture, the academic biblical scholars of the nineteenth century claimed the right to determine what rational interpretation of the Bible looked like based on scientific research. In effect, the academy determined what the church could responsibly teach. For this was the century when science moved from the society of gentlemen to the classroom of professors. What had been the "universal experience" of eighteenth-century gentlemen became the rigorous "method" that established the bounds of what counted as knowledge for nineteenth-century university professors. In Germany in particular, the places of learning that had served to train pastors as functionaries of the confessional state in the seventeenth and eighteenth centuries became research institutions serving the secular state in the nineteenth century, drawing not on the contested authority of religion but on the widely recognized authority of science. But these universities still trained pastors, who were still functionaries of the state. In this new kind of university, the most up-to-date scholarship made both the theology of the confessions and the traditional interpretations of Scripture on which they were based look increasingly irrational, unfounded, and parochial, a form of subjectivity rather than certainty. A theology that wanted to be objective and scientific—so the professors insisted—would have to begin with the established scientific results of historical-critical scholarship. This became a central methodological requirement governing liberal Protestantism in its service to modern society.

What It Meant and What It Means

The new methodological requirement for theology was laid down shortly before the beginning of the nineteenth century, during the same decade as Kant's essay, in a programmatic lecture by Johann Philipp Gabler, a biblical scholar trained at the Enlightenment universities of Jena and Göttingen.[27] Gabler argued that "dogmatic theology" (Christian theology in the traditional sense of the term, which could also be called confessional, doctrinal, or systematic theology) should not engage in Scriptural interpretation, but must draw its understanding of Scripture from a new discipline, called "biblical theology," which meant the kind of scientific investigation pursued by the historical-critical method, operating by reason alone apart from any doctrinal or confessional commitments to Scripture as revelation. In this foundational

27. Gabler, "Biblical and Dogmatic Theology" (1787). Histories of biblical scholarship often take Gabler's lecture as a watershed moment. See for example Ollenburger, "Old Testament Theology," as well as Childs, *Biblical Theology*, 3–10, which provides an extensive bibliography on the history of the concept of "biblical theology" going back to Gabler.

discipline, reason governs revelation, not merely (as in Locke) by proving that it *is* revelation, but by establishing the very meaning of the text in which Christian theology finds the revelation of God.

Over the course of the nineteenth century the results produced by "biblical theology" (in both its subdivisions, "New Testament theology" and "Old Testament theology") came to be quite out of harmony with traditional Christian doctrines, and theologians in Germany who wanted to claim to be scientific had to adjust. The outcome, by the end of the century, was that biblical theology came to look less and less like theology at all, as the biblical scholar William Wrede pointed out in another famous programmatic lecture.[28] What historical-critical scholarship uncovered in the Bible, Wrede concluded, was in fact not theology but ancient history: the history of ancient Israelite religion or of early Christian communities. Christian theologians and pastors were free to do with these results what they wished, but the job of the biblical scholar was not to assist them, but to investigate this ancient history in strict neutrality, letting the chips fall where they may, without bringing any confessional, doctrinal, or religious preconceptions into his research.

Until the rise of various forms of postmodern criticism in recent decades, the assumption that historical-critical scholarship was theologically neutral and epistemologically foundational was still accepted by liberal Protestant theology, together with the consequence that responsible theologians must police themselves and enforce boundaries set by the academy rather than by Christian orthodoxy. As the twentieth-century theologian Krister Stendahl put it in a classic essay,[29] theologians had the job of making normative proposals about what Christians should believe based on what historical-critical scholars had determined about the original meaning of the Bible. In his famous formulation, this involved starting with "what it meant" and moving to "what it means." A theologically neutral biblical scholarship must establish "what it meant," and on that basis Christian theology could construct "what it means." Again, we are very far from Luther's certainty about what Scripture teaches. But clearly part of what brought us here is the contending "certainties" unleashed by the Protestant Reformation, whose actual result was a great deal

28. Wrede, "Task and Methods of 'New Testament Theology'" (1897). The extra quotation marks are ironic scare-quotes; the phrase in the original German title could be translated more literally, "so-called [*sogennanten*] New Testament Theology." For an account of the history of biblical theology that compares Gabler and Wrede, representing historical-critical scholarship at the beginning and the end of the nineteenth century, see Boers, *What Is New Testament Theology?*

29. Stendahl, "Biblical Theology." Adams, *Making Sense of New Testament Theology*, 49–86, traces biblical theology from Gabler to Wrede to Stendahl, with a focus on the modernist prejudices they share.

of uncertainty and a growing preference for scientific research over Christian confessions as the arbiter of what Christians may believe. "Scripture alone" took on a new, modern meaning, as Scripture read apart from the Christian tradition of interpretation, which meant in effect that the secular academy governed the teaching of the church. Such is one central strand in the story of modernity, as initiated by Protestantism itself.

Right-Wing Postmodernism

Stories, however, are about contingent events that could have been different, and often they involve surprising twists and turns. In recent years the story of modernity has encountered the plot twist called postmodernism, which is of interest to Protestants who would like to do without claims to the wrong kind of certainty. The twist is most visible when we look back from where we now are to the Enlightenment of the eighteenth century, with its distinction between natural religion and revealed religion. We all know something about the history of the revealed religions, such as Judaism, Christianity, and Islam; their communities; and their tradition of teaching; but what is the history of natural religion—where did it come from? In retrospect, it looks very much like something made up by eighteenth-century gentlemen advocating their own prejudices as if they were the voice of universal reason itself. The content of natural religion, as it was conceived by the Deists, included belief in the existence of God, the importance of morality, and the reality of rewards and punishments for the soul after death. Ask any Hindu or Buddhist if this looks like the religion of reason, and the answer you can expect is that it looks much more like a form of watered-down Christianity. It is the imperialistic modern West, with a substantial residue of its own Christian past, thinking it speaks for universal reason.

From a postmodern perspective, Western modernity looks very much like Christendom in the process of secularizing itself, retaining a great deal of residual Christianity yet thinking that it actually represents the progress of universal reason. Thus to the postmodernist, modernity appears ironically as a tradition that cannot admit that it is a tradition, because it is ideologically opposed to all traditions. The kind of modern Enlightenment represented by Kant as well as the Deists takes traditional authorities, such as the church, to be the source of irrational prejudices and a failure to be intellectual adults. This results in a crisis for modernity itself when modern thinkers absorb the insight that contingent historical traditions and their authorities are the inevitable and inescapable social context of all human thinking, and that this includes even the university professors and their scientific research. Call this "the postmodern insight." I think the insight is true, along with its implication that modern intellectual projects cannot survive unscathed when they come to self-knowledge about their own placement within a tradition. For despite its antitraditional ideology, modernity itself is constituted by traditions—including the continuing religious traditions as well as political liberalism, modern Western philosophy, and the various sciences.[30]

The postmodern insight implies that reason is never the neutral secular judge that modernity supposes, as if it could supply a level playing field—one not already tilted, as it were, by the weight of various contending traditions. Whatever common ground we find is not neutral territory but is always already shaped by authorities who preceded us and who have made some beliefs seem more plausible or obvious than others. The beliefs we take for granted and don't think to question are always the product of particular traditions. Just as there is no such thing as human language or culture as such, but only particular languages and cultures, so also there is no such thing as natural religion or religion as such, but only particular religious traditions. And this helps us see that there is also no such thing as universal reason, but only the thinking that is at home in particular intellectual traditions, including those of modernity.

Responses to the postmodern insight can go in two directions, which I call left-wing and right-wing postmodernism. Left-wing postmodernism retains the modern suspicion that traditions and their authorities are inherently irrational. Hence if tradition is inevitable, then irrationality is inescapable. There is no getting away from the shifting and unequal landscapes of authority and social power, and no final solution to the problems that science and reason itself generate when they recognize that the foundational certainty Descartes and his followers sought is not to be had.[31] Right-wing postmodernism, on the other hand, denies that traditions must be irrational and affirms instead

30. My account of traditions here draws on MacIntyre, *Whose Justice? Which Rationality?*, especially chap. 18, "The Rationality of Traditions." MacIntyre's concept of traditions generalizes key concepts in the philosophy of science, including Thomas Kuhn's notion of scientific paradigms and Imre Lakatos's notion of research programs; see MacIntyre, "Epistemological Crises." What makes this form of postmodernism "right-wing," in my parlance, is that treating science and religion as traditions, capable of narrating their own history of inquiry, does not undermine their truth claims but shows why they have good reason for thinking their claims are true. The critical point is that traditions that don't recognize they are traditions—which is a typical feature of modern traditions—are in no position to narrate their own history in a way that is truthful. For a fuller account, see Cary, "Right-Wing Postmodernism and the Rationality of Traditions."

31. In the academic landscape of the recent past, the two great authorities for left-wing postmodernism are Michel Foucault and Jacques Derrida. Foucault's impact has mainly concerned the inescapable intellectual effects of social power, while Derrida's notion of deconstruction

that rationality always has its home in some tradition or other, such as ancient philosophy, rabbinic reasoning, Islamic jurisprudence, Christian theology, or modern scientific inquiry. None of these represent neutral or universal reason, but all of them include genuinely rational forms of inquiry in pursuit of truth, constituting particular intellectual traditions that (contrary to modern prejudice) are capable of being self-critical and of questioning their own prejudices.[32] You could say: all of them have a place for some version of the critical, Socratic spirit that questions what is taken for granted—and that spirit, rather than any foundation of certainty, is what makes them traditions that harbor an imperfect but real rationality.

The future of Christian theology, I am proposing in part 3, is best conceived not as a modernist project such as liberal Protestantism, but as a right-wing postmodernist project, which is to say an explicitly traditional form of reasoning. What this implies for Scriptural interpretation is a rejection of Gabler's requirement that Christian theology base its teachings on the prior results of "scientific" biblical scholarship. Quite the contrary: Christian theology has the obligation before God to do its own exegesis of Scripture, in service of the church rather than the academy. It therefore heeds the authorities of the Christian tradition, those ancient, medieval, Reformation, and also modern writers who have provided guidance in the past about how to read Scripture well—in ways that are not beyond critical questioning but that have proven themselves by serving to build up the church in faith, hope, and love.[33] In

---

began with an internal critique of the project of attaining Cartesian certainty in the phenomenology of Edmund Husserl.

32. The two most important figures for what I am calling right-wing postmodernism are Alasdair MacIntyre, in the works previously cited, and Hans-Georg Gadamer, in *Truth and Method*. "Right-wing" should not be taken in a crudely political sense. MacIntyre is hardly a classic political conservative; his view of traditions is closer to Karl Marx than to Edmund Burke, in that he sees ongoing conflict as essential to traditional reasoning: "What constitutes a tradition is a conflict of interpretations of that tradition," as he puts it ("Epistemological Crises," 11). The staying power of a tradition is not a given, but depends on the possibility of coming up with a truthful dramatic narrative of its conflicts and their resolutions, which always result in further questions, problems, and conflicts. Thus for MacIntyre rationality is inherently both traditional and conflictual, and never immune from the possibility of epistemic crisis, incoherence, and refutation.

33. The great and encouraging example here is Karl Barth, the most influential of twentieth-century Protestant theologians, who not only did his own biblical exegesis but listened intensively to the voices of the Christian theological tradition in the enormously instructive fine-print sections of his *Church Dogmatics*. In recent decades a movement of theological interpretation has flourished, exemplified in works by Fowl, Leithart, Levering, and Billings. See also the influential essays by Steinmetz, Lindbeck, and Yeago in the anthology by Fowl, *Theological Interpretation of Scripture*, as well as Yeago's important essay "The Bible." The Brazos Theological Commentary on the Bible series offers many book-length examples of what theological interpretation can look like, including my own *Jonah*. For work that undermines the Gablerian

company with these authorities, theology should bring explicit Christian convictions into the work of learning what Scripture meant as well as what it means. Theology should also learn from critical questioning, as it is found both within and outside the Christian tradition, including the now centuries-long tradition of modern academic biblical scholarship (often conducted by Christians with more-or-less implicit Christian interests, despite modern strictures against this), which has uncovered a great deal about the history and meaning of the Scriptural text.

What Christian theology should not do is wait for historical-critical scholarship to establish "what it meant" as the foundation for theological interpretation. Inquiry into "what it meant," like inquiry into "what it means," engages ongoing intellectual traditions that do not come to a full stop. We never finally arrive at "what it meant," so we are never in possession of scientific results that afford us a firmly established foundation for theology. The only lasting foundation is Scripture itself, to which Christian theology must constantly return as it keeps learning the Gospel afresh, in the conviction that the Scriptural witness to Jesus Christ continues to have something to say to the church in every era, because the church is the same community that the Scriptures have been addressing all along. All living intellectual traditions, whether in religion, science, philosophy, or politics, keep learning, which means they are free—whether they like it or not—to change their minds when necessary. So the Christian tradition also continues to have much to learn from the tradition of modern biblical scholarship, but is not bound to wait for its results before deciding what to teach about the meaning of Scripture.

With its roots in the church rather than the academy, Christian theology need not begin with the research of other disciplines nor with premises that are indubitably certain like an Aristotelian science. It grows rather from the Christian practice of worship, and it finds what Scripture means, to begin with, by using it in liturgy, hymn, prayer, and praise. Theological interpretations must above all be obedient to the faith Christians confess when they take the words of Scripture on their lips to honor God and build up the church in the gathered congregation, where the Bible is read aloud, the psalms are sung in prayer, the sacraments are administered according to their biblical institution, and the Gospel is preached so as to give people Jesus Christ as their own Beloved, to be received by faith alone. In this way, I think, Protestant theology can retain the great gift that Luther's theology

---

paradigm from the side of biblical theology, see Brevard Childs's landmark *Biblical Theology*, as well as Francis Watson, *Text and Truth*, vii, which programmatically "seeks to dismantle the barriers that at present separate biblical scholarship from Christian theology."

of the Gospel offers, while renouncing the claims to theological certainty whose contentiousness set the stage for modern biblical scholarship's turn away from the doctrines of the church. But this will require a particular instance of the kind of self-criticism that is a mark of a healthy intellectual tradition, to which I now turn.

The Certainty of Proof Texts

There is more than one kind of certainty, and there is such a thing as the wrong kind of certainty for a particular purpose. Certainty, as the Latin root of the word (*certa*) suggests, is a kind of firm fixedness, a definiteness that resists change. In philosophy this is usually taken to refer to a kind of knowledge that is unrevisable, because it could be demonstrated (by irrefutable proof) or seen (by intellectual vision, immediate intuition, or some kind of self-evidence) to be true. Hence philosophers were never willing to identify certainty with the mere feeling of assurance, which can easily change. Certainty was an intellectual or epistemic property based on logic, not feelings, and characterized by its permanent resistance to change. To be certain meant that it was logically impossible to discover you were wrong and needed to change your mind. This is the kind of certainty aimed at in ancient Aristotelian science as well as in modern Cartesian philosophy.

For the rest of this chapter I will be arguing that the certainty of Christian faith should be understood otherwise. Its ultimate basis is neither logic nor feeling but faithfulness, and in that sense it too involves resistance to change. Faithful people do not give up keeping their word, and Christian faith does not give up clinging to the word of the faithful God. The stubborn faithfulness of Christian faith, its "obstinacy in belief" as C. S. Lewis aptly describes it,[34] stems not from scientific proof but from the sometimes hard-won confidence that God will keep his promises. It is faith in another person's faithfulness. Luther speaks for this kind of certainty when he focuses on faith's dependence on the Word of God, which, as Isaiah puts it, "stands forever":

> It "stands," that is, it is steadfast, it is certain, it does not give way, it does not quiver, it does not sink, it does not fall, it does not leave you in the lurch. And where this Word enters the heart in true faith, it fashions the heart like unto itself, it makes it firm, certain and assured . . . for it knows that God's Word cannot lie to it.[35]

34. Lewis, "On Obstinacy in Belief," in *The World's Last Night, and Other Essays*, 13–30.
35. Luther, *On the Last Words of David*, LW 15:272.

I would add: such faith is personal, in that it rests on the truth of another person, his faithfulness in keeping his word. Its basis is not our ability to prove or see or establish scientifically the truth to which we cling, yet it does have a solid basis because God is indeed true to his word.

The resulting form of knowledge is what we would see in Othello if he had continued to believe in Desdemona rather than let Iago change his mind. Othello ceased to know Desdemona when he stopped believing her, having been persuaded by the "ocular proof"[36] that Iago arranged to provide (and that he led Othello to misinterpret). Othello should not have believed what he saw but rather what he heard from Desdemona, for her word was true. The obstinacy of such a faith does not make doubt impossible (it is not that kind of certainty), but neither does it assume that doubt is simply innocent (Othello's doubts about Desdemona surely were not). But it fights against doubt, clinging to the word of the other as faithfully as it can, in the conviction that the one who promised is faithful and true, despite appearances. Luther knows from experience what it is like for faith to cling to such a promise when all appearances are against it, but it was his mistake to attribute to such faith a kind of certainty whose great spokesman is Aristotle rather than the prophets and apostles of the Bible. This is the wrong kind of certainty for Christian faith.

If obstinate faithfulness is the kind of certainty that Christian faith aims for, then it will build on the authority of Scripture without trying to make it into the basis for scientific or logical certainty. And that allows us to see why disagreements over Scriptural interpretation do not demand the kind of proof-texting that has been so contentious and damaging in the history of Protestant theology. Luther bears heavy responsibility for this damage. The kind of proof-texting I have in mind does more than cite a Scriptural passage as an infallible authority (as has been done throughout the Christian tradition) in order to make claims of scientific certainty (as is common from the medieval period onward). It involves claims of scientific or logical certainty not just for the Scriptural text but for your own interpretation of the text—and in the face of similar claims of certainty made on behalf of rival interpretations by your theological opponents. Proof-texting, in other words, is a practice shaped by polemics, where the goal is to prove that your theology is irrefutable and indubitable, because only your interpretation of Scripture could possibly be correct, despite what your theological opponents say.

The distinctive basis of proof-texting is not the certainty that God's word is true but the success of your theological interpretation. A good proof text must therefore be clear and perspicuous, its meaning impossible to miss except

36. Shakespeare, *Othello* 3.3.360.

by opponents who are somehow blinded, either by ignorance and stupidity or by something worse, such as pride and willfulness. The kind of interpretation demanded by the practice of proof-texting is thus transparent in a peculiar way: it aims to render the work of interpretation invisible, making the meaning of the proof text appear so obvious that it hardly seems to need interpreting at all. A good proof text allows interpretation to disguise itself, putting on the cloak of the text itself, so that the interpreter can forcefully claim to be saying nothing other than what Scripture says.

Catholics can play at proof-texting, but the greatest proof-texters of the Christian tradition have always been Protestants, especially when they are arguing against other Protestants, on the ground of Scripture alone. Luther is a key example, being perhaps the first great theorist of Protestant proof-texting.[37] Starting from the conviction that "faith should and must be certain," he argues that this requires "plain, clear passages and altogether unambiguous words from Scripture as its basis."[38] Here the logic of scientific certainty is imposed on the conscience of believers: they must not doubt, which means their beliefs must be proved by Scriptural interpretations that are logically certain, which requires proof texts whose meaning is absolutely plain and clear. "The text must be simple and uniform," Luther writes, "having a single certain meaning, if it is to be clear and the basis of a certain article [of faith]."[39] For when it comes to proving articles of faith or Christian doctrine, "an uncertain text is the same as no text."[40]

The most important example of Luther's proof-texting can be seen in the very title of his treatise on the Lord's Supper, *That These Words of Christ, "This Is My Body" Etc. Still Stand Firm against the Fanatics* (1527). The "fanatics" are, in German, *Schwärmer*, meaning something like "rabble-rousers" (as the German word *Schwarm*, related to the English "swarm," can mean a riotous crowd or rabble). The suggestion is that his opponents are playing to the crowd rather than attending seriously to Scripture. In this case Luther is using the term to refer to the Swiss Protestant theologian Ulrich Zwingli and his colleagues, who denied that the body and blood of Christ were literally present in the bread and wine of the Lord's Supper, despite the words of institution spoken by Christ himself. "They won't admit that the

---

37. It is possible that Zwingli earned this title in the 1522 treatise *Of the Clarity and Certainty of the Word of God*.

38. Luther, *Against the Heavenly Prophets*, WA 18:150 (= LW 40:160). For an extended discussion of the nature of proof texts and the requirement of clarity or perspicuity, see Luther, *That These Words*, LW 37:25–35.

39. Luther, *Confession concerning Christ's Supper* (sometimes known as the *Great Confession*), WA 26:262 (= LW 37:163).

40. Luther, *Confession concerning Christ's Supper*, WA 26:263 (= LW 37:163).

Lord's body and blood are present," writes Luther, "even though the plain, clear words are standing there and saying: 'Eat, this is my body,' which are words that still stand there, firm and unharmed by them."[41] The clarity and certainty of the proof text is a crucial weapon for theological polemics, as "this single passage is strong and mighty enough against all their foul, frivolous twaddle."[42]

Luther's reading of his proof text is straightforwardly literal: when Christ says, "This is my body," he means this is his body. Luther sticks with the text "as the words read," as he often puts it. The literal meaning of the text plays a very specific role here. Luther is not a systematic literalist who reads every passage of Scripture literally, as if he had never learned from the Christian tradition that anthropomorphic descriptions of God in heaven having eyes and ears and a strong right hand must not be taken literally. Like Thomas Aquinas, however, he understands the logical point that demonstrative arguments cannot be based on words used in an equivocal sense,[43] which means that proofs of Christian doctrines cannot be based on figurative or metaphorical readings of Scripture. Much of Protestant literalism stems from this logical point about the need for literal interpretation of Scripture in order to produce proofs of theological doctrines. Luther's argument also employs a very restrictive version of the traditional "criterion of absurdity," according to which a Scriptural passage must not be taken literally if its literal meaning is something absurd or immoral.[44] Luther argues that if a figurative meaning is to be established as certain, it must first be proved that a literal reading is impossible or contrary to an article of faith. The burden of proof, in other words, lies with the advocates of figurative reading. This burden is easily met in the case of anthropomorphisms in the Bible, which would result in pagan nonsense if taken literally: the Creator of all flesh cannot be made of flesh, with literal eyes and ears and hands. But Luther is convinced it cannot be met in the case of Christ's words, "This is my body."[45]

Luther argues, on the contrary, that figurative readings of this particular text are conjectural and create an uncertainty that leaves Zwingli and his followers with a bad conscience.[46] They boast that their interpretation is irrefutable, but in fact they can't avoid knowing they're uncertain, Luther insists,

41. Luther, *That These Words*, WA 23:71 (= LW 37:18).
42. Luther, *That These Words*, WA 23:87 (= LW 37:29).
43. Aquinas, *ST* I, 12.5.
44. A sophisticated version of the criterion of absurdity can be found in Origen, *On First Principles* 4:2.9–4:3.4.
45. Luther, *That These Words*, LW 37:32.
46. Luther, *That These Words*, LW 37:30–33.

because "this saying of Christ, 'This is my body,' sticks like an everlasting splinter in their hearts from which they can never be free."[47] They attempt to hide their uncertain conscience, but it's clear in their writings that "they are acting against their own conscience."[48] Luther imagines what dishonest contortions he would have to go through if his own interpretation of Scripture were so lame and uncertain:

> If my conscience tried to reproach me, saying, "You take a good deal of liberty with your interpretation, Sir Martin, but—but—" etc., I would press until I became red in the face, and say, "Keep quiet, you traitor with your 'but,' I don't want the people to notice that I have such a bad conscience!"[49]

It is a point he makes repeatedly, summed up in an angry treatise on the same subject near the end of his life when he writes that his opponents "have shamelessly lied . . . against their own consciences."[50]

Luther's proof-texting is designed to show that his theological opponents cannot be making an honest mistake and proceeding in good conscience. Their own conscience is against them, for they must be consciously lying and deliberately twisting the words of the text in order to do away with its plain meaning, which is too obvious and certain for any honest, competent reader to understand it differently from the way Luther does. The result of Luther's proof-texting is thus a fiercely uncharitable and deeply unedifying form of polemics, whose aim is not to persuade those who disagree with him but to show those who agree with him, especially those who are unlearned and unsure of themselves, why they must never listen to his opponents. As he explains, he is writing against the fanatics "not for their sake but for the sake of the weak and simple. For I have no hope that the teachers of a heresy or fanaticism will be converted."[51] This kind of theological argument turned out to be unedifying even for his followers, however, as it led to a style of preaching that was less concerned with giving people Christ than with proving that Lutheran theology, rather than its competitors, had the certainty of Scripture on its side. This was one of the key complaints made by the Pietist movement that arose in the late seventeenth century in Germany: careerist pastors were functioning mainly as ideological support for the confessional state, making a living by polemicizing against

---

47. Luther, *That These Words*, LW 37:29.
48. Luther, *That These Words*, LW 37:34.
49. Luther, *That These Words*, LW 37:31.
50. Luther, *Brief Confession concerning the Holy Sacrament* (1544), LW 38:296.
51. Luther, *That These Words*, LW 37:19–20.

rival confessions rather than building up Christians in piety and the faith of Christ.[52]

Luther against the Jews

The logic of proof-texting is the backbone of the worst things Luther ever wrote, his treatises late in life against the Jews. These treatises show unmistakably that Luther's demand for certainty is wrong not just epistemologically but morally. They are the only writings I know by a great Christian theologian that are quite simply wicked. If Protestantism is to offer its theology to the whole church as good news for the world, then some serious Protestant self-criticism in light of these treatises is in order.

Luther's most important treatise against the Jews, called *On the Jews and Their Lies* (1543), is unbelievably virulent, and it cannot simply be blamed on the prejudices of his time. Luther gives only quick glances at standard medieval calumnies (that Jews poison wells and commit ritual murder, and similar paranoid fantasies)[53] and devotes more energy to accusing them of crucifying texts than of crucifying Christ.[54] The twisting and torturing of Scriptural texts is in fact at the center of his concern, because for him the Jews are at root hermeneutical enemies, rival interpreters who threaten his Christian grasp of the Scriptures. His anti-Judaism thus stands at the opposite end of the theological spectrum from the kind of gnostic or Marcionite theology that rejects the God of the Jews as if he were different from the God of Christian faith, or the genteel anti-Semitism of liberal Protestant theologians who found the Old Testament too saturated with ancient tribal Judaism to be normative for modern Christians.[55] Quite the contrary, the key point for Luther is that the Old Testament is the word of God that bears witness to Jesus Christ, which means it is properly a Christian book. He sees the Jews as a threat precisely

52. See the critique of the state of the clergy in Spener's 1675 book, *Pia Desideria*, 44–57, which is widely regarded as the founding document of Pietism.

53. He does give them a glance more than once: e.g., Luther, *On the Jews and Their Lies*, LW 47:217, 242, 264, 277. But they are never the mainspring of his argument. He is willing to entertain them as possibilities because of the maliciousness he attributes to the Jews on other grounds.

54. The language about crucifying the text appears in Luther, *On the Jews and Their Lies*, LW 47:178, 210. The notion of crucifying Christ appears as well in *On the Jews and Their Lies*, LW 47:215, 226, 232, 277, but it never bears the central burden of the argument.

55. On the rejection of the Old Testament by liberal Protestantism, see Francis Watson, "Erasing the Text: Readings in Neo-Marcionism," on Schleiermacher, Harnack, and Bultmann, in his *Text and Truth*. On the theme of "higher criticism" as "higher anti-Semitism," see Levenson, *Hebrew Bible*.

because they claim the Hebrew Scriptures as their own, as if Christian readings were illegitimate. His accusation is that "the Jews tear apart the text wherever they can, solely for the purpose of spoiling the words of Scripture for us Christians."[56] Therefore, he urges Christian interpreters "to recover Scripture from them as from public thieves."[57]

The point of the accusation comes into focus if we compare it with the much friendlier stance Luther took toward the Jews two decades earlier. In the little 1523 treatise *That Jesus Christ Was Born a Jew*, Luther argues that "Christ was a genuine Jew," born and bred.[58] This means, he tells his readers, that we Gentile Christians are merely "aliens and in-laws," while the Jews are "blood relatives, cousins and brothers of our Lord."[59] In this treatise the "us and them" contrast works in *their* favor: just think how much we have gained from Jewish generosity, Luther argues, and how we ought to return the favor rather than continuing to harass them.

> If the apostles, who also were Jews, had dealt with us Gentiles as we Gentiles deal with the Jews, there would never have been a Christian among the Gentiles. Since they dealt with us Gentiles in such brotherly fashion, we in our turn ought to treat the Jews in a brotherly manner in order that we might convert some of them.[60]

The treatise contains some of Luther's typical pungency, but it is directed against the papists, not the Jews. Given the way Jews were treated by popes and bishops and monks, he says, "If I had been a Jew and had seen such dolts and blockheads govern and teach the Christian faith, I would sooner have become a hog than a Christian."[61] Even the project of converting the Jews should be pursued gently, mainly by consorting with them in work and commerce, so that they might learn more about Christian life and teaching. And most strikingly, it is a project to be pursued without urgency and anxiety, for "if some of them should prove stiff-necked, what of it? After all, we ourselves are not all good Christians either."[62]

After such a friendly approach, how did things go wrong? You can see the clouds on the horizon in a couple of proof texts that Luther recommends using, in place of harassment and persecution, to convert the Jews. These

---

56. Luther, *On the Jews and Their Lies*, LW 47:244.
57. Luther, *On the Last Words of David* (1543), LW 13:344.
58. Luther, *That Jesus Christ Was Born a Jew*, LW 45:213.
59. Luther, *That Jesus Christ Was Born a Jew*, LW 45:201.
60. Luther, *That Jesus Christ Was Born a Jew*, LW 45:200.
61. Luther, *That Jesus Christ Was Born a Jew*, LW 45:200.
62. Luther, *That Jesus Christ Was Born a Jew*, LW 45:229.

are texts that had played a role for centuries in Christian writings against the Jews, but both of them are in fact remarkably obscure and prone to multiple interpretations: Genesis 49:10 ("the scepter shall not depart from Judah . . . until Shiloh comes") and Daniel 9:24–27, a passage about the end of sin and beginning of righteousness in Jerusalem after "seventy weeks of years."[63] According to Luther's interpretation, these are not only messianic prophecies (after all, the Jews already believe in messianic prophecies) but prophecies whose timing shows that they have already been fulfilled and cannot have been fulfilled by anyone but Jesus. Perhaps it does not need saying that biblical scholars today do not agree with Luther's interpretation of these passages. Yet their obscurity, and even Luther's admission that they have been interpreted in many contradictory ways over the years, do not keep the logic of proof-texting from kicking in when Luther finds, two decades later, that his interpretations have been challenged.

What led Luther to write *On the Jews and Their Lies*, he tells us at the outset, is news that Jews were trying to convert Christians, as well as a treatise he had recently read in which an author defends the Jews and "dares to pervert the scriptural passages which we cite in testimony to our faith . . . and to interpret them differently."[64] The key accusation against the Jews is thus not moral or political but theological and hermeneutical: that they lie, and that they lie most egregiously about the meaning of the Scriptures. They are like back-talkers who "give God the lie," for they continue to believe they are God's people in virtue of their ancestry, their circumcision, and their law,[65] despite all the Bible has said about their unworthiness earning God's wrath and rejection. In Luther's view, their most fundamental lie is to deny that the Hebrew Scriptures bear witness to Jesus Christ. So in the long central section of his treatise he turns to four proof texts on this subject, including the two that he discussed in *That Jesus Christ Was Born a Jew*.[66] His argument, as before, is that these are messianic prophecies that could only be fulfilled by Jesus.

The first thing he says about his first proof text is that it has been "tortured and crucified" by the Jews, "in violation of their own conscience. For

63. Luther, *That Jesus Christ Was Born a Jew*, LW 45:213–28.

64. Luther, *On the Jews and Their Lies*, LW 47:137.

65. These are the initial topics of the first part of the treatise, LW 47:140–77, in which the accusation is repeatedly made that they give God the lie: LW 47:143, 145, 164, 166. This means—to put the point in terms of one of Luther's most fundamental convictions—they deny that God is true to his word (*Deus verax*). Their sin, he concludes, is just like the papists' efforts to be justified by works rather than faith: "By means of their own deeds they want to manage to become God's people" (LW 47:175).

66. Luther, *On the Jews and Their Lies*, LW 47:178–254.

they realize fully that their twisting and perverting is nothing but wanton mischief."[67] This is the logic of proof-texting supporting the wrong kind of certainty in service to vicious theological polemics: Luther's opponents are violating their own conscience, for they must know perfectly well that their interpretation is forced. It is easy to prove (Luther thinks) that the correct interpretation is quite certain and unmistakable, since the meaning of the text is absolutely clear and obvious to all. The same conclusion follows concerning the interpretation of the second proof text: "We are certain that even the devil and the Jews themselves cannot refute this in their hearts and that in their own consciences they are convinced."[68] Similarly in introducing the third proof text, Luther is sure that "their conscience pales before this passage."[69] And likewise when he sums up his treatment of the fourth proof text: "No doubt it is necessary for the Jews to lie and to misinterpret in order to maintain their error over against such a clear and powerful text."[70]

The treatise goes on and gets much worse in the injustice of its accusations, the vileness of its insults, and the violence of its recommendations. Much of it will not bear repeating. But it should be mentioned that Luther's emphasis remains consistently on Jewish *speech*. His cruelest thoughts stem from his conviction that the Jews' blasphemous lies cry out to heaven and must not be tolerated, lest the wrath of God fall on all of Germany because of them. Hence his most distinctive policy recommendation is to make Jewish religious speech a capital crime: Jews should "be forbidden on pain of death to praise God, to give thanks, to pray, and to teach publicly among us and in our country."[71] In fact Luther wants to make it a matter of conscience to prevent Jews from speaking like Jews even in private:

> What will happen even if we do burn down the Jews' synagogues and forbid them publicly to praise God, to pray, to teach, to utter God's name? They will still keep doing it in secret. If we know that they are doing this in secret, it is the same as if they were doing it publicly. For our knowledge of their secret doings and our toleration of them implies that they are not secret after all, and thus our conscience is encumbered with it before God. . . . If we wish to wash our hands of the Jews' blasphemy and not share in their guilt, we have to part company with them. They must be driven from our country.[72]

---

67. Luther, *On the Jews and Their Lies*, LW 47:178.
68. Luther, *On the Jews and Their Lies*, LW 47:200.
69. Luther, *On the Jews and Their Lies*, LW 47:210.
70. Luther, *On the Jews and Their Lies*, LW 47:252.
71. Luther, *On the Jews and Their Lies*, LW 47:286.
72. Luther, *On the Jews and Their Lies*, LW 47:287–88.

Coming from a man whose central insights are about the power of words and whose greatest comfort is the word of God, this passage is as deeply dehumanizing as is possible for Luther, for it aims to deprive the Jews of the religious speech that makes them who they are. The violent policy recommendations that follow are more overtly wicked, but they grow out of this taproot of contempt and fear of those whose words threaten his own grasp on the word of God.

A Failure of Hope

Thinking about the future of Protestantism requires us to ask how Protestant theology can do things differently from Luther's uncharitable and unedifying polemics. My suggestion is that what goes wrong in Luther is not his faith but his theology, which demands of his faith the wrong kind of certainty, which in fact it never has. Not content with a faithfulness that clings to the Gospel in the face of doubts, he insists on the indubitable certainty of his proof texts. Part of his vehemence in writing against the Jews, one has to suspect, is due to the uncertainty of his own conscience as he offers dubious and obscure proof texts as the basis of his theological arguments. When he accuses the Jews of lying against their own conscience, it seems obvious that he is projecting his own uncertainties on his opponents. There is a similar vehemence, though less overt violence, in Luther's theological battles against the Roman Catholics and the Reformed. In every case, Luther's demand for certainty fuels fierce polemics that leave deep historical wounds and lead, by way of the irony of unintended consequences, to the uncertainty bred by the endless theological squabbles of confessional Europe in the next two centuries.

The failure of Luther's theology here is most obviously a failure to love. Christian faith should lead to love of neighbor, according to Luther's theology and everyone else's. If faith means looking to God for all good things, as Luther teaches, then love means seeking those same good things for our neighbors and even for our enemies. Not that we must desire our enemies to succeed in their ventures against us, but we should hope that they too might come to the same knowledge of Christ and eternal life that we desire for ourselves. Love of enemies is thus grounded in hope, the expectation that it really is possible in the end to share the best of all good things with our enemies. Hope means expecting that enemies may indeed become friends through some appropriate combination of repentance and conversion on both sides—as unlikely as that often seems. For Christian hope, grounded in faith, is based not on what we can see to be likely but on the promise of God's word. Luther knows this.

And yet Luther himself tells us that he refuses to entertain hopes for his theological opponents. In his last major treatise against "the fanatics" he writes, "I have abandoned all my hope for their improvement," and, "I did not want . . . to pray for them any more."[73] This is not just a passing moment of discouragement but a recommendation for all Christians, as he explains a few pages later: "No one among Christians should and can pray for the fanatics" because by their teachings they have "shamelessly lied . . . against their own consciences."[74] He writes similarly in the conclusion of a late treatise against Roman Catholics: "They are impenitent and blinded, delivered to the wrath of God. We must give room to the wrath and let God's judgment run its course. Nor shall we any longer pray for their sin . . . but pray about them and against them."[75] Strikingly, however, it seems the Bible itself does not allow Luther to abandon all hope for the Jews. Still, he does not expect any good to come to them until a far distant future when their exile and divine punishment "finally makes them pliable and they are forced to confess that the Messiah has come, and that he is our Jesus."[76] That future is not near enough to restore the hope he expressed in his earlier treatise that a brotherly attitude and a pair of proof texts would be sufficient to convert them. But apparently it does mean that even his later, violent onslaught against the Jews must conclude with a prayer for them, coming in the words of the very last sentence: "May Christ, our dear Lord, convert them mercifully."[77]

It appears that even in his bitter old age Luther could realize that hope was demanded of him. The deepest problems in Luther's theology, I would suggest, arise when his hope fails. For hope ought to follow from faith and lead to a love of enemies, including theological opponents, that can persevere in the face of an unbroken string of disappointments, including the age-long Jewish refusal to convert to the Christian faith. Hope opens us to the possibility that our opponents are not enemies but potential friends who have good things to give us, even when their words loosen our grasp on the meaning of God's word. This hope has actually begun to be fulfilled today in the growing Christian appreciation, even love, of Jewish exegesis and its tradition of creative interpretation called midrash.

The corrective we need when we are dismayed by the ferociousness of Luther's polemics, I suggest, is an insistence that theologians have a sacred obligation to hope. Theological writings must foster the hope that makes it

73. Luther, *Brief Confession*, LW 38:291.
74. Luther, *Brief Confession*, LW 38:296.
75. Luther, *Against Hanswurst* (1541), LW 41:255.
76. Luther, *Against the Jews and Their Lies*, LW 47:139.
77. Luther, *Against the Jews and Their Lies*, LW 47:306.

possible to love, which is to say: the Christian virtue of hope that frees us to pray for all our opponents, to desire good things for them, and to expect good things from them, including even those who undermine our theological interpretations of Scripture.[78] By the practice of such hope we put our trust not in our theological ability or irrefutable arguments but in the Holy Spirit, the God who has over the centuries of the Christian tradition borne witness to Jesus Christ and guided the church into all truth, according to our Lord's own promise (John 15:26; 16:13).

The hope required in Christian theological writing is thus quite different from the kind of certainty Luther demanded in his polemics. It offers Christians a possession that is not clear and plain like a proof text. Rather, it is based on faith in the promise of God, which gives us Christ as our present possession but does not allow us to see him or make him appear perspicuously in light of our theological reasoning—for as Luther rightly says, Christ is present only "in the darkness of faith."[79] Thus faith and hope give us no guarantee of escape from the uncertainties and anxieties of the future in a world full of sin, suffering, and death. But they do offer us reasons to treat our theological opponents differently than Luther did, which should be something we insist on in Protestant theology going forward.

78. In Cary and Phelizon, *Does God Have a Strategy?*, 5, I contend that "love is the enacted hope that I might find in the other a friend rather than an enemy or a slave," with particular attention to biblical exegesis and Jewish-Christian relations.

79. Luther, 1535 Galatians Commentary, *LW* 26:130. Cf. also 26:113.

10

Salvation

Faith in Christ's Promise Alone

For Protestants, faith and promise go together. Luther links them by insisting that proper Christian faith is based on the certainty that Christ will keep his promise to me. Likewise in the second generation of Protestant Reformers, John Calvin makes "the truth of the freely-given promise in Christ" essential to his definition of Christian faith.[1] Hence the uncertainties and anxieties Protestants wrestle with concern faith itself, which is not as reliable as the promise of God in which it believes.

As we saw in chapter 7, Luther is convinced that faith can be certain only by being unreflective—basing everything on God's promise alone and nothing on the belief that I believe. But although faith is properly unreflective, theology is not. Precisely because faith is not as reliable as the word of God, reflective questions about faith do arise in Luther's theology, and they loom increasingly large in later Protestant theology. As I shall argue in this chapter, however, Luther's sacramental conception of the Gospel allows him to be more successful than later Protestant theologians in getting us to put all our faith in the word of God alone.

Diverse Traditions of Anxiety

Diverse Protestant anxieties stem from the diverse ways in which the promises of the Gospel are and are not conditional upon faith. All the Protestant Reformers

---

1. Calvin, *Institutes* 3:2.7.

agreed that they are conditional in one sense, because unbelief means refusing the promise and therefore receiving none of the things promised. Yet in another sense the promises can be unconditional: they need not explicitly mention faith as a necessary condition or speak in conditional terms such as "*if* you believe in Christ, you are saved." At this point various traditions of Protestant theology begin to diverge in subtle but crucial ways, for they take different kinds of Scriptural promises to be the basis of Christian faith. Luther's thinking about the promise of the Gospel, for example, has us putting faith in a sacramental word such as "I baptize you in the name of the Father, and of the Son, and of the Holy Spirit" or "This is my body given for you." The sacramental word states no condition (it has no "if" clause) but simply addresses me directly, saying "you" in a way that includes me. Faith in such a word can be unreflective, simply believing that the word is true. By contrast, believing a conditional promise—or more precisely, believing it applies *to me*—means I must believe more than the word alone; I must believe I meet the condition. So if my salvation depends on a conditional promise such as "if you believe in Christ, you are saved" (or its logical equivalent, "whoever believes in Christ is saved"), then I cannot be assured of salvation unless I believe that I believe. This is what I call "reflective faith." It is an example of what Cajetan called an "acquired faith," not based on the revelation of God but on knowledge I acquire about myself. Luther in effect agrees with Cajetan that this is not proper Christian faith.

The different kinds of promise, conditional and unconditional, lead logically to different kinds of faith, reflective and unreflective, which lead in practice to different kinds of Christian life. And thus a great divergence arises between different strands of Protestant theology and the lives they shape. From this divergence stem many controversies within Protestantism, whose roots often go unnoticed because the contending theologians usually fail to realize that they are actually thinking of the promise of the Gospel in different terms. The task of this chapter is to uncover these roots and shed some light on the divergence and disagreements that grow from them. We need to see why reflective faith became important in later Protestantism and how it results in a different kind of Christian life and experience from faith in the sacramental promise of the Gospel as conceived by Luther. We can see this most clearly in Calvinist theology, which is helpful for our purposes because it is very close to Luther in many respects but also different in ways that had a deep influence on Protestant traditions well beyond the bounds of the Calvinist tradition. This chapter should help us understand, for example, why most Protestants today regard conversion rather than baptism as the beginning of the Christian life. More fundamentally, I shall be suggesting that when Protestant theology requires a reflective faith, it is caught in a logic that inevitably ends up demanding that believers engage in a kind of inward turn. Only a sacramental conception of the Gospel promise can avoid this Protestant inward turn and carry out the original Protestant intention of putting faith in the word of God alone.

To introduce Calvinist theology at this point is to speak of rival traditions within Protestantism, as Calvinism is the central strand within the Reformed tradition of Protestantism, and much of the Reformed tradition after Calvin is aptly described as the Calvinist tradition. The name "Reformed" does not refer to the whole Reformation, but to one tradition within it that took as its motto, "the Church reformed according to the word of God." Originating in Switzerland with Ulrich (or Huldrych) Zwingli and taking root also in Southern Germany under the leadership of Martin Bucer, it was reinforced in the next generation by John Calvin in Geneva and spread to the Netherlands (where it eventually became the state church), France (where the Reformed were known as Huguenots), Scotland (with the formation of the Presbyterian church), and England (where the Puritans became the Calvinist wing in the Church of England). The Reformed tradition is the great alternative to the Lutheran tradition within the "magisterial Reformation," a term designating the mainstream of the Reformation, which was willing to enlist European rulers and magistrates in the work of reforming the church (as Calvin worked with the magistrates in Geneva and Luther worked under the protection of a North German prince, the Elector of Saxony).

In contrast to the magisterial Reformation, the radical or left wing of the Reformation, represented most importantly by the Anabaptists, made no alliances with the rulers of Europe, because they thought these rulers were, like the vast majority of their subjects, not really baptized and not really Christian, belonging to the kingdom of this world rather than to the kingdom of God. Because the Anabaptist witness consisted largely in the life of an alternative community—their own disciplined life together under the word of God, which they contrasted with the kingdoms of this world—they laid less stress on the difference between faith and works than the magisterial Reformers. To a large extent, the Anabaptists' faith consisted in their communal life, which meant it was impossible, as well as unnecessary from the standpoint of their own theology, for them to draw a clear distinction between faith and works. Thus the anxieties that come with "faith alone" belong largely within the traditions of magisterial Protestantism, and when I speak of "Protestant theology" from now on, it is these traditions that I have in mind.[2]

---

2. One great scholar of the radical Reformation goes so far as to argue that "Protestant" is a label that does not apply to Anabaptists, who typically rejected the theology of "faith alone"

The fact that Protestantism of every sort has its anxieties is not an objection against it. In a world full of suffering, evil, and death, there is no escape from anxiety of one kind or another. Every tradition that shapes human lives tries to ward off various anxieties but also generates characteristic anxieties of its own, for every tradition has its own way of situating anxiety within the human lives it shapes. As we saw in chapter 5, the characteristic anxiety of medieval Catholicism concerned mortal sin which, in contrast to venial sin, is sufficient to destroy the new life of grace received in baptism and thus to earn damnation. This is an anxiety that Protestants do not have, mainly because Luther, early in his conflict with the pope, insisted that all sin was mortal. Combined with his conviction that Christians are always both sinners and righteous at the same time, this meant that every good work of a righteous Christian is in substance mortal sin if judged by God's strict judgment—which is to say that the only thing our good works can ever earn us in God's sight is damnation.[3]

The scandalous assertion that everything we do is mortal sin, which Luther defended at great length in the early 1520s, is not mere pessimism. It grew out of young Luther's campaign against monastic complacency,[4] which we examined in chapter 5, but in his mature theology it supports what Lutherans call the "evangelical use" of the law, which is to say, the preaching of the law that serves the good news of the Gospel. The law serves the Gospel when it drives people to despair of their own good works ("evangelical despair," as it came to be called) so that they realize they have no hope of salvation but in Jesus Christ. The intended effect, in the end, is not pessimism but freedom from performance anxiety; for there is no point worrying whether your good works are good enough when it's a foregone conclusion that they're not. Luther's scandalous claim became a decisive turning point from which Protestants never looked back. It is why Protestants never worry about whether they are in a state of mortal sin: there is no concept of venial sin to contrast with it.

(Williams, *Radical Reformation*, xxiii–xxv). The Anabaptists arising in the sixteenth century (including the Mennonites) should not be confused with the Baptists arising in the seventeenth century in England. The two movements did have contact with one another and some important points in common, including an insistence on adult believer baptism and a rejection of state-supported churches. Because the Baptist churches grew out of the Reformed tradition, however, much of what I say about Calvinist theology applies to the Baptists, but not to the Anabaptists.

3. Luther, *Defense and Explanation of All the Articles*, article 35 (*LW* 32:91), responding to the papal condemnation he received in 1520. See also articles 31, 32, 36. Luther defends his view in his 1521 treatise *Against Latomus*, *LW* 32:159–217.

4. As reflected for example in Luther, Romans Lectures, on Rom. 4:7, *LW* 25:276, where before his controversies with the pope began he argues that "there is no sin which is venial according to its substance and its nature. . . . Thus we sin even when we do good." Cf. also his defense of the thesis that "the righteous man also sins while doing good," in Luther, *Heidelberg Disputation* (1518), *LW* 31:60–70.

Hence the concept of mortal sin entirely drops out of Protestant thought, and most Protestants don't understand the term. If only faith in Christ can save you, the thing to worry about is not whether your sins are mortal but whether you really have faith. This is a new worry, which we need to understand.

There is no understanding a tradition and the lives it shapes until we understand its characteristic anxieties and how it deals with them. In particular, we do not understand a *Christian* tradition until we understand how its characteristic forms of pastoral care are directed toward its characteristic anxieties. For instance, the characteristic form of pastoral care for Catholics in the late Middle Ages was the sacrament of penance, in which they hoped to identify and confess all their mortal sins and have them absolved. In short: Catholics worry about mortal sin, so they go to confession. The logical basis of the worry, of course, is the teaching that those who die in a state of mortal sin end up in hell. The logical consequence is something that is literally unimaginable in Protestant theology: there are lots of Christians in hell. They are bad Christians, of course, devoid of charity and the life of grace because of their mortal sin, but they are Christians nonetheless, for theirs is the true Christian faith, not heresy. Dante's *Inferno* is full of bad Christians. By contrast, the whole point of Protestant belief in salvation by faith alone could be summed up in the thesis: there are no Christians in hell. That is why the Protestant worry is not "Are my sins mortal?" but rather, "Am I really a Christian?," which amounts to the worry, "Do I really have Christian faith?" And in contrast to patristic and medieval theology, the worry about faith is not whether what I believe is really the true Christian faith, but about whether I really, truly believe it. This is a worry that Lutherans and Calvinists share, but with subtle differences that we must now examine.

Perseverance and Predestination

Luther's insistence on the certainty of faith is not the same as the Calvinist insistence on the certainty of salvation.[5] As we saw, Luther forcefully rejects the Catholic notion that we cannot be certain we are in a state of grace, teaching instead that a proper faith in the Gospel makes me certain that Christ is mine

5. Interestingly, the Catholic Council of Trent, responding to the Protestant Reformation in 1547, recognized the difference and condemned these two teachings separately: first the characteristically Lutheran teaching that faith involves being certain of the forgiveness of sins (Session 6, chap. 9 and canon 13, in Schaff, *Creeds of Christendom* 2:98, 113) and then the characteristically Calvinist certainty of predestination and perseverance (Session 6, chaps. 12 and 13 and canons 15 and 16, in Schaff, *Creeds of Christendom* 2:103, 113–14). Protestants are seldom as clear as Trent was on the differences between them.

with all his grace and righteousness.[6] But this is not quite the certainty that later Protestants came to expect, for it is not a certainty that I am eternally saved. The sacramental word, grounded in the Gospel promise, gives me Christ himself but does not promise that I will continue to receive Christ for the rest of my life, because it does not promise that I will continue to have faith. This is crucial, because perseverance in faith to the end of life is required for salvation. The requirement of perseverance draws attention to the most important respect in which my faith is too unreliable to guarantee my salvation.

Augustine pointed out long ago, as we saw in chapter 4, that accepting the Christian faith today does not save me if I do not remain a Christian at the day of my death. For my eternal salvation, I need not only faith at the beginning of my spiritual journey but perseverance in faith to the end. Apostasy, or falling away from Christian faith, is always a possibility, and Augustine sees no way that my present faith can guarantee that I will still be a believer next year or even next week, much less at the end of my life. Hence Augustine has no doctrine of "eternal security," as it is called in the Calvinist tradition, because he thinks "no one can be secure [*securus*] about life eternal."[7] This is why Augustine distinguishes between being saved in hope (*in spe*), which happens in baptism, and being saved in reality (*in re*), which has not happened yet. No Christian has a present salvation, in Augustine's view, because we all have a life ahead of us, and nothing we presently believe or do can determine that we will still be Christians at the end of it. Only God can ensure that we will receive the gift of perseverance, which for all of us imperfect Christians is just as dependent on unmerited grace as the initial gift of faith is.

Luther is with Augustine rather than the Calvinists on this point. Since the Gospel is a sacramental word, it can give us Christ in the present but it cannot promise that we will continue to be believers in the future, and thus it cannot assure us that we will still have Christ at the end of our days. Such an assurance would amount to knowledge that we are predestined for salvation, and Luther, like Augustine and the whole Catholic tradition, does not see God giving us any such knowledge. We can see this in the famous distinction that Luther develops in his book *The Bondage of the Will*, where he contrasts God hidden and God revealed. There is a great difference, Luther teaches, between "the preached and offered mercy of God" and "that hidden and frightful will of God whereby he ordains by his own counsel which and what sort of persons

---

6. This insistence, which we saw in chap. 7 when Luther disagreed with Cajetan, remains in his later works, for example in the 1535 Galatians Commentary, on Gal. 4:6, *LW* 26:377–79, a passage whose concluding note is: "Let everyone accustom himself, therefore, to believe for a certainty that he is in a state of grace."

7. Augustine, *The Gift of Perseverance* 22.62.

he wills to be recipients and partakers of his preached and offered mercy."[8]
The difference, in a nutshell, is between Gospel and predestination. For it is
one thing when God reveals himself graciously in the promise of the Gospel,
and quite another when he chooses to give the gift of lifelong faith in the
Gospel to some undeserving sinners rather than others, which has the effect
of predestining the former to salvation and the latter to damnation. This has
always been seen in the Augustinian tradition as a choice God makes in the
hiddenness of his eternity, which is why Calvinists call it a "hidden decree."
Luther urges us to have nothing to do with this hidden aspect of God's will,
for "in this regard we have nothing to do with him, nor has he willed that we
should have anything to do with him. But we have something to do with him
insofar as he is clothed and set forth in his Word."[9] Hence our business is "to
pay attention to the Word and leave that inscrutable will alone."[10]

Urging people to turn from God hidden to God revealed is crucial to good
pastoral care in Luther's view, as we can see in a characteristic bit of table
talk recorded by one of his dinner guests:

> He spoke of predestination and said that when a man begins to dispute about
> it, it is like a fire that cannot be extinguished, and the more he disputes the more
> he despairs. Our Lord God is so hostile to such disputation that he instituted
> Baptism, the Word, and the Sacrament as signs to counteract it. We should rely
> on these and say: "I have been baptized. *I believe in Jesus Christ.* I have received
> the Sacrament. *What do I care if I have been predestined or not?*"[11]

The subtlety of the difference we are examining in this chapter is illustrated by
how we must interpret what Luther intends here by saying "I believe in Jesus
Christ." Calvinists use such a statement as the basis for discerning that they
are predestined for salvation. Luther uses it as an alternative to thinking about
predestination, because he wants to put his faith only in the God revealed
in baptism, word, and sacrament. Behind this difference is the logic of two
different kinds of divine promise, one sacramental and the other conditional.

Calvinist Syllogisms

The logic of Calvinist pastoral care concerning the certainty or assurance of
salvation is summed up in what Reformed theologians called "the practical

8. Luther, *Bondage of the Will*, WA 18:684 (= *LW* 33:139).
9. Luther, *Bondage of the Will*, WA 18:684 (= *LW* 33:139).
10. Luther, *Bondage of the Will*, *LW* 33:140.
11. Luther, *Letters of Spiritual Counsel*, 122 (= table talk #2631b).

syllogism." Syllogisms are the basic form of reasoning in Aristotelian logic, which theologians in any tradition in the West could use to make their thinking clear and explicit. The Reformed theologians formulated practical syllogisms to make explicit the kind of thinking that could assure me that I am eternally saved. The wording varied from one theologian to another, but it followed a definite pattern, which can be illustrated by a version of the practical syllogism taken from the seventeenth-century theologian Francis Turretin:

> (Major Premise) Whoever truly believes and becomes of a right spirit is elect.
>
> (Minor Premise) But I believe and am of a right spirit.
>
> (Conclusion) Therefore I am elect.[12]

The term "elect" is just a Latin way of saying "chosen" (*electus*), which here means that I am chosen by God for salvation—hence in the Augustinian tradition, including Calvinism, "elect" and "predestined for salvation" are equivalent terms. The premises take a form that is typical of Aristotelian syllogisms: the first, called the major premise, is a general principle. The second, called the minor premise, applies the general principle to a specific case—which in this case means me. The result is the desired conclusion: I am elect, so I am assured of salvation. In the Calvinist practical syllogism, the major premise is taken to be an implication of the Gospel promise. It is conditional (logically equivalent to "If you believe and are of a right spirit, you are elect"), and the way I know the Gospel promise refers to me is by knowing I meet the condition stated in the "if" clause. The reflective character of Calvinist assurance of salvation is plainly on display in the minor premise: in order to know I am saved, I need to know I believe.

The unstated but very clear assumption behind the practical syllogism is that true Christian faith always perseveres to the end. This is the distinctively Calvinist doctrine of perseverance, going back to Calvin himself[13] but formulated in classic fashion by the Synod of Dordt in 1619. It is the "P" (for "Perseverance of the saints") in the famous TULIP mnemonic representing the five canons, or doctrines, of the synod, which became famous as "five-point Calvinism."[14] The distinctive pastoral consequence of this doctrine is that if I

---

12. Muller, *Dictionary of Latin and Greek Theological Terms*, on *syllogismus practicus*, 293.

13. See Calvin, *Institutes* 3:2.40; 3:24.6.

14. See Schaff, *Creeds of Christendom* 3:592–95. The mnemonic summarizes the five canons (not in the same order as that in which they were presented in the original text) as Total depravity, Unconditional election, Limited atonement, Irresistible grace, and Perseverance of the saints.

know I have true faith, then I can know I am predestined for salvation, which means I am in fact already saved for eternity. In contrast to Augustine, I can say I am saved now, in present reality, not merely in hope. But knowing this depends on my being able to tell that I have true saving faith, the kind that perseveres rather than the temporary kind. That is why Turretin's syllogism adds "and becomes of a right spirit" in the major premise. There must be something about the spirit that comes with true faith that I can use to distinguish it from temporary faith.

This is what Augustine—and the whole Augustinian tradition up to and including Luther—had not imagined was possible. It did not occur to Augustine that a faith that failed to persevere was necessarily any less true and Christian, so long as it lasted, than a faith that persevered and resulted in salvation. Hence he never suggested there was anything I could discern in my own personal faith or its consequences that could assure me it would last until the end of my life. What is new about Calvinism begins with its insistence that saving faith is a different *kind* of faith from temporary faith,[15] and that there is some way of telling the difference. It is a deeper gift of the grace of God, and when I know I have been given this gift, then I know I am eternally saved. This leads to the great, radical innovation of Calvinist theology, which is the claim that I can know I am predestined for salvation. While Calvin's doctrine of predestination itself differs from Augustine's by no more than a hair's breadth,[16] his notion that I can *know* that I am predestined for salvation

15. The notion of a distinctively temporary faith is introduced by Calvin in *Institutes* 3.2.11. Given the pastoral need to distinguish this from saving faith, it is not surprising that later Reformed theologians insist that saving faith is not just more lasting than temporary faith but different in kind—technically speaking a different species, "specifically different" (Heppe, *Reformed Dogmatics*, 528).

16. Calvin frequently cites Augustine in support of his doctrine of predestination, perhaps most importantly in *Institutes* 3:22:8; 3:23.1. Critics trying to separate Calvinism from the larger Augustinian tradition have identified "double predestination" as its distinguishing mark. This is the doctrine that God not only predestines some for salvation but predestines others for damnation, in a hidden decree called "reprobation" (e.g., in Calvin *Institutes* 3:21.5; 3:23.1–3; cf. Heppe, *Reformed Dogmatics*, 156, 178–89). The Augustinian opponents of Calvinism think this is different—and much worse—from merely *not predestining* someone for salvation, though they cannot deny that it has the same effect in the end: those not predestined for salvation are damned, as surely as if they were predestined to be damned. Subtle differences in the doctrine of God and our understanding of his will may be at stake here (though I, for one, am not convinced), but at any rate the distinction makes no pastoral difference. By contrast, the radical innovation of teaching that we can know we are elect makes an enormous difference pastorally and in the shape of the resulting Christian life. It is this innovation, not double predestination or reprobation, that ought to be identified as the key point at which Calvinism diverges from the larger Augustinian tradition with regard to predestination. I would add that Augustine himself seems unaware of any difference between single and double predestination and takes no care to distinguish them, with the result that

is a momentous departure from the previous Augustinian tradition, a departure that shapes Christian life in a profoundly new way.[17] Although the decree of predestination remains hidden, in that I cannot know in general who is predestined for salvation, Calvin introduces the new teaching that in my own case I can be assured that I am among the elect, because I can know I have true saving faith.

And that is where distinctive Calvinist anxieties begin. Of course it is not Calvin's intention to stir up such anxieties,[18] but we must distinguish what a theologian intends from what he achieves. Calvin intends that the "very sweet fruit" of the doctrine of predestination should be preached as "our only ground for firmness and confidence."[19] And indeed we do not understand the Calvinist tradition until we see why so many Calvinists welcome the doctrine of predestination and find assurance in it. But as in other traditions, the source of anxiety in Calvinism lies very close to the ground of its certainties. For the opposite side of the coin from the Calvinist doctrine of predestined perseverance is the logical consequence that any faith that does not persevere to the end was never true Christian faith to begin with—and that such indeed might be *my* faith, even now. Christians who lose their faith never truly believed in Christ in the first place, Calvin teaches, for they "never cleaved to Christ with the heartfelt trust in which certainty of election has, I say, been established for us."[20] Yet he admits it is not uncommon for the reprobate (i.e., those eternally rejected by God and predestined for damnation) to feel in their heart that they are elect:

> For though only those predestined to salvation receive the light of faith and truly feel the power of the gospel, yet experience shows that the reprobate are

---

there are many passages in Augustine that Calvinists can cite in support of double predestination: e.g., *Enchiridion* 100 ("predestined to punishment"); *The Punishment and Merits of Sins* 2:17.26 ("predestined to condemnation"); *The Perfection of Human Righteousness* 13.31 ("predestined to destruction"); *The Nature and Origin of the Human Soul* 4:11.16 ("predestined to eternal death").

17. Calvin, *Institutes* 3:24.1–4, is quite clear that it is possible and desirable, though far from inevitable, that believers know they are predestined to salvation.

18. R. T. Kendall, while trying to make a sharp distinction between Calvin and later Calvinists, inadvertently shows how Calvinist pastoral care grows out of the anxiety that originates with Calvin's teaching about temporary faith in Kendall, *Calvin and English Calvinism*, 21–24. One should add: the concept of temporary faith is not one Calvin could have avoided, because it follows logically from the innovation he introduces in his doctrines of predestination and perseverance, which in turn follows from his insistence on the possibility of the assurance of salvation. Logically, you can't have Calvinist assurance of salvation without the specter of Calvinist anxiety about temporary faith.

19. Calvin, *Institutes* 3:21.1.

20. Calvin, *Institutes* 3:24.7.

sometimes affected by almost the same feeling as the elect, so that even in their own judgment they do not in any way differ from the elect.[21]

It is easy to be mistaken about whether you have true faith, because the feeling of temporary faith is, as Calvin says here, "almost the same." So you may feel you are a true Christian and yet be predestined for damnation. This is the consequence of defining true Christian faith by the state of the heart rather than the content of the creed. Reflective faith becomes the ground of assurance but also the source of deep new anxieties.

Protestant Conversions

The question for anxious Calvinists is: How do I tell whether I have true faith, the kind that is sure to persevere and result in salvation? Calvinist pastoral care has historically taken two different but mutually reinforcing approaches to this question. The first approach, which has had a momentous impact on Western religious life, especially in the English-speaking world, centers on the idea of a conversion experience that is a single, life-changing event of salvation. This can happen only once in a lifetime, because it is supposed to mark the irreversible transition from unbelief to saving faith. Other Protestant traditions also picked up the idea, though often without the Calvinist assurance that conversion is irreversible.

This Protestant idea of conversion looms so large in modern Western religious history that it has overshadowed the Reformation theology of justification—a term that is now largely forgotten even in the churches—with the result that nowadays the conversion experience is often simply identified with "getting saved." Already in the late sixteenth century Lutheran theologians were talking as if conversion were the decisive transition from death in sin to life in Christ, a notion that would have astonished Luther, for whom baptism was the only irreversible moment of becoming Christian.[22] Two centuries later, the theology that lost out at the Synod of Dordt, called Arminianism, made a great comeback in the Anglo-American world with the explicitly Arminian theology of John Wesley's Methodists, who treated the experience of conversion as essential to Christian life but rejected the Calvinist doctrines of

21. Calvin, *Institutes* 3:2.11.
22. The Lutheran *Formula of Concord* links conversion and regeneration (i.e., being born again) in Solid Declaration 2:2 and 6.1, in Tappert, *Book of Concord*, 520, 563, while also trying to connect both conversion and regeneration to baptism in Solid Declaration 2:65–68, in Tappert, *Book of Concord*, 534. The result is an amalgam that looks to me like part Luther, part Calvinism.

predestination and perseverance of the saints. Thus for the Methodists and other non-Calvinist Protestants, it was possible for people to be converted and saved, and then subsequently to lose their salvation.[23] Yet their experience of conversion, like the Protestant idea of conversion in general, is ultimately indebted to the Calvinist tradition.[24] You know you're listening to Protestants downstream from Calvin when you hear people arguing about "whether you can lose your salvation." Before Calvinism this was a question no one asked, because no one thought they already had a salvation to lose.

The novelty of the Protestant idea of conversion needs to be stressed, because it is an idea that tends to impose itself on readings of earlier theologians. Augustine's *Confessions*, for example, is often misread as if it centered on something very much like a Protestant conversion narrative, as we saw in chapter 4. Luther likewise is misread as if he regarded justification as a one-time event taking place at conversion rather than a lifelong process—despite his persistent use of process language, which we've examined in earlier chapters. Calvin himself uses the term "conversion" (i.e., the Latin *conversio*, which literally means "turning") in the traditional theological sense of a lifelong process of turning to God, which he identifies with repentance.[25] Yet Calvin initiated the Protestant concern with conversion in other terms when he spoke of the "effectual call" as evidence of election. This term designates the inner work of the Holy Spirit by which God initially produces saving faith in the heart and thus "manifests the election, which he otherwise holds hidden within himself."[26] Calvin also terms this the "inner call," in contrast to the external word of the Gospel, which is an outward call to faith and repentance that is preached indiscriminately to all and therefore does not identify who is saved.[27] "This inner call," says Calvin, "is a pledge of salvation that cannot deceive us."[28] To translate into later, more familiar terms: your conversion experience is how God lets you know, inwardly, that you're saved.

The need to be converted, in this distinctively Protestant sense, becomes a driving force in revivalism, which was a kind of social engine for producing conversion experiences. The theory and practice of revivalism began on Calvinist ground, with the Great Awakening in eighteenth-century America led by

23. For Wesley's frank rejection of the Calvinist doctrine on this point, see Wesley, "Serious Thoughts upon the Perseverance of the Saints," in *Works* 10:284–98.
24. For the roots of the Wesleyan "way of salvation" in the Calvinist "order of salvation" (*ordo salutis*) in Puritan theology, which gives a prominent place to conversion or "effectual call," see Campbell, *Wesleyan Beliefs*, chap. 2.
25. Calvin, *Institutes* 3:3.5, where *conversio* is rendered "turning" in the Battles translation.
26. Calvin, *Institutes* 3:24.1.
27. Calvin, *Institutes* 3:22.10.
28. Calvin, *Institutes* 3:24.2.

its foremost preacher, George Whitefield, and its foremost theorist, Jonathan Edwards, both of whom were Calvinists. John Wesley's involvement in revival preaching came after he read and was inspired by Edwards's *Faithful Narrative of the Surprising Work of God*, the first major theological work arising from the Great Awakening.[29] By the mid-nineteenth century the theology and practice of revivalism were more commonly Wesleyan than Calvinist, but the need that drove the revivals was the same: a powerful conversion experience was taken as a pledge of salvation and an assurance of divine forgiveness— though in Wesley's Arminian theology this did not amount to an assurance of eternal salvation.

The results, in any case, are forms of Christian life very different from one in which baptism marks the decisive moment of rebirth in Christ. Revivalism is not a phenomenon at home in traditions such as Catholicism, Eastern Orthodoxy, or Lutheranism, where being born again is what happens in baptism rather than in a once-in-a-lifetime conversion. In these traditions, children are baptized and raised Christian, rather than being taught that they must be converted in order to become truly Christian. This does not mean there can be no such thing as conversion experiences, but rather that no conversion experience is the foundation of the Christian life. Luther's theology, for example, leaves room for many conversion experiences, all of which are ways to repent and return to our baptism, which is the real foundation of Christian life.

The Continental branches of the Reformed tradition also did not embrace so strong a focus on conversion, which arose in English-speaking Calvinism largely because of some unusual developments in seventeenth-century America. The Puritan churches in New England at that time began requiring believers to narrate their experience of conversion as evidence of their regeneration and salvation, before they were admitted into full church membership.[30] This put immense pressure on people to have conversion experiences and resulted in the extraordinary phenomenon of congregations such as Jonathan Edwards's, where many baptized believers in the creed who were living a responsible Christian life—people that in other traditions would be model Christians—regarded themselves as unregenerate and unsaved because they had not had the required experience. These people were never given anything like Luther's pastoral advice to cling to the promise given to them in baptism.[31] Instead, they longed for what Edwards called a season of revival, a time of

29. See Outler, *John Wesley*, 15–16.

30. The story of this remarkable development, which is the presupposition of the revival led by Jonathan Edwards, is told in Morgan, *Visible Saints*.

31. This is the prime criticism of Edwards by Lutheran theologian Robert Jenson in his otherwise highly laudatory study, *America's Theologian*, 61–62, 72–73, 187–91.

weeks or months in the life of the church when many were converted and came to the assurance that they had true saving faith—something that they were taught only happened by a divine grace that could not be counted on because it was not promised to anyone in particular.

Sanctification as Evidence

In the Reformed traditions outside the English-speaking world, revivalism was much less widespread, in part because pastoral care concerning assurance of salvation emphasized a different approach, which centered on what happened *after* conversion. The aim was to discern the sanctifying work of the Holy Spirit in the heart of the believer. This approach can be combined with an emphasis on the necessity of conversion, as it was by Jonathan Edwards in his treatise *Religious Affections*, but it can also provide an alternative to the conversionist and revivalist traditions. For the focus in this approach is not on the one-time event of conversion, but on the ongoing life of Christian holiness that results from it.

To understand this approach, it is necessary to draw a sharp distinction between justification and sanctification, as these terms were used by theologians after Calvin. Justification, in the Calvinist view, is a purely forensic act of God declaring our sins forgiven and imputing to us the merits and righteousness of Christ, but making no inward change in us. Sanctification, by contrast, is the process by which the Holy Spirit works in us and with us, giving us a new heart to obey God's will in love, so that we grow in true inward righteousness and holiness.[32] Since sanctification, by God's design, inevitably follows justification, it serves as evidence that justification has taken place, which only happens in those who have true saving faith. Realizing that I am sanctified is thus a way of coming to know I have true faith and am saved. At this point the reflective character of Calvinism extends beyond the belief that

32. For a brief summary of this distinction, see the Westminster Confession, chaps. 11, 13 (Schaff, *Creeds of Christendom* 3:626–30). The distinction appears in many Reformed confessions, e.g., the Gallican or French Confession, in which Calvin had a hand, articles 18 and 22 (Schaff, *Creeds of Christendom* 3:369–72); the Belgic Confession, articles 23–24 (3:409–10); and the Heidelberg Catechism, questions 60 and 86 (3:326, 338). It should be noted that the terminology fluctuates, and sanctification may be discussed under the heading of good works, renovation, regeneration, mortification and vivification, conversion, or repentance (the last is the term primarily used by Calvin, *Institutes* 3:4.1–9). What is constant is the notion of real change in us and moral progress, which can be taken as evidence of true faith and thus of election. For further details, see Heppe, *Reformed Dogmatics*, chaps. 21–22. For later Lutheran versions of this distinction, see Schmid, *Doctrinal Theology*, §§42 and 48, where "renovation" is the preferred term for sanctification.

I believe, to include the belief that I am truly righteous and holy. For although sanctification never means that I have attained perfection in this life, it does mean I keep making progress in righteousness and holiness.

The sharp distinction between justification and sanctification, it should be said, is not found in Luther. Thinking in Latin, Luther often speaks of sanctification (*sanctificatio*) in connection with the work of the Holy Spirit (*Sanctus Spiritus*), who makes the believer holy (*sanctus*), but he does not explicitly contrast it with justification. He does not even connect the two terms, as if sanctification were a process in us that follows the one-time event of justification. The absence of such a connection is striking, because Luther loves using pairs of terms to make key distinctions, such as Gospel and law, faith and works, gift and example, and the two kinds of righteousness: alien and proper, passive and active. But you never find him pairing justification and sanctification like this. The most likely explanation is that he's never heard of such a pairing, so it never occurs to him to try to relate the two terms. Instead, he speaks unselfconsciously of sanctification or Christian holiness using the same process vocabulary he uses to describe justification or Christian righteousness: it begins and grows in us but is never perfected in this life.[33] In effect, sanctification for Luther is just one of many ways of talking about justification, drawing particular attention to the work of the Holy Spirit in the process.

There is a reason why we should not expect Luther to have anything quite like the Calvinist doctrine of sanctification. Given his doctrine of justification, it would be inconsistent for him to teach that there is anything we actively do, including our cooperation with the Holy Spirit in producing good works, that makes us more truly and inwardly righteous or holy than before. As we saw in chapter 8, that would be like saying the fruit makes the tree good, which gets things backwards. One becomes a new person, a good tree that can bear good fruit, by faith alone. So it is faith alone, not good works, that makes us inwardly righteous and holy, a different person than we were before, because it is by faith alone that we receive Christ together with his righteousness and holiness. So also it is only by the growth of our faith in Christ that we grow in real righteousness and holiness in the depth of our hearts, as this good tree grows inwardly stronger and therefore outwardly more fruitful. In contrast to the purely forensic doctrine of justification in later Protestantism (including the

---

33. E.g., Luther, *Large Catechism*, on the third article of the Creed, in Tappert, *Book of Concord*, 415–18; Luther, *On the Councils and the Church*, LW 41:114; Luther, Commentary on Psalm 45, 1532, LW 12:243–44, where the same Aristotelian process language is applied to both holiness and righteousness; Luther, Commentary on Psalm 51, 1532, LW 12:328, where alien righteousness and alien holiness are treated as equivalent.

Lutheran as well as Calvinist traditions), for Luther the righteousness of Christ by which we are justified is not restricted to the merit earned by Christ's sinless human life but includes the righteousness of God himself (*justitia Dei*, the key technical term in Luther's doctrine of justification), which is given to us in Christ incarnate.[34] This alone is the real righteousness that in us "grows, makes progress and is finally perfected through death."[35] Good works are merely the external fruit that is brought forth by this more inward righteousness.

However, good fruit can be taken as evidence that the tree is good. A faithful Christian does do good works, and even Luther sometimes points to this as comfort for the conscience (on what I called our "good days" in chap. 7).[36] But the Calvinist use of this comfort is much more systematic, because it is needed to support the belief that I have true saving faith. The difficulty here is that even those without faith can do outwardly good works. So the evidence of our sanctification, like the effectual call, must be inward, a change in motivation that we can somehow discern in the depths of our hearts. The result is a kind of Protestant inward turn, which we can see in another version of the practical syllogism:

(Major Premise) Whoever feels in himself the gift of sanctification, by which we die to sin and live unto righteousness, is justified, called, or presented with true faith and elect.

(Minor Premise) But I feel this by the grace of God.

(Conclusion) Therefore I am justified, called, and elect.[37]

34. The story of how Luther's concept of the righteousness of God in Christ incarnate was reduced in later Lutheranism to a purely forensic notion of the imputation of the human merits of Christ (which cannot be the righteousness *of God* because God does not earn merits) is best told by Vainio, *Justification and Participation in Christ*. Unfortunately, Vainio still adheres to a version of the justification/sanctification distinction, which he describes as two forms of "renovation." The important story he has to tell would be clearer and all the more compelling if he recognized that for Luther justification, in the strict and proper sense, is a process, and not one that can be distinguished from sanctification or real renovation in us.

35. Luther, *Two Kinds of Righteousness* (sermon, 1519), LW 31:299. See above, chap. 8, "The Word Forms Persons."

36. Zachman, *Assurance of Faith*, 80–87, provides some examples of this reasoning in Luther, though I do not think Zachman makes a clear enough distinction between Luther and the Calvinist uses of this "testimony of conscience." Luther does think believers ought to have a good conscience, in that they can be certain that their good works please God. This is a fundamental theme in Luther, *Treatise on Good Works*, LW 44:23–29, which is quite compatible with the insistence that apart from faith all our good works are mortal sins (*Treatise on Good Works*, LW 44:37–38). What Luther does not suggest, however, is that believers should use good works as evidence that they have saving faith and are elect. Only Calvinists have that problem.

37. Heppe, *Reformed Dogmatics*, 176. This syllogism is taken from the seventeenth-century Swiss theologian Johannes Wolleb, whose work was influential among American Puritans.

How one is to discern this feeling in oneself becomes a central concern of Calvinist pastoral care.

Of course the feeling is not how you are saved, but rather how you acquire certainty that you are saved. You can be saved without the assurance of salvation, and Calvinist theology typically distinguishes the two quite carefully. Thus the Westminster Confession in 1647 teaches that the certainty of salvation does not belong to the essence of saving faith, and that a true believer "may wait long, and conflict with many difficulties before he be partaker of it."[38] The wait may be long, in part because the bar is high. The certainty of salvation is not acquired by mere conjecture but is infallible, the Confession teaches, for it is based not only on the divine promise of salvation and the "inward evidence" of sanctification, but on the "the testimony of the Spirit" bearing witness inwardly to our spirit.[39] This inner testimony is not a special act of divine revelation given only to a few, but the knowledge any believer may have of the Holy Spirit working in his soul. For the believer "being enabled by the Spirit to know the things which are freely given him of God . . . may, without extraordinary revelation, in the right use of ordinary means, attain" the assurance of salvation.[40] Still, not every believer has this particular gift of the Spirit, though all should seek it.

The distinctive problems of a Calvinist life follow from this project of attaining assurance of salvation. Most famously, good works together with a strong inward motivation to produce them turn into crucial evidence that I have true saving faith. Thus Calvinists regularly give the lie to their opponents' objection that belief in predestination will remove all ethical motivation and make them morally lazy. Quite the contrary, it is much more likely to make them anxious workaholics, as the sociologist Max Weber observed.[41] From a theological standpoint, however, I think the most serious objection to Calvinism concerns how the project of assuring believers of their salvation *succeeds*. Those who feel sure of their salvation must believe they have a true inner righteousness brought about by the work of the Holy Spirit in their hearts, which is lacking in their neighbors—both overt unbelievers and all the so-called believers who do not really have true saving faith. In this sense, Calvinism requires a deep form of self-righteousness, the firm conviction that I am inwardly more righteous than my less-Christian neighbors—which is made worse, not better, by the requirement that I give all the credit and

38. Westminster Confession 18.3, in Schaff, *Creeds of Christendom* 3:638.
39. Westminster Confession 18:2, in Schaff, *Creeds of Christendom* 3:638. Cf. similarly Heppe, *Reformed Dogmatics*, 177–78.
40. Westminster Confession 18.3, in Schaff, *Creeds of Christendom* 3:638.
41. See Weber, *Protestant Ethic*, especially chaps. 4 and 5.

glory to God, who has been working so mightily in my soul, unlike the soul of my neighbor.

Over the years many Protestants have gotten themselves stuck in this kind of self-righteousness, not because they have inflated egos but because their theology demands that they believe this kind of thing or else they have to conclude they're going to hell. It is built into the logic of their faith, as illustrated by the minor premise in the various practical syllogisms, which is always about something going *right* in my life or my heart, some good thing in me that serves as evidence to distinguish true saving faith from temporary faith, and thus to distinguish me from my unsaved neighbors. The logic of Calvinist faith involves an inward turn that requires this kind of self-righteousness.

Confessing Unbelief

The great failure of the Calvinist syllogisms, which is also the failure of the Protestant inward turn, is its assumption that what I see when I look inward should be something going right, not something going wrong. The result is the opposite of repentance. It is a kind of introspection aimed at attaining the belief that I am truly righteous, by the grace of God working within me. This probably helps explain why the English word "righteousness," which was originally synonymous with "justice" (as explained in chap. 5), came to take on the meaning "self-righteousness." The word got caught up in Protestant anxieties about justification, including efforts people needed to make in order to convince themselves they were truly, inwardly righteous.

Luther, by contrast, instituted a different kind of pastoral care whose aim was to strengthen our faith by getting us to confess our unbelief and hear God forgive it. His *Small Catechism* includes a formula for people to use for confessing their sins and receiving absolution, the earliest version of which includes the confession that "I do not really believe the gospel" and "I also feel that God's Word is not bringing forth fruit in me. I hear it, but I do not receive it earnestly."[42] It should be emphasized: these are words for *Christians* to say. It is precisely believers who should regularly confess that they are unbelievers and that the word of God has not been fruitful in them. This is the exact opposite of the minor premises in the Calvinist syllogisms, but it is for Luther one of the most important ways that Christians grow in faith, as they come to receive the word of absolution and are allowed, indeed required,

---

42. Luther, *A Short Order of Confession before the Priest for the Common Man*, LW 53:117, originally included in the 1529 edition of the *Small Catechism*.

to believe with all confidence and certainty that their sins and unbelief are forgiven and that they have a gracious God in Christ.

Just as we should expect, given what we learned in chapter 7 about how Luther discovered the concept of Gospel in the sacrament of penance, the purpose of the whole rite is for us to hear the absolution, which is the Gospel word that strengthens our faith. In later versions, the confession begins, "Dear Pastor, please hear my confession and declare that my sins are forgiven for God's sake," and concludes with the pastor saying, "I forgive you your sins in the name of the Father and of the Son and of the Holy Spirit. Amen. Go in peace."[43] And it is prefaced with the admonition, "We receive absolution or forgiveness from the confessor as from God himself, by no means doubting but firmly believing that our sins are thereby forgiven before God in heaven."[44]

Luther's pastoral care clearly assumes that we are much better off when we have no need to find by introspection that we are inwardly righteous or true believers, but are free instead to confess our lack of faith and righteousness. When we turn to look at ourselves, we should find a sinner, which is to say an unbeliever, not a righteous person who knows for sure that he has true faith. And then we should turn away from what we find in ourselves and return to our baptism, beginning again at square one, taking hold of Christ in the Gospel promise and the word of absolution, and believing we have been given the gift of faith, just as the *Small Catechism* teaches us to say in the article on the Holy Spirit: "I believe that . . . I cannot believe in Jesus Christ. . . . But the Holy Spirit has called me through the Gospel . . . and preserved me in true faith."[45] In other words, when I look at myself I see a sinner and an unbeliever, but when I look at Christ in the Gospel I see that I have been given the gift of faith through the Holy Spirit, and that is what I should believe— not on the basis of introspection or reflective faith but on the strength and certainty of God's promise.

In short, just as I am righteous and a sinner at the same time, I am an unbeliever and a believer at the same time. And since Christ is mine by faith alone, this results in a Christological version of the *simul*: "I am a sinner in and by myself apart from Christ. Apart from myself and in Christ I am not a sinner."[46] Or quite simply: "Though I am a sinner in myself, I am not a

43. Luther, *Small Catechism*, on confession and absolution, in Tappert, *Book of Concord*, 350–51.

44. Luther, *Small Catechism*, on confession and absolution, in Tappert, *Book of Concord*, 349.

45. Luther, *Small Catechism*, on the third article of the Creed, in Tappert, *Book of Concord*, 345.

46. Luther, *The Private Mass and the Consecration of Priests*, LW 38:158.

sinner in Christ."[47] This is how justification and repentance fit together for the mature Luther. It is a distinctive way of penitence for which we will not have the strength unless we are free to put our faith in the promise of Christ alone, without the requirement of reflective faith. And for that we need to understand the Gospel as a sacramental word giving us an unconditional promise.

Lutheran Syllogisms

There is nothing in Luther quite like the Calvinist practical syllogism,[48] but his faith too has a logical structure that can be rendered in syllogistic form. Luther's pastoral advice for those who are worried about whether they are truly Christians (including himself) is to return to their baptism and say, "I am baptized." He tells the story of a holy woman who was tempted by assaults of the devil but drove him away by appealing to her baptism: "She made baptism her sole defense, saying simply, 'I am a Christian.'"[49] Faith in my baptism, which amounts to the assurance that I am a Christian, lies at the center of a distinctively Lutheran form of pastoral care, addressed to the specifically Lutheran anxiety of *Anfechtung*, which arises "on my bad days" (as I put it in chap. 7) when I look at my faith and life and see how inadequate and un-Christian they are, and am tempted to believe any devil that might come along to tell me that I am not really a Christian and that God could not possibly intend to save someone as faithless as I am.

To capture the logic of this pastoral care, we need two interconnected syllogisms.[50] First is a syllogism about the meaning of baptism:

(Major Premise) Those who are baptized have been born again in Christ.

(Minor Premise) I am baptized.

(Conclusion) Therefore, I am born again in Christ.

The major premise here is a statement of the doctrine of baptismal regeneration, which is the teaching that the Christian life begins in baptism rather

47. Luther, Commentary on Psalm 51, 1532, *LW* 12:311.

48. A principle akin to the major premise of the Calvinist syllogism, "If you only believe, you are saved," does appear in Luther's works, but he uses it to summarize the theology of his opponents, the Antinomians, who denied that believers in Christ must desist from sin and lead a new life; Luther, *Councils and the Church*, *LW* 41:114.

49. Luther, *Babylonian Captivity*, *LW* 36:50. Cf. the variant of this story in Luther, *Sermons on the Gospel of John*, on John 3:16, *LW* 22:356–57, where the devil makes an explicit appearance and it is clear that "I am baptized" and "I am a Christian" are equivalent claims.

50. In Cary, "Why Luther Is Not Quite Protestant," I tried to summarize the logic of Luther's baptismal faith using just one syllogism, but I now think it needs two to be really clear.

than conversion. Like Catholics and Orthodox, Luther teaches that we are born again through this sacrament, not by virtue of any decision or experience of ours. Baptismal regeneration is a form of sacramental efficacy, which means that the sacrament not only signifies a divine gift of grace but confers it. However, every Christian tradition is aware that some of those who are baptized later apostatize, falling away from the faith and rejecting Christ. So baptismal regeneration, in the traditions that teach it, involves a different conception of rebirth in Christ from in traditions that identify being born again with being eternally saved. To use Augustine's terms again, baptism in these traditions gives us salvation in hope (*in spe*), not yet in reality (*in re*).

The minor premise is what Luther wants me to say in response to any attack of the devil or conscience that tells me I am not really a Christian or a believer. It is a key moment of what Cajetan called "acquired faith," for it is not based directly on divine revelation but rather on something I must learn or find out about myself.[51] Unlike the Calvinist minor premise, however, it does not require an inward turn or reflective faith, the feeling of inward righteousness or the belief that I have saving faith. Rather, it requires me to remember my baptism or, if I was baptized as an infant, to trust the testimony of others who witnessed it, such as my godparents. Luther classifies this as faith in the work of God rather than the word of God, but insists that both are ways to believe God rather than human beings. Believing that I was baptized as an infant is like believing my father and mother when they tell me they are my parents. If I did not believe this, I would not know the work of God by which he gave me my natural life and being. Likewise, if I do not believe the testimony of my godparents that I was baptized, I will not come to know the work of God by which he gave me rebirth and new life. Hence it would be foolishness rather than piety to withhold belief in this human testimony just because it is not the word of God, for "when anyone bears witness to the work of God it does not mean believing men, but God."[52] This legitimizes my belief in my baptism, but Luther does not reckon frankly with the fact that it does not offer the kind of certainty that he usually demands of Christian faith. It would have improved his theology if he had recognized that the reasons he has to cling with obstinate faithfulness to his baptism do not afford him the kind of certainty that fueled the vicious polemics we examined in chapter 9.

We come to the usual and proper grounds of Luther's certainty with a second syllogism, which makes explicit the connection between the promise of

---

51. In his Augsburg treatises, Cajetan writes that acquired faith includes belief that "this person is rightly baptized," Cajetan, *Cajetan Responds*, 51.

52. Luther, *Concerning Rebaptism*, LW 40:236. Cf. also the story in Luther, *Sermons on the Gospel of John*, on John 3:16, LW 22:357–58.

God and the sacramental word in baptism, according to the double structure of God's word that we examined in chapter 7.

> (Major Premise) God said to me:
>> "I baptize you in the name of the Father, and of the Son, and of the Holy Spirit."[53]
>
> (Minor Premise) God is true to his word.
>
> (Conclusion) Therefore, I am baptized in the name of the Father, Son, and Holy Spirit.

The major premise here is not a general principle that I must apply to myself, much less a conditional promise whose condition I must meet. It applies to me because it says "you" and means me. It puts into words my remembrance of the particular occasion when the sacramental word was addressed to me. Here the word in which I am to believe is external in a logically decisive way: it is an external utterance limited to the particular time and place in which it was uttered, which is precisely why it can say "you" and mean me in particular. The same sentence uttered at a different time and place will not be about me and, depending on the circumstances, may not even be true. For example, I can utter the words, "I baptize you in the name of the Father, and of the Son, and of the Holy Spirit" while illustrating a point in a theology class, or I can write it in a book like this one, and the sentence is not true. No one is being baptized in my classroom or my book, because the sacramental word in this context is not part of an actual sacrament, as authorized by Christ's promise. In logical parlance, it is a different *token* of the same *type* of sentence, which is why it can have a different truth-value (i.e., it can be false rather than true). Unlike general principles or the conditional promise of the Calvinist syllogism, the truth of the sacramental word is thus dependent on the circumstances of utterance. To cling to this word for my salvation I must remember or call to mind my baptism, when these words were spoken to me in particular.

The result is an unreflective faith that clings to the word alone, as illustrated by the minor premise: "God is true to his word." For pastoral theology, this is crucially different from "I believe" in the minor premise of the Calvinist syllogism, which amounts to a requirement of reflective faith. Of course, to

---

53. In baptism, "the Lord sitting in heaven . . . [is] speaking to you upon earth with a human voice by the mouth of his minister," according to Luther, *Babylonian Captivity*, LW 36:62–63. Likewise, Christ "is himself the baptizer. . . . In baptism he can speak . . . through the mouth of the priest. . . . He is present, speaks and baptizes" (Luther, *Concerning Rebaptism*, LW 40:242–43).

believe Luther's minor premise is precisely to believe God and his word. But because Luther's minor premise says nothing explicitly about my belief, it does not require me to believe in my own belief. It leaves me free to confess my unbelief, even as I turn once again in repentance to remember my baptism and put my faith in it. For my faith is built on the truth in which it believes, not on the fact that I believe it. This explains why Luther can actually warn us against reflective faith, saying, "I cannot build on the fact that I believe,"[54] and urging, "Rely not on yourself, nor upon your faith."[55] In this way, surprising as it may seem, Luther's doctrine of justification by faith alone means *not relying on faith*. For faith does not rely on itself but on the truth of God's word alone. Hence the minor premise of this syllogism replaces reflective faith with Luther's pervasive insistence that God is true (*Deus verax*). My faith is not built up by discerning that I have true saving faith (for the fact is that I do not always believe so truly) but by remembering that what God said to me is true, because God is true to his word. So to strengthen my faith I keep returning to my baptism, saying, "I am baptized, and through my baptism God, who cannot lie, has bound himself in a covenant with me."[56] Faith grows in the heart precisely as it turns its attention away from faith in the heart and toward the external word, backed by the truth of God.

This is especially important in times of temptation. On our bad days, "when our sins or conscience oppress us," Luther urges us to talk back against the accusations of our conscience and say: "But I am baptized! And if I am baptized, *I have the promise that I shall be saved* and have eternal life."[57] Here it is important to bear in mind the subtle but profound difference between Luther's faith and the certainty of salvation that the Calvinist syllogism proposes to give us. The promise of salvation here does not assure me that I will be saved in the end, for it does not promise that I will persevere in faith to the end of my life, and therefore cannot assure me that I am elect and predestined for salvation. Rather, it is a promise of salvation to which I can always return whenever I feel what a sinner and unbeliever I am. It is a standing invitation to take comfort in the grace of Christ, which is always there every time I turn to it, so that I may once again believe what the word of God says about me rather than my own conscience, which quite rightly accuses me of being an unbeliever. Baptism thus builds up my faith by turning my attention away from my failure to believe and toward the truth of God's word. Luther's sacramental conception of the Gospel thereby provides an escape from the

54. Luther, *Large Catechism*, on infant baptism, in Tappert, *Book of Concord*, 443.
55. Luther, *Sermons* 6:164.
56. Luther, *Holy and Blessed Sacrament of Baptism* (sermon, 1519), LW 35:36.
57. Luther, *Large Catechism*, on baptism, in Tappert, *Book of Concord*, 442.

anxieties of reflective faith, but at a cost: it cannot offer us assurance of ultimate salvation, because it does not promise that we shall persevere in faith to the end. It is a standing invitation to which we must always return, not a promise of eternal security.

By a similar reasoning, Luther rejects the medieval teaching that the sacrament of penance is "the second plank after shipwreck,"[58] as if our baptism were a ship that has been sunk by our sins and we have only one piece of it left to keep us afloat. Quite the contrary, according to Luther: our baptism, based on God's promise alone, remains in force and unchanged, and we unfaithful sinners simply need to return to it, which is the whole function of repentance. The ship is still safe and sound, but we are like fools who have jumped overboard and need to get back on board. This ship carries "all those who are brought to the harbor of salvation, for it is the truth of God giving us its promise in the sacraments."[59]

The same logical structure, with the same exclusive dependence on the truth of God's promise, can be seen in all the sacraments as Luther understands them. In every sacrament I can hear an external word, based on Christ's promise, that says "you" and includes me. This is not just how Luther thinks about the sacraments; it is the pattern for all his thinking about the Gospel, as he explains:

> God deals with us in no way other than by his holy word and sacraments, which are like signs or seals of his words. The very first thing necessary, then, is faith in these words and signs, for when God speaks and gives signs, man must firmly and wholeheartedly believe that what he says and signifies is true, so that we do not consider him a liar or juggler, but trust him to be faithful and true.[60]

Hence the theme of *Deus verax*, God being true to his word, is at the heart of Luther's concept of the Gospel, as we saw in chapter 7. Always, the Gospel demands "a faith that relies confidently on this promise, believes Christ to be true in these words of his, and does not doubt that these infinite blessings have been bestowed upon it."[61] Always, Christian faith is not the confidence that I have such a faith, but the confidence that Christ, my God, will not lie to me.[62]

---

58. Luther, *Babylonian Captivity*, LW 36:58. Cf. similarly Luther, *Large Catechism*, on baptism, in Tappert, *Book of Concord*, 446.

59. Luther, *Babylonian Captivity*, LW 36:61.

60. Luther, *Defense and Explanation of All the Articles*, article 1, LW 32:15.

61. Luther, *Babylonian Captivity*, LW 36:40, on the words of institution in the Lord's Supper.

62. Cf. Luther, *Sacrament of Penance* (sermon, 1519), LW 35:12: "Christ, your God, will not lie to you."

No Right Not to Believe

Calvin does not see the promise of God in the sacraments quite the same way as Luther, though he tries. In the first edition of his *Institutes* he is sharply critical of earlier Reformed theologians, mainly Zwingli and Bucer, who carried their criticism of the Roman Catholic sacramental system too far. They saw a great gulf between the power of salvation, which belongs to God alone, and the superstitious, magical thinking that ascribed salvific power to mere external rituals, including baptism and the Lord's Supper. Calvin saw this as a false dichotomy. He wanted to develop a genuine sacramental piety, which did not reduce the sacraments to a mere public manifestation of faith, as in the Zwinglian teaching that "baptism is nothing more than a token or mark by which we confess our religion before men."[63] Calvin emphatically agreed that God alone has power to save us, but he also insisted that God used the sacraments to *do* something, and what they did was a real help to us. To spell out what this was he turned to Luther's *Babylonian Captivity* and picked up the connection between promise and sacrament. His key claim is that the sacraments are seals of the promise, given by God to strengthen our faith. What the sacraments *do* is expressed by Calvin using a characteristic set of verbs that explicate the Augustinian concept of sacraments as signs whose function is to signify grace: the sacraments present, offer, and exhibit, as if before our very eyes, the things that God has promised us.

Thus Calvin's sacramental theology occupies a distinctive middle ground between the "low" view of the sacraments characteristic of Zwingli (and later of the Anabaptists and Baptists) and the "high" view in Catholicism, Eastern Orthodoxy, and Lutheranism. On the one hand, he avoids the low view of baptism as merely a symbol or token for the public manifestation of our faith, which was vulnerable to the Anabaptist inference that, given such a view, only adult believers, not infants, should be baptized. On the other hand, he cannot teach baptismal regeneration, because no one, least of all the Reformed, thinks that baptism guarantees that we are chosen and predestined by God for salvation—and in the Calvinist view (in contrast to the "high" sacramental traditions) everyone who is regenerated is saved in the end, which means that only those predestined for salvation are regenerate, which certainly does not include all the baptized.

Reformed theologians after Calvin can go quite far in the direction of baptismal regeneration, but never beyond the bounds set by the doctrine of election. Hence they can teach that in baptism "the things promised are by the

---

63. Calvin, *Institutes of the Christian Religion: 1536 Edition*, 4:13.

Holy Spirit not only offered to believers but also actually exhibited and conferred; God is true in sealing his promises."[64] But the phrase that must not be overlooked here is "to believers." Baptism gives no grace of salvation to those who do not have true saving faith and are not elect. This is why there could be so many people in Jonathan Edwards's congregation who were baptized but believed they were not regenerate. Reformed theology always allows for the possibility that the baptized are not regenerate and often (as in Edwards' theology) insists on it. By contrast for Luther, as we have seen, everyone who is baptized should insist, "I am a Christian," and none of the baptized can legitimately say, "I am not regenerate," for that would be calling Christ a liar.

The difference here is both stark and subtle: it makes a great difference in the practice of the Christian life, but it stems from a fine point of logic, which is easy to overlook because it appears at first to be splitting hairs. We can bring the logic into focus by recalling the sacramental semiotics that Luther, Calvin, and the whole Augustinian tradition have in common (introduced at the beginning of chap. 7). They all think of the sacraments as consisting of an outward sign (*signum*) that signifies something (a *res*), and that the thing signified by the sacrament (its *res significata*) is a spiritual gift of grace. Most importantly, they all agree that unbelief separates *signum* and *res*—just as they agree, as we noticed at the beginning of this chapter, that unbelief separates the promise from what is promised. The result is that the unbeliever receives the word or external sign but not the grace it signifies. Thus unbelievers can receive a valid baptism, an external sign that needs to be given only once, but they do not receive the inner grace of regeneration, rebirth, and new life that it signifies (or, in the Catholic view, they actually do receive new life in baptism but then forfeit it by the mortal sin of unbelief).

What makes Luther's view distinctive is the peculiar sense in which the baptized have no right to their unbelief, as we saw at some length in chapter 7. The sacramental word spoken in my baptism makes an unconditional demand that I believe, for otherwise I am in effect calling Christ a liar by saying he did not give me what he promised. No matter what kind of unbeliever I am, whether merely weak in faith or an adamant anti-Christian, if I am baptized I have no right to believe I am unregenerate—even when my unbelief constitutes a quite effective rejection of my regeneration and new life. I am simply, unconditionally commanded to believe that what Christ told me in my baptism is true, and therefore I have no right to believe about myself

---

64. Heppe, *Reformed Dogmatics*, 617, quoting the Leiden Synopsis 44:32. Note also that in the numerous definitions of baptism by Reformed theologians quoted in Heppe, 611, what is given through baptism is always given *to the elect*.

what Jonathan Edwards's anxious congregants were taught to believe about themselves: that they were not regenerate. Much less should I wait until I have had a conversion experience—or have found evidence of true saving faith in my heart—before believing that Christ has kept his word and given me the new life he promised.

The peculiar sense in which I have no right to my unbelief is tied to the very direct way that the sacramental word says "you" and means me (when it says: "I baptize *you* . . .") and to the fact that, due to the double structure of God's word, this word is actually Christ's word. When Calvin picked up the connection of promise and sacrament from Luther, he did not pick up this double structure, in part because it is not so clearly spelled out in the *Babylonian Captivity* as it is in the series of sacramental treatises where it was first elaborated in 1519. A sacramental theology without this double structure has a fundamentally different logic from Luther's, because it cannot rely in the same exclusive way on the truth of God's word.

The Truth of God

Perhaps the clearest way to illustrate the logical difference between Luther and most other Protestants is to consider the word of absolution. After the *Babylonian Captivity*, Protestants no longer treat penance as a distinct sacrament, but Luther insisted that "confession and absolution should by no means be allowed to fall into disuse in the church,"[65] and Calvin too found much to value in the word of absolution spoken by one Christian to another. Calvin recommends confession and absolution as a pastoral practice, so long as it is explicitly conditional upon faith. "For absolution is conditional upon the sinner's trust that God is merciful to him," Calvin writes, which means that the sinner "can, indeed, embrace clear and true absolution when that simple condition is applied of embracing the grace of Christ."[66] Calvin evidently assumes a logic of faith that could be expressed in something like the following syllogism:

(Major Premise) Christ promises absolution of sins to those who believe in him.

(Minor Premise) I believe in Christ.

(Conclusion) Therefore, I am absolved of my sins.

65. Luther, *Smalcald Articles* 3.8, in Tappert, *Book of Concord*, 312.
66. Calvin, *Institutes* 3:4.22.

As with the other Calvinist syllogisms, the minor premise makes it clear that reflective faith is required. It is a prerequisite condition: I must first believe in Christ—indeed I must believe that I believe in him—before I can believe that my sins are absolved.

John Wesley's faith is historically downstream from the logic of this syllogism, as we can see from his account of how he came to assurance of divine forgiveness:

> I felt my heart strangely warmed, I felt I did trust in Christ, Christ alone for my salvation, and an assurance was given me that he had taken away *my* sins, even *mine*.[67]

Here is an inner assurance of pardon without any external word of absolution, for it is reflective faith alone, not a sacramental word saying "you" and meaning me, that assures Wesley he can say salvation in Christ is *mine*. And here again we must distinguish a theologian's intention from his achievement. Wesley clearly does not intend to put his faith in anything but God's word, but he also cannot believe his sins are forgiven until he feels sure that he trusts in Christ—which is to say he must believe that he truly believes, before he can believe that he is pardoned and saved. And only the experience of his strangely warmed heart, not the truth of God's word, can assure him that he truly believes. For both Wesley and Calvin, therefore, reflective faith is a prerequisite condition without which I am in no position to believe I am forgiven, justified, or saved. This creates serious psychological as well as logical difficulties, for it means that in an important sense, I must believe I believe before I am allowed to believe.

For all their disagreements, Wesley and Calvin both differ sharply from Luther, for whom believing in Christ is not a prerequisite for believing I am absolved or pardoned, because believing I am absolved when I hear the word of absolution simply *is* believing Christ. Ever since 1519, as we saw in chapter 7, Luther taught that you should hear the word of absolution "as though Christ himself were absolving you."[68] The resulting logic can be displayed by constructing a syllogism parallel to the one on baptism above.

(Major Premise) Christ, who is God, said to me,
  "I absolve you of your sins in the name of the Father, the Son, and the
   Holy Spirit."

---

67. From Wesley's narration of his famous "Aldersgate Experience" in Outler, *John Wesley*, 66.
68. Luther, *Sermon on Preparing to Die* (1519), LW 42:110.

(Minor Premise) God is true to his word.

(Conclusion) Therefore, my sins are absolved.

Once again the characteristic minor premise is not about my faith but about the truth of God and his word. This is much more suitable for building up my faith than a premise such as "I believe in Christ," which I often find hard to believe. There is no prerequisite condition requiring me to believe that I believe in Christ before I am allowed to believe that my sins are forgiven. Indeed, there is nothing quite like being "allowed" to believe my sins are forgiven. I am simply commanded to believe in the absolution of my sins, for otherwise I am calling God a liar. Here is a *must* in service of a *may*: I may believe I am forgiven because I must believe the word of absolution.

Luther continues to think along the lines of this syllogism long after dropping penance from his list of sacraments, as we can tell by his tireless insistence on the theme of *Deus verax*, the God who is true to his word. For instance, in his 1530 treatise *The Keys*, he returns to the promise of Christ that was the ground of the sacrament of penance, and he uses it to repudiate any attempt to make him doubt that his sins are forgiven:

> Let no one remind me of my sins any longer. All are gone, forgiven, forgotten. He who promises me, "Whatever you loose shall be loosed" [Matt 16:19], does not lie; this I know. If my repentance is not sufficient, his Word is; if I am not worthy, his keys are: He is faithful and true. My sins shall not make a liar of him.[69]

If my sins cannot make a liar of Christ my God, then neither can my unbelief, which is the root of my sins. Hence there is no good thing in me, not even my faith, that I must be confident in before I can believe in his promise. This is deep comfort for those who are weak in faith. It only makes logical sense, however, if I may put all my confidence in the truth of his word, quite regardless of how inadequate I see and feel my faith to be, along with everything else in me. I must not be trapped in a logic that requires a minor premise like those in the Calvinist syllogisms, which requires me to find in myself some good thing such as faith or the right spirit.

Luther can be very vehement in affirming the logic of unreflective faith, because he remembers the agonies of his time as a monk when he could never be penitent enough. In one lecture he reminds his students how much better off they are than he was at their age, when he was endlessly trying to have enough contrition to be convinced that his sins were forgiven. His rejection

69. Luther, *Keys*, LW 40:375.

of the requirement of adequate contrition, which first came to light when he insisted on justification by faith alone despite Cajetan's insistence to the contrary, is based on the same logic that leads to the absence of the requirement of reflective faith—which is to say, the freedom from the need to ascertain that I have true saving faith. We can see this when he turns once again to the *Deus verax* theme, in connection with the word of absolution that he now thinks any Christian brother, not just a priest, can speak to me on the basis of Christ's promise:

> If I have not been perfectly contrite, what is that to me . . . ? But this does pertain to me, and on this I do build, that God says to me through the brother, "I absolve you in the name and merit of Christ." I believe this word is true, nor will my faith fail me. It is built on the rock of the words of the Son of God, who cannot lie.[70]

This is a faith that will not fail me, Luther is saying, precisely because it is based on the truth of God's word alone, not on confidence in my contrition or even in my faith. And whenever I doubt that I have true faith—which it is quite reasonable for me to do very often—I am free to repent of my unbelief and turn to the truth of the promise of forgiveness, without first having to believe that I believe it.

Here, I think, the theological achievement of Luther matches his intention. All Protestant theologians intend for us to put our trust in the word of God alone, but I think this chapter has shown that to achieve this intention they need a sacramental conception of the Gospel. They need to have us clinging to a promise of Christ that is not conditional, being the basis of an external word that can say "you" and mean me. In that sense Protestantism needs to be closer to Catholic sacramental faith than most later Protestants realize, even while they rightly insist, against the strand of Catholic theology represented by Cajetan, that forgiveness and salvation come to us by faith alone.

---

70. Luther, Commentary on Psalm 51, 1532, *LW* 12:372.

11

Sacrament

Turning Outward to Divine Flesh

f the previous two chapters are correct, there are two kinds of certainty that we do not have and that it is not actually good for us to want. There is the certainty that our interpretation of Scripture is correct, and there is the kind of certainty that Calvinists call the assurance of salvation. To claim these certainties is to insist on a kind of unchangeability in ourselves, which excludes possibilities in the future that we might well be anxious about. The one kind of certainty intends to exclude the possibility that I might find my faith is mistaken; the other intends to exclude the possibility that I might lose my faith. Excluding such possibilities has its attractions, but I think proper Christian faith faces the anxieties of the future differently. It clings stubbornly to the promise of God and prays in hope, "Thy kingdom come," which means it awaits a future it cannot secure for itself, in which Christ the King, now hidden at the right hand of the Father, keeps his word and appears in glory, and we with him (Col. 3:3).

We need an epistemology for this, an account of what it means to know Christ in the flesh when he is hidden from our sight and we await his coming. The basis of such an account will be the doctrines of the Trinity and incarnation, together with the practice of the sacraments. It will not secure scientific or Cartesian certainty for us. It will not enable us to refute all objections to our faith and prove that we are right. It therefore will not satisfy the kind of modern epistemology that assumes that real knowledge consists in the certainty of knowing that we know and being able to prove it. The knowledge of God given in the Gospel is not knowledge we can prove we have, for it is dependent on a certainty that is beyond our capacity to prove or verify, which is the truth of God's promise. In the end we will certainly see God being true to his word, when Christ is manifest in glory as promised, but until that day we walk by faith, not by sight. Even the presence of Christ in the flesh, which is as certain as the word of God, is something we know not by seeing it, observing it, or experiencing it, but by hearing about it. Hence an epistemology of hearing is implicit in the outward turn to the flesh of Christ.

In this chapter our guide to the epistemology of hearing shall be Luther's account of the sacrament of Christ's body and blood. I will be contrasting it both with Augustine's inward turn to intellectual vision and with the sacramental theology of the Reformed tradition. As in the previous chapter, the contrast between Luther and Calvin will be especially subtle but also especially instructive. Once this contrast is clear, it will be evident that in his sacramental theology, Luther is closer to Thomas Aquinas, while Calvin is closer to Augustine. The question that divides them is whether God and his saving power can be found by clinging to external signs. In answering this question with a resounding Yes, Luther puts himself closer to medieval Catholicism than to Calvin and Augustine.

An Epistemology of Hearing

As chapters 9 and 10 have suggested, the proper certainty of faith is an obstinate faithfulness, based on trust in God's word alone, not on reflective belief in our own belief, our capacity to prove or secure our own knowledge, our correctness of Scriptural interpretation, or our inner experience. Luther's account of this kind of faith is his great contribution to the Christian knowledge of God. His misguided claims to theological certainty are not in fact necessary to his theology of the Gospel, which is built not on the success of his theological or interpretive arguments, but on the simple conviction that by believing the Gospel is true, we receive and know God in the flesh. For it is not the strength and certainty of our own faith, much less the certainty of our theology, that brings Christ into our hearts, but rather the power of the word of God itself to give what it promises.

The ground of our certainty is therefore not within us but outside us. Christian faith is knowledge based on the Gospel as an external means of grace that, like the sacraments, gives us the hidden Christ in the flesh, so that he may dwell in our hearts by faith. The Gospel is a word of saving power even and indeed especially in its sheer externality, a physical thing made of sound waves that reach our ears—not an inner thought or choice or experience, nor a universal principle or intelligible truth, but a sacramental word spoken aloud at a particular time and place. At the core of Luther's theological imagination is the inescapable sense that this external word has something to say to me in particular that I cannot in good conscience deny, because I have no right to talk back at God when he insists on giving me his own Son in the promise of the Gospel. Hence I must believe that I know God incarnate simply by hearing his word and believing it, lest I call God a liar.

Luther's insistence on faith alone thus rests on an epistemology of hearing in which our knowledge stems from what we have heard or learned from other persons rather than seen for ourselves. The "hearing" in this epistemology need not be literal hearing; its essential meaning is dependence on the word of others, whether spoken or written. It means putting our faith in external authorities: for example in a teacher who knows what we don't or a witness who has seen what we haven't. The result is an essentially secondhand form of knowledge, relying on what someone else has to say, which means we must trust this other person to be telling the truth. This is the kind of epistemology needed to account for our knowledge of other persons, I have elsewhere argued, based on their unique authority to speak for themselves and say who they are.[1] Through their words and especially their promises, people can tell us who they are and who they will be for us and for our sake. When they make such promises and keep them, they give themselves to be known, like a bride and bridegroom giving themselves to each other in their wedding vows. In this way, the knowledge of other persons is not an achievement of the knower but a gift of the known, because the known are persons who can give themselves to be known in their words. Consequently, we cannot know people merely by observing them, for knowing other persons requires us to respect them *as* persons, which means we cannot ignore what they have to say for themselves.

This is why I think that the knowledge of God does not ultimately amount to the vision of God. In the Scriptures we encounter a person who has something to say for himself, and we cannot know him if we do not hear him. Even when we see his coming in glory, it is as the fulfillment of his promise—seeing that he is in fact true to his word. Thus an epistemology of hearing is needed to account for our knowledge of God, rather than the epistemology of intellectual vision that is at the heart of Augustine's Christian Platonism,

1. Cary, "Believing the Word."

which we encountered in chapter 3. The metaphor of vision has been natural to Platonism ever since the allegory of the cave, because the aim of Platonist spirituality is for us to see for ourselves rather than to rely on what we've heard from others. The mind according to Platonism is like an eye designed to see the truth and the very essence of things, their eternal and spiritual being. Hence it is not surprising that in Platonism—including a Christian Platonism like Augustine's—epistemology is inseparable from ethics and spirituality, because the epistemology of intellectual vision offers a powerful, indeed seductive account of our spiritual ascent to God and the ultimate happiness of beatific vision.

Luther's theology also brings epistemology, ethics, and spirituality together, but in a different and more biblical way than Augustine. Instead of an ascent to the vision of God, Luther's spirituality bases our knowledge of God on a piety of the word, in which our primary obligation is to hear what God tells us about himself and to believe it. In this chapter the task is to see how Luther's theology, including his epistemology of hearing, fleshes out the spiritual connection between God and us by way of an outward turn to the divine carnality of Christ's flesh, rather than an inward turn to the human spirituality of intellectual vision.

Against Augustine: Where to Find God

Luther's outward turn is about where to turn our attention to find God: not upward to an intelligible realm beyond space and time, nor inward to a dimension inside ourselves, our souls, our consciousness, or our experience, but outward to bodily things such as the bread of the sacrament. Luther's epistemology of hearing supports this outward turn by focusing our attention on God incarnate, who gives himself to be known in the external word of the Gospel and found in the external sign of the sacrament. For the Gospel tells us where to find God: "He is present in his Word and in the outward things of which his Word speaks."[2] And according to his word, God is to be found where he is present in the flesh: "He wishes to make us certain as to where and how we are to lay hold of him. There is the Word, which says that when you eat the bread you eat his body, given for you."[3] Faith finds God where he has promised to be, which means it can find him by eating.

---

2. Luther, *That These Words of Christ, "This Is My Body," Etc., Still Stand Firm against the Fanatics* (1527), LW 37:137.

3. Luther, *The Sacrament of the Body and Blood of Christ—against the Fanatics* (1526), LW 36:346.

But Luther immediately adds: "If the Word were not there, I would not pay any heed to the bread."[4] Luther's outward turn is based not on a broadly sacramental view of the world but on the very particular sacraments instituted by the word of Christ. For all their beauty and glory, we cannot use the things of this world to come to God, but must let God use particular things in this world to come to us. It is not just that we are unable to come to God by our own spirituality and good works. More fundamentally, God is a person who has something to say to us about how he is to be known, and we do not know him if we do not hear what he has to say. For "he has set down for us a definite way to show us how and where to find him, namely the Word."[5] So he is present in all things, but we find him in the particular things he gives us through his external word. As Luther explains:

> Although he is present in all creatures . . . yet he does not wish that I seek him there apart from the Word. . . . He is present everywhere, but he does not wish that you grope for him everywhere. Grope rather where the Word is, and there you will lay hold of him in the right way.[6]

We grope for God in bread, because that is where his own word puts him. "He has put himself into the Word, and through the Word he puts himself into the bread also."[7]

Luther's outward turn gives a deeply un-Augustinian answer to a key problem of Augustinian spirituality: How are we to find God when God is invisible to us precisely in his spiritual being? For God is everywhere, but nowhere to be seen. In his *Confessions*, Augustine gives us a sense of the crisis this problem caused for him when he was a young man wandering far from the truth. The spiritual being of God is omnipresent, young Augustine realized, yet he found it impossible to imagine God's presence. For our imagination depends on images of external things that take up space, whereas God's omnipresence means that his mode of being is nonspatial, not dependent on any physical place. God is present without taking up space, because he does not need room in the created world in order to exist. He is not extended in space, spread out part-by-part, as if part of God were in one place and part of him in another—like water in a sponge—and more of him in an elephant than in a sparrow.[8] So to conceive of God we need to turn our attention away from external things, Augustine

---

4. Luther, *Sacrament of the Body and Blood of Christ*, LW 36:346.
5. Luther, *Sacrament of the Body and Blood of Christ*, LW 36:342.
6. Luther, *Sacrament of the Body and Blood of Christ*, LW 36:342.
7. Luther, *Sacrament of the Body and Blood of Christ*, LW 36:343.
8. For these two images, see Augustine, *Confessions* 7:1.2; 7:5.7. For Augustine's very deliberate way of setting up this problem and its Platonist solution, see Cary, "Book Seven."

contends—and that requires a kind of purity of mind that detaches our soul from its interest in bodily things extended in space. For in Augustine's thinking the human soul by itself, in its own spirituality apart from bodily things, is the great clue to the spiritual and nonspatial being of God.

But this is also where young Augustine needed help, he writes, for "I was so gross of heart—not seeing even myself clearly—that whatever was not extended in space . . . I thought must be nothing whatsoever."[9] If only he could turn away from mental images of external things and look right at his own mind (Augustine the bishop, years later, is convinced), he would see something quite different, his own nonspatial and incorporeal being, which will never be seen by the eyes of the body. "My heart was in search of such images as the forms my eye was accustomed to see," he writes, "and I did not realize that the attention [*intentionem*] by which I formed these images was not itself a bodily image; yet it could not have formed them, unless it were something—and something great."[10] The activity of the human soul or mind or heart (in Augustine, as in the Bible, these terms are often interchangeable) is a kind of greatness that is very different from bodies, which are great only in size. But to see this greatness we need to experience and recognize a different kind of vision, which is beyond sense and imagination but ultimately capable of seeing the incorporeal Truth that is God. That is why Augustine had to learn from the Platonists how to turn inward.

Augustine found the help he was looking for in "some books of the Platonists," which he read at a crucial juncture in his life, just a few months before his decisive return to the Catholic church.[11] He does not tell us exactly which books these were, and they may have included nothing by Plato himself. But we do know one Platonist book to which he alludes in the *Confessions*, the essay "On Beauty" by Plotinus, the great pagan philosopher who founded the Neoplatonist tradition late in the third century AD. In a chapter from that essay that clearly stuck with Augustine over the years,[12] Plotinus teaches that

9. Augustine, *Confessions* 7:1.2.

10. Augustine, *Confessions* 7:1.2, translation modified. Sheed uses "mind" to translate *cor* here, despite translating it more accurately as "heart" in the previous sentence. I prefer to preserve Augustine's reference to the heart, which accords with biblical usage, admitting no split between mind and heart because the term for "heart" includes mind, will, and emotion all in one. See Wolff, *Anthropology of the Old Testament*, 41–58, on the Hebrew term for "heart."

11. Augustine, *Confessions* 7:9.13. Scholars disagree about which books these are, but most agree that they included works of Plotinus, with Plotinus's essay "On Beauty" (*Enneads* 1:6) usually first on the list. For overviews of this long scholarly discussion, see O'Meara, "Augustine and Neo-platonism"; O'Connell, *St. Augustine's Early Theory of Man*, chap. 1.

12. Plotinus, "On Beauty," *Enneads* 1:6.8. Augustine, *City of God* 9:17, quotes from this chapter the same passage to which he alludes in *Confessions* 1:18.28, some twenty years earlier.

in order to see what is divine, we must "awaken a different kind of vision," using the eye of the mind, not the body. This requires us to enter "into the inside" (*eis to eiso*), Plotinus says, in language that inspired Augustine's inward turn.[13] For Augustine tells us he was admonished by these books "to return to my own self" and "enter into my inmost place," by the help of God's grace, with the result that he "saw with the eye of my soul . . . the unchangeable Light," which was "not the common light obvious to all flesh . . . but other, wholly other."[14] The unchangeable inner Light is God, the immutable Truth shining above the soul, wholly other than all external things. Augustine wants to make sure we don't take the spatial imagery here literally. The inner space of the soul is "a more inward place, which yet is no place,"[15] and the inner Light of Truth is above his soul not "as oil is above the water it floats on, nor as the sky is above the earth," but as the Creator is above the creation: "It was above because it made me, and I was below because made by it."[16]

Augustine's inward turn involves finding God by a distinctive movement of the soul: in then up. It is not a literal movement in space but a turning of the heart's attention. First he turns his attention inward, examining the various powers of his soul, rising up from the senses to the superior power of the intellect, and then uses the intellect to look upward, to what is above his soul and all its powers. The first step of the journey is to enter the inner space of his own soul to awaken the intellectual vision that the eye of the body is not capable of, which we heard him describing at length in chapter 3. The inner vision he wants is intellectual vision, the eye of the mind catching a glimpse of the spiritual being of God, seeing him as the inner Light of Truth shining above his soul. This gives him a way of conceiving divine omnipresence. For earlier, he had thought that anything not spread out in space must be "nothing, absolutely nothing,"[17] but now he asks himself: "Is Truth then nothing at all, since it is not extended either through finite spaces or infinite?"[18] Just in case the answer to this highly rhetorical question is not obvious, Augustine spells it out later in one of his letters:

> God is not extended or spread out in space, whether finite or infinite (as if there could be more of him in one part than in another) but is *present as a whole*

13. For a much fuller account of the inspiration Plotinus provided for Augustine's inward turn, see Cary, *Augustine's Invention of the Inner Self*, chap. 3.

14. Augustine, *Confessions* 7:10.16.

15. Augustine, *Confessions* 10:9.16. On the nature of this inner space as Augustine conceives it, see Cary, *Augustine's Invention of the Inner Self*, chap. 10.

16. Augustine, *Confessions* 7:10.16.

17. Augustine, *Confessions* 7:1.1.

18. Augustine, *Confessions* 7:10.16.

everywhere—just like Truth, which no one in their right mind would say is partly in this place and partly in that; for after all *Truth is God*.[19]

Turning inward is Augustine's way of finding God, the Creator of all things who cannot be seen in any external thing but must be perceived by an inward intellectual vision.

By turning our attention away from external things, we embark on a journey that is "not for the feet," as Plotinus says in the chapter that inspired Augustine.[20] Nor is it by chariots or ships, Plotinus adds, that we come back home to the Fatherland where our Father is. In the *Confessions*, Augustine uses this imagery to describe the journey of his own soul, comparing it to the prodigal son coming back to his father after he went into a far country, which is itself an image for our wandering far from God and returning to him. So Augustine combines biblical and Platonist imagery as he lays his life before God in prayer:

> It is not on our feet or by movement in space that we go from Thee or return to Thee: Thy prodigal son did not charter horses or chariots or ships, or fly with wings or journey on his two feet.[21]

Augustinian spirituality is Platonist, in that Platonist concepts define both the goal, which is the vision of God as intelligible Truth, and the nature of the movement toward it: the journey "not for the feet" that Plotinus described and that, in Augustine's reading, the parable of the prodigal son symbolizes.

Augustine thinks Christ himself called us to this inward journey, even when he came in the external form of flesh. As we saw in chapter 3, according to Augustine's semiotics the best that words and other outward signs can do, whether from Scripture or the books of the Platonists or from the mouth of Christ incarnate, is to remind us of what is within and admonish us to turn inward to find it. Thus no word has the power to give us salvation or the knowledge of the Truth, not even the words of Christ. As Augustine explains in his book on *The Teacher*, words are external signs that cannot give us what they signify, for "we don't learn anything by these signs called words."[22] Rather, whenever we learn so as to really understand, we are learning from the one inner teacher, which is Christ as inner Truth, "the Truth that presides within

---

19. Augustine, Letter 118:23, my translation.
20. Plotinus, "On Beauty," *Enneads* 1:6.8.
21. Augustine, *Confessions* 1:18.28. The same Plotinian imagery recurs in his description of his conversion in 8:8.19.
22. Augustine, *The Teacher* 10.34.

over the mind itself."[23] Though words can admonish us to consult the inner teacher, the source of our knowledge of intelligible things is never the words themselves but always the inner teacher, who is "the everlasting Wisdom of God, which *every rational soul* does consult."[24] This inner teacher cannot be Christ in the flesh, because flesh is external and not available to be consulted by every rational soul at every time and place. Hence when the eternal Wisdom of God becomes incarnate, a particular man living and teaching at a particular time and place, he is becoming external in order to use external signs, including words, to admonish us to turn away from external things and toward the inner Truth, his eternal being as God:

> For a kind of reminder can be made by men through words as signs, but only the inner Teacher, the one true teacher, the incorruptible Truth itself, teaches—who also *became external so as to call us away from external things* to inner things.[25]

Augustine believes therefore that Christ incarnate, the external teacher, does not want us clinging to external things, not even the human flesh that he assumed for our salvation. His humanity is the road we take to get to his divinity, and he wants to speed us on our way, not detain us on the road.[26]

The turn away from external things is not an accidental feature of Augustine's pursuit of intellectual vision. It is essential to the moral purification by which we make progress on our way to the vision of God. We need pure hearts to see God (Matt. 5:8), which for Augustine is a biblical way of saying what Plato and Plotinus say about the need to purify the soul by virtue in order to find the truth.[27] What we need to be purified from is our attachment to external things, which get the soul tainted with bodily pleasures and desires that pull it away from the inner presence of God and cloud its capacity for intellectual vision. This Platonist interpretation of Christian purity may have been suggested to Augustine by a little-known African Platonist named Fonteius of Carthage, who died a baptized Christian but was still a pagan when he wrote a book titled *On Purifying the Mind in order to See God*. Early in his career Augustine presents an excerpt from this book addressing the problem about

---

23. Augustine, *Teacher* 11.38.

24. Augustine, *Teacher* 11.38. That this inner Truth and unchanging Wisdom is available for every rational soul to consult—whenever, for example, one learns the unchanging truths of mathematics—is a key feature of the conception of God Augustine develops in *On Free Choice* 2:8.20–14.37.

25. Augustine, *Answer to the Letter of Mani Known as "The Foundation"* 36.41, my translation.

26. Augustine, *On Christian Doctrine* 1:34.38. See above, chap. 3, "God's Way into the Cave."

27. Plato, *Phaedo* 67b–69d; Plotinus, "On Virtues," *Enneads* 1:2. Cf. above, chap. 3, "Epistemology as Ethics."

how to see the omnipresent God that had caused him so much trouble as a young man. "God is everywhere present," Fonteius writes, but he "is present in vain to defiled souls, since the mind in its blindness cannot see him."[28] For Platonist spirituality, finding God is possible not because an external word gives us some physical place to take hold of him, but because the mind can be purified, healed, and strengthened so as to recover its natural inward power of intellectual vision.[29]

Luther explicitly rejects this Platonist notion and Augustine's attempts to combine it with biblical teaching. Preaching on the passage in the prologue to the Gospel of John where Christ the eternal Word is described as "the light of men," Luther rejects "all human, Platonic, and philosophical thinking, which leads us out of Christ into ourselves."[30] He insists that the light in this passage is the grace of Christ incarnate, not the natural light of reason by which "the Word of God in its divinity could be a light, which naturally shines and has always given light to human reason, even among the heathen."[31] The authority of his beloved Augustine does not sway Luther on this point. "The Platonists with their useless and unintelligent twaddle first brought Augustine to this interpretation of this text," and afterward "Augustine carried us all with him."[32] Luther is not willing to be carried along with Augustine in this respect. He is not looking for the immutable Light of Truth within, available to be consulted by every rational soul who learns from the inner teacher. The truth of God is not something we see in an inner light but something we hear in an external word, for that is where we find the God who is true (*Deus verax*), precisely because he is true to his word and keeps his promise when he gives himself to us in Christ incarnate.

Against Karlstadt: Clinging to Externals

Luther does not accept the inward turn that is central to Augustine's spirituality, because he has a very different solution to the problem of how to find an omnipresent God we cannot see anywhere. We must believe that we have found God where God has promised to be present for us. As Luther explains:

28. Augustine, *Eighty-Three Different Questions*, question 12.
29. See Augustine, *Soliloquies* 1:6.12–7.14 and 1:13.23, where Augustine uses imagery derived from the allegory of the cave.
30. Luther, Third Sermon for Christmas Day, WA 10/1.1:202 (= Luther, *Sermons* 1:190).
31. Luther, Third Sermon for Christmas Day, WA 10/1.1:202 (= Luther, *Sermons* 1:190).
32. Luther, Third Sermon for Christmas Day, WA 10/1.1:210 (= Luther, *Sermons* 1:196). Luther could be thinking of how Augustine insists on the agreement of John 1 with the "books of the Platonists" in *Confessions* 7:9.13 and with Plotinus in *City of God* 10:2.

It is one thing if God is present, and another if he is present *for you*. He is there for you when he adds his Word and binds himself, saying, "Here you are to find me." Now when you have the Word, you can grasp and have him with certainty and say, "Here I have thee, according to thy Word."[33]

This is why we can find God by eating, if what we eat is the bread the word of God gives us. Faith in the word makes anything we do spiritual; for "all that our body does outwardly and physically, if God's Word is added to it and it is done through faith, is in reality and in name done spiritually. Nothing can be so material, fleshly or outward, but it becomes spiritual when it is done in the Word and in faith."[34]

This is a distinctive notion of spirituality, based on an outward turn which becomes explicit in Luther's arguments against Andreas Karlstadt, an early leader of the radical Reformation who was an inspiration for some of the first Anabaptists. Karlstadt advocated a kind of inward Christian spirituality that Luther wanted nothing to do with, because it "seeks to fool the people with the word 'spiritual' and undertakes to make everything spiritual which God has made bodily."[35] Karlstadt, in effect, "makes inward whatever God makes outward."[36] Whereas Karlstadt insists on "the Spirit, the Spirit, the Spirit,"[37] Luther pointedly insists on "the Word, the Word, the Word."[38] What Luther has in mind here is clearly an oral word, an external Gospel we can literally hear with our ears, so that God comes to us from the outside through our senses: "He comes into the heart . . . and is grasped only through the Word and hearing."[39]

The external comes first. Luther's theology is not a form of "experiential-expressivism,"[40] a theology that begins with inner experience that is then expressed or symbolized by words and other outward signs. Quite the reverse: the Spirit of God gives us faith and all other spiritual gifts by working from the outside in.

---

33. Luther, *That These Words*, LW 37:68.
34. Luther, *That These Words*, LW 37:92.
35. Luther, *Against the Heavenly Prophets* (1525), LW 40:191.
36. Luther, *Against the Heavenly Prophets* (1525), LW 40:184.
37. Luther, *Against the Heavenly Prophets* (1525), LW 40:147.
38. Luther, *Against the Heavenly Prophets* (1525), LW 40:212.
39. Luther, *Sacrament of the Body and Blood of Christ*, WA 19:490 (= LW 36:341).
40. Lutheran theologian George Lindbeck analyzes "experiential-expressivism" as a typically modernist approach to religion, characteristic of Protestant liberalism, in *Nature of Doctrine*, chaps. 1 and 2. I present Augustine's "expressionist semiotics" as the distant origin of experiential-expressivism in *Outward Signs*, xv, noting that much of what makes Luther seem paradoxical is that he uses Augustine's expressionist semiotics in ways that defeat the purpose of Augustinian inwardness.

> Now when God sends forth his holy Gospel he deals with us in a twofold way,
> first outward, then inward. Outwardly he deals with us through the oral word
> of the Gospel and through bodily signs, namely, baptism and sacrament. In-
> wardly he deals with us through the Holy Spirit and faith, together with other
> gifts. But the measure and order of it all is that the outward part should and
> must come first. The inward follows and comes through the outward. For he
> has resolved to give no one the inward part of it without the outward part. For
> he wants to give no one the Spirit or faith without the external word and signs
> that he has instituted.[41]

Luther's outward turn does not deny the inner work of the Spirit, but finds
the Spirit and all other divine gifts by directing attention outward to the oral
word, just as it finds God externally in the flesh of Christ. For Luther, God is
in us to the extent that we find him outside us. This may seem paradoxical,
but in fact it fits the Aristotelian theory of perception mentioned in chapter
8, according to which the mind is formed by the external things it perceives.
You get the form of a favorite song in your heart by listening attentively to
the external sound of it; in the same way you can be formed by the Gospel
when, for example, you learn the Lord's Prayer by heart. Whenever you take
the word of Christ to heart, your heart begins to be shaped by Christ's own
heart. And that is the work of the Holy Spirit in you, giving you faith and all
the inward gifts of God.

This is quite different from the inward emphasis in Luther's early theology,
which we encountered in chapter 6. In his lectures on the Psalms beginning
in 1513, Luther thought of the Gospel as an inward judgment of the Spirit in
contrast to the outward letter of the word. This was the first course he taught
in his new position as professor at the University of Wittenberg, where at
the time Karlstadt was his colleague on the faculty. Evidently both men were
reading *The Spirit and the Letter*, the foundational treatise in Augustine's
doctrine of inner grace,[42] where Augustine uses the contrast between the letter that kills and the Spirit that gives life to interpret Paul's contrast between
law and grace, making both contrasts parallel to the contrast between outer
and inner. In Augustine's treatise, any external word or sign must count as

---

41. Luther, *Against the Heavenly Prophets*, WA 18:163 (= LW 40:146). Cf. Luther, *Smalcald
Articles* 3.8, in Tappert, *Book of Concord*, 312: "God gives no one his Spirit or grace except
through or with the external Word, which comes before."

42. That Luther was reading *The Spirit and the Letter* is evident from his frequent citations
of the treatise in his early lecture courses at Wittenberg, on the Psalms and the letter to the
Romans. That Karlstadt was reading it at the same time or not long afterward is evident from
the commentary he composed on the treatise. For the continuities between Augustine's doctrine
of grace and his Platonist inward turn, see Cary, *Inner Grace*, especially chaps. 1 and 3. The key
connection is that Christ, as the Truth and Wisdom of God, is the inner teacher.

letter, not Spirit, which implies that it cannot be a source of life and salvation. This left no room for a conception of the external word as a means of grace, which would help explain why it evidently did not occur to young Luther that there could be such a thing as what he later calls the Gospel, an external word that gives us Christ and his grace. It took Luther a great deal of agonizing before he came to see that he could add a kind of codicil to the Augustinian heritage, as I put it chapter 8, which directs our attention to an external word to find an inner grace.

Karlstadt, meanwhile, was turning in another direction. While still at his academic post in Wittenberg, he wrote a commentary on Augustine's treatise *The Spirit and the Letter*, in which one of Karlstadt's key conclusions was "external things do not save."[43] No outward turn here! For a while Luther too is willing to continue speaking in this way, for example in a misleading passage early in *The Freedom of a Christian* in 1520, when he says, "No external thing has any influence in producing Christian righteousness or freedom."[44] He is thinking of the external good works of observant monks, which he has been criticizing for years, as we saw in chapter 5. "It does not help the soul," he goes on to explain, "if the body is adorned with the sacred robes of priests or dwells in sacred places or is occupied with sacred duties or prays, fasts, abstains from certain kinds of food, or does any kind of work that can be done by the body or in the body."[45] The contrast between body and soul turns out to make no difference, however, because even the works of the soul, such as contemplation and meditation, do not help make a Christian righteous and free, as Luther insists in the very next paragraph. What makes all the difference is nothing in us, body or soul, inner or outer, but only "the most holy word of God, the gospel of Christ," which is the source of our salvation.[46] Luther clearly was not anticipating that his strictures against external things might be turned against the external word of God. But that is exactly what happened in the theology of Karlstadt and those like him, as Luther explains years later:

> When we began to teach based on the Gospel that an external thing cannot save, since it is a mere bodily creature . . . people, even great and learned people, got the idea that baptism as external water, the word as external human speech, Scripture as an external letter made with ink, the bread and wine being baked by the baker, must be nothing but mere external, fleeting

43. *Quae foris sunt non salvant*; in Karlstadt, *Karlstadt und Augustin*, 84.
44. Luther, *Freedom of a Christian*, LW 31:344–45.
45. Luther, *Freedom of a Christian*, LW 31:345.
46. Luther, *Freedom of a Christian*, LW 31:345.

things. So they came up with the outcry, "Spirit! Spirit! The Spirit must do it! The letter kills!"[47]

Again, Luther's piety finds the Spirit only by turning to the external word, which is "the thing that performs all miracles, effects, sustains, carries out and does everything."[48]

By the time he comes to write the *Large Catechism* in 1530, Luther is thoroughly disenchanted with "sects who proclaim that . . . external things are of no use."[49] Their rejection of external things undermines faith, he teaches, for they "separate faith from the object to which faith is attached and bound, on the ground that the object is something external."[50] To reject external things is to detach Christian faith from what it is faith in. This kind of spirituality does not understand that

> faith must have something to believe—something to which it may cling and upon which it may stand. Thus faith clings to the water and believes it to be Baptism in which there is sheer salvation and life, not through the water . . . but through its incorporation with God's word and ordinance and the joining of his name to it. When I believe this, what else is it but believing in God as the one who has implanted his Word in this external ordinance and offered it to us so that we may grasp the treasure it contains?[51]

By this stage in his career Luther is absolutely clear that external things *do* save, if they are the things given to us by the external word of the Gospel. This is the sense in which Luther's faith is thoroughly sacramental; it is always a matter of clinging to external means of grace in which we find justification, salvation, and eternal life in Christ.

Against Zwingli: Real Presence

Behind sacramental faith is always incarnational faith. The sacramental efficacy by which external signs confer an inner gift is grounded in the power of Christ's flesh, the external thing by which God gives not only his grace but himself. The outward turn in Christian faith is thus a turn to the flesh of Christ, which is hardly unique to Luther. In a lovely and recurrent image, the

---

47. Luther, *On the Councils and the Church* (1539), WA 50:646 (= *LW* 41:170).
48. Luther, *On the Councils and the Church* (1539), *LW* 41:150.
49. Luther, *Large Catechism*, on baptism, in Tappert, *Book of Concord*, 437.
50. Luther, *Large Catechism*, on baptism, in Tappert, *Book of Concord*, 440.
51. Luther, *Large Catechism*, on baptism, in Tappert, *Book of Concord*, 440.

medieval tradition saw the sacraments flowing from the flesh of Christ like the blood and water from his side. The notion that the power of salvation resides in this unique human flesh, which is the very humanity and flesh of God, was enshrined in the Christian tradition most decisively in the era of Augustine—but not through Augustine, who died a year before it happened, on the other side of the Mediterranean. At the ecumenical Council of Ephesus in 431, led by bishop Cyril of Alexandria, the worldwide church made it an official part of its teaching that Christ's body is "life-giving flesh."[52] This phrase embraces a paradox, for in both biblical and philosophical thinking the spirit gives life to the flesh, not the other way round, just as the soul animates the body and keeps it alive—for a body without a soul is a corpse. When we receive Christ's body in faith, however, the power of life flows in the opposite direction, from his flesh to our souls, because his flesh is spiritual food that gives us eternal life. The phrase "life-giving flesh" thus serves to sum up the connection between incarnation and Eucharist.

The Christian tradition embraces this phrase because of its reading of the sixth chapter of the Gospel of John, where Christ calls himself the bread of life and explains what he means: "The bread that I will give for the life of the world is my flesh" (John 6:51). It is possible to read the chapter otherwise, however, by focusing on John 6:63 instead, where he says, "The Spirit gives life, but the flesh is of no avail." This is what happened when the first generation of Reformed theologians, led by Ulrich Zwingli and John Oecolampadius, used John 6:63 to support their argument that the flesh of Christ is not present bodily in the sacrament. Why would Christ institute a sacrament to give us what is of no avail? Luther's retort is that "there is a very great difference between Christ's flesh and ordinary flesh."[53] To show the difference, he applies their argument to the bodily presence of Christ in the whole story of the Gospel, from Mary's womb to the cross to the right hand of God, and asks whether Christ's flesh was of no avail in all these places. For it is the same flesh, and it remains flesh, "whether in the stomach, bread, the cross . . . whether in heaven, spirit, manger, mother, or wherever you will."[54]

But it turns out that the real sticking point concerns where Christ's flesh is present now, at the right hand of God the Father in heaven. This becomes especially clear when John Calvin, in the generation after Zwingli, returns Reformed theology to the mainstream Christian tradition by insisting in no

52. See the third letter of Cyril to Nestorius, §7, accepted as orthodox teaching by the Council of Ephesus in 431, translated in McGuckin, *Saint Cyril of Alexandria*, 268–69. Note also the eleventh of the famous twelve anathemas, 275.
53. Luther, *That These Words*, LW 37:79.
54. Luther, *That These Words*, LW 37:83–84.

uncertain terms that Christ's flesh is indeed of great avail, for it is food for the soul. Calvin makes no use of John 6:63 in his sacramental thinking[55] and instead builds on the conviction that those who receive the Supper in faith partake of Christ's life-giving flesh as a kind of spiritual nourishment. Yet Calvin is also very clear that our partaking of Christ's flesh is not a literal eating, as if the body of Christ were present right there in our mouths along with the bread. For he joins the rest of the Reformed tradition in disagreeing with Luther and the Lutherans at a key point about the presence of Christ's flesh: it cannot be in bread, because it is in heaven. Reformed theologians reason that a human body needs to be someplace—contained in a particular, circumscribed location like any other bodily thing—and the place of Christ's body is now in heaven, not on earth. Combining this Reformed reasoning with the theme of Christ's life-giving flesh, Calvin teaches that when we receive the sacrament in faith, Christ's Spirit unites us on earth with Christ's body in heaven. Therefore "it is not necessary for the essence of the flesh to descend from heaven in order that we be fed upon it," Calvin writes, because "the secret virtue [i.e., power] of the Spirit makes things separated in space to be united with each other, and accordingly enables life from the flesh of Christ to reach us from heaven."[56] Thus we partake of Christ's flesh spiritually—by the power of the Holy Spirit, not by chewing it with our teeth.

Here Luther, as elsewhere in his disagreements with Reformed theologians, belongs with the medieval tradition in a way that puts him closer to Catholicism than most Protestants are. In his doctrine of "real presence," as it is now called, he agrees with the medieval church in teaching that Christ's flesh is present as a reality (*res*) in the sacrament, not separated from us in space but present bodily, in such a way that it can literally be held in our mouths and pressed with our teeth. And yet, just as it is not visible to the eye like ordinary flesh, it is not chewed up, torn apart, and digested like ordinary flesh or meat. It is bodily present but not physically consumed. For it is truly human flesh but it is also utterly unique flesh, being the flesh of God incarnate at the right hand of the Father. Hence "no one sees or grasps or eats or chews Christ's body in the way he visibly sees and chews any other flesh," Luther writes, even though it is true that "he who crushes this bread with teeth or tongue, crushes with teeth or tongue the body of Christ."[57] There is a kind

---

55. Strikingly, in fact, according to the comprehensive Scripture index in the Battles edition, Calvin does not quote John 6:63 at all in the whole of the *Institutes*.

56. Calvin, *The Best Method of Obtaining Concord, Provided the Truth Be Sought without Contention,* in *Theological Treatises,* 328–29.

57. Luther, *Confession concerning Christ's Supper* (also known as the "Great Confession"), *LW* 37:300. Here Luther affirms one of the most striking formulations of the real presence in

of sacramental union, as Luther puts it, between bread and body, so that it becomes a single thing, and what happens to the one happens to the other. It is analogous to the way that, because of the union of body and soul, stepping on my toe hurts *me*, and seeing my body is seeing *me*. Therefore, although Christ's body is invisible to us, "whoever sees the bread sees Christ's body" and although we do not feel it, whoever "takes hold of this bread, takes hold of Christ's body."[58] And what is true of the eye that sees and the hand that holds is true also of the teeth that chew and the mouth that swallows.

What Luther aims to do in this teaching is strike the same balance as the medieval church, insisting on the one hand that Christ's flesh is literally in the mouth just like bread, and yet on the other hand that it is not present in such a way as to be consumed, digested, and destroyed by us, for it is the life-giving flesh of God, "imperishable, immortal, incorruptible flesh."[59] Precisely because it is at the right hand of God—which is present everywhere, not restricted to some place far away as if God's heaven were a location in physical space—Christ's flesh is not contained in the bread like meat in pie, nor is it cut up in pieces so that part of it is in one place and part in another. In the sacrament we receive the whole living, glorified body of God incarnate with our hands and mouths.

> When you receive the bread from the altar, you are not tearing an arm from the body of the Lord or biting off his nose or a finger; rather, you are receiving the entire body of the Lord; the person who comes after you also receives the same entire body, as does the third and the thousandth. . . . He does not say: "Peter, there, devour my finger; Andrew, devour my nose; John, devour my ears," etc.; rather, he says, "It is my body, take it and eat it," etc. Each person receives it whole.[60]

Clearly, Luther is thinking: "This is my body" does not mean "This is part of my body." It is Christ giving himself to us whole, not in pieces. Here again

---

the Roman Catholic tradition, the decree against Berengar of Tours, which demanded that Berengar confess that the body of Christ is "pressed and crushed by the teeth of the faithful, not only sacramentally but in reality" (Luther, *Confession concerning Christ's Supper*, LW 37:300).

58. Luther, *Confession concerning Christ's Supper*, LW 37:300. The term "sacramental union" is the best brief label for Luther's view—not "consubstantiation," a term often applied to the Lutheran view but that the Lutheran churches typically reject. "Consubstantiation" suggests a metaphysical theory to rival Roman Catholic transubstantiation, whereas the kind of explanation Luther has in mind is not metaphysical but grammatical, i.e., the "mode of speech about diverse beings as one [that] the grammarians call 'synecdoche,'" as he proceeds to say in *Confession concerning Christ's Supper*, LW 37:301–2.

59. Luther, *That These Words*, LW 37:124.

60. Luther, *Brief Confession concerning the Holy Supper*, LW 38:292.

Luther is happy to take a page from the medieval church, this time from a hymn of Thomas Aquinas, which he proceeds to quote: "One takes it, a thousand take it; this one takes as much as that one; nor, being taken, is it consumed."[61] The preceding verses also make Luther's point: "It is not cut or broken apart or divided by those who take it, but received whole."[62]

It is true, of course, that Luther was a critic of Roman Catholic eucharistic theology and that he rejected its doctrine of transubstantiation, according to which the whole of the bread and wine is converted to the substance of Christ's body and blood, leaving only the appearance of bread and wine. Yet unlike many later Protestants, he does not treat this doctrine as a horrible abomination. In his view, "this error is not very important if only the body and blood of Christ, together with the word, are not taken away."[63] In Luther's view, the Roman Catholic doctrine retains what is essential to the sacrament, which is the real presence of Christ's flesh, and merely adds a superfluous and unnecessary miracle by getting rid of the substance of bread and wine. Luther treats this as an error but not a heresy; it is even a legitimate theological view, "which may be held as an opinion, but need not be believed."[64] It becomes intolerable only if it is made into a requirement, a doctrine that Christians are forced to believe. For, as always in Luther's theology, the church has no authority to make such requirements for Christian faith without a basis in Scripture (as we saw in chap. 9, this is the meaning of the Protestant doctrine of *sola scriptura*, "Scripture alone").

So Luther disagrees with both Roman Catholics and Reformed on the doctrine of the Supper, but his disagreement with the latter is far deeper, because he thinks Zwingli and his colleagues miss the whole point of the sacrament, which is to bring Christ to us in the flesh. The medieval affirmation that we can chew his body with our teeth is a way of insisting on a key feature of any kind of bodily presence: that it is there whether we believe it or not, just like bread or wine in the mouth. (If you were mistaken and thought you had

61. Luther, *Brief Confession concerning the Holy Supper*, LW 38:293.
62. Thomas Aquinas, "Lauda, Sion, salvatorem," stanza 8, from the mass for Corpus Christi (= hymn 96 in Walsch and Husch, *One Hundred Latin Hymns*), my translation. The whole stanza reads:
> A sumente non concisus,
> Non confratus, non divisus,
> Integer accipitur;
> Sumit unus, sumunt mille,
> Quantum isti, tantum ille,
> Nec sumptus consumitur.
63. Luther, *Adoration of the Sacrament* (1523), LW 36:287.
64. Luther, *Babylonian Captivity*, LW 26:29.

eaten rice-cake instead of bread, the truth would still be that it was bread in your mouth, whether you believed it or not.) But again, this true bodily presence is also a unique bodily presence, for it is the presence of divine flesh, glorified and hidden at the right hand of the Father. It is present in particular portions of bread and wine not because we receive it properly in faith but solely because this is what God promises in the Gospel. Thus Luther teaches that the sacrament "is not founded on the holiness of men but on the Word of God" and that "the Word by which it was constituted a sacrament is not rendered false because of an individual's unworthiness or unbelief."[65] We are commanded to receive the sacrament in faith, of course, but as in Luther's other disagreements with the Reformed, reflective faith is not necessary. I do not have to believe that I have true faith in order to believe that I am partaking of Christ's flesh, for "the godless person or Judas receives orally just as well as St. Peter and all the saints."[66] As we shall see, this dependence on the word alone, not on our faith, is characteristic of sacramental validity as understood in the Augustinian tradition.

Against Calvin: Flesh as Sign

The reason why Protestants came to be permanently divided about the sacrament of the Supper is best illustrated in the writings of John Calvin, who worked persistently to overcome the division but failed. Calvin's theological career was launched a decade after the controversy between Luther and Zwingli began in 1526. The first edition of Calvin's masterpiece, the *Institutes*, published in 1536, is deeply influenced by Luther's epochal treatise on the sacraments, *The Babylonian Captivity of the Church* (1520), as well as Luther's earliest publication on the Supper, the little 1519 sermon *The Blessed Sacrament of the Holy and True Body of Christ, and the Brotherhoods*. Though Calvin eventually became the most important theologian of the Reformed tradition, he was not happy with the sacramental theology of the first generation of Reformed theologians.[67] He wanted nothing to do with a doctrine

---

65. Luther, *Large Catechism*, on the sacrament of the altar, in Tappert, *Book of Concord*, 448; this characteristic passage is quoted by the *Formula of Concord*, Solid Declaration 7:24–25, in Tappert, *Book of Concord*, 573.

66. Luther, *Brief Confession*, LW 38:304, another passage quoted in the *Formula of Concord*, Solid Declaration 7:33, 575.

67. The general treatment of the sacraments in the first edition of Calvin's *Institutes* is a resolute attack on the low view of the sacraments held by Zwingli and Bucer, in support of a sacramental piety that owes a great deal to Luther and Melanchthon, as can be seen in the notes to the Battles translation of Calvin, *Institutes of the Christian Religion: 1536 Edition*, 87–94.

that separated Christ's flesh from the Supper, and he was deeply dissatisfied with Zwingli's notion that the sacraments were simply a way for believers to testify publicly to their faith. In the sacraments we partake of Christ in the flesh, Calvin teaches, for it is God who is testifying—confirming our faith by giving us signs that serve as a kind of seal of the promises by which he gives us Christ.

In Calvin's *Short Treatise on the Lord's Supper* (1541), his last major publication on the subject before Luther's death, he tried to push Reformed theology as far as it could go in Luther's direction, insisting that "Jesus Christ gives us in the Supper the real substance [*propre substance*] of his body and his blood."[68] Picking up on the theme of union with Christ that is the foundation of Luther's doctrine of justification, Calvin teaches that we receive no benefit from Christ unless we are united with him by faith, which "is not only a matter of being partakers of his Spirit; it is necessary also to partake [*participer*] of his humanity."[69] This is why "our Lord gives us in the Supper what he figures [*figure*] by it, and we thus truly receive [*recevons vraiment*] the body and blood of Jesus Christ."[70] Calvin sees word and sacrament performing the same function, which is to offer and present to us Christ incarnate: "For what is said of the word fitly belongs also to the sacrament of the Supper, by means of which our Lord leads us to communion with Jesus Christ."[71] Because the sacrament serves to seal the promise of God, who is true to his word, it too must be a means by which we partake of Christ: "If God cannot deceive or lie, it follows that he performs all that it signifies [*signifie*]. We must then truly [*vraiment*] receive in the Supper the body and blood of Jesus Christ."[72]

In later writings meant to address Lutheran concerns, Calvin frequently returns to the emphasis on God being true, the *Deus verax* theme that is so important to Luther. If God is true, then the sacrament cannot be an empty sign, devoid of what it signifies. Hence Luther's great concern, as Calvin understood it, was to make sure the sacraments were not regarded as "void and empty figures," whereas in fact "God truly testifies in them what he figures, and at the same time, by his secret agency, performs and fulfills what he

68. Calvin, *Short Treatise on the Lord's Supper*, in *Theological Treatises*, 148. French original in volume 5 of the works of Calvin in *Corpus Reformatorum* (CR) 33:440.

69. Calvin, *Lord's Supper*, 146 (= CR 33:438).

70. Calvin, *Lord's Supper*, 163 (= CR 33:456). Translation modified. Unfortunately, in Calvin's sacramental writings translators often render words like *vrai* and *vraiment* ("true" and "truly") with "real" and "really," thus obscuring an important connection with Luther's *Deus verax* theme.

71. Calvin, *Lord's Supper*, 144 (= CR 33:435).

72. Calvin, *Lord's Supper*, 148 (= CR 33:440). Translation modified.

testifies."[73] In semiotic terms inherited from Augustine, Calvin insists that the sacraments are "signs distinct from the things signified," but "the signs are not devoid of the things, as God conjoins the effectual working of his Spirit with them."[74] To separate sign from thing signified is to separate the sacrament from its truth and make it an empty symbol:

> For unless a man means to call God a deceiver, he would never dare assert that an empty symbol is set forth by him. . . . For why should the Lord put in your hand the symbol of his body, except to assure you of a true participation in it? But if it is true that a visible sign is given us to seal the gift of a thing invisible, when we have received the symbol of the body, let us no less surely trust that the body itself is also given to us.[75]

Yet Calvin also contends that the sacrament is indeed separated from the thing it signifies when it is received unworthily. This too follows from the sacramental semiotics of Augustine, who, as Calvin reminds us, often noted the distinction between *sacramentum* and *res*, which meant "not only that the figure and the truth are contained in the sacrament, but that they are not so linked that they cannot be separated."[76] He goes on to explain:

> A sacrament is thus separated from its truth by the unworthiness of the recipient, so that nothing remains but a vain and useless figure. But that you may have not a sign empty of truth but the matter [*res*] with the sign, you must apprehend in faith the word which is included there.[77]

Here Calvin's unfortunate confusion of the truth (*veritas*) of the sacrament with the thing (*res*) it signifies (as if the terms "figure" and "truth" were parallel with sign and thing signified, respectively) obscures an important point of agreement with Luther, which is a consequence of the Augustinian semiotics they share. Every theologian downstream from Augustine agrees that unbelief separates the sign from the thing signified in the sacrament.

---

73. Calvin, *Exposition of the Heads of Agreement*, also known as his first defense of the Zurich Consensus, in *Tracts and Letters*, 2:224.

74. Calvin, *Exposition of the Heads of Agreement*, 224–25.

75. Calvin, *Institutes* 4:17.10. So far as I can tell, Calvin makes no distinction between *signum* and *symbolum* when discussing the sacraments, so we should treat the two terms "sign" and "symbol" as synonyms.

76. Calvin, *Institutes* 4:14.15 (= CR 30:951). Battles translates *res* in this section as "matter," which does not quite convey the Augustinian semiotic language of *signum* and *res* that Calvin is using. Elsewhere Calvin does use the terms *materia* (in Latin) and *materiere* (in French) to describe Christ as what is signified in the sacrament, and it is useful to be aware when Calvin is using this alternative vocabulary to do the work of Augustine's semiotics.

77. Calvin, *Institutes* 4:14.15 (= CR 30:951).

But Luther would never agree that unbelief compromises the truth of the sacrament.

The key disagreement between Calvin and Luther, in fact, stems from a divergence in what they identify as sign (*signum sacramenti* or *signum* or simply *sacramentum*) and as thing signified (*res sacramenti* or *res significata* or simply *res*). For Luther, the flesh of Christ is part of the sacramental sign in the Supper, which means it is there every time the sacrament is there, because strictly speaking, the sacrament *is* the sign (since "sacrament" is defined as a specific kind of sign, as discussed early in chap. 7). Hence in every valid sacrament, Christ's flesh is always present along with the visible signs of bread and wine ("in, with, and under" them, as Lutherans like to say). Hence Christ's body and blood, along with bread and wine, are present in the mouths of those who receive the sacrament whether they believe it or not, and whether they are worthy or not. That is why Luther never adopts anything like Calvin's unfortunate language about unworthiness separating the sacrament from its *truth*. The truth of the sacrament is the truth of the sign itself, which is not dependent on our faith or worthiness but solely on the truth of God's word. Christ's body is always present as the sacramental sign precisely because Christ's word, which tells us this is his body, is always true. Calvin thinks differently because he identifies Christ's body not with the sacramental sign but with the thing signified. And as all Augustinian theologians agree—Calvin and Luther alike—unbelievers do not receive the thing signified by a sacrament.

The Augustinian principle that Calvin and Luther agree on can be spelled out in terms of the distinction between sacramental validity and sacramental efficacy. The validity of a sacrament simply means it actually is a sacrament, properly constituted by word and sign. In a valid sacrament we have not merely water or bread, but the water of baptism and the bread of the Lord's Supper, sacred signs consecrated by the word of Christ and signifying a divine gift of grace. Plain bread does not signify Christ's body unless it is consecrated by the word ("This is my body, given for you"), and ordinary water does not baptize anyone unless it is consecrated by the word ("I baptize you in the name of the Father, and of the Son, and of the Holy Spirit"). This is what Augustine means by his oft-quoted formulation, "The word comes to the element, and it becomes a sacrament" (*accedit verbum ad elementum, et fit sacramentum*).[78] The elements, water or bread and wine, become valid sacramental signs— which is simply to say, there really is a sacrament—whenever they are properly consecrated according to Christ's word in Scripture, quite independently of whether the word is believed.

---

78. Augustine, *On the Gospel of John* 80:3, my translation.

The efficacy of the sacrament, however, is something more. The sacrament is efficacious when the thing signified by the sacramental sign is not only offered, presented, and exhibited but actually conferred, which means that the person who receives the sign receives also the thing signified, as we saw in chapter 7. In Calvin's view as well as Luther's, the efficacy of the sacrament is very much like the efficacy of the word, which bestows the mercy and grace it promises only on those who believe it. Thus the sacrament is *valid* by virtue of the word of God alone, quite apart from faith, but it is *efficacious* only for those believe. That is the principle that Luther and Calvin agree on, together with all Augustinian theologians.

The difference between Luther and Calvin about real presence is best understood as a disagreement about what belongs to the validity of the sacrament, not its efficacy. For mere validity in a sacrament, even without efficacy, has important consequences. To illustrate with baptism, where Luther and Calvin agree, the consequence of a valid sacrament is that the person who received it should not seek to be baptized again, even if he initially received baptism in a state of unbelief. As Luther explains:

> When the Word accompanies the water, Baptism is valid, even though faith be lacking. For my faith does not constitute Baptism but receives it. Baptism does not become invalid even if it is wrongly received or used, for it is bound not to our faith but to the Word.[79]

The difference between validity and efficacy comes into view when Luther explains how it is that baptism can indeed become an empty sign, valid but without efficacy:

> The external sign has been appointed not only on account of what it confers [i.e., its efficacy] but also on account of what it signifies [i.e., its validity]. Where faith is present with its fruits, there Baptism is no empty symbol, but the effect [i.e., its efficacy] accompanies it, but where faith is lacking it remains a mere unfruitful sign [i.e., a valid sacramental sign but not efficacious].[80]

So far we have the same Augustinian principle that Luther and Calvin agree on: a sacrament received without faith is valid but empty and lacking efficacy, because it does not confer the grace it signifies.

The difference between Luther and Calvin emerges when we apply the same distinction to the sacrament of the Supper and ask what follows from

---

79. Luther, *Large Catechism*, on infant baptism, in Tappert, *Book of Concord*, 443.
80. Luther, *Large Catechism*, on infant baptism, in Tappert, *Book of Concord*, 445.

mere validity without efficacy. How one applies the distinction, of course, depends on what one identifies as the sign and as the thing signified. If Christ's body and blood are sacramental *signs*, then they are present in every valid sacrament—which is to say, every time there really is a sacrament of the Supper. Because of the recipient's unbelief the valid sacrament may be without efficacy, which makes it an empty, fruitless sign, conferring no grace—but it is still a sign that includes Christ's flesh. For Christ's life-giving flesh gives no life to those who receive it in unbelief, like Judas or Pilate, who received Christ's flesh and had it crucified. That is why, in Paul's terms, those who eat and drink unworthily eat and drink condemnation (1 Cor. 11:27–29).

From his earliest writings on the Supper, it is clear that Luther thinks of the body and blood of Christ as sacramental *signs*. In his first treatise on the Supper, he says that Christ "gave his true natural flesh in the bread, and his natural true blood in the wine, that he might give a really perfect sacrament or sign."[81] According to the same treatise, as we saw in chapter 7, the thing signified in the Supper includes the communion of the saints (*communio sanctorum*). Hence in another treatise written in the same year, Luther connects this particular sign with this particular thing signified, when he speaks of "the holy body of Christ, which is a sign and promise of the communion of all angels and saints."[82] A year later he calls the sacrament "a powerful and most precious seal and sign: his own true flesh and blood under the bread and wine."[83] Likewise in 1520, in *The Babylonian Captivity*, he describes Christ's body and blood as a sign that confirms the Gospel promise: "It is as if Christ were saying: 'I shall give my body and pour out my blood, confirming this promise by my very death, and leaving you *my body and blood as a sign* and memorial of this same promise.'"[84] All these writings come before the controversies with Karlstadt and Zwingli. But by 1523 the controversies are on the horizon, as Luther is aware that "there have been some who have held that in the sacrament there is merely bread and wine."[85] They do so, he explains, because they identify the body and blood of Christ as merely the thing signified in the sacrament. "They have taught nothing more than that the bread signifies the body and the wine signifies the blood of Christ."[86] He is

81. Luther, *The Blessed Sacrament of the Holy and True Body of Christ, and the Brother-hoods* (sermon, 1519), LW 35:59.

82. Luther, *Sermon on Preparing to Die* (1519), LW 42:111.

83. Luther, *Treatise on the New Testament, That Is, the Holy Mass* (1520), LW 35:86.

84. Luther, *Babylonian Captivity*, LW 36:40. He repeats the point a little later, *Babylonian Captivity*, LW 36:44.

85. Luther, *Adoration of the Sacrament*, LW 36:279.

86. Luther, *Adoration of the Sacrament*, LW 36:279 (= WA 11:434). Throughout this passage, "to signify" renders the German *bedeuten*.

evidently thinking of an influential recent letter by the Dutch writer Cornelius Hoen, who interpreted the words "This is my body" to mean "This *signifies* my body,"[87] an interpretation that was soon adopted by Zwingli. The implication is clear: in the sacrament "the body of Christ is not there, but it signifies it like a sign."[88] For Luther, by contrast, everything depends on Christ's flesh being present bodily, just as truly as the visible sign of the sacrament.

Though Calvin does not adopt Hoen's interpretation of "is" as "signifies," he does clearly classify the body and blood of Christ as things signified by the sacrament rather than signs. Quite simply, "the bread and wine are visible signs, which represent to us the body and the blood."[89] The same classification is implied by Calvin's frequent reference to Christ's flesh as the matter and substance of the sacrament.[90] (These terms should not be interpreted in their Aristotelian sense, which would bring Calvin's thinking within the framework of medieval scholasticism and its doctrine of transubstantiation, which he heartily despises, but rather in terms of Augustinian sacramental semiotics, which he consistently finds useful.) Christ's flesh is the matter and substance of the sacrament precisely because it is, in Augustinian terms, the thing signified by the sacramental signs of bread and wine. And that means that those who receive the sacrament without faith receive only bread and wine, not body and blood. It is still a valid sacrament, but for them it is not efficacious, for it is devoid of the thing signified.

The difference between Luther and Calvin on the Supper, in other words, stems from their different ways of identifying what is the sign and what is the thing signified in the Supper—its *signum* and its *res*. Calvin identifies Christ's body as the thing signified (*res*), whereas Luther identifies it as the sacramental sign (*signum*). Consequently, the Augustinian principle they agree on—that unbelief separates sign from thing signified, making a valid sacrament inefficacious—results in two different conclusions. If Christ's body is

87. An English translation of this letter is available in Oberman, *Forerunners of the Reformation*, 268–78. For Zwingli's uptake of Hoen's interpretation, see Hillerbrand, *Reformation*, 150–51. Luther explicitly rejects this interpretation in *Confession concerning the Lord's Supper*, LW 37:170–77. The issue came up for debate in the face-to-face discussion between Zwingli and Luther at Marburg in 1530, LW 38:22, 40.

88. Luther, *Adoration of the Sacrament*, WA 11:434 (= LW 36:279). Here I use "sign" to render the German *zeichen*.

89. Calvin, *Short Treatise*, 147. Cf. similarly, "The signs are bread and wine, which represent for us the invisible food that we receive from the flesh and blood of Christ" (Calvin, *Institutes* 4:17.1).

90. "I am accustomed to say that the matter and substance [*matiere et substance*] of the sacraments is the Lord Jesus Christ" (Calvin, *Short Treatise*, 146 [= CR 33:437]). Cf. Calvin, *Institutes* 4:14.16; 4:17.11 (= CR 30:952, 1010), where the vocabulary in the Latin is *materiam* and *substantia*.

the thing signified, as Calvin thinks, then unbelievers receiving the sacrament do not receive Christ's body. But if Christ's body is the sign in the sacrament, as Luther teaches, then it is present every time the valid sacrament is present, by virtue of the word alone, whether it is believed or not.

Calvin's identification has far-reaching pastoral consequences that lead in the opposite direction from Luther's theology. It means, to begin with, that the external, sacramental sign is not something to which faith can cling, finding life and salvation in it. Rather, the sign in the Supper points away from itself, directing our attention to the life-giving flesh of Christ, which is literally far away from us in heaven. The sign itself cannot unite us with this distant flesh, which is why, in Calvin's view, we partake of Christ's body only by the power of the Holy Spirit. For believers who receive the sacrament, "the Spirit truly unites things separated in space."[91] That is how "Christ's flesh, separated from us by such great distance, penetrates to us, so that it becomes our food."[92] On this point Calvin criticizes the Lutherans for thinking that partaking of Christ's flesh requires us to "swallow Christ's flesh under the bread."[93] Christ does not come to us in bread or other visible signs, but rather "the secret power of the Spirit is the bond of our union with Christ."[94] For "it is not necessary for the essence of the flesh to descend from heaven in order that we be fed upon it," because the power of the Spirit "is sufficient to break through all impediments and surmount any distance of place."[95]

With Aquinas: Faith in External Things

Calvin resonates with Augustine's semiotics when he teaches that "we are not to cling to the visible signs and there seek our salvation."[96] He also appeals to the ancient liturgical exhortation, "lift up your hearts" (*sursum corda*), which he takes to mean that we must not be like "those who are halted at the outward sign" but rather raise the attention of our hearts to heaven, where Christ is.[97] In the ancient church, he says, "the people were solemnly exhorted to lift their hearts on high, to show that *we must not stop at the visible sign*, to adore Jesus Christ rightly."[98] The sacramental signs are not devoid of truth, but "in

91. Calvin, *Institutes* 4:17.10.
92. Calvin, *Institutes* 4:17.10.
93. Calvin, *Institutes* 4:17.33.
94. Calvin, *Institutes* 4:17.33.
95. Calvin, *Best Method*, 328.
96. Calvin, Geneva Catechism, in *Theological Treatises*, 132.
97. Calvin, *Institutes* 4:17.36.
98. Calvin, *Short Treatise*, 159.

order to enjoy the truth of the signs our minds must be raised to heaven where Christ is," for "in these earthly elements [of bread and wine] it is improper and vain to seek him."[99]

I think we can see now why Calvin's efforts to overcome the division between Reformed and Lutheran theologians were bound to fail. The pastoral difference is immense—as far apart as heaven and earth, or the power of the Spirit and flesh in the mouth. It comes down to a difference in where believers are to direct their attention and devotion, as signaled by the verb "to cling." Augustine loved the psalm that says, "My good is to cling to God."[100] The question for anyone in the wake of Augustine is where the heart turns its attention, love, and desire when it seeks to cling to God. For Augustine, we turn inward, where Christ is the inner teacher, and words and signs merely direct us along the road of this inner journey. For Calvin, we are united to Christ's flesh in heaven by the supernatural and incomprehensible power of the Spirit. And for Luther, we grope for God in bread and wine, where Christ gives himself bodily to us by his word. Luther insists that faith lives by clinging to these external things, whereas Calvin has Augustine on his side, not to mention Karlstadt, when he warns us not to "cling too tightly to the outward sign."[101] For Luther, there is no such thing as clinging too tightly to the outward signs given us by God, the external word of the Gospel and the sacrament in which Christ's body and blood are present. Our whole salvation depends on clinging as tightly as we can to these outward signs, and nothing else. Luther's outward turn thus brings him closer to medieval sacramental theology and such teachers as Thomas Aquinas than to Calvin and Augustine.

The point of clinging to these outward signs, for Luther, is that in their externality they give us something to believe that is not dependent on our belief or faith—and precisely this strengthens our faith. Our justification and salvation depend on our faith, but the presence of Christ's life-giving flesh does not, any more than the presence of bread and wine. It is therefore possible to take hold of God incarnate by faith alone, believing that he is present even in our mouths, without believing our faith is worthy or strong or sufficient. In this way those who are weak in faith, believers who find that much of the time they are also unbelievers, may receive justification and salvation and all other blessings in Christ's life-giving flesh, while still believing their faith is weak and inadequate—which, after all, is the truth. As we saw with the Gospel word in the previous chapter, so also we now see in the sacrament:

99. Calvin, Geneva Catechism, 137.

100. Ps. 73:28, translated from the Latin version used by Augustine: *mihi autem adhaerere Deo bonum est.*

101. Calvin, *Institutes* 4:14.16.

everything in our faith depends on God being true to his word, not on the worthiness or strength of our faith. *Faith needs to cling to something that is not dependent on faith*. From this perspective, Calvin's teaching that only those who worthily receive the sacrament partake of Christ's distant flesh defeats the key purpose of the sacrament, which is to strengthen and confirm our faith. You cannot strengthen Christian faith by requiring it to believe in its own worthiness.

Of course this does not mean faith is unnecessary. Christ's body in the sacrament "cannot be perceived except by faith," as Thomas Aquinas puts it.[102] To quote another of Aquinas's eucharistic hymns, "Since the senses fail, *faith alone* suffices."[103] For medieval sacramental piety as for Luther, "faith alone" means a dependence on the truth of God's word alone, which requires an epistemology of hearing, because as Paul says, "Faith comes from hearing, and hearing through the word of Christ" (Rom. 10:17). Hence in a hymn attributed to Aquinas, which addresses the "hidden Truth" (*latens veritas*) of the Eucharist:

> Seeing, touching, tasting are in thee deceived;
> What says trusty hearing? That shall be believed;
> What God's Son has told me, take for truth I do;
> Truth himself speaks truly, or there's nothing true.[104]

In the sacrament Christ's body and blood are given to us as a sign, *external yet invisible*, perceptible by the hearing of faith alone.

It is odd, of course, to depend on faith alone to perceive external things such as flesh and blood, which are normally the sort of things you can see for yourself. It is even more odd to depend on faith to perceive an external *sign*. In this regard, Calvin's identification of Christ's body as thing signified

---

102. Non potest conspici nisi per fidem (Aquinas, *ST* III, 7.6.7).

103. From "Pange, lingua," stanza 4 (= hymn 98 in Walsch and Husch, *One Hundred Latin Hymns*), my translation:
>   Et, si sensus deficit
>   ad firmandum cor sincerum
>   sola fides sufficit.

104. From "Adoro te devote," stanza 2 (= hymn 99 in Walsch and Husch, *One Hundred Latin Hymns*).
>   Visus tactus gustus in te fallitur,
>   sed solus auditus tute creditur.
>   Credo quidquid dixit Dei filius,
>   nihil veritatis verbo verius.

The hymn is traditionally attributed to Aquinas, but recent scholars have regarded the authorship as uncertain. I use the wonderful translation by Gerard Manley Hopkins in Clark, *An Aquinas Reader*, 540.

rather than sign is not unreasonable. What kind of sign is it that is invisible, hidden from us at the right hand of God, beyond every bodily sense? It certainly doesn't look like an outward and visible sign. So it is reasonable to locate Christ on the other side of the *signum-res* distinction, together with the grace signified by the sacrament, as the spiritual food that nourishes our souls.[105] Yet this identification too is odd, for Christ's flesh does not seem to fit the role of *inner* grace, which is the thing signified by a sacrament. There is, after all, nothing more external than flesh. Confronted with this two-sided dilemma—an outward sign that cannot be perceived and an inner grace that consists of flesh—medieval theologians ended up saying yes to both sides, by formulating a new category which they called "sacrament and thing" (*sacramentum et res*). It is a third category, what logicians call a *tertium quid*, added to the simple duality of "sacrament alone" (*sacramentum tantum*), which is only the sign, and "thing alone" (*res tantum*), which is only the thing signified. It is the kind of hybrid category that we would nowadays call a "both/and." To classify Christ's flesh as "sacrament and thing" is to say it is both sign and thing signified in the sacrament. This is the classification used in the twelfth-century *Summa sententiarum* (Summary of sentences),[106] which is picked up by Peter Lombard in his *Sentences*, the most influential theology text of the Middle Ages,[107] and from there the classification spreads throughout medieval theology, including most importantly Thomas Aquinas.[108]

The classification "sacrament and thing" was used in medieval theology to describe the power of several different sacraments, but its original use in the *Summa sententiarum* was to answer a question Augustine left unanswered about what happens when the sacrament of the Eucharist is received without faith. In a very influential sermon on John 6,[109] Augustine contrasted the mere physical eating of the sacrament (which the medieval theologians labeled

105. As Calvin puts it, in terms with which Luther would heartily agree, "Christ's flesh itself . . . is a thing no less spiritual than our eternal salvation" (Calvin, *Institutes* 4:17.33).

106. Anonymous, *Summa sententiarum* 6:3. Authorship of this treatise used to be attributed to Hugh of St. Victor.

107. Lombard, *Sententiae* 4:8.7. This hybrid category clearly originates in eucharistic theology, but Lombard already knows of theologians extending it to the sacrament of penance (4:22.2).

108. Aquinas uses this hybrid category in his discussion of baptismal character (*ST* III, 61.1), interior repentance in the sacrament of penance (*ST* III, 84.1, ad 3), and Christ's body and blood in the Eucharist (*ST* III, 73.1). In each case what is in view is a spiritual gift that is not, strictly speaking, an interior grace.

109. Augustine, *On the Gospel of John* 26, one of the most important eucharistic texts in medieval theology, especially for debates on whether the unworthy receive Christ's literal body and blood when they eat the sacrament, a point on which Augustine's sermon is maddeningly ambiguous.

"sacramental eating") with the spiritual eating that actually profits the soul. "Why do you make ready your teeth and your stomach?" he famously says in the preceding sermon. "Believe and you have eaten."[110] Believing *is* spiritual eating, for Augustine. He thus offers us a neat division between validity and efficacy: on the one hand is the valid outward sign received by teeth and stomach, which both believers and unbelievers are capable of, and on the other hand is the efficacious inner grace that benefits only those who receive the outward sign worthily.

But Augustine did not say—and did not even ask—whether the valid outward sign received by everybody includes Christ's body and blood. Elsewhere, I have argued that this is because his Platonism left no room for a concept of Christ's flesh as life giving—an external thing with salvific power.[111] He probably did believe, following what had long been the dominant tradition of the church at the time, that Christ's body and blood were present in the sacrament itself.[112] But he didn't know what to do with this tradition theologically (to use his own terms, he believed it but did not yet understand it), and developed no piety or devotion around the concept of Christ's life-giving flesh. Instead, when he wanted to explain the efficacy of the sacrament, he insisted that believers participate in the thing signified, which he consistently identified as the unity, peace, and love of the church as the Body of Christ.

This left later medieval sacramental theology with the unanswered question of how Christ's life-giving flesh can be conceived both as a divine gift, like an inward and spiritual grace, and as an external thing, like all flesh. The hybrid category of "sacrament and thing" was invented to answer the question. Medieval sacramental theology made it explicit that the unworthy eat Christ's flesh sacramentally but not spiritually, which is to say they receive it as sacramental sign (*sacramentum*) but not as thing signified (*res*). They receive his flesh but not its life-giving power. By contrast, those who receive worthily receive Christ's flesh as both sacrament and thing signified (*sacramentum et res*).

110. Augustine, *On the Gospel of John* 25:12, my translation.
111. I present a detailed analysis of the sermon in Cary, *Outward Signs*, 248–52, arguing that the source of its ambiguity is that Augustine does not have a conception of Christ's life-giving flesh, much less a eucharistic piety built around it.
112. See Augustine, Sermon 227: "The bread which you see on the altar, sanctified by the word of God, is the body of Christ." See also the one passage where Augustine says pretty clearly that the unworthy eat Christ's body: "It was none the less the body of the Lord and the blood of the Lord, even in those to whom the apostle said, 'He that eateth unworthily, eateth and drinketh damnation to himself'" (Augustine, *On Baptism against the Donatists* 5:8.9 [the quotation combines 1 Cor. 11:27 and 29]).

With Christian Worship: Hidden Flesh

The fact that Christ's life-giving flesh does not fit neatly into Augustine's semiotics is a consequence of the fact that divine carnality does not fit neatly into a Platonist framework. As we saw in chapters 2 and 3, if you try to locate Christ's flesh in Plato's allegory of the cave, you end up seeing the Sun, the supreme Good itself, shining inside the cave. But the problem is not merely Plato's or Augustine's. The divine carnality of Christ is too great a thing to fit into any conceptual framework. It is the humanity of God, divinized, glorified, and exalted, as hidden as God yet as external as any flesh, for Christ is indeed true God and true man in one person, rightly sitting on the throne of God. This, as we have seen in chapter 2, is the very starting point of Christian faith, the focus of Christian worship, and the origin of the doctrine of the Trinity. Everything that is most distinctive, glorious, and puzzling about Christian faith is centered here.

The Protestant debate about the presence of Christ's flesh in the Supper is rooted in a deep question about the presence of Christ's flesh at the right hand of God the Father. What could such presence possibly mean? Calvin, objecting against the Lutheran view, argues that the externality of Christ's flesh means that, like all human flesh, it must be located literally in one place—and that place is in heaven, a great physical distance from any bread and wine on earth. Luther heard very similar objections from earlier Reformed theologians and found them ridiculous. On this point he is emphatically opposed to literalism.

> Now if we ask how they interpret God's "right hand" where Christ sits, I suppose they will dream up for us, as one does for the children, an imaginary heaven in which a golden throne stands, and Christ sits beside the Father in a cowl and golden crown, the way artists paint it.[113]

It is obvious, to Luther's mind, that the right hand of God is not a literal hand with five fingers, the throne of God is not a literal throne made of gold, and therefore Christ in heaven is not located in some literal place far above us. As we might put it today: there is no rocket ship we could take to get there, no planet where we could travel to see him. That kind of presence is not what it means to be at God's right hand, in Luther's reading of Scripture.

> The Scriptures teach us . . . that the right hand of God is not a specific place in which a body must or may be, such as on a golden throne, but is the almighty

113. Luther, *That These Words*, LW 37:55.

power of God, which at one and the same time can be nowhere and yet must be everywhere.[114]

The right hand of God is a figure of speech picturing his divine power, as the throne of God is a figure of speech picturing his sovereignty, and its placement in heaven, far above the earth, is a figure of speech picturing his power and sovereignty over all things. The Old Testament goes further, picturing God's throne room *above* the visible heavens, with the beams of his chamber laid on the waters above the dome of the sky over our heads (Ps. 104:3).[115] The point of the picture is that God is beyond the framework of heaven and earth, not by distance but by power, so that—in another important biblical picture—heaven is his throne but earth is his footstool (Isa. 66:1). His presence in heaven never means his absence from earth, but precisely his sovereignty over the whole creation, both heaven and earth.

The point of the biblical pictures can be restated in terms of worldviews other than the ancient Near Eastern cosmology of the Old Testament. Dante, for example, conveys the same point using the Ptolemaic astronomy of the Middle Ages, when he pictures the place of God located outside the revolving spheres of the visible heavens, in the limitless and unmoving "fiery heaven" of the empyrean, beyond all the planets and stars whose movements measure the passage of time (days measured by the movement of the sun, months by the moon, years by the sun and the stars). Yet the power by which the heavens turn in their huge cosmic dance, giving time and growth and strength and life to things below (as the sun gives new life to the earth every spring), is precisely the love of God "which moves the sun and other stars," as Dante says in the famous concluding line of the whole poem.[116] It is a vivid poetic picture of God located "outside" both space and time yet governing all things within space and time, giving them their temporal life and power and being.

But of course to be outside space cannot literally mean to be *spatially* outside it. The metaphor of "outside" must refer to a nonspatial mode of being, which (as Augustine learned from Plotinus) means that God is present everywhere as a whole, indivisible, not spread out part-by-part in particular places like water in a sponge. Being "outside" space therefore does not mean God is distant from us, but that he is fully present in every place, just

---

114. Luther, *That These Words*, LW 37:57.

115. In the version of ancient Near Eastern cosmology used in most of the Old Testament, the earth was flat and the heavens were a transparent dome (or "firmament" in the language of the King James Version) above which was water, which made the sky blue. To picture the beams of God's chamber laid on top of these waters was therefore to "locate" God beyond both heaven and earth.

116. Dante, *Paradiso* 33:145.

as his eternity does not mean he is absent from the temporal world, but that he is fully present at all times. Luther endorses this Augustinian concept of divine omnipresence, teaching that God is "simultaneously present in all places whole and entire," and insists that it is "beyond our reason and can be maintained only with faith, in the Word."[117] He is evidently unaware that the concept originates with the pagan philosopher Plotinus. What is properly beyond our reason—in the terms I have been using, it cracks open our conceptual frameworks—is Luther's willingness to apply this concept of divine omnipresence to Christ's humanity in the doctrine later known, in technical terms, as the "ubiquity" of Christ's *flesh*.[118]

Whatever metaphysics we develop to speak of the omnipresence of divine power must apply also to the Lord Jesus Christ, living in flesh at God's right hand. There might be more than one plausible metaphysics for this. Luther is undogmatic, indeed rather uninterested, in exactly which metaphysical account of the presence of Christ is best, so long as it is clear that wherever the right hand of God is, there is Christ Jesus in the fullness of his humanity, including his body and blood. As we have seen, that is why Christ's flesh is unlike all other human flesh: incorruptible, indivisible, hidden from sight, and perceptible by faith alone.

Yet precisely because we perceive Christ by faith alone, we cannot perceive him anywhere and everywhere. To find his hidden and exalted flesh we must turn at particular times and places to particular external things consecrated by his word. Only thus can we say, "Here I have thee, according to thy Word." As Luther explains:

> Just as I say of the right hand of God: although this is everywhere, as we may not deny, still because it is also nowhere, as has been said, you can actually grasp it nowhere, unless for your benefit it binds itself to you and summons you to a definite place. This God's right hand does, however, when it enters into the humanity of Christ and dwells there. There you surely find it, otherwise you will run back and forth throughout all creation, groping here and groping there yet never finding, even though it is actually there; for it is not there for you.[119]

Christ's flesh is unique, breaking every metaphysical framework in which our reasoning seeks to place it, whether Augustine's Platonism, or the Ptolemaic astronomy of Luther's day, or our modern science, or the ancient Near Eastern cosmology of the Bible itself. Only faith finds it, hearing Christ's own word as he promises us: This is my body, given for you.

---

117. Luther, *Confession concerning Christ's Supper*, LW 37:216.
118. Luther, *Confession concerning Christ's Supper*, LW 37:219.
119. Luther, *That These Words*, LW 37:68–69.

12

Trinity

God Giving Himself in Person

The Protestant Gospel makes absolutely no sense without the Trinity. That is one of its strengths, theologically speaking, for it grounds Protestant theology in the most fundamental Christian teaching about who God is. The Gospel cannot be a saving word unless the person it gives us is God in the flesh, which is an absurd notion unless the orthodox doctrine of the Trinity is telling us the truth about who God is. We miss the point of the doctrine of the Trinity if we do not recognize that taking hold of Jesus Christ in faith and worship means being united to God in person. We can see the logical connection between Gospel and Trinity more clearly, therefore, if we think further about the consequences of Luther's account of how the word gives us a person and about the epistemology of hearing this entails. This shall lead us in the present chapter to defend the Augustinian doctrine of the Trinity that Luther took for granted, but also to be critical of the use to which Augustine put the doctrine in his spirituality.

Faith and Love

We are justified by faith alone, according to Protestant theology, because it is faith, not love, that receives the person the Gospel has to give. This is the great difference that Luther makes in the Augustinian theology of grace: instead of coming to God by the grace-filled power of love, he insists we receive God by the grace-filled power of faith. The way of grace, in other words, is not our way to God but God's way to us. Faith still results in love for God, as Augustine teaches, but love is no longer the force of attraction that moves us toward God and unites us with him. The love of God and neighbor that grows in us is the fruit of the faith that *alone* unites us with God in Christ, making all the decisive changes in our hearts, causing us to become a good tree that can bear good fruit—which is to say, an inwardly good person, transformed by the grace of Christ, who can do works of love.

As we saw in chapter 8, in Luther's account of the process of justification, faith means repeatedly beginning anew, as if every day were Christmas when the newborn king comes for the first time to us helpless sinners who cannot come to him. It is precisely by always starting at square one, receiving Christ by faith alone, that we grow in the righteousness of faith (the "alien" righteousness which makes us who we are as Christians) as well as works of love (the "proper" righteousness which is for the sake of our neighbors). Our Lord Jesus keeps coming to us in the Gospel, giving himself to us, making us new, living in us and producing in us the works of love.

This has always raised important questions about the place of love for God in Protestant theology. The deep Augustinian notion that faith seeks understanding by love—so that all love of truth is ultimately the love of God—motivates a kind of spirituality that is not Protestant, for in Protestantism faith, love, and truth are related in a different way. Of course love desires its Beloved, but according to Luther love for God only gets what it desires by faith in his word. We take hold of Christ by clinging to the Gospel because it is the promise of God—and God is true to his promise even though every man be a liar (Rom. 3:4), including our sinful selves who love God only half-heartedly. So in contrast to Augustine, it is faith, not love, that unites us to our Beloved. It is (once again) like a marriage: no amount of love makes two people married if they have not given and received wedding vows, which are the promises that establish the covenant of marriage. Marital love does not establish this covenant but flows from it, for there is no married love without married persons, who only begin to exist *as* married persons because of the marriage promises. In just this way, Luther teaches that the Christian person must exist before doing good works, with the implication that faith comes before love.[1]

According to Luther, we have a divine Beloved not because of our love but because our Beloved has given himself to us, so that in faith we can say: "My

1. See the series of analogies illustrating the relation of person and work in Luther, *The Freedom of a Christian*, LW 31:360–63.

Beloved is mine and I am his."[2] Faith alone can say this, for our imperfect love is never worthy of such a Beloved and never has the power to make him ours. This is why Luther describes faith as a passive righteousness:[3] unlike Augustinian love, it is not something we do to come to God. Rather, it believes that God has already come to us. Its only work and activity is to take hold of the promise that tells us the Beloved is already ours, because he has given himself to us in his promise, as a bridegroom gives himself to his bride.

This has profound consequences for preaching, which are encapsulated in Luther's distinction between law and Gospel. When the Gospel is preached, it is not—as one old saying has it—like one beggar telling another beggar where to get bread. Telling people what to do to get what they need is law, not Gospel. It is unwittingly cruel, for a beggar may die of starvation before he manages to get himself to where the bread is. Preachers need not be so cruel, because they can preach the Gospel instead, which gives a beggar nothing less than Christ himself, the bread of life, in person. As ministers of the word they have the authority to promise sinners, on the basis of Christ's own word, that he is theirs. Thus the Gospel is not one beggar telling another beggar where to get bread, but one beggar actually giving another beggar bread. In the sacrament, on the basis of Christ's own promise, one beggar can put the bread of life right into another beggar's mouth.

Spirituality and God in Person

Receiving God in the flesh becomes the basis of a different kind of spirituality from the one we examined in chapter 3, where Augustine takes Christ as man to be the way to Christ as God. For Augustine, faith must seek understanding because believing in Christ in the flesh merely puts us on the road to a pure intellectual vision of God that has no need of flesh. By contrast, the goal of Luther's spirituality is not for the mind to see God but for God to be ours in person—a goal already achieved by the gift of faith, because God incarnate is formed in our hearts when we believe the Gospel. Hence Christ as man is not the way to Christ as God, but rather Christ as man is the way that God is given to us in person, in his own flesh.

Faith alone receives the goal of spirituality, because only by faith do we take hold of this one person in his word. Knowing and loving God are a result of the goal of spirituality being achieved by the sheer gift of God, which is

2. See Luther's definition of true faith in his Theses on Faith, thesis 22, *LW* 34:110.

3. "Passive righteousness" is a key description of the righteousness of God that is ours by faith alone in Luther's important preface to his 1535 Galatians Commentary, *LW* 26:4–12.

to say: achieved by grace alone and received through faith alone. The whole Christian life therefore grows out of what is received by faith alone, which is Christ himself given in the Gospel. Works of love do not bring us to Christ as God but are the work of Christ as God within us, already present in the heart because we believe the Gospel. This is why, as we saw in the previous chapter, the inward gift of the Spirit directs our attention outward: to find God in person is to find him in the flesh, which is to find him externally. As the Eucharist in particular shows us, we find his flesh not by seeing but by hearing, for he dwells in our hearts precisely to the extent that we take hold of him by faith in his external word. To have this one person in us is to have all that is God, because the person of Christ has the fullness of divine being, inseparable from the person of God the Father and the Holy Spirit.

In this way, Luther's outward turn to the Gospel makes relationship with God distinctly personal. Instead of seeking an inner vision of the Truth like the eye's enjoyment of light,[4] it means learning to trust the word of someone who promises to be your Beloved, a person who is your friend sharing with you everything he is and has. As in all friendship, your friend is someone you cannot know by turning inward and looking inside yourself. Even loving him is not sufficient to give you knowledge of him. He must give himself to be known by giving you his word, speaking and testifying to who he is and will be, as in the great biblical wedding vow that unites the LORD God to Israel in covenant: "I will take you to be my people, and I will be your God."[5] This is why "faith comes from hearing, and hearing through the word of Christ" (Rom. 10:17). Like any beloved person who is other than you, God incarnate becomes yours as you pay attention to what is outside yourself. Hence to know God is to believe an external word, listening to what another person has to say for himself when he says, "I will take you to be my people," or, "This is my body, given for you." Like the inner experience of music, the presence of the beloved in the depths of the heart depends on what comes from outside, through the ears.

Protestant theology thus presents to the Christian tradition a proposal about how the knowledge and love of God are ours through faith in the external word of the Gospel. Protestants are convinced that from the beginning, this has always been the power of Christian faith. All Luther's theology of the Gospel does is make explicit how this happens: how the Holy Spirit

---

4. As in Augustine's account of beatitude in *City of God* 8:8, discussed in chap. 3, "Strengths and Weaknesses of Platonism."

5. Exod. 6:7 (cf. Lev. 26:12). The "new covenant" in Jer. 31:31–33 and the "everlasting covenant" in Ezek. 37:26–27 are a renewal and deepening of this same promise, not a repudiation of it.

has always been using the word of God to give people Christ and thus bring them to God the Father.

To speak of God giving himself in person is not to deny the usefulness of impersonal Platonist categories like immutable Truth, supreme Good, and eternal Beauty. But it is to say that we perceive the ultimate Truth, Goodness, and Beauty most clearly by believing the story of one particular person, Jesus Christ.[6] This is of course an extraordinary claim, which Plato could not have anticipated: that the intelligible form of all things, from which comes all that is true and good and beautiful, is best seen in the life and death and resurrection of one man, who sits now at the right hand of God the Father and will come again in glory. But if the Protestant theology is right, this has always been what the Christian doctrine of the Trinity is about.

In that sense, again, Protestant theology is not saying anything new. It is a reprise of the most central, distinctive, and extraordinary thing that Christian faith says about who God is. As we saw in chapter 2, the doctrine of the Trinity arose from Christian reflection about how it is possible to worship this one man without being idolaters. The doctrine of the Trinity is the teaching about who God is that makes sense of the Gospel and what it tells us about Christ. It supports the outward turn toward this one person in whom we find the Truth and Goodness and Beauty that is God. It is therefore also the way to understand Christian spirituality as a relationship with God in person, someone who can be trusted as a friend and received as a Beloved. Christian faith is distinctively personal, not because it is experienced in the depth of the heart like every strong feeling—as if "personal" simply meant "emotional"— but because it is about this one person, Jesus Christ.

Three Persons

Talking about God in person gets complicated in Christian theology, however, because in the doctrine of the Trinity it has become customary to speak of God as three persons. But it is not quite as complicated as it is sometimes made to look. The phrase "three persons" does not designate the object of Christian faith—or rather, it designates it in a very abstract way that is not essential to Christian faith, but is useful for some purposes in Christian theology. Unlike the phrase "one God," the phrase "three persons" is not part of the creed. It belongs to a theology whose aim is, in every case, to direct our attention to

6. That Christ is the Truth has been a key claim of Christian theology ever since John 14:6. For a philosophical elaboration of the claim, see Marshall, *Trinity and Truth*. For a meditation on Christ as the supreme form of Beauty, see Balthasar, *Seeing the Form*.

one object of Christian faith, not three. As a consequence, the word "God" itself tends to be rather vague in Christian usage. It can refer to God the Father or God the Son or God the Holy Spirit, or to the one God who is nothing other than Father, Son, and Holy Spirit. If you want to know what Christian theology really means by the word "God," therefore, you have to direct your attention in worship to the Father, the Son, and the Holy Spirit. You can't really say what Christians believe in without using some version of that three-fold name, as is done throughout Christian worship as well as in the Creed.

But by the same token, you don't really need the phrase "three persons." You can be a perfectly good trinitarian Christian without ever having heard that God is three persons or "three in one"—or for that matter without ever hearing the word "Trinity." All you need, in order to believe in the holy Trin-ity, is right there in the Creed, which never uses the word "three" or "Trinity" and always speaks of God in the singular, not the plural. Still, if you want to reflect theologically on what makes Christian faith Christian, you will find the phrase "three persons" indispensably handy, for reasons that have to do with the history of Christian doctrine. Hence to explain theologically the sense in which, through the Gospel of Christ, God gives himself to us in person, we need to say something about the history of trinitarian doctrine.

Strikingly, the main reason the word "person" has become an important term in modern thought is that it was used in the doctrine of the Trinity.[7] In ancient thought "person" (Latin *persona* or Greek *prosopon*) was not an important term in descriptions of human nature, which was conceived rather in terms of soul and body. At the core of the concept of a human being was the soul, spirit, mind, or heart, not personality or personhood. In fact the word "person" had not yet acquired the meanings and implications that have developed in modern usage. To use the word in the ancient world is not to talk about someone's personality or consciousness or inner experience, but to refer to them from a distinctively external perspective. Originally, *persona* meant "mask," from the verb *per-sonare*, literally "to sound through," because of how someone's voice sounded through a mask. The term came to be used in the theater because ancient plays were performed by actors wearing masks, which indicated the role they were playing on stage. There was a Ulysses mask, a Helen mask, a Dionysus mask, and so on, each representing a differ-ent person in the play. Hence to this day, the list of characters in a playbill is often called *dramatis personae*, literally "the drama's masks."

Loosely connected to the dramatic sense of the term "person" is a gram-matical sense, still in use when we talk about first-person, second-person,

7. See Cary, "Person before God."

and third-person pronouns or verb forms. In a drama, one character speaks to another in a way that many others can hear, as *I* (the first person) speak to *you* (the second person), overheard by *him* or *her* (a third person).[8] What all persons have in common is that in gendered languages we do not refer to them as neuter but as masculine or feminine. In Latin, for example, a person may be called *unus* (masculine for "one") or *una* (feminine for "one") but not *unum* (neuter for "one"). To put it in English, we could say: "person" always means some*one*, not some*thing*.[9] Hence Tertullian, the third-century church father who introduced the term *persona* into trinitarian theology, notes that Father, Son, and Holy Spirit are one, in the sense that they are *unum* but not *unus*.[10] Loosely translated, these three are one, but not the same someone.

In the Bible, God is portrayed as a person in both the dramatic and the grammatical senses of the term. He is someone who speaks to another one, a first person who speaks to a second person with words that can be heard by third persons. He is one who enters into relations of covenant and promise with other persons, one whose word is to be believed and obeyed, but also one to whom other persons may address words of appeal, complaint, thanks, and praise. And when the Son of God comes into the world, he also is a person who speaks in prayer and praise to God his Father, and who in turn is spoken to. "You are my beloved Son; with you I am well pleased," says the first person to the second person, and many third persons—ourselves—learn what is said (Mark 1:11). Elsewhere in the drama, the Son tells his disciples he will ask the Father to send them another one—another *unus*, we could say—who will be their Comforter, the Holy Spirit (John 14:16). So God is found in three different persons in the biblical drama, which is to say, each one of these three persons is God.[11]

To believe the Gospel of Christ is to find oneself in the same drama with these three persons: as those to whom the Son promises that the Father will send his Spirit (John 14:26), as those receiving the promised Spirit poured

8. Tertullian, *Against Praxeas*, chap. 11, develops this connection between dramatic and grammatical senses of *persona* in connection with the Father, Son, and Holy Spirit.

9. For this approach to the notion of "person," see Spaemann, *Persons*. For a philosophically sophisticated account of the irreducible importance of the concept of "person" in sociology, see Smith, *What Is a Person?*

10. Tertullian, *Against Praxeas*, chap. 25: "These three are *unum*, not *unus*." Cf. likewise chap. 22, where Tertullian points out that when Jesus says, "I and the Father are one" (John 10:30), he uses *unum*, not *unus* (the original Greek, likewise, is neuter, not masculine).

11. Ancient readers identifying who is speaking to whom in a dramatic narrative or poetic text were engaging in what has been labeled "prosopological exegesis" (from *prosopon*, the Greek equivalent to Latin *persona*). Bates, *Birth of the Trinity*, has recently uncovered prosopological exegesis being used by the New Testament and early Christian writers to identify the persons of the Trinity speaking in the Old Testament Scriptures.

out by the Son sitting at the right hand of God (Acts 2:33), as those who are given eternal life with Christ, whom the Spirit declares to be the Son of God by the power of his resurrection (Rom. 1:4). We could say: in Christ, God has entered the drama of human history. But it might be more accurate to say that through Christ human history is caught up in the drama between Father, Son, and Holy Spirit unfolding in the Gospel. For to receive Christ in faith is to participate in his story and share his life. By faith alone we abide in Christ as he abides in us (John 15:5), so that our life is hidden with Christ in God (Col. 3:3), and when he appears we shall appear with him and be like him (1 John 3:2). Being incorporated into Christ's body, we are brought into the drama that is the eternal life of the Trinity.[12]

So the word "person," which describes the life of Father, Son, and Holy Spirit in dramatic terms, has its uses in trinitarian theology. It assists the outward turn of the Gospel by directing our attention to persons outside ourselves, those in whose drama we participate. But it reveals no secrets about the being of God and invites no speculations about God's inner experience. It has nothing to say about God's "personality" in the modern sense of the term, and indeed does not even imply that there is such a thing. The term is much more modest than that, as well as much more abstract. Knowing God does not mean understanding the concept of a divine person, as if we came to know God through metaphysical inquiry about the nature of personhood—still less through psychological inquiry into God's personality traits. Rather, we know God by participating in the drama of Father, Son, and Spirit through faith in the Gospel. Philosophical inquiry has its place, for there are some useful abstract things to say about the three divine persons, as there are also about the immateriality and eternity of God's being (*ousia*), as we saw in chapter 1. But none of these things gives us knowledge of who God is. For that, we need to believe God's own word, which is how we learn what God himself has to tell us about who he is.

As the church kept listening to the word of God in its regular worship of Christ over the first few centuries of its life, it came to articulate the doctrine of the Trinity using terms like "person" and "being" in ways that reflect the conviction that the philosophers got a number of things right about divine immateriality, immutability, and eternity. But the orthodox church also hedged these terms about with strong warnings concerning their limitations and

---

12. For an explicitly dramatic theology, see the massive and influential project of Catholic theologian Hans Urs von Balthasar, *Theodrama*. In a different but related vein, Lutheran theologian Robert Jenson in his *Systematic Theology* contends that the identity of God is a narrated dramatic coherence. The crucial difference is that Balthasar makes the effort to retain, and Jenson rejects, a broadly Platonist view of immutability as an essential attribute of the being of God. In this respect Luther himself remains with the Catholics.

indeed their inadequacy. The being of God is incomprehensible, the church fathers insisted, and we certainly cannot define what it is (an important point made repeatedly against the heretic Eunomius by the church fathers whose thinking led to the standard form of the Nicene Creed at the Council of Constantinople in 381). A generation later Augustine pointed out the limitations and inadequacy of the term *persona*, which Latin theology used to answer the question, "Three *what*?" We use the term, Augustine warns us, not to say what kind of thing there are three of in the Trinity, but because it is better than having nothing to say.[13] We can't say there are "three gods," but neither can we say there are three things of any other kind. No term for a species or kind of thing can be used in the plural in the doctrine of the Trinity, for there is no *kind* of thing that there are three of in God.[14] A century later, a Latin confession of faith inspired by Augustine illustrated this point by saying, "The Father is eternal, the Son is eternal, and the Holy Spirit is eternal, but there are not three Eternals, but one Eternal."[15] The confession proceeds to say the same thing using the terms "uncreated," "immeasurable," "omnipotent," and "God." All of these terms can be used of the Triune God, Father, Son, and Holy Spirit, only in the singular. We can say, "The Father is omnipotent, the Son is omnipotent, and the Holy Spirit is omnipotent," but we cannot draw the conclusion that there are three Omnipotents.[16] And likewise, the confession insists, "The Father is God, the Son is God, and the Holy Spirit is God, and yet there are not three Gods, but God is one."[17]

Thus the term "person" turns out to be handy precisely because it is not a species term, a word that could be used for a specific *kind* of thing. In that way it is unlike "human" or "god," or for that matter "nymph" or "satyr." All of these are ancient terms for kinds of creatures who are persons in the dramatic sense—they could show up as *dramatis personae* in an ancient drama. But "person" is not a classification that includes all these kinds, the way a genus or general biological classification like "mammal" includes species such

13. Augustine, *Trinity* 5:9.10. In Edmund Hill's translation: "When you ask, 'Three what?' human speech labors under a great dearth of words. So we say three persons, not in order to say that precisely, but in order not to be reduced to silence."

14. Augustine, *Trinity* 7:4.7–9. See Cross, *"Quid tres?"*

15. The *Quicunque Vult*, or "Athanasian Creed," §§10–11, my translation from Schaff, *Creeds of Christendom* 2:67. The name *Quicunque Vult*, taken from the first two words of the document, is more accurate than the traditional title, "Athanasian Creed," since it is not exactly a creed and it certainly does not originate with Athanasius.

16. The *Quicunque Vult*, or "Athanasian Creed," §§13–14, in Schaff, *Creeds of Christendom* 2:67.

17. The *Quicunque Vult*, or "Athanasian Creed," §§15–16, in Schaff, *Creeds of Christendom* 2:67.

as humans, dogs, and cats. Rather than a classification or general category, "person" is a term for anyone who can play a role in a drama, of whatever species or category. A talking dog, if there were such a thing, would be a person. Similarly, in science fiction today, we often imagine weirdly shaped extraterrestrial beings who are persons but are not human. They are not members of the same biological species as we are, and they have no relation to any other animal species on earth, so we could not classify them as "mammals" or "reptiles" or any other category in the biology of our planet. But they can play a role in the same drama as humans do, and that means that when we imagine them, we are imagining persons.

The fact that the phrase "three persons" does not tell us what kind of thing the Father is, or the Son or the Spirit, is part of what makes it a handy grammatical placeholder for what is three in God, on the rare occasions when we want to do what the creed does not do, and count to three after talking about Father, Son, and Holy Spirit. When we do that in Western theology, "person" is the noun that goes with "three," as "God" is the noun that goes with "one." And we can certainly say that God is three in one (it is perfectly orthodox to do so), but it does not tell us much at all about the Trinity. After all, this is the same vocabulary we use when we say there are three peas in a pod. So teaching the doctrine of the Trinity does not mean explaining how it is that God can be "three in one." That phrase, legitimate as it is, does not tell us much about the doctrine or what it is about.

A Doctrine to Make Sense of the Gospel

It is not important to explain how God can be "three in one," but it is important to show how faith in Father, Son, and Holy Spirit is faith in one God. Hence the important thing to say about God as three persons is that we cannot think of three divine persons the same way we think of three human persons. Three human persons make three humans, but three divine persons do not make three gods. This is because the doctrine of the Trinity has a logic that does not invite ordinary counting. We could say: in the Trinity, things don't add up.

No one grasped this more astutely than Augustine, from whose writings we can extract a summary of what I call the "bare bones logic" of the doctrine of the Trinity. It is a summary that has no need of the words "three," "persons," or "being."[18] The only substantive terms required are the word "God" and the

18. I have extracted the following summary by combining things Augustine says in *Trinity* 8:1.1 and *On Christian Doctrine* 1:4.5. A very similar summary was constructed from the *Quicunque Vult* by Richard Cartwright, "Problem of the Trinity," 188.

threefold name: Father, Son, and Holy Spirit. The summary consists of a mere seven statements, containing two triads and a final statement as a clincher. The first triad names the God in whom Christians believe:

1. The Father is God.
2. The Son is God.
3. The Holy Spirit is God.

The second triad makes it clear that these are not three names for the same thing:

4. The Father is not the Son.
5. The Son is not the Holy Spirit.
6. The Holy Spirit is not the Father.

Then the clincher insists on monotheism:

7. There is only one God.

The elegance of this summary lies to a large extent in what it does not say. It does not count up to three or identify any kind of thing that there are three of in God. It does not make the mistake of saying that Father or Son or Holy Spirit is "part of" God. (It tells us the Father *is* God—not *part of* God—and likewise the Son and the Spirit.) It even avoids formulations that are orthodox but distract from the point of the doctrine, such as saying there are three persons *in* God or, conversely, that God is *in* three persons, both of which are orthodox but not very helpful. And it shows that handy technical labels, such as "person" and "being," are not essential; the labels are expressions of a more fundamental logic, whose purpose is not to explain how God is three in one but to make sense of the drama of the Gospel.

The logic of the doctrine of the Trinity needs the whole drama of the Gospel to put flesh on its bones: the whole story of Jesus Christ, his coming from God the Father in the power of the Holy Spirit, his being promised by the prophets of Israel as the fulfillment of the covenant, his incarnation in the womb of Mary, his birth and life and death and resurrection and ascension and coming again in glory, his being head over all things for the sake of the church, his Body. The bare bones summary serves a purpose like the list of names, the *dramatis personae*, on a playbill. It is no substitute for the drama itself, but it does help you keep track of who's who and who's doing what.

And the mere label, "Trinity"—like the label *dramatis personae*—is far less informative than the names it introduces.

The reason we have a doctrine of the Trinity in the first place is to make sense of the Gospel and the persons in it. The doctrine of the Trinity does this mainly by helping us make sense of the doctrine of the incarnation, the teaching that one person, Jesus Christ, is the Son of God incarnate—which is to say that this one person is both God and man, a human being who has the same divine being as God the Father. To combine the doctrines of incarnation and Trinity in this way is to use one mystery to make sense of another; it should not be mistaken for an attempt to explain how it is all possible. But the two doctrines together do clarify some things, supporting key convictions of the Christian faith and excluding bad ideas and false teachings.

And there are a lot of bad ideas to exclude when you start doing what Christians have always done, worshiping a man who sits on the throne of God. Is this idolatry, worshiping the creature rather than the Creator? No—the doctrine of the Trinity answers—for this one whom we worship is the Son of God, and the Son *is* God (statement 2). So are we saying that Jesus is no different from God the Father? No—the doctrine of the Trinity answers again—because the Father is not the Son (statement 4). Then are we saying they are two different Gods? No again, comes the answer, for there is only one God (statement 7). This is the logical structure embedded in Christian worship from the beginning, but it took centuries to make the logic explicit.

It was inevitable that difficult questions had to be answered about the logic of Christian worship. The question, "Is Jesus the same as God the Father?" had to be answered with a clear no but also a partial yes. For on the one hand, the Father is not the Son (statement 4), but on the other hand the Son is God (statement 2), and there is only one God (statement 7), so he is not a different God from the Father. The logical conclusion to draw is that in his divine attributes he is exactly the same as the Father: equally divine, equally eternal, equally omnipotent, and equally the Creator of heaven and earth. As we saw in chapter 2, this is what the Council of Nicaea had in mind in AD 325 when it introduced the term "being" (*ousia*) into the doctrine of the Trinity by teaching that the Son is "of one being" (*homoousios*) with the Father. This key phrase reinforces the stark affirmation of statement 2: not only is it true that the Son is God ("true God from true God," as the creed says), but the Son is God in exactly the same sense that the Father is God, having everything that belongs to the divine being of the Father. He is not a different God created by or subordinate to the Father. If he were, he would not deserve to be worshiped equally with the Father. And the bishops at the

Council of Nicaea clearly saw that this would violate the fundamental logic of Christian faith and worship.

Likewise, as we saw in chapter 2, about a century after Nicaea another difficult question arose: Can Mary be called the mother of God? In the end, the same basic logic prevailed: Mary's baby is the Son of God, and (as statement 2 says) the Son is God. When she gave birth to him, therefore, she gave birth to God. So Mary is indeed the mother of God. But of course this does not mean she originates the divine being or *ousia* of the Son of God. So here again there is a kind of yes and no, because what needs to be said about Jesus' divine being is different from what needs to be said about his humanity. In his divine being he is God (statement 2), but his humanity makes it clear that he is not the Father (statement 4). In the standard formula, he is one person having two natures, both divine and human. But the Nicene Creed's language is simpler and subtler than this later formula, with no need of the technical terms "person" and "nature." The key point is made by a series of verbs in the second article of the creed that all have the same grammatical subject. The same one who is eternally begotten of the Father or (to translate more precisely) "born from the Father before all ages," and who is therefore "true God from true God," is also the same one (the same grammatical subject) who for our salvation "came down from heaven and was incarnate by the Holy Spirit from the Virgin Mary and was made human."[19] The same one thus has two births, as Cyril of Alexandria emphasized. The church fathers at the Council of Chalcedon in 451 underlined this point by using the phrase "the same one" (*ton auton*) seven times in their brief statement on the doctrine of the incarnation.[20] The repetition is so emphatic and obtrusive that English versions often fail to translate every occurrence of the phrase. But they should, for it makes the point clearer than abstractions like "person" and "nature." We are talking about the same someone when we say "born of the Virgin Mary" as when we say "born from the Father before all ages."

A century later, as we saw, the church tackled an even more difficult question: Was it God who suffered and died on the cross? Once again the logic of Christian worship ultimately prevailed. The Son of God whom we worship equally with the Father is no less truly God than the Father is, and he is the same person who suffered and died on the cross. As the Second Council of Constantinople put it in 553, "Our Lord Jesus Christ who was crucified in the flesh is true God."[21] This is the same logic as the creed, as read by the Council

---

19. For the Greek and Latin texts, see Schaff, *Creeds of Christendom* 2:57–61.

20. In this understanding of the Chalcedonian statement as essentially a reading of the Nicene Creed, I am much indebted to McGuckin, *Saint Cyril of Alexandria*, 233–43.

21. Leith, *Creeds of the Churches*, 50.

of Chalcedon: the same someone who is "true God from true God" is the same one who "was crucified under Pontius Pilate, suffered and was buried." But again there is a "no" as well as a "yes." The Father did not suffer and die on the cross, for the Father is not the same one as the Son (a very important consequence of statement 4). Hence the doctrine of the Trinity allows the church to affirm Deipassionism (that God suffered) but not Patripassionism (that the Father suffered).

To speak of the suffering and death of God is to speak of the person of Christ, the same one who was both eternally begotten of the Father and born of the virgin Mary. When God died on the cross, there was no loss of his divine nature or being, but rather the divine Son in all his unchangeable eternity—the same one who is eternally begotten of the Father—was the same one as that dead man, not a different person, so that for three days it was true to say, "that dead man is the eternal God," just as it was true some thirty years earlier to say, "that baby in Mary's womb is the eternal God." This is where the great formula we learned from Gregory of Nazianzus in chapter 2 leads in the end: "What he was, he remained; what he was not, he assumed."[22] The Son of God, remaining true God from true God, immortal and eternal, assumed or took up our mortality and made it truly his own; hence even during the three days when he was dead, Jesus was still the immortal, eternal God. Our language reaches the borders of intelligibility here: a dead man is the immortal God. Yet here too the doctrine of the Trinity is not senseless but helps make sense of what Christians need to say about Christ: that the Son of God, who is not the same one as the Father, chose in his eternity to be the same one as this man in his life and death and resurrection and exaltation to the right hand of the Father. Just as Jesus' human life is the life taken up and lived by this one person, the Son of God, so his death is the death that the Son of God took up and made truly his own.

Another formulation we encountered in chapter 2 points to something similar: Cyril of Alexandria's description of the Son of God as one who "suffered impassibly,"[23] a paradox that could also be described as his "impassible passion." Since "passion" is related to "action" as passivity is to activity (or, in older English, as suffering is to doing), I suggest that what we have here is a unique combination of divine activity and human passivity. Augustine put it this way, emphasizing the point that the activity of the Trinity is always the activity of all three persons: "The Father of course did not suffer, but

---

22. Gregory of Nazianzus, Oration 29:19 (the third "Theological Oration").
23. Cyril of Alexandria, "Scholia on the Incarnation" §35, in McGuckin, *Saint Cyril of Alexandria*, 332.

the suffering of the Son was the work of both the Father and the Son."[24] He could even go on to say that the suffering of the Son was "*done* by the Son" as well as "*done* by the Father."[25] The strange language here gets at the fact that the suffering of the Son of God was not, at root, something *done to* him (for nothing is done to the impassible God) but something *done by* him, something he actively *did*, as the one act of the one God, Father, Son, and Holy Spirit working together. What he *did* was choose from eternity (i.e., in his divine nature) that the Son would be none other than this one human sufferer, Jesus Christ.

Hence the suffering of God is radically unlike ours in that, in the most fundamental sense, it is his own doing. He does not merely suffer it, enduring it passively as something done to him—which indeed does happen to him in his human nature when he is nailed to the cross—but also and more fundamentally, he actively takes up this human suffering and makes it his own,[26] out of pure love for us, in a way that is possible only for the impassible God. So "impassible suffering" means that in God alone, his suffering is fully his own doing. Of all the human beings who have ever suffered, only the incarnate Son of God chose from the beginning to make suffering his own, just as only he, of all human beings who were ever born, *chose* to be born, to be human and mortal and vulnerable. The rest of us are in no position to make our suffering our own in this fundamental way, and thus our suffering is less truly ours than God's suffering is his. In that sense God suffers more truly than anyone else.

And it is this God who is given to us, in person, in the Gospel of Jesus Christ.

The Use of Trinitarian Metaphysics

What we have seen is a pattern in the history of trinitarian doctrine: because Christians worship the man Jesus Christ as a person who rightly sits on the throne of God, difficult metaphysical questions about the being of God arise and need some kind of answer. This means there is a place for metaphysical inquiry as intellectual service to Christ—for example when we clarify how it is that Christians can believe that Father, Son, and Holy Spirit is one God. It

24. Non est quidem passus Pater, sed Filius: passionem tamen Filii et Pater et Filius operatus est (Augustine, Sermon 52:8).

25. Passionem Filii et a Patre factam et a Filio factam (Augustine, Sermon 52:12).

26. Cf. Cyril's formulation: "He impassibly appropriated the suffering of his own flesh" (third letter to Nestorius, §6, in McGuckin, *Saint Cyril of Alexandria*, 270). Similarly, Maximus the Confessor says, "Divinely, if I may so speak, he experienced suffering, for he suffered willingly" (*Ambigua* 5 [PG 91:1056], translated as *Difficulty* 5 in Louth, *Maximus the Confessor*, 176).

would be a mistake, however, to reverse the connection and take the worship of Christ as a clue to the ultimate metaphysical meaning of the doctrine of Trinity, as if the goal of Christian faith were to see how God can be both three and one, or to understand what "person" means when we say there are three of them in the Trinity. That would put metaphysics in the position of defining the goal of Christian thought. It would make the mistake of putting the Gospel in the service of metaphysical inquiry, rather than the other way round. And that would be misunderstanding what it means to know who God is.

To know who God is, is to know God as a person. This is possible because the man Jesus Christ is God in person—a human person in the same ordinary sense that we are, and also the same person who is eternally begotten of the Father, true God from true God. We know God, Father, Son, and Holy Spirit, by faith in this one person, as well as by the worship, prayer, and praise that flow from this faith, involving us in the drama of the life of the Triune God. Because this is all the Spirit's work in us, it is the focus of Christian spirituality as well as the point of the doctrine of the Trinity: everything grows out of the outward turn in faith to the person of Christ in the flesh. Metaphysical inquiries into the triune being of God lead beyond this, because abstract questions do arise about how it is possible to say that this person is God. Christian theology needs to give a responsible answer to such questions, but they are not the road to a deeper or more personal knowledge of God. For there is a difference between knowing a person and knowing what a person is; it is the difference between knowing someone and knowing something. Trinitarian metaphysics concerns knowing something about God, whereas trinitarian worship concerns knowing God. The metaphysics has a beauty of its own, hinting at the incomprehensible depths of the being of God, but it should not be used to set up a spirituality that aims to take us beyond faith in the person of God incarnate.

In this regard, the metaphysics of the Trinity is like the metaphysics of logic itself. You can think logically without ever having heard of the discipline of logic, just as you can speak grammatically without ever studying grammar, and in the same way you can be a believer in the Trinity without ever learning technical trinitarian vocabulary such as "Trinity" or "three persons." Still, learning logic can help you think more logically, just as studying grammar can help you speak more clearly, and learning the technical trinitarian vocabulary can enrich your understanding of trinitarian faith. What is more, if you have a knack for abstract thought, the sheer beauty of logical theory can become an object of contemplation and a source of intellectual joy, as mathematical theories are for mathematicians. And something similar can happen when theologians contemplate trinitarian doctrine. But when that does happen, the doctrine is cut loose from the original grounds for studying it. Just as the logician contemplating the pure abstract beauty of logical theory is leaving behind or soaring beyond the simple desire to speak and think logically, so the theologian contemplating the metaphysical beauty of trinitarian doctrine is going beyond the faith that brings together a congregation to worship in the name of the Father, the Son, and the Holy Spirit. This cutting loose or going beyond is what I mean by calling it "abstract."

The abstract contemplation of trinitarian metaphysics may well evoke a kind of devotion—and so, for that matter, may the love of abstract logical theory, which pays homage to the *Logos* of God, the divine Reason from which comes the rational discipline of logic (the Greek word *logos* in John 1:1 can be translated both "reason" and "word," and is the word from which we get our word "logic"). Both kinds of contemplation have their legitimate joys, but neither one is a way to the knowledge of who God is. Most importantly, the contemplation of trinitarian metaphysics, legitimate as it is, should not be confused with the goal to which the church's worship ultimately leads. If you are a Platonist, you may well think that the soaring ascent to a contemplative vision of the eternal *Logos* or divine Reason is the real meaning and goal of the discipline of logic. Likewise, if you are a Christian Platonist, you may come to think that the contemplation of the eternal Trinity, quite apart from the incarnation of God in the man Jesus, is the ultimate goal of Christian faith, life, and worship. A serious choice lies here—two diverging theological paths—and I think Luther takes us along a different path from Augustine.

This brings us back to the criticism of Augustine's Christian Platonism in chapter 3, this time from a specifically trinitarian perspective. Augustine's astute grasp of the logical and metaphysical issues in the doctrine of the Trinity remains a permanent gift to the Christian tradition, but his thinking about the Trinity still takes the form of an inward turn and spiritual ascent, a movement "in then up," in which Christ in the flesh is not the goal but the way of ascent—the means by which the heart is purified so as to see the being of God in a Platonist intellectual vision. This means that in Augustine, Platonism ends up defining the goal of Christian faith. In fact, in his treatise *The Trinity* Augustine uses a quotation from Plato to explain what the goal of Christian faith is. "Truth is to faith as eternity is to what has a beginning," he says, quoting Plato's *Timaeus*.[27] What has a beginning is temporal, which means it eventually passes away; so faith, for Augustine, is an aspect

---

27. Augustine, *Trinity* 4:18.24. Augustine is quoting Cicero's translation of Plato's *Timaeus* 29c. The original Greek could be translated more closely: "As being is to becoming, so truth is to belief." In either case, the basic contrast is between unchanging truth and temporal belief.

of the mortal condition we are hoping to overcome. Hence as Christians expect mortality to give way to eternal life, he says, they also long for faith to give way to the vision of truth "in all its clarity, which is as distant from our faith as eternity is from mortality."[28] Developing a Christian interpretation of Plato's point, Augustine tells us that the usefulness of Christian faith in this mortal life is that "we now put faith in *things done in time on our behalf* and thus are purified, so that when we come to vision, eternity may replace mortality as *truth replaces faith*."[29] The "things done in time on our behalf" are Christ's human life, death, resurrection, and ascension, which Augustine elsewhere calls the "temporal dispensation," equivalent to what is called in Greek the "economy" (*oikonomia*) of salvation.[30] So faith in Christ's human life, according to Augustine's Christian Platonism, puts us on a road of purification that arrives in the end at a vision of truth that faith itself is not capable of. Christian hope, for Augustine, means expecting that the vision of God "replaces faith" in the end, precisely because Platonist vision is the goal of Christian faith.

Hearing the Other

Here I think Luther's theology of the Gospel serves to correct Augustine in a fundamental way. For Luther, true knowledge of God is not like an eye enjoying the light or a mind enjoying the vision of Truth. It does not have the immediacy of "seeing for yourself" but the opacity of relying on what another person has to say to you. In Luther's theology, we do not know God without believing his word, which means we must hear what this person, this Beloved, tells us about who he is. Luther's theology thus relies on what I called, in the previous chapter, an epistemology of hearing, because it makes our knowledge dependent on "hearing the word," in the sense of learning what another person has to say, whether by reading or literally hearing. It is an epistemology of secondhand knowledge, which is the kind of knowledge we have of other persons, whom we cannot know without their say-so.

28. Augustine, *Trinity* 4:18.24.

29. Augustine, *Trinity* 4:18.24. Cf. the same point made in the same vocabulary, but without explicit reference to Plato, in Augustine, *On Christian Doctrine* 1:38.42: "The vision [*species*] we see shall replace [*succedet*] faith." The verb here, *succedere*, refers to things that follow one another in a series or succession in time, so that what comes later replaces what came earlier.

30. Augustine uses the phrase *dispensatio temporalis* as a technical term in, e.g., *Of True Religion* 7.13; *On Faith and the Creed* 4.6; *On Christian Doctrine* 1:35.39. Its function as an equivalent to the Greek *oikonomia* is reflected in later theological usage, including the use of "dispensation" to translate *oikonomia* in the King James Bible, e.g., Eph. 1:10; Col. 1:25.

Knowledge of another person, according to this epistemology, is not an achievement of the knower so much as a gift of the known. We can only know persons if they give themselves to be known, because they have an authority to speak for themselves that we cannot ignore. It is not like a math class, where we begin by believing what our teacher tells us but then proceed to figure it out for ourselves. In mathematics, the motto "faith seeking understanding" would mean we are not content with secondhand knowledge but aim to see the point for ourselves. But knowing other persons is not that kind of seeing, for it is knowledge that cannot be cut loose from or soar beyond what the objects of knowledge have to say for themselves. Failing to respect their authority to speak for themselves is failing to respect them as persons, which means failing to know them *as persons*. Therefore, knowledge of other persons, as opposed to merely knowing something *about* them, depends on their freely choosing to give themselves to be known in their words. This kind of personal knowledge is the fundamental structure of Luther's theology, where everything depends on God giving himself to be known in his word, the Gospel of Jesus Christ. Indeed, we can say that a proper account of how we know persons ought to model itself on Luther's account of how we know God.[31]

Augustine, however, wants to know something more: he longs for faith in the word of Christ to be replaced by a vision of God as Truth, as our knowledge of Christ the man gives way to knowledge of Christ as God. This means, to borrow the terms he uses in the *City of God*, that the knowledge of God is not like knowing a friend but like seeing the light.[32] In his great treatise *The Trinity* Augustine describes this as a movement through the knowledge of temporal things (*scientia*) to wisdom about eternal things (*sapientia*), as "through him we go straight toward him, through knowledge to wisdom, without ever turning aside from one and the same Christ."[33] For one and the same person is both true man and true God, both creature and Creator, both temporal friend and eternal Truth, the object of knowledge in time as well as of wisdom in eternity. For Augustine, the one aspect is related to the other as means to end, or journey to destination. To put it in later theological language, Augustine wants to move from knowledge of the *economic Trinity* (God as made known in the temporal dispensation or economy of salvation, centered on Christ's incarnation) to understanding the *immanent Trinity* (God in himself, the eternal being of God as it has always been, quite apart from his work of creation, incarnation, and redemption).

31. I have sketched such an account in philosophical terms, without mentioning Luther, in Cary, "Believing the Word."
32. Augustine, *City of God* 8:8.
33. Augustine, *Trinity* 13:19.24.

Unfortunately this later language has proved to be both unhelpful and inescapable, in large part because of a misleading formulation by the influential twentieth-century Catholic theologian Karl Rahner, who put into circulation a kind of trinitarian axiom: "The 'economic' Trinity is the 'immanent' Trinity and the 'immanent' Trinity is the 'economic' Trinity."[34] The formulation is misleading because it talks as if there were two Trinities that needed to be equated with one another. Of course, as Rahner knew perfectly well, there was never more than one Trinity. But because of the incarnation, we need to speak of the one Trinity in two different ways: in terms of God's eternal being and in terms of God's work in the economy of salvation. What Rahner seems to have overlooked is that making a clear distinction between these two ways of speaking is indispensable to Christian theology; it is not a problem to be solved or a dichotomy to be overcome. To identify these two ways of speaking, as if they were saying the same thing, is simply to create confusion. To avoid such confusion, the Eastern Orthodox tradition in particular takes care to distinguish between speaking "according to the *theologia*" and speaking "according to the *oikonomia*" (or speaking "theologically" and "economically"), which corresponds to the immanent and the economic descriptions of the Trinity, respectively.[35] The distinction is plain to see in the second article of the Nicene Creed, which is organized around the difference between the two births of the one Son of God: first his eternal begetting from the Father (according to the *theologia*), and then his being incarnate and born of the virgin Mary (according to the *oikonomia*). This is two births, not two persons or two sons—and therefore not two Trinities that somehow need to be reconciled with one another. It has always been one Trinity, just as it has always been, as Augustine rightly puts it, "one and the same Christ."[36]

34. Rahner, *Trinity*, 22.

35. See, most explicitly, John of Damascus, *Exposition of the Orthodox Faith* 1:2, where this distinction serves to organize the whole treatise, which summarizes the legacy of the Eastern Orthodox church fathers up to the eighth century (quite in contrast to Rahner's account of trinitarian theology, as I argue in Cary, "On Behalf of Classical Trinitarianism"). I mention this here because one of the bad effects of Rahner's intervention was to reinforce the kind of polemics that sought to drive a wedge between Eastern and Western orthodox theology, with Augustine typically cast as the villain who perverted Western theology. See for example Zizioulas, *Being as Communion*, 40–41, which seems to be lifting a page from Lossky, *Mystical Theology of the Eastern Church*, 57–58. When it comes to blaming Augustine, however, Western theologians are usually at the forefront, including notably Gunton, *Promise of Trinitarian Theology*, chap. 3, and LaCugna, *God for Us*, chap. 3. Resistance to the wedge and to the villainizing of Augustine has been led by Rowan Williams, "*Sapientia* and the Trinity"; Michel Barnes, "Augustine in Contemporary Trinitarian Theology"; and Lewis Ayres, *Augustine and the Trinity*, joined by Gioia, *Augustine's "De Trinitate."* While I think the wedge is flat wrong, I find the resistance sometimes relies on making too facile a separation between Augustine's Platonism and his trinitarianism.

36. Augustine, *Trinity* 13:19.24.

The criticism I am making of Augustine therefore should not be confused with Rahner's unhelpful intervention in trinitarian theology, which addressed a serious problem in early twentieth-century Catholicism but has created a great many new problems of its own. When I object to Augustine moving from Christ as man to Christ as God, and thus from the economic Trinity to the immanent Trinity, it is not because I think this somehow divides Christ or splits the Trinity in two. On the contrary, Augustine in this regard simply recognizes what Cyril of Alexandria and the Eastern Orthodox tradition emphasized: that there are two births of the one Son of God,[37] and accordingly two different ways of describing the one holy Trinity. My objection, rather, is epistemological and spiritual: Augustine wants to use the kind of faith we put in the temporal birth, Christ's being born of Mary and all that follows it in his human life, as a means of intellectual ascent beyond faith to a pure understanding of what is eternal in God. Augustine is right that we need a metaphysical understanding of the eternal birth (according to the *theologia*) in order to make sense of the temporal birth (in the *oikonomia*); this is what I described as metaphysics in the service of the Gospel. But this metaphysical understanding is not a form of intellectual vision that should turn into the goal of Christian faith, reached by a spirituality that becomes a kind of anagogy—which is to say, a philosophical project of ascending to a pure knowledge of God. Rather, we should recognize that the knowledge of God is given to us through God's descending to us, as proclaimed in the Gospel.

Luther warns against the project of anagogy, or ascent to God, in a sermon on the Gospel of John. This is often thought to be the most philosophical of all the Gospels, but Luther sees it quite differently:

See, this is what St. John in his Gospel absolutely insists on in every word, that we must let go of every high and mighty thought with which reason and clever people concern themselves, seeking God in his Majesty apart from Christ. He intends, in Christ, to lie in the cradle and in his mother's lap, or else to hang on the cross. . . . If you want to take and hold what God is and does and has in mind, then seek it nowhere else but where he has put it and set it himself. . . . Hence a Christian should know not to seek or find God otherwise than in the Virgin's lap and on the cross, or however and wherever Christ shows himself in the word.[38]

To find God in this way is to see the point of the doctrine of the Trinity differently from Augustine. Instead of an invitation to spiritual ascent, purifying

37. That Augustine is explicitly aware of this theme of the two births can be seen in his exposition of the Creed in Sermon 215:3.
38. Luther, sermon on John 17:9–10, Sept. 12, 1528, WA 28:135–36.

the mind in order to see God in his eternal being, the point is that believing in the baby in Mary's lap and the man on the cross, as given to us in the Gospel, is nothing less than knowing the eternal God in person.

Karl Barth, the great twentieth-century Protestant theologian, quotes this same passage to illustrate Luther's well-known aversion to *speculatio maiestatis*, the attempt to see the divine majesty rather than to rest content with faith in the Gospel of Christ.[39] Elsewhere Barth remarks that for Luther this was "no less than a principal rule of all knowledge of God. . . . We must seek Him where He Himself has sought us."[40] We could call this "Luther's rule," noting, along with Barth, that it was fundamental to other Protestant Reformers as well, including Melanchthon and Calvin.[41] It is a consequence of Luther's epistemology of hearing, which implies that we must find God where God has chosen to give himself to us through his word. As Luther puts it, in another passage Barth quotes at length: "I must only listen and cling to the Word, basing everything on the Word of God alone," for a Christian "is not guided by what he sees or feels. . . . He listens to Christ's words and follows Him into the darkness."[42] The metaphor of darkness here is the signal that Luther is relying entirely on an epistemology of hearing rather than intellectual vision or inner experience. As Barth appreciated, Luther's insistence on neither seeing nor feeling God distances him from the modern turn to experience in Protestant liberalism as well as from Augustine's ancient project of spiritual ascent. The latter, in Barth's view, involves "abandoning, or at any rate wanting to abandon, the place where God encounters man," because in our ascent "we hurry past God, who descends in His revelation into this world of ours."[43]

Inner Ascent

The Nicene doctrine of the Trinity itself poses obstacles to the project of spiritual ascent, as Augustine realizes. Ascent needs hierarchy: a gradation of beings, some lower, some higher, which we may ascend like a ladder. Of course the higher beings are not literally above the lower in space but rather

39. Barth, *Church Dogmatics*, I/1, 170. Luther's rejection of *speculatio maiestatis* is found expressly in the 1535 Galatians Commentary, *LW* 26:29.

40. Barth, *Church Dogmatics*, II/1, 18.

41. Barth, *Church Dogmatics*, I/1, 418.

42. Luther, *Sermons on the Gospel of John*, on John 3:11, *LW* 22:305–6, quoted more fully in Barth, *Church Dogmatics*, I/1, 169–70.

43. Barth, *Church Dogmatics*, II/1, 11–12. Barth is commenting on the vision at Ostia, described in Augustine, *Confessions* 9:10.23–25.

superior in being—better and more divine in some way. A hierarchy of divine beings is a pervasive feature of ancient Platonism, but it is precisely what the Council of Nicaea eliminated from the Christian view of God. The theology Nicaea rejected pictured the divine in a way that resembled the kind of ontological hierarchy found in ancient Platonism, which seems perfectly designed to support the mind's ascent to God. For example, Plotinus's theory of a gradation of three divine beings would have us turning our minds away from bodily things to contemplate the divine Soul of all things (rather like today's reverence for Gaia, or life-force), then raising our mind's eye to the vision of the divine Intellect, Mind, or *Nous* (the epitome of all understanding, as found in the intelligible world above Plato's cave), and finally rising to union with what Plotinus calls the One, the supreme divinity that is the source of all being, unity, and goodness (also called the Good, as it is identified with the dazzling sun in Plato's allegory of the cave).[44] One can see the attraction of this kind of hierarchy for ancient Christian intellectuals, who could use it as a model for the mind's ascent by the life-giving power of the Spirit through the mediation of the Son to arrive in the end at the divine Father that is the source of all.[45] But Nicene theology decisively rejected this kind of hierarchy when it insisted that Father and Son are coequal, deserving of the same worship. There is no means of ascent here, no lower being leading upward to a higher and more fully divine being.

One of the crucial consequences of Nicaea is that the eternal Son of God is not the mediator between God and creation. As we saw in chapter 2, the divine being of the Son is not *between* the divine being of the Father and our created being, as if the Son were lower than the Father and therefore closer to us, the way an intelligible *Logos* or divine Reason would be closer to us in being than is the incomprehensible divine One in Plotinus. And as we saw in chapter 3, Augustine understands this consequence and draws the apt conclusion that Christ is the mediator between us and God not in his divinity but in his humanity. Logically speaking, Christ is not a *tertium quid* (a third thing) but a both/and. That is to say, his divinity is not a third kind of being between the being of God the Father and the being of things he has created. Rather, Christ is both Creator and creature. As God, he is Creator in the same sense as the Father is, because he has exactly the same being as the Father (which is what the *homoousios* clause says in the Nicene Creed). As man, he is a creature in exactly the same sense that we are, having the same kind of being as any created

---

44. See especially Plotinus's essay "On the Three Primary Hypostases," *Enneads* 5:1.1–5.

45. Augustine explicitly points out the parallel between pagan Platonists and the Christian Trinity in *City of God* 10:29, as well as the crucial difference, which is the Christian belief in the incarnation of the Son.

thing. The divinity of Christ (as the eternal Word or *Logos*) therefore cannot mediate between Creator and creature; it is not a rung on the ladder leading up to God the Father. That is why, in Augustine's account, Christ as God is what we ascend *to*, and Christ's humanity becomes the way to his divinity.

By the same token, however, Augustine thinks we will not arrive at Christ's divinity by clinging stubbornly to his humanity. This is the deep difference between Augustine and Luther. When Augustine treats Christ's humanity as the way, not the goal, this means, as we saw in chapter 3, that "nothing should detain us on the way, since the Lord himself, insofar as he deigned to become our way, wanted not to detain us but for us to travel onward—not clinging in weakness to temporal things."[46] The temporal things that must not detain us, Augustine explains, are precisely the things that he made his own in the incarnation, the human things which were "taken up by him and accomplished for our salvation."[47] We are not to be detained by these things, because the Lord Jesus wasn't. Rather, we should be "running through them eagerly so as to advance and deserve to arrive at himself, who has liberated our nature from temporal things and set it at the right hand of the Father."[48] We want to arrive where Christ is with God, still human (for in his own person he has freed human nature from death, not abolished human nature) but no longer concerned with temporal and human matters such as birth, suffering, death, and resurrection from death.

Hence for Augustine, coming to Christ at God's right hand requires an inward turn, away from external and temporal things, including everything having to do with Christ's individual humanity. The Lord Jesus himself is our example here, for in his brief life on earth "he did not delay but ran, calling out by word and deed, death and life, descent and ascent—calling out that we should return to him. And he withdrew from our eyes so that we might return to the heart and find him."[49] To find him in our hearts is to find him in his divinity rather than his flesh. For the flesh of another person is external, not something we can find by turning to our hearts. Therefore in sharp contrast to Luther, for Augustine the external things in Christ's human life, everything from his birth to his crucifixion and ascension, are not where we look to find God, but rather are signs admonishing us to turn back to the inwardness of the heart, where we will find Christ in his divinity.

Thus in Augustine's theology the means by which we ascend to God is not a gradation of divine beings, but neither is it something external like the flesh of Christ. It is an inner ascent, requiring us to return to the heart and enter

---

46. Augustine, *On Christian Doctrine* 1:34.38, my translation.
47. Augustine, *On Christian Doctrine* 1:34.38, my translation.
48. Augustine, *On Christian Doctrine* 1:34.38, my translation.
49. Augustine, *Confessions* 4:12.19, my translation.

into the inner world of the soul. In the *Confessions*, Augustine dramatizes his search for God by asking, "Who is He that is above the topmost point of my soul?" In answer, he resolves that "by that same soul I shall ascend to Him."[50] The ladder to ascend is the hierarchy of powers in the soul, starting with the senses, which are oriented toward external things, but leaving them behind as we purify ourselves from attachment to sensible things and climb step by step to the highest cognitive power in us, the intellect, which must finally look above itself to see the unchanging intelligible Truth, which is God. The soul's inward ascent in the *Confessions*, moving in then up, is the culmination of a project of inward turn that is sketched in earlier works of Augustine,[51] and it continues to shape his spirituality in later works, especially in the second half of his treatise *The Trinity*. In the *Confessions* and earlier versions of this inward turn, the soul is a clue to the nonmaterial being of God. In *The Trinity*, things get more complicated, as Augustine looks for triadic structures in the soul that might serve as incorporeal images of the Triune God. Augustine argues that the most inward activities of the human soul are distinct and coequal, yet each is coextensive with the whole soul in a way that makes for a distant resemblance to the way Father, Son, and Spirit, though distinct and coequal, are one God. For example, early on in this long investigation Augustine asks us to consider the triad of mind, knowledge, and love, and then the triad of memory, understanding, and will, as images of the divine Trinity in the human soul.[52]

Divine Images in the Soul

There has been much misguided criticism of these "psychological analogies" of the Trinity, as they were later called. Augustine has been accused of conceiving God as nothing but one mind with three functions or faculties—a view that would bring him near to the heresy called "modalism." But it should be

50. Augustine, *Confessions* 10:7.11.

51. The key examples of an inward turn in Augustine's earlier work are in *On Free Choice* 2:3.8–12.34 and *Confessions* 7:10.16; 7:17.23; 10:6.8–27.38. These are examples of a project of philosophical inquiry, not mystical experiences, as I argue in Cary, *Augustine's Invention of the Inner Self*, chaps. 5 and 6. The inward turn in these texts is designed to lead readers to see in their own souls an incorporeal form of being that can be a clue to the incorporeal being of God. The same structure of inward turn is used to lead readers to see an alternative to the materialist conception of God in Manichaeanism, in *Answer to the Letter of Mani known as The Foundation* 20.16–18. Augustine makes a gesture toward this kind of inward turn to see God as the incorporeal Truth and Goodness in *Trinity* 8:1.2–3.5, but this is only the beginning of ascent, preliminary to tackling the more difficult problem of trying to understand God as Trinity.

52. Augustine, *Trinity* 9:4.4; 10:11.17.

obvious to anyone who reads Augustine's *The Trinity* that he would have no work to do in the treatise if he did not recognize that each of the three persons is God and that this raises the problem of how God is one. This problem, which makes the oneness of God the *goal* of Augustine's inquiry rather than the starting point, is clearly on Augustine's agenda from the very beginning of the treatise, and it is precisely in order to tackle this problem that he asks us to consider triadic structures in the soul.

The fact that understanding the oneness of God is the goal of Augustine's treatise rather than its starting point is important, because one of the most pervasive criticisms of Augustine has been that he "starts with" the oneness of God's being and downplays the threeness of the divine persons. It is hard to imagine this criticism gaining traction except in the wake of Protestant liberalism, with its inveterate tendency to confuse how we think about God with how God is. (It is in the wake of liberalism that theologians could warn that "Your God is too small" and sometimes forget that there really is no danger that thinking could make it so.) Likewise, modern critics of Augustine and Western theology have worried about expositions of the doctrine of the Trinity that start with the oneness of the divine being or essence and then proceed to discuss the three persons, as if this meant that somehow God himself started with the divine being and only subsequently and secondarily consisted of three persons. Because ancient and medieval thinkers were trained in rhetoric, they all knew better. They understood that where an exposition starts is a choice that depends on a writer's pedagogical or persuasive strategy, not on metaphysical principles. This is why expositions of the Trinity have often started with the one divine being: not just Thomas Aquinas's *Summa Theologica* in the West, for example, but also John of Damascus's *On the Orthodox Faith* in the East. What neither West nor East does is treat the divine being as the *ontological* starting point, the primal source (*arche* or *principium*) of the three persons, for the simple reason that this is quite alien to both Scripture and creed. The Nicene Creed common to both East and West says nothing about the being (*ousia*) of God other than that the Father and the Son both have it. When it comes to how God "starts," the creed describes the Father as origin of the Son, who is begotten, and of the Spirit, who proceeds, while identifying no origin whatsoever of the Father. Accordingly, East and West alike agree that the Father is the primal starting point, the unoriginated origin of the Son and the Spirit, and thus "the source of all that is divine," as Augustine puts it.[53]

---

53. Augustine, *Trinity* 4:20.29: "principium totius divinitatis." See Aquinas's exposition of this point, *ST* I, 33.1.

Augustine's "psychological analogies," or as he rather calls them, the images of the Trinity in the soul, don't change any of this. They are merely one inadequate way of imagining how Father, Son, and Holy Spirit could be one God. Augustine himself insists on their inadequacy. In the concluding book of his treatise *The Trinity*, he turns to what is evidently his favorite image, comparing our mind's memory, understanding, and love to Father, Son, and Holy Spirit, respectively—but then adds that we cannot say the Father has no understanding and love of his own, nor that the Son has in himself no memory and love, nor that the Holy Spirit lacks a memory and understanding of his own.[54] Augustine thus makes it impossible to miss the limitation of any analogy that compares God to a single mind, by reminding us of the kind of social analogy that compares God to three human persons, including a father and a son, each of whom has his own mind with its own memory, understanding, and love. Neither kind of analogy, psychological or social, is actually adequate, because no image for God is ever adequate. This is a familiar point in Platonism, where lower things are never fully adequate images of higher things (as we can see already in Plato's allegory of the cave, where lower things are shadows of what is more real than themselves).

Augustine's insistence on the inadequacy of all images of the Trinity shows that he is not playing the modern game of constructing "models" of the Trinity to show how God can be both three and one. He knows—better than his critics—that no single model can capture all the important logical features of the doctrine of the Trinity. The aim of his psychological analogies, rather, is to provide a starting point that, as in all forms of Platonist anagogy, can be refined and purified and eventually left behind as the human mind ascends to a vision of what is higher than itself. In the context of anagogy, the notion of "starting with" the image of the Trinity in the soul actually has a clear meaning. But the movement of anagogy is not from oneness to threeness or vice versa. It is a turning of attention, starting with the lower aspects of the soul and ending with God above the soul, like the inward turn in Augustine's *Confessions*, which is a movement "in then up."[55] The point of the psychological analogies is not to "explain" the Trinity but to provide guideposts on this path of anagogy.[56]

54. Augustine, *Trinity* 15:17.28.
55. Augustine, *Confessions* 7:10:16; 10:7.11. For the modification of Platonism involved in the movement "in then up," see Cary, *Augustine's Invention of the Inner Self*, 38–40.
56. The great contribution of Rowan Williams to the renewal of interest in Augustine's trinitarianism is an anagogical reading of Augustine's psychological investigations (in "*Sapientia* and the Trinity" and "Paradoxes of Self Knowledge") that paraphrases Augustine's Platonism in deconstructive terms emphasizing the inadequacy of every image. Williams's deconstructionism, as developed more fully in "Language, Reality and Desire," is meant to emphasize

As with Platonism in general, the point at which Augustine's trinitarianism needs a Protestant critique is his epistemology: hence not his metaphysics of God but his conception of how we grow in the knowledge of God through the work of anagogy. This becomes especially clear as the spiritual ascent in *The Trinity* draws near to its conclusion with a consideration of the triad of memory, understanding, and love, giving special attention to how the mind remembers, understands, and loves *itself*.[57] There are reasons for this turn to the self. When the mind is turned away from what is not itself, it is to that extent more like the eternal being of God, whose knowledge is not dependent on anything outside himself. God could remember, understand, and love himself even if he had never created the world. The objection to raise against Augustine's psychological analogy at this point is that our minds are not in fact like that. Our mental life is never wholly self-contained—not even when we are remembering, understanding, and loving ourselves. Whenever we remember, understand, or love ourselves, it is in the context of events in time and space, a story of how we grow, learn, and change that is impossible to tell without including a great deal of the world outside us, for we are creatures completely dependent for our existence on belonging to the world God created. In that way we are inevitably quite unlike God.

Augustine acknowledges the human mind's dependence, but not its dependence on what is outside it. He insists that the mind remembering, understanding, and loving itself is foolish if it does not also remember, understand, and love *God*,[58] but throughout *The Trinity* he insists, as usual, that God is found within the mind, not outside. Even when a man loves his brother, Augustine says, "he can already have God better known to him than his brother, certainly better known because more present, better known because more inward to him."[59] Beginning in book 8, the whole investigation of triads in the mind is a movement inward and upward, ascending through the soul to a God who is not remembered, understood, or loved as one among external things. Even the exception proves the rule, when Augustine backtracks to look at a triad in the "outer man" of the senses in book 11, after introducing the more inward triad of memory, understanding, and love at the end of

---

the openness and incompleteness of all desire, and thus moves in the opposite direction from Luther's Protestant insistence that the Gospel actually gives us what it signifies, as in the famous motto "Believe, and you have it" (Luther, *Holy and Blessed Sacrament of Baptism* [sermon, 1519], LW 35:38).

57. Augustine, *Trinity* 14:10.13.
58. Augustine, *Trinity* 14:12.15.
59. Augustine, *Trinity* 8:8.12.

book 10. For what he discovered when he looked closely at memory in book 10 was that our sinful desires, drawing us in love and attachment to external things, easily lead us astray, so that the mind's memory forgets what it is and confuses itself with things outside it, thus generating materialist theories of mind that Augustine wants us to overcome.[60] So he backtracks to the "outer man" precisely to accomplish the work of anagogy more thoroughly, starting with what is more familiar to us in our mortal and fleshly lives[61] so that we can distinguish it clearly from the higher triad of the inner man, beginning in book 12—thus purifying the mind (its memory, understanding, and love) from its inveterate attachment to things outside it.

The foolishness of failing to remember, understand, and love God is intimately connected, in Augustine's estimation, with our attachment to external things, which deforms the image of God in us. Hence the deformed image needs to be reformed, as Paul puts it, "by the renewal of your mind" (Rom. 12:2), which means putting on "the new man, who is renewed in the knowledge of God according to the image of him who created him."[62] Augustine carefully distinguishes this inner renewal of our minds from the resurrection of our bodies, when even outwardly we will be "conformed to the image of [God's] Son" (Rom. 8:29) because of our eternal life in the risen Christ.[63] The ultimate renewal Augustine hopes for is perfected not by resurrection in Christ but by intellectual vision, which will restore to us a knowledge of God that renews in our minds the full image and likeness of God.

But from a perspective like Luther's, this makes things worse, for it means Augustine wants us to become wiser, better, and more like God by a movement inward and upward that involves turning away from all external things, including the Gospel and Christ incarnate—when in fact it is faith in Christ alone that inwardly renews the mind. The Gospel does not direct our attention inward, but outward to Christ in the flesh. And Christ came not to admonish us to purify and reform our minds by turning inward and looking upward, but to draw us out of ourselves in love for one another, precisely by the authority of an external word, the word of our incarnate Beloved, which comes to us from outside our own minds. At no stage from infancy to eternal life in Christ is our own being constituted by a love, understanding, or memory that is independent of what comes to us from outside ourselves. Our minds are closest to God, as they are also closest to our neighbors, our friends, sisters, and brothers, when they are turned away from themselves

60. Augustine, *Trinity* 10:5.7–10:8.11.
61. Augustine, *Trinity* 11:1.1.
62. Augustine, *Trinity* 14:16.22, quoting Col. 3:9 (my translation).
63. Augustine, *Trinity* 14:18.24.

toward outward things. We do not get closer to God by purifying ourselves from all external attachments.

As we can see in Augustine's treatise *The Trinity* and in many other works, it is the concept of intellectual vision that makes his inward turn conceivable. Without it, we would have no alternative but to turn to Christ incarnate to find the perfection of the knowledge of God. What Luther's theology offers on this score is an account of the knowledge of God that does not depend on the notion of a power or faculty of intellectual vision, and that therefore has no alternative to Christ incarnate as the basis and goal of the knowledge of God. For all those of us who find it impossible to believe in a Platonist notion of intellectual vision, as well as those who share Barth's aversion against the liberal Protestant turn to experience, this is good news indeed.

The Election of the Beloved

The point of the doctrine of the Trinity is not to give us a goal for anagogy, re-forming the inner triadic structure of the mind until it more closely resembles God in his triune being, but rather to show why calling on Jesus Christ in faith, prayer, and worship gives glory to none but the true God, the LORD, the God of Israel, who made heaven and earth. An inward turn misses the point, insofar as it directs our attention away from this one man, without whom there is no living by the Spirit of God in the presence of God the Father. The doctrine of the Trinity supports an outward turn to faith in God in the flesh, as given to us in the external word of the Gospel.

Because of the doctrine of the Trinity, we can say that knowing God means believing a person who has chosen to be our Beloved in the flesh. He is a person, which means he can give himself to be known in his word. To know this person, the philosophical love of God as Truth is less important than biblical faith in the God who is true (*Deus verax*), who makes promises and keeps them. As Karl Barth puts it, the choice of God (in what theology calls the doctrine of election) is his decision to be the covenant partner of humanity by becoming incarnate in Jesus of Nazareth. This decision to be for us in Christ is "the beginning of all the works and ways of God."[64] It is a free decision: God could have remained nothing other than the immanent Trinity, an eternal communion of love and knowledge between Father, Son, and Holy Spirit, lacking nothing. Instead, he chose in the sheer goodness and generosity of love to open up the triune life for our participation, first

64. Barth, *Church Dogmatics*, II/2, 3.

by creating us, then by giving us Christ as covenant partner, redeeming us through his blood, and incorporating us into his body and thereby into the life of the Trinity. As Barth emphasizes, this is God's eternal decision about how he shall be God: that he shall promise himself to creatures who are not God by becoming one of them in the incarnation and giving himself to them in his word. We could add that the election or eternal decision of God is his choice that the Gospel of Christ shall be the story of the world and that the Son of God shall be the central character in the story, leading the list of its *dramatis personae.*[65]

What Protestant theology proposes, from Luther to Barth, is that there is no knowledge of God that takes us beyond this choice of God: his decision to be for us in God incarnate, promised to us in the Gospel. There is no intellectual vision that sees deeper than this decision of God and no experience that gives us reliable access to God apart from this promise. It is like the way the bride and bridegroom in a good marriage do not try to know each other apart from their covenant with each other, because the promises of the covenant give them their identity as husband and wife. But it goes further: for this bridegroom has chosen to be our Beloved from before the foundation of the world, deciding to create us as those whom he calls to join him in this life-giving covenant, which forms both our identity and his. There is no God to know who is other than the God who made the promises of this covenant, just as there is no person of the Son of God who is other than the one who has chosen to be Christ incarnate. There are indeed some abstract truths about the metaphysics of God that the ancient pagan philosophers have grasped, which have a kind of metaphysical loveliness that we should not ignore, but there is no way of finding God in person apart from the promise of the Gospel of Jesus Christ.

This means we need a different interpretation of "faith seeking understanding" than we find in Augustine. It is not like trusting the word of our teacher until we can see for ourselves. It is trusting that our Beloved will be who he says he is. The relation between faith and understanding is not the difference between believing what we hear and seeing for ourselves, but rather the relation between believing the promise we hear from our Beloved and seeing how he keeps his word. What faith seeks to understand is the whole story of divine faithfulness, which is the story in which we live with God as he shares his eternal life with us. The goal it seeks is not a beatific vision of the being of God but something more like the Transfiguration narrated in the New Testament, where we see "the glory of God in the face of Jesus

65. Robert Jenson's *Systematic Theology* proposes such a view of the story of the world.

Christ."[66] But the metaphor of vision needs expanding, for what we see in the face of Christ our Beloved is one who is our host in the marriage supper of the lamb (Rev. 19:9), where there will be feasting and dancing and singing—tasting and touching as well as hearing and seeing—as we glorify God and enjoy him forever.

Until then, our Beloved remains hidden at the right hand of the Father (Col. 3:1–3), in divine carnality as external as flesh and as invisible as God. The hiddenness has a structure, however, that is familiar to all who await the promised coming of someone they love. The flesh whose presence is promised cannot be seen, because it will be visible to us only in the future, when the promise is completely fulfilled. Therefore faith in the promise of Christ always has the structure of hope, as we await his coming in glory. Yet by the same token, the hiddenness of Christ's exalted flesh and blood in bread and wine is the presence of this future in the midst of the life of the Body of Christ today, as the church both remembers his death and proclaims the day of his coming, and worships already with the angels around the throne of God, singing "Holy, holy, holy." The sacramental supper is a foretaste of the marriage supper of the Lamb, from which the Lamb himself, though invisible, is not absent or distant, but present as our spiritual food.

Without the doctrine of the Trinity we could not even begin to speak about the presence of the Beloved in flesh among us. We could not even begin to believe the Gospel, because we would not know Christ as God, and therefore we would not know that the promise of Christ is the promise of the *Deus verax*, the living God who is true to his word. Thus the Protestant devotion to the word of the Gospel cannot do without the patristic doctrine of the Trinity. Theologically, that is a strength, not a weakness. But conversely, the point of the doctrine of the Trinity becomes clearer when we see, with Luther, that what the Gospel has always done is give us God in person.

To think of God like Luther is therefore to separate our metaphysics from our spirituality, in a way that departs from a major strand in Western theology whose greatest early representative is Augustine. We are not on a spiritual journey whose culmination is beatific vision, the fullness of the vision of the mind's eye, as represented for example in Plato's allegory of the cave. Rather, we have a place in the story of the Gospel of Jesus Christ, who died for us and rose for our justification, so that all who believe in him may be born anew and have eternal life, being created in Christ so that we might walk in

---

66. 2 Cor. 4:6. Cf. the beholding of divine glory in 2 Cor. 3:18 (where "the glory of the Lord" means the glory of the Lord Jesus) and John 1:14, as well as the vision of Christ incarnate in 1 John 1:1–3 and 3:2, all of which can be read as interpretations of the Transfiguration narratives in the gospels, especially Matt. 17:2; Mark 9:2–3; Luke 9:29.

works of love (Eph. 2:10). A spirituality that does not require a metaphysics of intellectual vision as its foundation and goal is a key gift that Protestant theology has to offer the church as a whole, including all of us who do not believe in Platonic souls and their power of intellectual vision, but who do believe in Jesus Christ.

When God Says "You"

What changes us inwardly into a true and better image of God is not metaphysical spirituality or intellectual vision but finding ourselves in the story God tells us about who he is, which is the Gospel of Jesus Christ. We are those for whom Christ came, those who live in Christ and in whom Christ lives. We know this about ourselves because we believe it, which is to say our knowledge consists in our faith in the Gospel. We belong to the Gospel story because we belong to Christ, and we belong to Christ because through the Gospel he has claimed us as his own. So we are in the Gospel as Christ's own because the Gospel is in us giving us Christ. He claims us by giving himself to us, as a bridegroom claims his bride by giving himself to her in his promise. Like a wedding vow, the Gospel promise is an external word that says "you" and means me, so that everyone who believes it can say with confidence, "My Beloved is mine and I am his." By addressing us in his promise with the second-person pronoun—saying "you" and meaning me, and in the end each one of us—he makes himself ours and makes us his own, which is to say he makes us new persons who are born again in him, as a wedding vow makes a husband and a wife where there were none before.

The epistemology that accounts for this kind of knowledge makes persons central without giving us a metaphysical account of what persons are, and this is a real advantage. We know persons by hearing what they have to say for themselves, not by being able to give an account of what personhood is. We know particular persons by learning their story, especially as they tell it themselves. And we know persons most deeply when they address their story to us: when someone says "you" and means me, so that I am a second person hearing the word of a first person as he tells me who he is and gives himself to me in his promise. This puts me on the receiving end of the word, as the object rather than the subject of the active verbs in his story—as someone he knows and loves rather than someone who knows and loves him. For if I want to know another person, then the important thing to perceive is not how I love him but how he loves me. And for that I need to be the second person, not the first person: the one who hears "you" rather than the one who says

"I." This is why Luther's insight that the Gospel is about what God does, not what we do, is so important. The Gospel does not say "I believe" but rather "Christ died for you" and "this is my body, given for you." By addressing us with the second-person pronoun, it locates us in Christ's story so that we may put all our faith in him alone, and none in our own doings—not even in our own believing. It thus shows us how to find ourselves in Christ rather than getting us trapped in the quagmire of looking for Christ in ourselves, our lives and our experience. It gets Christ into us by directing our attention away from ourselves and toward someone else—the one who in the Gospel says "you" and means me.

Believers do of course say "I" also, but they do so in response to the Gospel word that says "you." This is the implication of Luther's saying that "faith first makes the person, who afterward performs works," and that the doer of the law is "one who, having already become a person through faith, then becomes a doer."[67] It is like saying that you only start living a married life once the wedding vow has made you into a new kind of person, a husband or a wife. The new person we each become in Christ is the doer of good works who comes into being by believing the promise of the Gospel when it says "you" and means me. It is this new person who can say not only "Christ died and rose to redeem me" (which is the Gospel, where the first-person pronoun referring to me is the object in sentences with an active verb, because I am on the receiving end of what Christ does) but also "I believe in Christ" and even "I love my neighbors" (where I am the subject of the active verb, because I am telling the story of my imperfect but real obedience to the law of God, including both my growing faith and the works of love which are its fruit).

The promise that makes us new persons has to have a sacramental kind of power, because it must be an external word spoken at a particular time and place in order to say "you" and mean me in particular. By addressing me in this external way the Gospel tells me that I am God's beloved for whom Christ died and rose, so that my own first-person speech and self-understanding—who I think and say I am and how I live my life—are determined by the second-person address that comes to me from God himself, preveniently, before anything I can do about it. We could adopt the language of Martin Buber and call this an "I-Thou" relationship, but it goes in a different direction from Buber's philosophy. Buber focused on the relationship that arises when I say "You" instead of "It,"[68] whereas Luther would have us attend first

---

67. Luther, 1535 Galatians Commentary, on Gal. 3:10, *LW* 26:255, 260. See above, chap. 8, "Person and Work."

68. This is clear from the programmatic opening page of the book: "The attitude of man is twofold in accordance with the two basic words he can speak. . . . One basic word is the word

to what happens when I *hear* "you" spoken to me in the external word of the Gospel. Faith clings to this word as the truth that makes me the person I am by giving me the person I love. Call this a "second-person" approach rather than an "I -Thou" approach. To grasp how this approach works is to understand much that seems counterintuitive or paradoxical about Luther's theology. The appearance of paradox is due in large part to the fact that our philosophical tradition has thought so little about what it means to be a second person addressed by a first person. Luther's theology would be easier to understand if we were accustomed to recognizing, as philosopher Amy Richards puts it, that "we become first persons—agents—only because we are first (and always) second persons, called into being through the address of others and constituted by our relationship to them."[69] If we paid more attention to the way children learn how to be persons as they are addressed by their parents, who love and understand them better than they love and understand themselves,[70] we would find Luther's theology far less paradoxical.

The way we learn how to be persons in Christ is inevitably a central topic of Christian theology, which we could define in a way compatible with Luther if we call it "disciplined reflection on Christian teaching," where "teaching" is understood as including both what to teach and how—both the content of Christian doctrine and the kind of spirituality, worship, and church life required to teach it well. "Spirituality" here refers to the work of the Holy Spirit (as at the end of chap. 2). Luther's intense focus on the word of God leads to the classic Protestant understanding of the inseparability of word and Spirit, according to which the most important work of the Holy Spirit is to give us faith in the word of Christ. This is how the Spirit unites us with Christ, so that Christ lives in us and we in Christ. For by faith Christ is formed within me as I am incorporated into the life of his Body, the church—so Christ is in me precisely as I am in Christ. This is what Luther means by sanctification, the process of becoming holy that makes progress as the Holy Spirit deepens our faith in the Gospel and causes us to share ever more fully in the blessings of the *communio sanctorum*, which is both the communion of holy people and the sharing of holy things that belong to them, including the truth about who God is, the incorruptible good of eternal life, and the beauty of holiness.

---

pair I-You. The other basic word is the word pair I-It" (Buber, *I and Thou*, 53 [While retaining the earlier English title, Walter Kaufman, the translator of the new edition, quite rightly renders the German *du* as "you" rather than "thou" throughout the text]).

69. Richards, "Response to Tollefson," 120.

70. For a "second-person approach" to infants' understanding of self and other in developmental psychology, see Reddy, *How Infants Know Minds*.

To believe the Gospel is to cling to a kind word of grace in which Christ says "you" and means me, knowing that the word gives every good thing that it promises, because God is true to his word and Christ is God. Our clinging to this word in faith is the work of God the Holy Spirit, who by this faith makes us members of Christ's body so that in the end we may stand in the presence of God the Father together with all his holy ones, in perfection and great joy. It is an immense privilege to teach this: that the Spirit through the word brings us in Christ to the Father, so that we are partakers in the life of the holy Trinity.

Conclusion

Why Luther's Gospel?

I n the late medieval world into which Luther was born, priests were instructed to provide pastoral care to the dying by holding a crucifix in front of their eyes and speaking words such as these:

> Put all thy trust in his passion and in his death, and think only of it and nothing else. Wrap yourself in his death . . . and have the cross before thee, and say: ". . . Lord, father in heaven, the death of our lord Jesus Christ, thy Son, which is here imaged, I set between Thee and my evil deeds, and the merit of Jesus Christ I offer in place of what I should have merited but haven't."[1]

Readers of the fourteenth-century theologian Julian of Norwich will be familiar with the gesture of holding a crucifix before the eyes of the dying, and with the kind of Christ-centered consolation that can result from it. Luther's proposal to the church can be seen as an extension of this medieval version of eleventh-hour pastoral care to cover the whole of life. His counsel to Christians terrified at the prospect of dying in mortal sin was to despair over their own merits and put all their trust in Christ. But he went one step further when he added what I called "the Lutheran codicil" in chapter 8. We are not only to pray for the grace of Christ, his forgiveness and redemption and the power to fulfill his commandments, but we are also to be confident that we have them, because he has promised them all to us in the Gospel.

---

1. Duffy, *The Stripping of the Altars*, 315. I have translated from the Middle English. For an introduction to Luther's relation to the tradition of *ars moriendi*, see Wicks, "Applied Theology at the Deathbed."

Thus Augustine's theology of law and grace became Luther's theology of law and Gospel, teaching us to find in the promise of God grace in the face of sin and death, consolation in the face of terror, certainty in the face of anxiety, obedience in the face of the law's demands, and Christ himself in the face of every trial and temptation.

The Lutheran codicil depends on the Gospel as the word of God that gives us Christ. As Luther understands it, the Gospel has the same kind of power as a sacrament: it gives the grace it signifies to those who believe it. Faith in the Gospel saves us because the grace signified by the Gospel of Jesus Christ is nothing less than Christ himself, which is to say God in person, with all that he is and all that he has, including salvation, righteousness, holiness, blessing, and eternal life. This sacramental conception of the Gospel is at the basis of the Protestant faith in the saving power of the word of God and thus also of the Protestant doctrine of justification by faith alone. In this respect Protestant theology has always relied, without always knowing it, on a Catholic conception of the sacramental efficacy of external means of grace. Far from denying the sacraments' power, Luther insists on making more of it than medieval Catholicism was willing to countenance, beginning with his insistence that Christians who hear the word of absolution in the sacrament of penance ought to be quite certain that their sins are absolved and forgiven, because it is Christ himself who promises that it is so—and who are we to talk back to Christ our God as if he were not true to his word? This kind of certainty—grounded on the external word of the Gospel uttered at a particular time and place, so that it can say "you" and mean me in particular—determines everything in Luther's theology.

Why should any of us—including the rest of the church outside Protestantism—accept Luther's concept of the Gospel as the word that gives us Christ?

First of all, we can know nothing of Christ apart from the Gospel. No icon has any meaning for those who do not know the story of Christ, no sacrament is possible without it, and no word can have saving power unless it is the word that gives us God in the flesh. Every means of grace comes back to Christ in person, who is accessible to us only in this story and its promises. The confidence that the Gospel gives us Christ is essential to Christian life even in traditions where distinctively Protestant doctrines such as justification by faith alone have no place.

Second, we all do need the comfort of the Gospel. No tradition, within Christianity or outside it, escapes anxiety in this world full of evil, suffering, and death. And some of us still suffer the same anxieties as those medieval Catholics on their deathbeds, terrified of our own sin and finding nothing in our lives that is sure to meet with divine approval. The Gospel is the good news that we can look away from our lives and at Christ instead. It gives all of us the freedom to despair of our good works, to look at ourselves and find a sinner who needs to repent rather than a righteous Christian with true saving faith.

Third, when the Gospel comforts us, we do learn to love. The Gospel is a kind word that cheers us up and teaches us to delight in the goodness and mercy of God given to us in his beloved Son. With this cheerfulness and delight, the love of God and neighbor grows in our lives, like good fruit from a good tree. For when Christ the Beloved gives himself to us in the Gospel, he gets into our hearts through our ears like music, reshaping everything and remaking us from the bottom up. He inwardly forms us in his own image, so that we may have strength to take up our cross and follow him in the hard, hard work of love. The Gospel justifies us by faith so that we may freely love, not driven by the need to justify ourselves, to assuage the performance anxieties of our spiritual life, or to assure ourselves that we really are good, loving Christians. Thus the Gospel frees love to *be* love, by freeing it to be about others rather than ourselves. It allows us to ask better questions: instead of worrying, "Am I really a good, loving Christian?," we can worry, "Are the things I'm doing genuinely good for my neighbor?" This is the kind of worry that love has, as it seeks the wisdom to do the work of love well.[2]

Fourth, Protestants especially need to learn or relearn Luther's distinction between law and Gospel. Roman Catholics and Eastern Orthodox do not need to make this distinction so explicit, because their liturgies are full of the Gospel, rich in words that give us Christ. But Protestants, who often depend more on preaching than on liturgy, are in a bad way when they think they can form Christians by telling them what to do or giving them good advice about how to live the Christian life. This confuses law and Gospel, or rather treats the law as if it were the Gospel, which is an unintended kind of cruelty. Instead of giving us a kind and gracious God, it binds us without mercy to the anxieties that result from our own imperfect achievements. It misses the point that was already clear to Augustine, which is that telling you what to do does not help you do it—not if the thing that needs doing is to love God with a whole heart and your neighbor as yourself. For that, you need an inward

---

2. I take this to be an important part of moral wisdom, which is hard for Christians to learn when they have a theology that directs their attention to the motivations of their own spiritual life rather than the good of their neighbors. I discuss this in a pastoral vein in Cary, *Good News for Anxious Christians*, chap. 5 ("Why You Don't Have to Be Sure You Have the Right Motivations: Or, How Love Seeks the Good"). See also Wolterstorff's argument against the idea that Christian love is characterized by its distinctive motivation in *Justice in Love*, chap. 10: when Jesus commanded us to love our neighbors, he did not command us to have a particular kind of motivation for our love.

gift of grace that the law of God cannot give you—for only the Gospel, not the law, is God giving you himself in grace and mercy and kindness. Only the Gospel can give you the glad heart that gladly loves God and neighbor.

Fifth, we need a word of God that supports an outward turn, so that we are free to direct our attention away from ourselves and cling to Christ in his word alone. This means we need a Gospel that is not a principle to apply to our lives but an external word addressed to us, in which God himself says "you" and means me. Precisely because the external word, unlike a universal principle, can address each of us in particular, we can learn to trust what God says about us rather than turn inward or look at ourselves to find out who we are and how we stand before God. We are not Christians because of our decision for Christ or our inward experience but because Christ has given himself to us, and we know he has given himself to us because that is what the Gospel promises. Thus we find ourselves in Christ, not in ourselves. We know who we really are by looking away from ourselves at our Beloved. We find ourselves in his story—the Gospel story—as those for whom he came, those to whom he gives himself in love, those for whom he gave up his life, those who will be raised up with him in eternal life in the presence of God the Father. We find ourselves in him rather than finding him in ourselves, which means we are not trapped in the dreary, anxious business of finding him in our experience, our hearts, or our lives. Precisely for that reason our experience, hearts, and lives are free to be about our neighbors and our God rather than ourselves. Once again, the outward turn means that love is free to *be* love. It also means that faith is free to be unreflective—not a faith that has to put faith in faith. We can put faith in the word alone and not in our success in believing it. The task of faith is to believe that our God is true to his word— that is hard enough—rather than to believe that we have true saving faith.

Sixth, we should accept Luther's conception of the Gospel knowing that it can be separated from the need to possess the wrong kind of certainty, which proved to be so destructive in the history of Protestantism. The sacramental conception of the external word giving us Christ is not the modern conception of Scripture as a depository of inerrant propositions used to construct an infallible theology. Christian faith does not live by proving it has the only possible correct view of this or that passage of the Bible. Rather, faith takes hold of Christ by clinging to the Gospel even in the face of doubts and uncertainties, trusting that God will be true to his gracious word. By the same token, Christian faith is not dependent on academic biblical scholarship to secure in advance a foundational understanding of the Scripture and "what it meant," and neither is Christian theology. Christian faith grows out of the hearing of the Gospel in Christian life, worship, liturgy, preaching, teaching, prayer, praise, song, and sacrament. Christian theology is not a science based on deduction from Scripture, but disciplined reflection on how and what believers should be taught in these settings, and in particular how Scripture should be taught, which takes account of what is learned in academic and other settings, but whose first obligation is faithfulness to the life of the church.

Seventh, the Gospel gives us a way of knowing God that depends on what God has to say for himself. Such knowledge fits an epistemology of hearing—that is, of heeding the word of the other, which is the appropriate way to account for how we know other persons. Thus the Gospel gives us an alternative to dependence on the philosophical spirituality of intellectual vision, which is in turn the basis of concepts of the immortality of the soul that have often usurped the place of resurrection of the body in Christian accounts of eternal life. Knowing God does not require an intellect that sees incorporeal truths, but a heart that hears the Gospel and trusts that God is true to his word (*Deus verax*). This is good news for all of us who think of the human mind differently from the Platonist concepts of soul and intellect that so impressed Augustine. It gives us a more appropriately critical form of the critical appropriation of classical philosophy.

Finally, the Gospel ought always to be the fundamental criterion used by Christian thought in its critical appropriation of any other form of thought, from ancient Platonism to modern science. The crucial example to follow here is that of the church fathers, the early theologians who formulated the orthodox doctrines of Trinity and incarnation, which are the church's great reckoning with ancient classical philosophy. These two doctrines are best understood as conceptual, indeed philosophical interpretations of the story of Christ, as told in Scripture and summarized in the Nicene Creed. Likewise, the doctrine of justification by faith alone should be understood as a conceptual, indeed philosophical interpretation of the effect the Gospel has on us when it says "you" and means me, giving to all who hear and believe it the Beloved whose story it tells.

Appendix 1

Luther's Devils

There is something peculiar about Luther's frequent references to the devil, which needs explaining. He does more than trace the work of evil powers in this world that lead us away from Christ back to the activity of the devil. Any Christian in the sixteenth century could talk like that. Luther goes further: he tells us that he regularly argues with the devil, who comes in person to dispute with him in the middle of the night. I think it is important to see how we can take these references seriously without coming to the conclusion that Luther is crazy or hallucinating. We need a better understanding of Luther's devils than the silly story that has gotten about—I don't know from where—that Luther once threw an inkpot at a devil he saw lurking in the shadows. That is not at all like Luther, who *hears* his devils rather than seeing them. In this regard he has a great deal of company in the Christian tradition, which will help us understand what he's talking about.

Two points of comparison are particularly helpful. One is the medieval notion of the devil assaulting the conscience, an assault called *impugnatio* in Latin or *Anfechtung* in German. As mentioned in chapter 5, we have pictures of this kind of assault. We can see it in late medieval woodcuts of people lying on their deathbed with a mob of devils gathered around them, whispering the names of their sins in their ears, trying to drive them to despair so that they give up hope of salvation. This is evidently an experience that people regularly expected to have—and not just on their deathbed. It is the voice of conscience turned into a terrifying accusation. Although no doubt it was possible for this voice to become an auditory hallucination and literally be heard, the basic form of "hearing" here is simply persistent, unwanted thoughts—what psychologists nowadays call "perseveration."

This leads to the second point of comparison. The battle with persistent, unwanted thoughts has been a part of the Christian tradition since at least the time of the desert fathers in the third century, who often described their inner battle with *dialogismoi*, the thoughts that (as we now say) kept "running in their heads" and which urged them to sin or distracted them from prayer. Given the worldview of the time, it is hardly surprising that they described these unwanted thoughts as coming from a devil.[1] Luther is not doing anything new when he identifies his own unwanted thoughts as a devil speaking.

If we set Luther in the context of these two features of the Christian tradition, and bear in mind also that he spends nearly all his waking hours with his head filled with theology—writing it, preaching it, or lecturing on it—then we will not be surprised that the devil who attacks him is an avid and skillful theologian. Luther was an insomniac who seldom got a good night's sleep. "Almost every night when I wake up," he wrote, "the devil is there and wants to dispute with me."[2] He means "dispute" in the usual medieval sense of an academic argument, which in his case means theological argument—the same kind of argument that occupies his mind throughout the day. I suggest that Luther is like many a writer or teacher or leader who cannot "turn his mind off" when it's time to get some sleep. The theological disputations that preoccupied him during the day take over his mind at night and won't let him go, assaulting him with persistent, unwanted, and often very critical thoughts.

I know myself what it is like to wake up in the middle of the night with thoughts running in my head that amount to a detailed refutation of some writing on theology that I had done the day before. I can't turn it off, because I know I'm hearing a good argument that I have to take account of. When something like that happens to Luther, it is not so surprising that he attributes the arguments against him to the devil. Nor is it surprising that the devil turns out to be a formidable theologian, much superior to Luther's human opponents: this devil is Luther's own theological genius turned against him. Whereas his human opponents "have only annoyed me," Luther says, "the devil is able to confront me with arguments."[3]

This helps explains the startling nonchalance with which Luther sometimes speaks of his devils. There are nights when he would rather not argue,

1. For a sophisticated account of these "thoughts" or *dialogismoi* by the great theorist of early Christian asceticism, see Evagrius of Pontus, *To Eulogios* and *On Thoughts*, in *Greek Ascetic Corpus*.

2. Luther, table talk #469, *LW* 53:78.

3. Luther, table talk #518, *LW* 53:93.

and he can sometimes get rid of them by turning over in bed and farting at them.[4] They tend to be persistent, however, and their arguments demand an answer. I take it this is what Luther has in mind when he complains that if the devils attacking him "can't get anywhere in my heart, they grab my head and torment me there."[5] The clever devils give up trying to scare him, in other words, and just plague him with theological disputations instead. They give him a headache, not a palpitating heart.

I can propose a way to test this explanation of Luther's devils. I would challenge anyone to make better sense of the extraordinary passage near the beginning of his 1533 treatise *The Private Mass and the Consecration of Priests*, where he introduces an important change in his theological position by saying: "Once I awakened at midnight and the devil began the following disputation with me in my heart."[6] This is followed by four pages in which the devil speaks—evidently not aloud but "in my heart"—addressing Luther and refuting his earlier defense of the validity of the private mass. After a brief, failed attempt by Luther to defend himself,[7] the devil speaks for another page, wrapping up his argument. Luther reports this whole encounter in a tone that is absolutely deadpan, with no indication that this is an exaggeration or a joke or any kind of fiction. He does indicate that he's not quoting the devil *verbatim*, for he concludes with the remark, "This was the gist of the disputation."[8] In other words, he is reporting the substance of a long argument the devil made against him, silently, in the middle of the night. What's more, he proceeds to admit that the devil won the argument. For the point of the devil's disputation was that Luther had compromised too much with the abominable papist practice of the private mass, and Luther came to see that this was correct: that he must abandon his current theological position and be more thorough in condemning something he had done regularly in earlier years, in his days as a Catholic priest.

The notion that the devil can be such a fine theologian lands Luther in a couple of quandaries, however, which he must immediately resolve. To begin with, the devil is a liar—so how can the point of his disputation be true and correct? The answer is that like any clever liar, he uses a partial truth to his

---

4. Luther, table talk #469, *LW* 53:78. Cf. Luther, table talk #491, *LW* 53:83: "I'll turn my behind on them." Likewise Luther, table talk #122, *LW* 53:15: "I resist the devil, and often it is with a fart that I chase him away," and Luther, table talk #590, *LW* 53:106: "If I can hold on to the distinction between law and gospel, I can say to him any and every time that he should kiss my backside."

5. Luther, table talk #491, *LW* 53:83.

6. Luther, *The Private Mass and the Consecration of Priests*, *LW* 38:149.

7. Luther, *Private Mass and the Consecration of Priests*, *LW* 38:155.

8. Luther, *Private Mass and the Consecration of Priests*, *LW* 38:156.

advantage whenever he can. And it is certainly true (Luther now realizes) that his life as a priest under the pope was filled with abominations. Hence "the devil does not lie when he holds before us our manifest evil works and life. . . . However, he is lying when he tries to force me to despair."[9] So here we have the usual situation of the devil accusing him of being a sinner. This puts Luther on familiar ground when it comes to the second quandary: How is he supposed to respond when the devil wins the argument? He must not despair like Judas but repent like Peter, remembering what the Gospel has to tell him about Christ: "For the devil has made you admit that you have sinned and been justly condemned, like Judas. But now like St. Peter turn back to Christ, and look at what he has done for you."[10]

The conclusion at which Luther arrives is that "I am a sinner in and by myself apart from Christ. Apart from myself and in Christ I am not a sinner."[11] This is one of his most succinct and lucid statements of the doctrine of justification, which shows the Christological basis for the *simul*, his conviction that we are both sinners and justified at the same time. So that is the outcome of his nocturnal disputation. Evidently there is a lot you can learn by losing an argument with the devil. No doubt this is why Luther insists that a good theologian must have extensive experience of *Anfechtung*.[12]

9. Luther, *Private Mass and the Consecration of Priests*, LW 38:157.
10. Luther, *Private Mass and the Consecration of Priests*, LW 38:157–58.
11. Luther, *Private Mass and the Consecration of Priests*, LW 38:157.
12. See Luther's preface to his German writings, LW 34:287.

Appendix 2

Gospel as Sacrament

Luther's Sermon on Christmas Day 1519

This sermon, which I have not found previously translated in full, is Luther's most explicit statement about how the Gospel works like a sacrament. It is contained in a collection of Luther's sermons made by Johannes Graumann, called Poliander, who in the years 1519–21 wrote down a large number of the sermons and lectures that Luther delivered orally. Unlike many who took notes when Luther spoke in later years, Poliander never worked up his notes for publication. His manuscript lay unnoticed until the 1880s, when it was rediscovered in time to be included in an early volume of the Weimar edition of Luther's complete works (= WA 9:439–42).

The manuscript contains what appear to be notes taken down on the spot, bearing all the marks of extemporaneous speech, including sudden grammatical shifts of pronoun and person. At the risk of jarring the reader, I have retained most of these in the translation, as they afford a vivid sense of the urgency and warmth of Luther's preaching. The sermon is in Latin, which means it was probably preached in the monastery rather than in the town church. The audience for this sermon thus consisted of monks, who were accustomed to practicing the kind of sacramental text-meditation that Luther advocates here, a style of reading that has also been called *lectio divina*.

Poliander begins with a note on what Luther read aloud as background for the sermon.

First he read aloud the story of the nativity according to Luke, and said he would put off expounding it until another time, for now was the time for starting the Gospel.

Text: "The Book of the Birth of Jesus Christ" [Matt. 1:1].

This birth is what we are to speak of.

But here at the beginning I will point out that we must treat the whole life of Christ, all of Christ's deeds, in two ways: both as sacrament and as example.[1] For throughout Christendom far and wide Christ is poorly preached— merely as an example, placed before our eyes as nothing more than an example to be imitated, no different from other saints like Peter, Paul, or John, who are proposed in the same way as examples for us. So is Christ no better than they are? By far, of course! From John you seek an example of humility, and you seek the same thing from Christ. But listen to the difference. (Oh, that you would rightly pursue the whole aim of the Gospel! Nothing holier or more profitable can be heard or taught.) From John you ask an example of humility—not that he actually grants humility but that, captivated by love of his virtues, you are eager to imitate what he has done, as much as you can. But from Christ you seek not only an example but at the same time the virtue itself. That is to say: Christ not only presents the appearance of virtue to be imitated but transfuses the virtue itself into people. And the humility of Christ becomes our humility, in our own breast. Now that is what I mean by "sacramentally," which is to say: all the words, all the Gospel stories are sacraments of a sort, that is, sacred signs through which God brings about, in those who believe, whatever the story designates.

"The Birth of Jesus Christ." These words are a kind of sacrament, through which, if anyone believes, we are born again. Just as baptism is a kind of sacrament through which God makes a person new, and as absolution is a sacrament through which God remits sins, so the words of Christ are sacraments through which he works our salvation. Thus the Gospel is to be regarded sacramentally; that is, the words of Christ are to be meditated on as symbols [*symbola*] through which is given the same righteousness, virtue, and salvation that the words themselves set forth.

1. The notion that Christ's life and death are for us both *sacramentum* and *exemplum* goes back to Augustine, *The Trinity* 4:3.6, a passage that played an important role in Luther's earlier thinking (e.g., Romans Lectures, on Rom. 4:25; 6:3, *LW* 25:284, 309–10). In his later explanations of the nature of the Gospel Luther will say, equivalently, that Christ is both gift and example (e.g., the preface to his first book of sermons, written about a year after this, *Brief Instruction on What to Look for and Expect in the Gospels*, *LW* 35:117–24).

Now you understand the difference between the Gospel and human stories. The history by Livy,[2] for example, presents various portraits and repre-
sentations of the virtues, which cannot cause them in others. But the Gospel
presents portraits of the virtues which are at the same time instruments
by which God transforms and renews us in the church. The Gospel is for
the salvation of all who believe; just as there is undoubtedly grace through
baptism, and through absolution there is forgiveness of sins, so undoubtedly through meditation on the words of Christ there is grace and salvation.

But three things are required for this. First of all, preaching or else some
kind of meditation or reading—it doesn't matter which. Next, we must regard
the deeds as ours, and that what is preached pertains to us. That is, if I hear
the story of Christ and don't think that it all pertains to me, so that it is for
me that Christ is born, suffered, and died, then the preaching or knowledge
of the story isn't worth a thing. Ultimately, faith in these things is denied,
which is by far the most important point of all. No matter how sweet or
good Christ is, he is not recognized, he will not cheer us up, unless I believe
that *to me* he is sweet and good—unless I say, *"Mother, this baby is mine!"*[3]

So let us begin now at the bottom step and meditate on Christ's infancy.
But let us meditate on how all these things were truly accomplished just
as we see them happen with our own infants. Let no one think Christ was
already showing signs of his majesty back then. He was needy in every way,
just like our infants. I don't want you to contemplate the deity in Christ, to
look up at the majesty, but call the thoughts of your mind to this flesh, this
child Christ. There can be no divinity that is not a terror to man; there can
be no man that is not terrified by this unheard-of majesty. That's why Christ
clothed himself in humanity and also whatever human affections there are
apart from sin, so that he might not terrify us but that you might begin to
embrace his favor and love and be consoled and strengthened. Thus Christ
is to be set forth as the one who came to give salvation and grace.

I say this especially to worried consciences, those that are anxious and
sad, so that you may gaze intently at this child and meditate in faith on his
being the one who made satisfaction for us. There's just no doubt, because so
much comfort comes to the soul—try it out and you'll feel it. Look! Christ is
there in the cradle, in the arms of this girl, this youngster, a maiden. First of
all, what is lovelier than a child, gentler than a girl, nicer than a sweet young
woman, a maiden? But look also at the ignorant child. All these things pertain

---

2. Titus Livius Patavinus, ancient Roman writer whose history of Rome was standard reading in schools at this time.

3. Here Luther breaks into German.

to him, lest your conscience be terrified and you fear to come to this child and take comfort from him. Let there be no doubt: this bouncing baby boy playing in the girl's arms, if you embrace him, dote on him, smile at him— that is, if you meditate on him—your soul will be utterly calm and at peace.

Look how God lures you in! He sets forth a child to whom you may flee, whom no one can be afraid to approach, because nothing is more lovable to us. You are afraid—but just do it! Just flee to this child, there in the arms of this sweet, lovely girl—for that's how great the goodness of God is, wanting anything but that you should despair. Trust him, trust him! Look, here is the child, from whom you can expect and demand salvation.

It seems to me that no more efficacious consolation is given to the whole human race than this, that for all of us Christ is a man, a child, a baby in this girl's arms, playing at his sweet mother's breast. Who is there who would not grasp this sight and be consoled? Now is the power of sin, hell, and the sting of conscience overcome, if you flee to this beckoning child. Only believe this, that he said he came not to judge but to save [John 12:47]—take that as settled. Just as baptism most certainly works grace, just as absolution most certainly effects the forgiveness of sins, so beyond doubt meditation on this child playing here will be joy to the laboring conscience and strength to the fearful soul.

And let me say, by the way: don't contemplate any sign of divine majesty, don't be afraid, but call to mind the flesh, the smile, the sheer attractive-ness of a child. Know this, that Christ was truly an ignorant child, knowing no more than we did as infants. This is clear from what Paul said to the Philippians, "Who being in the form of God," etc. [Phil. 2:6]. Here Christ the man is spoken of, for even when Christ did things from which a divine radiance shone, still he didn't want to put on anything but the form, that is, the appearance, of a servant—that is, of human servants. And then, being established in the likeness of human beings, the point is that he associated intimately with human beings. He was found in appearance (Greek *schema*, i.e., in bearing or attitude[4]) as a man. That is to say, just as there are all the ages of our life to bear or live through, so it was also with Christ—and just as we bear or live through childhood, so it was also with the child Christ.

I do not accept what some people teach, that even then Christ had ab-solute and certain knowledge of all things. Rather, he was truly an ignorant

---

4. In Poliander's MS the word *schema* (taken from Phil. 2:7) is written in Greek characters. Luther proposes to interpret this word with the Latin *gestus*, which has the literal sense of car-rying something but can also mean how one bears up under various challenges in life, one's attitude toward them, as well as how one conducts business or lives through the ages of one's life (*aetatem gerere*).

child and later grew in age, in years and in wisdom, as Luke says [Luke 2:52]. And also in Mark he is surprised, saying he had not found so much faith in Israel [Matt. 8:10]. And again, in his hometown of Nazareth he could do no miracles because of their unbelief [Mark 6:5]. Surely if he was caught by surprise, it follows he was ignorant. And the words of Scripture are not to be treated as playacting [hypokrita][5] but in their true sense. Also Paul says to the Hebrews, "Christ learned from the things he suffered" [Heb. 5:8]. And as the eye of Christ did not see when closed but he truly slept, so also his soul did not see all things. For the deity was joined as intimately to the body as to the rational human soul of Christ: it did not take away the weakness of the body nor the ignorance of the soul. In the same way also Christ's temptation in the desert must be understood as real, not feigned, which means he had no foreknowledge of it. That's my digression.

In sum: Christ was man, he assumed human things and willingly took them all, except sin. I say this so that we won't be afraid to embrace this child, to ask him for salvation. That's enough to say about sacramental meditation on the Gospel.

We surely do meditate on the Gospel sacramentally, which means the words work in us by faith the same thing that it sets forth. Christ is born: believe that he is born for you, and you are reborn. Christ conquered death and sin: believe that he conquered for you, and you will conquer. And the Gospel has this characteristic, which is not there in human stories. In the Gospel "righteousness is revealed," etc. [Rom. 1:17]. Christ's nativity is the cause of ours. To think of examples [rather than sacramentally] look at him setting aside his majesty, disregarding the flesh; you also set aside arrogance, etc. See the example of peaceableness; you also be a servant of concord and peace. See, Christ does all things for others: you also serve others. But in order to be able to do this, meditate on Christ sacramentally; that is, trust that he is the one who will give you this.

5. In Poliander's MS the word *hypokrita* is written in Greek characters. It means hypocrisy or deceitful speech or pretending, as when someone acts in a play. Luther is evidently thinking of biblical commentators who said that Christ only pretended to be surprised and not to know things in advance.

Bibliography

Adams, A. K. M. *Making Sense of New Testament Theology*. Macon, GA: Mercer University Press, 1995.

Allen, Diogenes, and Eric O. Springstead. *Philosophy for Understanding Theology*. 2nd ed. Louisville: Westminster John Knox, 2007.

Althaus, Paul. *The Theology of Martin Luther*. Philadelphia: Fortress, 1966.

Anonymous. *Summa sententiarum*. In *Patrologia Latina*, edited by J.-P. Migne, 176:42–174. Paris, 1844–55.

Anselm. *Proslogion*. In *A Scholastic Miscellany: Anselm to Ockham*, edited by Eugene R. Fairweather, 69–93. Philadelphia: Westminster, 1956.

Aristotle. *The Basic Works of Aristotle*. Edited by Richard McKeon. New York: Random House, 1941.

———. *Selections*. Translated by Terence Irwin and Gail Fine. Indianapolis: Hackett, 1995.

Arnobius. *The Case against the Pagans*. Translated by George E. McCracken. 2 vols. Westminster, MD: Newman Press, 1949.

Athanasius. *Against the Arians*. Translated by John Henry Newman. In *St. Athanasius: Select Works and Letters*, edited by Archibald Robinson, 307–447. Vol. 4 of *The Nicene and Post-Nicene Fathers*, second series, edited by Philip Schaff and Henry Wace. 1891. Reprint, Grand Rapids: Eerdmans, 1987.

———. *On the Incarnation of the Word*. Translated by John Henry Newman. In *The Nicene and Post-Nicene Fathers*, series 2, edited by Philip Schaff and Henry Wace, 4:367. Reprint, Peabody, MA: Hendrickson, 1994.

Augustine. *Answer to the Pelagians*. Translated by Roland Teske. 4 vols. Hyde Park, NY: New City Press, 1997–99. Includes *The Punishment and Forgiveness of Sins, The Spirit and the Letter, Nature and Grace, The Perfection of Human Righteousness*, and *The Nature and Origin of the Human Soul* (in vol. 1); "*Answer to the Two Letters of the Pelagians*" and "*Marriage and Desire*" (in vol. 2); and *Grace and Free Choice, Rebuke and Grace, The Gift of Perseverance*, and *The Predestination of the Saints* (in vol. 4).

———. *Augustine: Earlier Writings*. Edited by J. H. S. Burleigh. Philadelphia: Westminster, 1953. Includes *Soliloquies, Faith and the Creed, Of True Religion, The Usefulness of Belief*, and *The Nature of the Good* as well as less-recommended translations of *The Teacher* and *On Free Will* (translated under the title *On Free Choice of the Will*, below).

———. *City of God*. Translated by Henry Bettenson. New York: Penguin, 1984.

———. *Confessions*. Translated by F. J. Sheed. 2nd ed. Indianapolis: Hackett, 2006.

———. *Eighty-Three Different Questions*. Translated by David L. Mosher. Washington, DC: Catholic University of America Press, 1982.

———. *Enchiridion on Faith, Hope and Love*. Translated by J. F. Shaw. Washington, DC: Regnery, 1996.

———. *Letters*. Translated by Roland Teske. 4 vols. Hyde Park, NY: New City Press, 2001–5.

———. *The Literal Meaning of Genesis*. Translated by John Hammond Taylor. 2 vols. New York: Newman Press, 1982.

———. *The Lord's Sermon on the Mount*. Translated by John J. Jepson. Westminster, MD: Newman Press, 1956.

———. *The Magnitude of the Soul*. Translated by John J. McMahon. In *The Immortality of the Soul, The Magnitude of the Soul, On Music, The Advantage of Believing, On Faith in Things Unseen*, 59–149. Washington, DC: Catholic University of America Press, 1947.

———. *The Manichean Debate*. Translated by Roland Teske. Hyde Park, NY: New City, 2006. Includes *The Catholic Way of Life and the Manichean Way of Life* and *Answer to the Letter of Mani known as The Foundation*.

———. *On Baptism against the Donatists*. Translated by J. R. King. In *St. Augustine: The Writings against the Manichaeans and against the Donatists*, 411–514. Vol. 4 of *The Nicene and Post-Nicene Fathers*, first series, edited by Philip Schaff. 1887. Reprint, Grand Rapids: Eerdmans, 1983.

———. *On Christian Doctrine*. Translated by D. W. Robertson Jr. New York: Macmillan, 1958.

———. *On Faith and Works*. Translated by Gregory J. Lombardo. New York and Mahwah, NJ: Newman Press, 1988.

———. *On Free Choice of the Will*. Translated by Thomas Williams. Indianapolis: Hackett, 1993.

———. *On Order*. Translated by Sylvano Borruso. South Bend, IN: St. Augustine's Press, 2007.

———. *On the Gospel of John*. Translated by John Gibb and James Innes. In *St. Augustine: Homilies on the Gospel of John, Homilies on the First Epistle of John, Soliloquies*, 7–452. Vol. 7 of *The Nicene and Post-Nicene Fathers*, first series, edited by Philip Schaff. 1888. Reprint, Grand Rapids: Eerdmans, 1986.

———. *Opera Omnia*. Complete works in Latin. In *Patrologia Latina*, edited by J.-P. Migne, vols. 32–45. Paris, 1844–55. http://www.augustinus.it/latino.

———. *Sermons*. Translated by Edmund Hill. 10 vols. Brooklyn and Hyde Park, NY: New City Press, 1990–97.

———. *The Teacher*. Translated by Peter King. In *"Against the Academics" and "The Teacher,"* 94–146. Indianapolis: Hackett, 1995.

———. *The Trinity*. Translated by Edmund Hill. 2nd ed. Hyde Park, NY: New City Press, 2012.

Ayres, Lewis. *Augustine and the Trinity*. New York: Cambridge University Press, 2010.

———. *Nicaea and Its Legacy: An Approach to Fourth-Century Trinitarian Theology*. New York: Oxford University Press, 2006.

Bainton, Roland. *Here I Stand: A Life of Martin Luther*. Nashville: Abingdon, 1987.

———. *The Martin Luther Christmas Book*. Philadelphia: Westminster, 1948.

Balthasar, Hans Urs von. *Seeing the Form*. Vol. 1 of *The Glory of the Lord: A Theological Aesthetics*. San Francisco: Ignatius Press, 1982.

———. *Theodrama*. Translated by Graham Harrison. 5 vols. San Francisco: Ignatius, 1988–98.

Barnes, Michel. "Augustine in Contemporary Trinitarian Theology." *Theological Studies* 56/2 (1995): 237–50.

Barth, Karl. *Anselm: Fides Quaerens Intellectum*. Translated by Ian W. Robertson. London: SCM, 1960.

————. *Church Dogmatics*. 13 vols. Translated by G. W. Bromiley et al. Edinburgh: T&T Clark, 1956–69.

————. *The Holy Spirit and the Christian Life: The Theological Basis of Ethics*. Translated by R. Birch Hoyle. Louisville: Westminster/John Knox, 1993.

Bates, Matthew W. *The Birth of the Trinity: Jesus, God and Spirit in New Testament and Early Christian Interpretations of the Old Testament*. New York: Oxford University Press, 2015.

Bauckham, Richard. *Jesus and the God of Israel*. Grand Rapids: Eerdmans, 2009.

Bayer, Oswald. *Promissio: Geschichte der reformatorischen Wende in Luthers Theologie*. Göttingen: Vandenhoeck and Ruprecht, 1971.

Behr, John. *The Nicene Faith*. 2 vols. Crestwood, NY: St. Vladimir's Seminary Press, 2004.

Bernard of Clairvaux. *Letters*. Translated by Bruno James Scott. Kalamazoo, MI: Cistercian Publications, 1998.

Billings, J. Todd. *The Word of God for the People of God: An Entryway into the Theological Interpretation of Scripture*. Grand Rapids: Eerdmans, 2010.

Bizer, Ernst. *Fides ex Auditu: Eine Untersuchung über die Entdeckung der Gerechtigkeit Gottes durch Martin Luther*. 3rd ed. Neukirchen: Kreis Moers, 1966.

Boers, Hendrikus. *What Is New Testament Theology?* Philadelphia: Fortress, 1979.

Bourke, Vernon. *The Essential Augustine*. 2nd ed. Indianapolis: Hackett, 1974.

Braaten, Carl, and Robert Jenson, eds. *Union with Christ: The New Finnish Interpretation of Luther*. Grand Rapids: Eerdmans, 1998.

Brown, Peter. *Augustine of Hippo: A Biography*. 2nd ed. Berkeley and Los Angeles: University of California Press, 2000.

Buber, Martin. *I and Thou*. Translated by Walter Kaufmann. New York: Charles Scribner's Sons, 1970.

Burnaby, John. *Amor Dei: A Study in the Religion of St. Augustine*. Reprint, Eugene, OR: Wipf & Stock, 2007.

Burns, J. Patout. *The Development of Augustine's Doctrine of Operative Grace*. Paris: Études Augustiniennes, 1980.

Cajetan, Tommaso de Vio. *Cajetan Responds: A Reader in Reformation Controversy*. Translated by Jared Wicks. Eugene, OR: Wipf & Stock, 2011.

Calvin, John. *Institutes of the Christian Religion*. 2 vols. Translated by Ford Lewis Battles. Philadelphia: Westminster, 1960.

————. *Institutes of the Christian Religion: 1536 Edition*. Translated by Ford Lewis Battles. Rev. ed. Grand Rapids: Eerdmans, 1986.

————. *Theological Treatises*. Edited by J. K. S. Reid. Louisville: Westminster John Knox, 2006.

————. *Tracts and Letters*. 7 vols. Translated by Henry Beveridge et al. Reprint, Grand Rapids: Baker, 1983.

Campbell, Ted A. *Wesleyan Beliefs: Formal and Popular Expressions of the Core Beliefs of Wesleyan Communities*. Nashville: Abingdon, 2010.

Cartwright, Richard. "On the Logical Problem of the Trinity." In *Philosophical Essays*, 187–200. Cambridge, MA: MIT Press, 1987.

Cary, Phillip. "Augustine and Luther." In *Augustine and Modern Theology*, edited by Chad Pecknold and Tarmo Toom, 151–73. Edinburgh: T&T Clark, 2013.

————. *Augustine's Invention of the Inner Self: The Legacy of a Christian Platonist*. New York: Oxford University Press, 2000.

————. "Augustinian Compatibilism and the Doctrine of Election." In *Augustine and Philosophy*, edited by Phillip Cary, John Doody, and Kim Paffenroth, 79–102. Lanham, MD: Lexington Books, 2010.

————. "Believing the Word: A Proposal about Knowing Other Persons." *Faith and Philosophy* 13/1 (January 1996): 78–90.

————. "Book Seven: Inner Vision as the Goal of Augustine's Life." In *A Reader's Companion to Augustine's "Confessions,"* edited by Kim Paffenroth and Robert P. Kennedy, 107–26. Louisville: Westminster John Knox, 2003.

———. *Good News for Anxious Christians: Ten Practical Things You Don't Have to Do.* Grand Rapids: Brazos, 2010.

———. "The Incomprehensibility of God and the Origin of the Thomistic Concept of the Supernatural." *Pro Ecclesia* 9/3 (Summer 2002): 340–55.

———. *Inner Grace: Augustine in the Traditions of Plato and Paul.* New York: Oxford University Press, 2008.

———. *Jonah.* Brazos Theological Commentary on the Bible. Grand Rapids: Brazos, 2008.

———. "On Behalf of Classical Trinitarianism: A Critique of Rahner on the Trinity." *The Thomist* 56/3 (July 1993): 365–405.

———. *Outward Signs: The Powerlessness of External Things in Augustine's Thought.* New York: Oxford University Press, 2008.

———. "The Person before God." In *Religion and the Social Sciences: Conversations with Robert Bellah and Christian Smith*, edited by R. R. Reno and Barbara McClay, 59–68. Eugene, OR: Wipf & Stock, 2015.

———. "Right-Wing Postmodernism and the Rationality of Traditions." *Zygon: Journal of Religion and Science*, forthcoming.

———. "United Inwardly by Love: Augustine's Social Ontology." In *Augustine and Politics*, edited by John Doody, Kevin L. Hughes, and Kim Paffenroth, 3–33. Lanham, MD: Lexington Books, 2005.

———. "The Weight of Love: Augustinian Metaphors of Movement in Dante's Souls." In *Augustine and Literature*, edited by Robert P. Kennedy, Kim Paffenroth, and John Doody, 15–36. Lanham, MD: Lexington Books, 2006.

———. "Why Luther Is Not Quite Protestant: The Logic of Faith in a Sacramental Promise." *Pro Ecclesia* 14/4 (Fall 2005): 447–86.

Cary, Phillip, and Jean-François Phelizon. *Does God Have a Strategy?* Eugene, OR: Wipf & Stock, 2015.

Childs, Brevard. *Biblical Theology of the Old and New Testaments.* Minneapolis: Fortress, 1992.

Cicero, Marcus T. *Tusculan Disputations.* Translated by J. E. King. Loeb Classical Library. Cambridge, MA: Harvard University Press, 1971.

Clark, Mary T., ed. *An Aquinas Reader.* New York: Doubleday, 1972.

Cross, Richard. "*Quid tres?* On What Precisely Augustine Professes Not to Understand in *De Trinitate* 5 and 7." *Harvard Theological Review* 100/2 (2007): 215–32.

Crouzel, Henri. *Origen: The Life and Thought of the First Great Theologian.* Translated by A. S. Worrall. San Francisco: Harper & Row, 1989.

Cullmann, Oscar. *Immortality of the Soul or Resurrection of the Dead?* Reprint, Eugene, OR: Wipf & Stock, 2000.

Dahl, Nils A. "The Arrogant Archon and the Lewd Sophia: Jewish Traditions in Gnostic Revolt." In *Sethian Gnosticism*, edited by Bentley Layton, 689–712. Vol. 2 of *The Rediscovery of Gnosticism.* Leiden: Brill, 1980.

Dante. *Paradiso.* Translated by John D. Sinclair. New York: Oxford University Press, 1977.

———. *Purgatorio.* Translated by John D. Sinclair. New York: Oxford University Press, 1977.

Descartes, René. *Selected Philosophical Writings.* Translated by John C. Cottingham, Robert Stoothoff, and Dugald Murdoch. New York: Cambridge University Press, 1988.

Dieter, Theodor. *Der junge Luther und Aristoteles: Eine historische Untersuchung zum Verhältnis von Theologie und Philosophie.* Berlin: Walter de Gruyter, 2001.

Dillon, John. *The Middle Platonists: 80 B.C. to A.D. 220.* 2nd ed. Ithaca: Cornell University Press, 1996.

———. "Origen and Plotinus: The Platonic Influence on Early Christianity." In *The Relationship between Neoplatonism and Christianity*, edited by Thomas Finan and Vincent Twomey, 7–26. Dublin: Four Courts Press, 1992.

———. "*Pleroma* and Noetic Cosmos: A Comparative Study." In *Neoplatonism and Gnosticism*, edited by Richard T. Wallis and Jay Bregman, 99–110. Albany: State University of New York Press, 1992.

Duffy, Eamon. *The Stripping of the Altars: Traditional Religion in England, 1400–1580*. New Haven and London: Yale University Press, 1992.

Earman, John. *Hume's Abject Failure: The Argument against Miracles*. New York: Oxford University Press, 2000.

Edwards, Jonathan. *A Faithful Narrative of the Surprising Work of God*. In *The Great Awakening*. Vol. 4 of *The Works of Jonathan Edwards*, edited by C. C. Goen, 144–211. New Haven and London: Yale University Press, 1972.

———. *Religious Affections*. Vol. 2 of *The Works of Jonathan Edwards*, edited by John E. Smith. New Haven and London: Yale University Press, 2009.

Eire, Carlos. *Reformations: The Early Modern World, 1450–1650*. New Haven and London: Yale University Press, 2016.

Epictetus. *The Discourses. The Handbook. Fragments*. Edited by Christopher Gill. London: J. M. Dent, 1995.

Erikson, Erik H. *Young Man Luther: A Study in Psychoanalysis and History*. New York: Norton, 1958.

Evagrius of Pontus. *The Greek Ascetic Corpus*. Translated by Robert E. Sinkewicz. New York: Oxford University Press, 2003.

Evans, C. Stephen. *The Historical Christ and the Jesus of Faith*. New York: Oxford University Press, 1996.

Evans, G. R. *Augustine on Evil*. New York: Cambridge University Press, 1982.

Fowl, Stephen E. *Engaging Scripture: A Model for Theological Interpretation*. Malden, MA: Blackwell, 1998.

———, ed. *The Theological Interpretation of Scripture: Classic and Contemporary Readings*. Malden, MA: Blackwell, 1997.

Frei, Hans W. *The Eclipse of Biblical Narrative: A Study in Eighteenth and Nineteenth Century Hermeneutics*. New Haven and London: Yale University Press, 1974.

Friedman, Richard Elliott. *Who Wrote the Bible?* San Francisco: HarperSanFrancisco, 1987.

Gabler, Johann Philipp. "An Oration on the Proper Distinction between Biblical and Dogmatic Theology and the Specific Objectives of Each." 1787. In *Old Testament Theology: Flowering and Future*, edited by Ben C. Ollenburger, 498–506. Winona Lake, IN: Eisenbrauns, 2004.

Gadamer, Hans-Georg. *Truth and Method*. Translated by William Glen-Doepel. London and New York: Bloomsbury Academic, 2013.

Gavrilyuk, Paul L. *The Suffering of the Impassible God: The Dialectics of Patristic Thought*. New York: Oxford University Press, 2004.

Gay, Peter. *Deism: An Anthology*. Princeton: Van Nostrand, 1968.

Gioia, Luigi. *The Theological Epistemology of Augustine's "De Trinitate."* New York: Oxford University Press, 2008.

Gregory, Brad S. *The Unintended Revolution: How a Religious Revolution Secularized Society*. Cambridge, MA: Harvard University Press, 2012.

Gregory of Nazianzus. *The Theological Orations*. In *Christology of the Later Fathers*, edited by Edward R. Hardy, 128–214. Philadelphia: Westminster, 1954.

Gunton, Colin. *The Promise of Trinitarian Theology*. Edinburgh: T&T Clark, 1977.

Gyllenkrok, Axel. *Rechtfertigung und Heiligung in der frühen evangelische Theologie Luthers*. Uppsala: Lundequistska, 1952.

Hacker, Paul. *The Ego in Faith: Martin Luther and the Origin of Anthropocentric Religion*. Chicago: Franciscan Herald Press, 1970.

Hacking, Ian. *The Emergence of Probability: A Philosophical Study of Early Ideas about Probability, Induction and*

Statistical Inference. New York: Cambridge University Press, 1975.

Hamm, Berndt. *The Early Luther: Stages in a Reformation Reorientation*. Translated by Martin J. Lorhmann. Grand Rapids: Eerdmans, 2014.

Hanson, R. P. C. *The Search for the Christian Doctrine of God: The Arian Controversy, 318–381*. Edinburgh: T&T Clark, 1988.

Hardy, Edward R. *Christology of the Later Fathers*. Philadelphia: Westminster, 1954.

Harrison, Carol. *Rethinking Augustine's Early Theology: An Argument for Continuity*. New York: Oxford University Press, 2006.

Heppe, Heinrich. *Reformed Dogmatics Set Out and Illustrated from the Sources*. Translated by G. T. Thomson. Grand Rapids: Baker, 1978.

Hillerbrand, Hans J. *The Reformation: A Narrative History Related by Contemporary Observers and Participants*. Reprint, Grand Rapids: Baker, 1982.

Holl, Karl. *Gesammelte Aufsätze zur Kirchengeschichte*. Vol. 1, *Luther*. 6th ed. Tübingen: J. C. B. Mohr, 1932.

Howard, Thomas. *Protestant Theology and the Making of the Modern German University*. New York: Oxford University Press, 2006.

Hughes, Robert Davis, III. *Beloved Dust: Tides of the Spirit in the Christian Life*. New York: Continuum, 2008.

Hume, David. *An Enquiry concerning Human Understanding*. Indianapolis: Hackett, 1977.

Humphrey, Edith. *Ecstasy and Intimacy: When the Holy Spirit Meets the Human Spirit*. Grand Rapids: Eerdmans, 2006.

Hurtado, Larry. *Lord Jesus Christ: Devotion to Jesus in Earliest Christianity*. Grand Rapids: Eerdmans, 2005.

Irenaeus. *Against Heresies*. Translated by A. C. Coxe. In *The Apostolic Fathers with Justin Martyr and Irenaeus*, edited by A. C. Coxe, 315–567. Vol. 1 of *The Ante-Nicene Fathers*, edited by

Alexander Roberts and James Donaldson. 1885. Reprint, Grand Rapids: Eerdmans, 1987.

Jenson, Robert W. *America's Theologian: A Recommendation of Jonathan Edwards*. New York: Oxford University Press, 1988.

———. *Systematic Theology*. 2 vols. New York: Oxford University Press, 1997.

Jerome, *Biblia Sacra* (Vulgate translation of the Bible). Stuttgart: Deutsche Bibelgesellschaft, 1994.

John of Damascus. *Exposition of the Orthodox Faith*. Translated by S. D. F. Salmond. In *St. Hilary of Poitiers, John of Damascus*, 1–101. Vol. 9 of *The Nicene and Post-Nicene Fathers*, second series, edited by Philip Schaff and Henry Wace. Reprint, Grand Rapids: Eerdmans, 1979.

Jonas, Hans. *The Gnostic Religion*. 2nd ed. Boston: Beacon Press, 1963.

Justin Martyr. *Dialogue with Trypho*. Translated by A. C. Coxe. In *The Apostolic Fathers with Justin Martyr and Irenaeus*, edited by A. C. Coxe, 194–270. Vol. 1 of *The Ante-Nicene Fathers*, edited by Alexander Roberts and James Donaldson. 1885. Reprint, Grand Rapids: Eerdmans, 1987.

Kant, Immanuel. *Perpetual Peace, and Other Essays*. Translated by Ted Humphrey. Indianapolis: Hackett, 1983.

Karlstadt, Andreas. *Karlstadt und Augustin: Der Kommentar des Andreas Bodenstein von Karlstadt zu Augustins Schrift "De Spiritu et Littera."* Edited by Ernst Kähler. Halle: Max Niemeyer, 1952.

Kelly, J. N. D. *Early Christian Doctrines*. 5th ed. New York: Continuum, 2000.

Kendall, R. T. *Calvin and English Calvinism to 1649*. Oxford: Oxford University Press, 1979.

LaCugna, Catherine. *God for Us: The Trinity and Christian Life*. San Francisco: HarperSanFrancisco, 1973.

Leith, John H., ed. *Creeds of the Churches*. 3nd ed. Atlanta: John Knox, 1973.

Leithart, Peter. *Deep Exegesis*. Waco: Baylor University Press, 2009.

Levenson, Jon D. *The Hebrew Bible, the Old Testament, and Historical Criticism: Jews and Christians in Biblical Studies*. Louisville: Westminster/John Knox, 1993.

Levering, Matthew. *Participatory Biblical Exegesis: A Theology of Biblical Interpretation*. Notre Dame, IN: University of Notre Dame Press, 2008.

Lewis, C. S. *The Last Battle*. New York: HarperCollins, 1984.

———. *The World's Last Night, and Other Essays*. New York: Harcourt Brace Jovanovich, 1973.

Lienhard, Joseph. "*Ousia* and *Hypostasis*: The Cappadocian Settlement and the Theology of 'One *Hypostasis*.'" In *The Trinity*, edited by Stephen Davis, Daniel Kendall, and Gerald O'Collins, 99–121. New York: Oxford University Press, 1999.

Lindbeck, George. *The Nature of Doctrine: Religion and Theology in a Postliberal Age*. Philadelphia: Westminster, 1984.

Locke, John. "A Discourse of Miracles." In *"The Reasonableness of Christianity," with "A Discourse of Miracles" and Part of the Third Letter concerning Toleration*, edited by I. T. Ramsey, 78–87. Stanford, CA: Stanford University Press, 1958.

———. *An Essay concerning Human Understanding*. Oxford: Clarendon, 1991.

Lombard, Peter. *Sententiae*. Rome: Collegii S. Bonaventurae ad Claras Aquas, 1971.

Lossky, Vladimir. *The Mystical Theology of the Eastern Church*. Crestwood, NY: St. Vladimir's Seminary Press, 1976.

Louth, Andrew, ed. *Maximus the Confessor*. London and New York: Routledge, 1996.

———. *The Origins of the Christian Mystical Tradition: From Plato to Denys*. 2nd ed. New York: Oxford University Press, 2007.

Luther, Martin. *D. Martin Luthers Werke* (= *WA*). Weimar: H. Böhlau, 1883–1993. The complete critical edition of Luther's writings in the original languages, commonly known as the Weimar edition or

Weimarer Ausgabe. http://www.luther dansk.dk/WA/D.%20Martin%20Luthers %20Werke,%20Weimarer%20Ausgabe %20-%20WA.htm.

———. *Letters of Spiritual Counsel*. Edited by Theodore G. Tappert. Louisville: Westminster John Knox, 1955.

———. *Luther: Early Theological Works*. Edited by James Atkinson. Philadelphia: Westminster, 1962.

———. *Luther's Works* (= *LW*). Jaroslav Pelikan, general editor. St. Louis: Concordia (vols. 1–30); Philadelphia: Fortress (vols. 31–55), 1955–76.

———. *Pro veritate inquirenda et timoratis conscientiis consolandis* [For truly inquiring and comforting frightened consciences]. Translated in *Lutheran Forum* 44/4 (Winter 2010): 34–35.

———. *Sermons*. Edited by John Nicholas Lenker. 8 vols. Reprint, Grand Rapids: Baker, 1988.

MacIntyre, Alasdair. "Epistemological Crises, Dramatic Narrative, and the Philosophy of Science." In *The Tasks of Philosophy*, 3–23. New York: Cambridge University Press, 2006.

———. *Whose Justice? Which Rationality?* Notre Dame, IN: University of Notre Dame Press, 1988.

Mannermaa, Tuomo. *Christ Present in Faith: Luther's View of Justification*. Minneapolis: Fortress, 2005.

Marshall, Bruce D. *Trinity and Truth*. New York: Cambridge University Press, 2000.

McGinn, Bernard. *The Foundations of Mysticism: Origins to the Fifth Century*. New York: Crossroad, 1999.

McGuckin, John. *Saint Cyril of Alexandria and the Christological Controversy*. Crestwood, NY: St. Vladimir's Seminary Press, 2004.

Melanchthon, Philip. *Apology of the Augsburg Confession*. In *The Book of Concord*, edited by Theodore G. Tappert, 97–285. Philadelphia: Fortress, 1959.

Meyendorff, John. *Christ in Eastern Christian Thought*. Crestwood, NY: St. Vladimir's Seminary Press, 1987.

Middleton, Richard. *A New Heaven and a New Earth: Reclaiming Biblical Eschatology*. Grand Rapids: Baker Academic, 2014.

Morgan, Edward. *Visible Saints: The History of a Puritan Idea*. Ithaca: Cornell University Press, 1963.

Morse, Christopher. *The Difference Heaven Makes: Rehearing the Gospel as News*. London and New York: T&T Clark, 2010.

Muller, Richard A. *Dictionary of Latin and Greek Theological Terms: Drawn Principally from Protestant Scholastic Theology*. Grand Rapids: Baker, 1985.

Nisula, Timo. *Augustine and the Functions of Concupiscence*. Leiden: Brill, 2012.

Nygren, Anders. *Agape and Eros*. Translated by Philip S. Watson. Chicago: University of Chicago Press: 1982.

Oberman, Heiko. *Forerunners of the Reformation*. New York: Holt, Rinehart and Winston, 1966.

O'Connell, Robert J. *The Origin of the Soul in St. Augustine's Later Works*. New York: Fordham University Press, 1987.

———. *St. Augustine's Confessions*. Cambridge, MA: Harvard University Press, 1969.

———. *St. Augustine's Early Theory of Man*. Cambridge, MA: Harvard University Press, 1968.

Ollenburger, Ben C. "Old Testament Theology: A Discourse on Method." In *Biblical Theology: Problems and Prospects*, edited by Steven J. Kraftchick, Charles D. Myers Jr., and Ben C. Ollenburger, 81–103. Nashville: Abingdon, 1995.

O'Meara, John J. "Augustine and Neoplatonism." In *Studies in Augustine and Eriugena*, 146–65. Washington, DC: Catholic University of America Press, 1991.

———. *The Young Augustine: The Growth of St. Augustine's Mind up to His Conversion*. London: Longmans, Green & Co., 1954.

Origen. *On First Principles*. Translated by G. W. Butterworth. Gloucester, MA: Peter Smith, 1973.

Outler, Albert C. *John Wesley*. New York: Oxford University Press, 1964.

Ozment, Steven E. *The Reformation in the Cities: The Appeal of Protestantism to Sixteenth-Century Germany and Switzerland*. New Haven and London: Yale University Press, 1975.

Palamas, Gregory. *The Triads*. Translated by Nicholas Grendle. Mahwah, NJ: Paulist Press, 1983.

Pelikan, Jaroslav. *Christianity and Classical Culture: The Metamorphosis of Natural Theology in the Christian Encounter with Hellenism*. New Haven and London: Yale University Press, 1993.

———. *The Emergence of the Catholic Tradition*. Vol. 1 of *The Christian Tradition: A History of the Development of Doctrine*. Chicago: University of Chicago Press, 1971.

Plato. *Complete Works*. Edited by John M. Cooper. Indianapolis: Hackett, 1997. Includes *Euthyphro, Meno, Phaedo, Phaedrus, Republic, Symposium, Timaeus*, etc.

Plotinus. *Enneads*. Translated by A. H. Armstrong. 7 vols. Loeb Classical Library. Cambridge, MA: Harvard University Press, 1966–88.

Rahner, Karl. *The Trinity*. Translated by Joseph Donceel. New York: Herder and Herder, 1970.

Reddy, Vasudevi. *How Infants Know Minds*. Cambridge, MA: Harvard University Press, 2008.

Richards, Amy Gilbert. "Response to Tollefson." In *Subjectivity: Ancient and Modern*, edited by R. J. Snell and Steven F. McGuire, 115–23. Lanham, MD: Lexington Books, 2016.

Robinson, James M., ed. *The Nag Hammadi Library in English*. 3rd ed. San Francisco: HarperCollins, 1990.

Rombs, Ronnie J. *Saint Augustine and the Fall of the Soul: Beyond O'Connell and*

His Critics. Washington, DC: Catholic University of America Press, 2006.

Schaff, Philip. *The Creeds of Christendom.* 3 vols. Reprint, Grand Rapids: Baker, 1990.

Schmid, Heinrich. *The Doctrinal Theology of the Evangelical Lutheran Church.* Translated by Charles A. Hay and Henry E. Jacobs. Reprint, Minneapolis: Augsburg, 1961.

Shakespeare, William. *The Riverside Shakespeare: Complete Works,* edited by G. Blakemore Evans. 2nd ed. Boston: Houghton Mifflin Company, 1997.

Smith, Christian. *What Is a Person? Rethinking Humanity, Social Life and the Moral Good from the Person Up.* Chicago: University of Chicago Press, 2010.

Spaemann, Robert. *Persons: The Difference between 'Someone' and 'Something.'* Translated by Oliver O'Donovan. New York: Oxford University Press, 2006.

Spener, Philip Jacob. *Pia Desideria.* Translated by Theodore G. Tappert. Philadelphia: Fortress, 1964.

Stead, Christopher. *Philosophy in Christian Antiquity.* New York: Cambridge University Press, 1996.

Stendahl, Krister. "Biblical Theology: A Program." In *Meanings: The Bible as Document and as Guide.* Philadelphia: Fortress, 1984.

Stephen, Leslie. *History of English Thought in the Eighteenth Century.* 3rd ed. New York: P. Smith, 1949.

Stevenson, J., ed. *Creeds, Councils, and Controversies: Documents Illustrative of the History of the Church, A.D. 337–461.* London: SPCK, 1983.

Tappert, Theodore, ed. *The Book of Concord: The Confessions of the Evangelical Lutheran Church.* Philadelphia: Fortress, 1959.

Tatian. *Address to the Greeks.* Translated by J. E. Ryland. In *Fathers of the Second Century,* edited by A C. Coxe, 65–83. Vol. 2 of *The Ante-Nicene Fathers,* edited by Alexander Roberts and James Donaldson. Reprint, Grand Rapids: Eerdmans, 1989.

Tentler, Thomas N. *Sin and Confession on the Eve of the Reformation.* Princeton: Princeton University Press, 1977.

Tertullian. *Tertullian's Treatise against Praxeas.* Translated by Ernest Evans. London: SPCK, 1948.

Thomas Aquinas. *Summa Theologica* (= *ST*). Translated by Fathers of the English Dominican Province. 5 vols. Westminster, MD: Christian Classics, 1981.

Turner, John D. *Sethian Gnosticism and the Platonic Tradition.* Québec: Les Presses de l'Université Laval; Leuven and Paris: Peeters, 2001.

Vainio, Olli-Pekka. *Justification and Participation in Christ: The Development of the Lutheran Doctrine of Justification from Luther to the Formula of Concord (1580).* Leiden and Boston: Brill, 2008.

Valla, Lorenzo. *The Treatise of Lorenzo Valla on the Donation of Constantine.* Translated by Christopher B. Coleman. Toronto: University of Toronto Press, 1993.

Visser, Arnoud S. Q. *Reading Augustine in the Reformation: The Flexibility of Intellectual Authority in Europe, 1500–1620.* New York: Oxford University Press, 2011.

Wallis, Richard T., and Jay Bregman, eds. *Neoplatonism and Gnosticism.* Albany: State University of New York Press, 1992.

Walsch, Peter G., and Christopher Husch, eds. *One Hundred Latin Hymns: Ambrose to Aquinas.* Cambridge, MA: Harvard University Press, 2012.

Watson, Francis. *Text and Truth: Redefining Biblical Theology.* Grand Rapids: Eerdmans, 1997.

Weber, Max. *The Protestant Ethic and the Spirit of Capitalism.* New York: Charles Scribner's Sons, 1976.

Weinandy, Thomas G. *Does God Suffer?* Notre Dame, IN: University of Notre Dame Press, 2000.

Wesley, John. *The Works of John Wesley.* 14 vols. Reprint, Peabody, MA: Hendrickson, 1984.

Wicks, Jared. "Applied Theology at the Deathbed: Luther and the Late-Medieval Tradition of the *Ars Moriendi*." *Gregorianum* 79 (1988): 345–68.

———. "*Fides sacramenti—fides specialis*: Luther's Development in 1518." In *Luther's Reform: Studies on Conversion and the Church*, 117–47. Mainz: Verlag Philipp von Zabern, 1992.

———. *Man Yearning for Grace: Luther's Early Spiritual Teaching*. Washington, DC, and Cleveland: Corpus Books, 1968.

Williams, A. N. *The Divine Sense: The Intellect in Patristic Theology*. New York: Cambridge University Press, 2009.

Williams, George Huntston. *The Radical Reformation*. Philadelphia: Westminster, 1962.

Williams, Rowan. "Language, Reality and Desire in Augustine's *De Doctrina*." *Journal of Literature and Theology* 3/2 (July 1989): 138–50.

———. "The Paradoxes of Self-Knowledge in the *De Trinitate*." In *Augustine: Presbyter Factus Sum*, edited by Joseph T. Lienhard, Earl C. Muller, and Roland J. Teske, 121–34. New York: Peter Lang, 1993.

———. "*Sapientia* and the Trinity: Reflections on the *De Trinitate*." In *Collectanea Augustiniana: Mélanges T. J. van Bavel*, edited by B. Bruning, M. Lamberigts, and J. van Houtem, 317–22. Leuven: Leuven University Press, 1990.

Wolff, Hans Walter. *Anthropology of the Old Testament*. Translated by Margaret Kohl. Philadelphia: Fortress, 1974.

Wolterstorff, Nicholas. *Justice in Love*. Grand Rapids: Eerdmans, 2011.

Wrede, Wilhelm. "The Task and Methods of 'New Testament Theology.'" 1897. In *The Nature of New Testament Theology*, edited by Robert Morgan, 68–116. Naperville, IL: Allenson, 1973.

Wright, N. T. *Surprised by Hope: Rethinking Heaven, Resurrection, and the Mission of the Church*. New York: HarperCollins, 2008.

Yeago, David. "The Bible." In *Knowing the Triune God: The Work of the Spirit in the Practices of the Church*, edited by James J. Buckley and David S. Yeago, 49–93. Grand Rapids: Eerdmans, 2001.

Zachman, Randall C. *The Assurance of Faith: Conscience in the Theology of Martin Luther and John Calvin*. Minneapolis: Fortress, 1993.

Zizioulas, John. *Being as Communion*. Crestwood, NY: St. Vladimir's Seminary Press, 1997.

Zwingli, Ulrich. *Of the Clarity and Certainty of the Word of God*. In *Zwingli and Bullinger*, edited by G. W. Bromiley, 59–95. Philadelphia: Westminster, 1953.

Index